JOHN WILSON'S
FISHING ENCYCLOPAEDIA

While guide Bola looks on, retaining stringer at the ready, John battles away with a huge mahseer amongst the rock strewn river rapids in southern India. An epic struggle lasting for over an hour resulted eventually in a golden mahseer of over 90lb.

John Wilson's
FISHING
ENCYCLOPAEDIA

BⵞXTREE

First published in Great Britain in 1995 by Boxtree Limited

1 3 5 7 9 10 8 6 4 2

Designed and typeset by
Gregory Mason Graphic Design Consultancy
Printed and bound by New Interlitho Spa, Milan, Italy for

Boxtree Limited
Broadwall House
21 Broadwall
London SE1 9PL

A CIP catalogue entry for this book is available from the
British Library.

ISBN 1 85283 466 8

INTRODUCTION

I think it is true to say that only a small proportion of angling authors are ever given the privileged, albeit rather daunting, assignment of putting their entire life's fishing experiences and knowledge into one huge volume. My initial reaction to the task, having spent weeks deciding upon a structure which would make sense not only to you the reader, but also to me as I went along, was where on earth to stop.

Having been blessed, or cursed (take your pick), with the gift of the gab, my problem has naturally not been choosing subjects about which to write, but deciding which should be left out. In the end, this encyclopaedia is personal to my own knowledge, experiences and life-span, covering over forty-five years at the waterside starting with a toddler's first encounter with minnow and loach and I hope the reader will be able to relate accordingly to his or her own personal fishing experience.

Actually, the easiest decision of all came from trying to select which sea, game and coarse fish to include from the staggering amount (I truly never before realized there were so many) of species on the 'British Record Fish List', no less than 181 individual fishes. I have simply mentioned them all, plus a selection of tropical sports fish from both fresh and saltwater, and as more and more anglers now travel abroad to experience new challenges, I hope this inclusion will prove valuable. As records frequently change however, the entry for each species' weight should only be considered an approximation of the potential size to which each may be caught.

I hope that listing everything in alphabetical order provides the quickest access to a particular subject. Comprehensive cross-references to other entries are given in *italics* throughout. I hope most of all that whenever and wherever the wonderful sport of fishing takes you, this encyclopaedia can be a helpful reference.

Good fishing

John Wilson
Great Witchingham, 1995

ACKNOWLEDGEMENTS

So many friends have, without knowing, helped in the making of this encyclopaedia simply by providing me with encouragement, advice and the opportunity of fishing beautiful locations, both at home and abroad, that it is indeed impossible to thank everyone personally.

My particular thanks, however, go to fellow fishermen Dave Lewis and Bruce Vaughan, who are so often behind the camera whilst I am fishing, and to my long-suffering typist Jan Carver, who always manages to turn 'Wilsonisms' into readable English.

Instructional fishing books cannot work without clear and concise diagrams, for which I have two artists to thank: fishing buddy Dave Batten, who has illustrated most of my books, and Greg Mason, who was also responsible for the overall design and cover of this encyclopaedia.

Angling authors also have extremely understanding wives to thank for their tolerance during those long periods of penning when few words are spoken lest concentration wanes, and I am fortunate that my wife, Jo, appears to be blessed with the patience of Job.

Lastly, because this work rates as the pinnacle of my career under the Boxtree imprint, much gratitude is deserved by the company's directors, Sarah Mahaffy and David Inman; it was their vision that led to my commission to write the first *Go Fishing* book to accompany the TV series. For me, it was the book that started it all.

DEDICATION

This book is for Nanda and Susheel, Bola and Suban, and for my dad, whose arm being longer than his young son's always managed to sweep the garden cane net into deeper areas where the sticklebacks and minnows were larger, thus giving birth to a sense of mystery that remains today as strong as it ever was, wherever I see water.

Aa

ANCHORS & MUDWEIGHTS

Many anglers pay little attention to anchors and mudweights. Yet sea fishermen who venture off shore and freshwater game and coarse fishermen who boat fish could not function without them.

ANCHORS

Proper steel anchors of the fixed, or better still, the 'hinged' type (fig. 1), are imperative for holding a boat steady in the desired position at sea. Reservoir and lakeland trout fishermen also use them. A chain is attached to the lower, hinged end of the anchor shaft. It runs along the shaft and is tied to the other end with a length of weak cord that will break easily under pressure (fig. 1). This arrangement enables the angler to prise the anchor from the snaggiest bottom strata by pulling at it from an uptide direction.

Another most effective method of retrieving anchors at sea over particularly rough ground is to slide a separate retrieval line on a large ring (an Alderney Ring) that runs freely along the anchor stem, with a buoy at the surface end. To up-anchor you then simply pull on the buoy line while motoring up tide, using the engine's power to pull the anchor free from the bottom (fig. 2).

MUDWEIGHTS

Mudweights are better than steel anchors for anchoring a boat in lakes and rivers. A heavy chain, for instance, crunching over the side of a dinghy is bound to scare the more wary freshwater species. A ½in-thick soft rope (easier on the hands than hard, thin rope) is preferable, secured to the top of the mudweight. It is easy to make a pair of simple mudweights (fig. 3A).

When lifting mudweights into the boat, remember to swish them about to release any silt or mud that has attached to them as a messy boat is no fun to fish from.

ANCHORING A BOAT

Remember that to anchor effectively in freshwater, and even more so at sea, you sometimes need to let out at least twice, and sometimes three times, the anchor line as the depth you are fishing in. An anchor or mudweight lowered straight down below the boat will not hold, so allow the current or wind to swing the boat into a comfortable position on a long rope before tightening up. In exceptionally strong currents, such as at sea or in a tidal river, it is imperative that you anchor at the bow end only. The current force alone ensures that the boat stays steady. However, when fishing in freshwater lakes, pits and broads, or slow-moving rivers, the wind force is invariably greater than the sub-surface drift or tow. In such cases, use a mudweight at each end of the boat to prevent it being blown about. Plan to fish side-on to the wind when possible, and bows-on only in really gusty weather (fig. 3B).

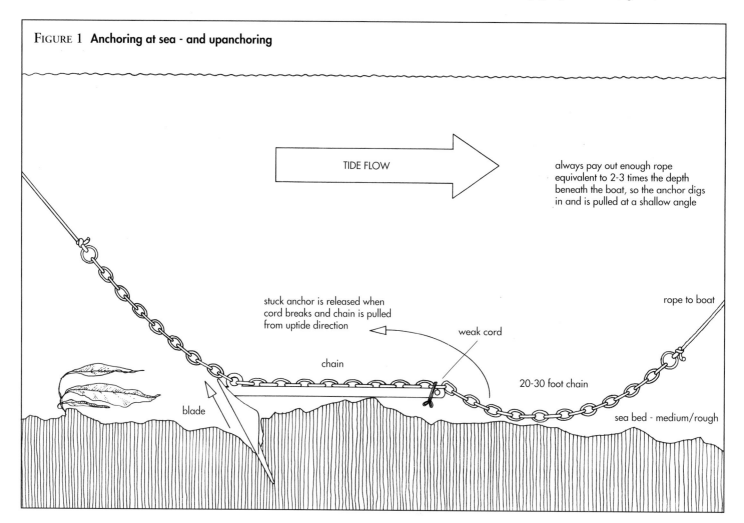

FIGURE 1 **Anchoring at sea - and upanchoring**

TIDE FLOW

always pay out enough rope
equivalent to 2-3 times the depth
beneath the boat, so the anchor digs
in and is pulled at a shallow angle

stuck anchor is released when
cord breaks and chain is pulled
from uptide direction

weak cord

rope to boat

chain

blade

20-30 foot chain

sea bed - medium/rough

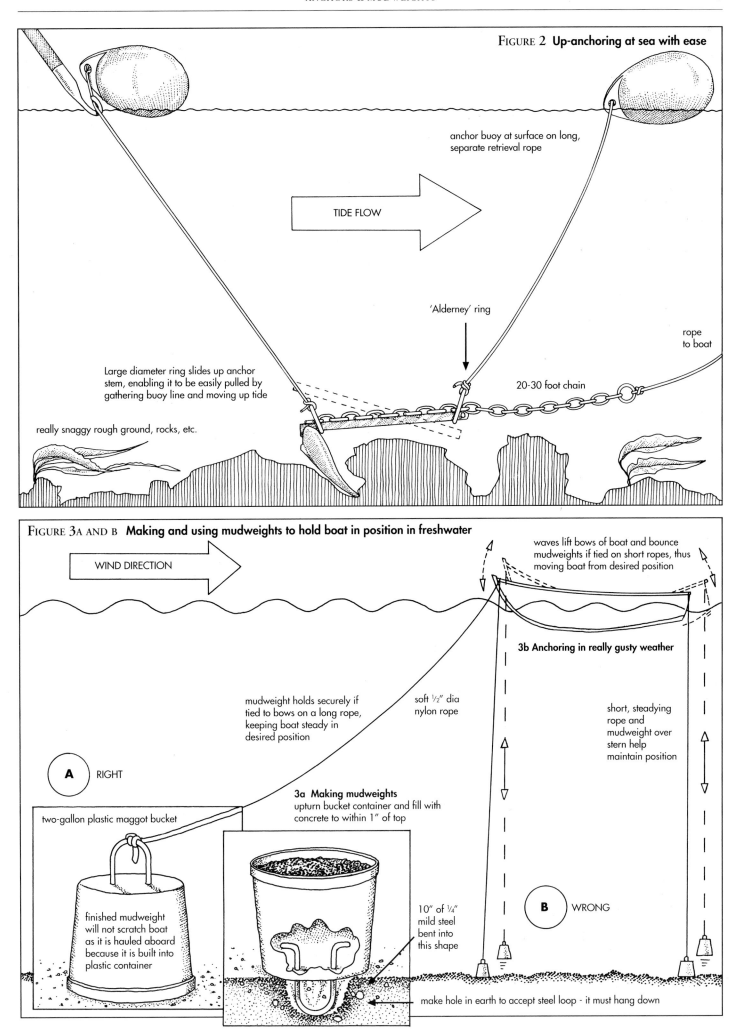

FIGURE 2 **Up-anchoring at sea with ease**

anchor buoy at surface on long, separate retrieval rope

TIDE FLOW

'Alderney' ring

rope to boat

Large diameter ring slides up anchor stem, enabling it to be easily pulled by gathering buoy line and moving up tide

20-30 foot chain

really snaggy rough ground, rocks, etc.

FIGURE 3A AND B **Making and using mudweights to hold boat in position in freshwater**

WIND DIRECTION

waves lift bows of boat and bounce mudweights if tied on short ropes, thus moving boat from desired position

3b Anchoring in really gusty weather

mudweight holds securely if tied to bows on a long rope, keeping boat steady in desired position

soft ½" dia nylon rope

short, steadying rope and mudweight over stern help maintain position

A RIGHT

3a **Making mudweights**
upturn bucket container and fill with concrete to within 1" of top

two-gallon plastic maggot bucket

finished mudweight will not scratch boat as it is hauled aboard because it is built into plastic container

10" of ¼" mild steel bent into this shape

B WRONG

make hole in earth to accept steel loop - it must hang down

ANCHORED FLOAT RIGS

See *Freshwater float fishing techniques.*

ANCHOVY

(*Engraulis encrasicolus*)

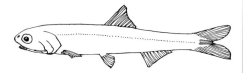

British record: 1½oz (42g)

This slender, cylindrical, silvery little sea fish rarely exceeds 7-8in. It has large, easily dislodged scales, a distinct, underslung mouth and a rounded snout. It masses in huge shoals close inshore and in estuaries during the warmer months, feeding on minute planktons. It is an important southern European food fish, but is rarely caught by anglers on rod and line.

ANGLER FISH

(*Lophius piscatorius*)

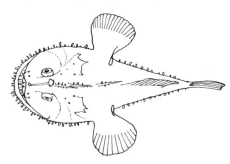

Average size: 30-40lb
Mega specimen: over 60lb
British record: 94lb 12¼oz (42kg 985g)

This strange, almost prehistoric sea fish is not unlike the freshwater bullhead in shape, with a steeply tapering body, a bulbous, wide, flat head and a cavernous mouth. It is equipped with a line of long, inward-pointing teeth in both its top and lower jaws, from which its prey stands no chance of escape. It has huge pectoral fins, with a pair of spines on the body immediately above them, and two dorsal fins.

It is aptly called the angler fish because it attracts its food (other fish) by wriggling a flap of skin, joined to the first spine of its first dorsal fin, that hangs forward over its mouth.

Its blotchy, grey-brown, scaleless body has an unmistakable outline of small skin

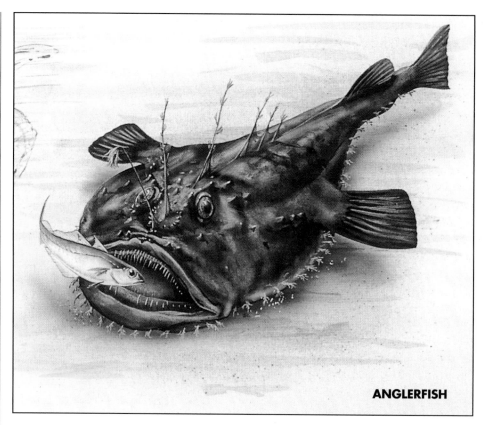

ANGLERFISH

flaps, and the belly is pure white.

It spawns in late spring/early summer, depositing a ribbon-like sheet of eggs up to 3ft wide and over 20ft long. The eggs remain near the surface in a long trail until they hatch.

HABITAT AND DISTRIBUTION

It spends its entire life mostly in deep water, lying on the bottom over sand, gravel and, sometimes, rocks. It cannot be specifically fished for, and is caught only very occasionally, when an angler's bait happens to be lowered close to those powerful jaws.

Also very occasionally caught in British waters is the black-bellied angler fish (*Lophius budegacea*). This is a much smaller species, identified by its noticeably grey underside.

TECHNIQUES

See *Downtide boat fishing.*

ANGLERS CONSERVATION ASSOCIATION (ACA)

The ACA (incorporating the Pure Rivers Society) is the only British independent organization committed to restoring contaminated fisheries in both still and running water and prosecuting the pol- luter under common law. Anyone can join the ACA for a small yearly subscription. The association currently boasts over 15,000 members, and encourages all fishermen to become waterside watchdogs.

ACA, 23 Castlegate, Grantham, Lincolnshire, NG31 6SW. Tel: 01476 61008; fax 01476 60900.

AQUATIC PLANTS

See *Waterside flora - rivers; Waterside flora - stillwaters.*

ARGENTINE

(*Argentina syphraena*)

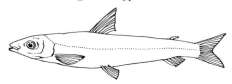

British record: 5oz 3dr (147g)

This deep-water shoal fish, as its unusually large eyes suggest, feeds on molluscs, crustacea and tiny fish. It averages 6-9in when adult and has a slender body, green-pewter along the back with a silver flash along the flanks. A distinct, pointed snout and tiny adipose fin are its other identifying features. It is rarely caught on rod and line.

ARLESEY BOMB

See *Ledger weights - freshwater.*

ARTERY FORCEPS

Artery forceps are indispensable for removing hooks when coarse, game and light sea fishing. A locking, long-nosed pair removes hooks from size 14 upwards quickly and efficiently. Below hook size 16, barrel-nosed disgorgers are more effective, particularly for spade-end hooks.

All good tackle shops stock both straight and curved-nosed models, 5-12in long, in stainless steel (they are rejects from the medical profession). Most fishermen find curved-nosed forceps easier to use, but the choice is yours. For general work, a 6-8in pair is ideal. For pike, 10-12in models are advisable to prevent contact between those sharp teeth and your fingers. It is, however, perfectly in order to slip the nose of shorter forceps gently through the gill slit of a pike (be careful of the rakers) to dislodge a deeply embedded hook and to remove it via the jaws.

Forceps bend along the stems if used to remove sea hooks in sizes 2/0 upwards. For those, long-nosed pliers are superior.

ARTIFICIAL FLIES

DRY FLIES

Dry flies are tied to imitate a vast variety of insects, both aquatic and wind-blown terrestrials, and vary in size from tiny midge and caenis patterns to large mayflies and daddy long legs at the other end of the scale.

The one requirement of all dry flies is that they float on or just in the surface film. In order to achieve this, dry flies need to be tied on hooks that are lighter in the wire and incorporate light, water-repellent materials in their dressing. Most commonly used are stiff cock hackles, while buoyant deer hair is also popular.

In recent years, emerger patterns that sit in the surface film and give the impression of an insect in the process of hatching, have become increasingly popular among reservoir trout fishermen.

LURES

Lures are tied both as attractors, which trigger off aggression in trout, and to imitate natural food forms, particularly small fish. They are usually tied on big, long-shank hooks and feature substantial wings made either of feathers (streamers) or hair (hair wings).

While fish-imitating lures can be quite muted in their dressing, attractors are highly coloured and sometimes quite lurid, with day-glo and fluorescent-coloured bodies and wings. Bright silver, gold and light-reflecting materials are also popular for making lure bodies.

Tin heads and dog nobbler patterns, which incorporate a weighted ball (in a variety of materials) just behind the eye, have become very popular on stillwaters. The weight ensures that the fly sinks rapidly and creates an exaggerated and jerky swimming action during the retrieve.

Salmon flies are, for the most part, designed to produce an aggressive response from the salmon rather than to imitate something that features in the fish's diet. This is because salmon cease feeding when they return to freshwater to spawn. Shrimp and prawn patterns are the exception as they imitate the naturals on which salmon feed at sea. Salmon flies vary from the extremely gaudy to the plain black, and are tied in a wide range of sizes on strong treble, double and single hooks in sizes 10 to 4, to tackle any water conditions that might occur. *(Tube flies; Waddington.)*

Though not strictly artificial flies, because they are tied to represent bumble bees, amphibians, tiny voles and other edible surface swimmers, popping bugs made from deer hair fall into this section *(Flyfishing - Fly rodding).* These American-style creations bring out the aggressive nature in pike and chub when twitched and jerked across the surface of clear water.

NYMPHS

Nymphs represent a variety of aquatic insects. Some, such as the caddis grub (sedge), are designed to imitate the larval stage, while others copy the pupal stage. Some represent creatures - such as shrimp and corixa - that live their entire lives in water but are not aquatic flies.

As with dry flies, nymph patterns come in many shapes and sizes from tiny buzzers and midges to mayflies, damselflies and dragonflies. Colours tend to be muted, greens, greys and browns being popular, while some patterns incorporate leaded underbodies or wire ribs to speed up their descent to the bottom layers.

Booby nymphs are a new concept in fishing. They consist of flies that incorporate small balls or squares of highly buoyant foam tied in at the head. They are intended to be fished on a fast-sinking line and are connected to it by a very short leader. This ensures that while they rise off the bottom, they are held down close to it to represent something swimming or scurrying about close to the lake bed. Their great advantage is that they can, and should, be fished very slowly without snagging up as conventional nymphs are prone to do.

A colourful and comprehensive selection of mayfly patterns which are tied to imitate the largest of our British upwinged aquatic flies.

There are literally thousands of different patterns of artificial flies. Many are tied to imitate the live aquatic insect in its larval, pupal or adult (winged fly) form. Some are weird and wonderful creations designed purposefully to attract and bring out the aggressiveness in predatory species, by the use of fluorescent wools, tinsels and other gaudy materials. Some benefit from the addition of strip lead along the shank or a weighted ball immediately behind the eye to create an exaggerated action on the

retrieve, as in the dog nobbler and tin head patterns, etc., while others work in reverse with balls of buoyant foam tied in at the head so they float tantalizingly above a wet fly line and actually dive down when retrieved. There are even patterns sculptured from buoyant deer hair and rubber strands tied to imitate frogs and mice scuttering across the surface. They all work. And they are all classified as artificial flies when used in conjunction with a fly rod and fly line.

WET FLIES

Wet flies generally fish below the surface. They are tied on heavier hooks than are dry flies, using softer materials, and are given wings and hackles that curve back over slim bodies to produce an overall streamlined effect. The exceptions are flies designed to cause a wake or surface disturbance when retrieved. Wet flies incorporating bushy hackles that extend the full length of the body are known as palmered patterns and fished on the top dropper. While many wet-fly patterns are supposed to represent insects, others are bright and flashy, acting as attractors that play on the trout's aggressive and inquisitive nature.

ARTIFICIAL LURES

Whether made from wood, stainless steel, aluminium, copper, brass, perspex, high-density plastic, soft rubber, chrome tubing, or even a mixture of hair, fur, feathers and wool, artificial lures catch most species of predatory coarse, game and sea fish. To be successful when working artificials, however, you need to know the purpose for which each type is designed.

BUZZ BAITS

These surface attractors, with names like Buzzard, Clacker, Sputter Buzz, Brush Popper and Uncle Buck's Buzzer, are similar to *spinner baits* in that they have a V-frame of sprung wire. However, the vibratory blade is replaced by a large plastic or aluminium propeller that churns the surface to catch the attention of predators down below, chub and pike in particular.

Some models come fitted with weedguards to protect the large single hook and can be whisked through the thickest surface greenery. In-line buzz baits such as the Goldwing and Snagless Sally have a blade or propeller at the head, with a double-pronged weed-guard in front of a single, keel-weighted hook and rubber skirt.

DEVON MINNOWS

These fast-revolving, propeller-headed bodies thread onto a special wire mount that has a treble at one end and a swivel at the other. Sleeved onto the eye of the treble is a red tulip bead so that the body, which is made of metal (for deep, fast water) or balsa wood, spins freely and does not wedge down over the hook. Sizes vary from 1in to 3in, the smaller models being aimed at trout, the larger at salmon. The colour and pattern variations are endless,

the most popular being the famous Yellow Belly, with blue and silver and red and gold coming close behind.

A similar lure made by Mustad, called the Tasmanian Cobra, comes in a variety of colours and in sizes ¼-½oz (7-14g).

KONA HEADS

These blue-water, surface-trolling lures, designed to attract swift-moving pelagic species such as wahoo, marlin and sailfish, have a highly reflective head made from hard, high-density resin/plastic, through which a nylon tube passes. A long, brightly coloured, plastic, squid-type skirt is firmly attached behind the head, helping to conceal the large, forged hook.

So that the hook is positioned correctly with the bend almost level with the tail ends of the coloured skirt, use a second crimp up the wire, or a mono-trace between hook and head (fig. 4).

PIRKS

Pirks are large bar spoons used for sea fishing. They are designed not to be cast, but to be lowered down into deep water over rough ground or a wreck and jigged up and down to attract species such as cod, ling, pollack and coalfish, which grab hold thinking the pirk is a small shoal fish.

The body can be round (bar pirks) or triangular in cross section, like the Norwegian Jiggers by Mustad. Tassels of red plastic, tubing or feathers are added to the strong, galvanized treble hook for extra attraction. Although most anglers prefer the reflective properties of chromium plate, coloured pirks are also effective, such as Mustad's 'Jenson' range, which comes in sizes from 5¼oz (156g) to 11oz (300g) and several bright colours, and has a scale-like finish.

Another unusual but extremely effective pirk is the Leadhead. Available in sizes up to 16oz (450g), it has a large, cadmium-plated single hook and a plastic, worm-like, twister-attractor tail.

To avoid the expense of losing shop-bought pirks to the rusting hulks of wrecks, many sea fishermen make their own. Heavy chromium-plated door and boot handles salvaged from really old cars are one source. Unfortunately, modern cars are fitted with unsuitable handles, so you need to search around in breakers' yards. Drill a hole at each end of the handle, having first removed the stem with a hacksaw (fig. 5) and fit the swivel and treble via large split rings.

Another way of making really excellent

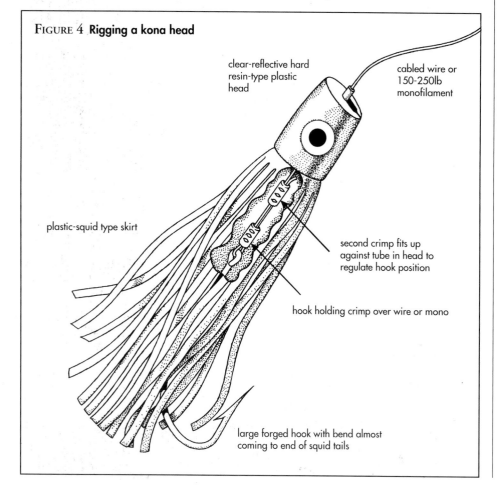

FIGURE 4 **Rigging a kona head**

clear-reflective hard resin-type plastic head

cabled wire or 150-250lb monofilament

plastic-squid type skirt

second crimp fits up against tube in head to regulate hook position

hook holding crimp over wire or mono

large forged hook with bend almost coming to end of squid tails

pirks is to fill short lengths of ¾-1in diameter chromium-plated steel tube (as used in bathroom towel rails) with molten lead, leaving 1½in clear at each end. Both can then be flattened in the vice or with a hammer, and holes drilled through to accommodate split rings, hook and swivel (fig. 6). A range weighing between 8oz (25g) and 20oz (500g) should suit all but the most challenging situations.

When you need to cast smaller pirks long distances, such as off the rocks or shore in search of species like pollack and coalfish, choose models with a really lifelike action. The Lance, made by Bridun Lures, is a great caster and is available in numerous colour finishes, in sizes 10-50g (⅜-1¾oz). Also recommended is the Dexter Wedge, which has a highly reflective finish in a choice of several colours, and comes in sizes 10-80g. It has a superb wobbling action and casts like a bullet. Mustad's Jensen Pirken has an authentic, scale-like

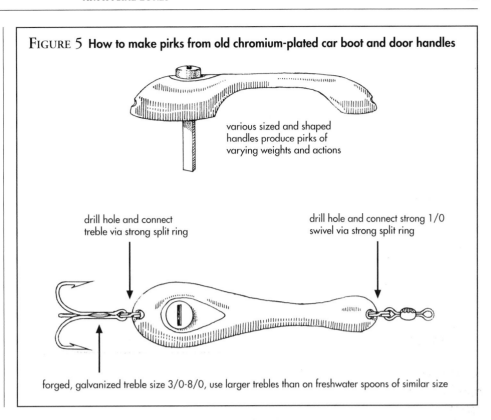

FIGURE 5 **How to make pirks from old chromium-plated car boot and door handles**

various sized and shaped handles produce pirks of varying weights and actions

drill hole and connect treble via strong split ring

drill hole and connect strong 1/0 swivel via strong split ring

forged, galvanized treble size 3/0-8/0, use larger trebles than on freshwater spoons of similar size

This armoury of artificial saltwater lures includes both coloured and chromium-plated pirks weighing up to 20oz, plastic and rubber eels, worm tails, a set of handline jigs, plastic squids and several sets of feathers.

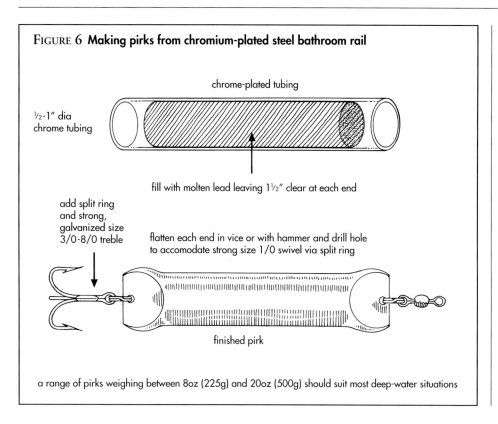

FIGURE 6 **Making pirks from chromium-plated steel bathroom rail**

chrome-plated tubing

½-1″ dia chrome tubing

fill with molten lead leaving 1½″ clear at each end

add split ring and strong, galvanized size 3/0-8/0 treble

flatten each end in vice or with hammer and drill hole to accomodate strong size 1/0 swivel via split ring

finished pirk

a range of pirks weighing between 8oz (225g) and 20oz (500g) should suit most deep-water situations

bass fishermen for luring members of the sun bass family, soft plastic and synthetic worms are now widely used for catching a number of freshwater and saltwater species. Worms are generally available from 3in to 10in long, either straight or with twister-type tails for added attraction, and come in every conceivable colour.

Some have ribbed, lifelike bodies; some are perfectly smooth and exceptionally supple. Some have legs and newt-like contours. Some are impregnated with various attractor oils and essences. Some glow in the dark, some have a highly reflective or metallic sheen. To the touch they even feel like the real thing, and all will catch predatory fish.

Small synthetic worms can be threaded onto the single lead-headed hook of a spinning jig, while the larger sizes are best presented 'Texas rigged'. Simply thread a small coned 'worm weight' (a small, drilled bullet will suffice, or even a swan shot) onto

finish, casts well, and comes in sizes ¼oz (7g) to 2oz (60g) and a variety of colours.

PLASTIC SQUID/MUPPETS

Called muppets by sea fishermen, these imitation squid made from soft, rubbery plastic are available 3-9in long and in numerous colours from luminous green, which glows in the dark, to jet black, which stands out well in heavily coloured water. Muppets can be threaded on the line above a pirk or a live worm bait to provide added visual attraction. Alternatively, they can be made up with 40-50lb test mono filament on snoods constructed from blood-dropper loops (*Knots*) in sets of two or three, each concealing a large single hook (fig. 7A).

A most effective and inexpensive bluewater trolling lure for catching pelagic species such as bonito and other tunas can be made quickly and easily with a single medium to large-sized muppet. Pink and hot orange are great blue-water trolling colours. Make a tiny hole with a hook point or needle in the head, and sleeve the reel line through it, followed by a ½in-diameter lead bullet or a couple of large, coloured beads. Then tie on a suitable hook. The bend and point of the hook should be concealed by the muppet's skirt (as in fig. 7B). A muppet sleeved up the line above mounted whole fish or fish-strip bait also makes trolled baits more attractive.

PLASTIC WORMS

Originally conceived by American black-

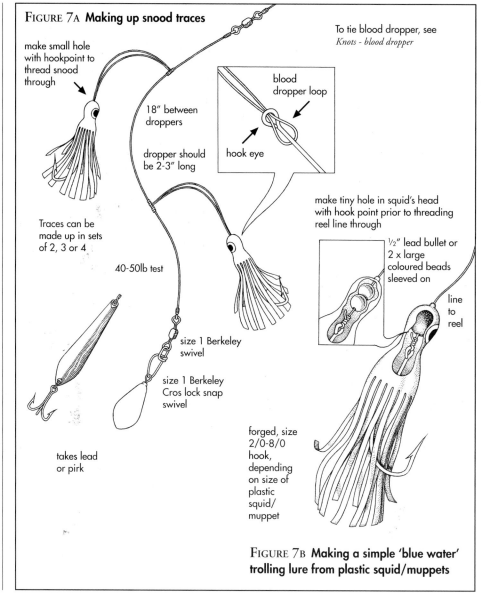

FIGURE 7A **Making up snood traces**

make small hole with hookpoint to thread snood through

To tie blood dropper, see *Knots - blood dropper*

18″ between droppers

dropper should be 2-3″ long

blood dropper loop

hook eye

Traces can be made up in sets of 2, 3 or 4

40-50lb test

size 1 Berkeley swivel

size 1 Berkeley Cros lock snap swivel

takes lead or pirk

make tiny hole in squid's head with hook point prior to threading reel line through

½″ lead bullet or 2 x large coloured beads sleeved on

line to reel

forged, size 2/0-8/0 hook, depending on size of plastic squid/ muppet

FIGURE 7B **Making a simple 'blue water' trolling lure from plastic squid/muppets**

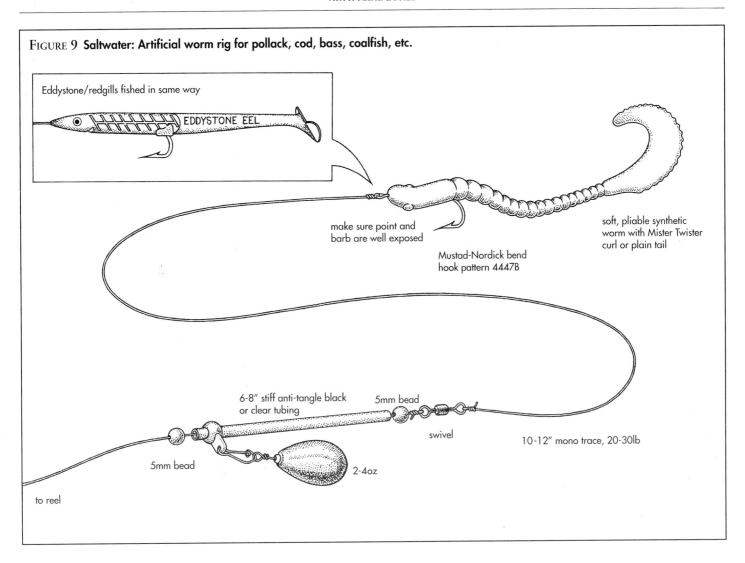

FIGURE 9 **Saltwater: Artificial worm rig for pollack, cod, bass, coalfish, etc.**

Eddystone/redgills fished in same way

EDDYSTONE EEL

make sure point and barb are well exposed

soft, pliable synthetic worm with Mister Twister curl or plain tail

Mustad-Nordick bend hook pattern 4447B

6-8″ stiff anti-tangle black or clear tubing

5mm bead

swivel

10-12″ mono trace, 20-30lb

5mm bead

2-4oz

to reel

---

the line, and tie on a fine-wire hook. Mustad's blued, Nordick-bend, pattern 4446B, is ideal. Insert the hook point into the centre of the head of your chosen worm and thread it carefully through the worm, concealing much of the shank. Bring the point out of the side of the worm and then ease it back into the worm again but without piercing the other side (fig. 8).

The worm is now 'Texas rigged' and can be cast into and retrieved through the very thickest beds of weed and lilies without getting caught up, yet the fine-wire hook will pull easily through the worm and into the fish's jaw on the strike.

Plastic worms are also extremely effective for sea species like coalfish, bass, cod and pollack shoaled up in deep, clear water. Use the forged version of the same Nordick-bend hook, Mustad 4447B, and thread on the worm, ensuring that the point and half the bend are exposed (fig. 9). Then tie a swivel onto the other end of the worm trace, which should be at least 10-12ft long. Above this goes a 2-4oz lead (depending on the tide) rigged on a sliding 6-8in length of anti-tangle tubing,

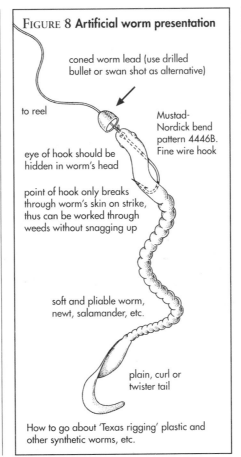

FIGURE 8 **Artificial worm presentation**

coned worm lead (use drilled bullet or swan shot as alternative)

to reel

Mustad-Nordick bend pattern 4446B. Fine wire hook

eye of hook should be hidden in worm's head

point of hook only breaks through worm's skin on strike, thus can be worked through weeds without snagging up

soft and pliable worm, newt, salamander, etc.

plain, curl or twister tail

How to go about 'Texas rigging' plastic and other synthetic worms, etc.

stopped by a bead against the swivel.

PLUGS

Although it is not always easy to tell which plug will do what from the displays in a tackle shop, these deadly artificials, whether used for freshwater or saltwater species, generally fit into one of three categories: surface plugs, or poppers; floating divers, that is, plugs that float but which, owing to their large, angled lips, will also dive down on the retrieve; and sinking divers.

Surface plugs or poppers

This fascinating range has been purposefully designed to displace the surface film by spluttering, popping, gurgling, chugging, rattling, throbbing and so on, thus attracting and inviting predatory species into attacking them from below. Some remain on the surface all through the retrieve regardless of speed, others will dive a foot or two when cranked in really hard. Most are used effectively along reed lines, through or beside beds of lilies and above dense beds of soft weeds where predators such as pike like to hide.

Rebel's Buzz 'n' Frog has rear legs that

These surface plugs and popping lures really irritate predators into spectacular attacks

Top row: **Buzz 'n' Frog, Mann's Ghost, Thundertoad, Moss Boss, Heddon's Crazy Crawler**

Second row: **Zara Mouse, Creek Chub Mouse, Throbber, Dying Flutter**

Third row: **Torpedo, Baby Torpedo, Nip-I-Diddee, Sputterbuzz**

Bottom row: **Trouble Maker, Chugger Spook, Zara Spook, Bass Oreno**

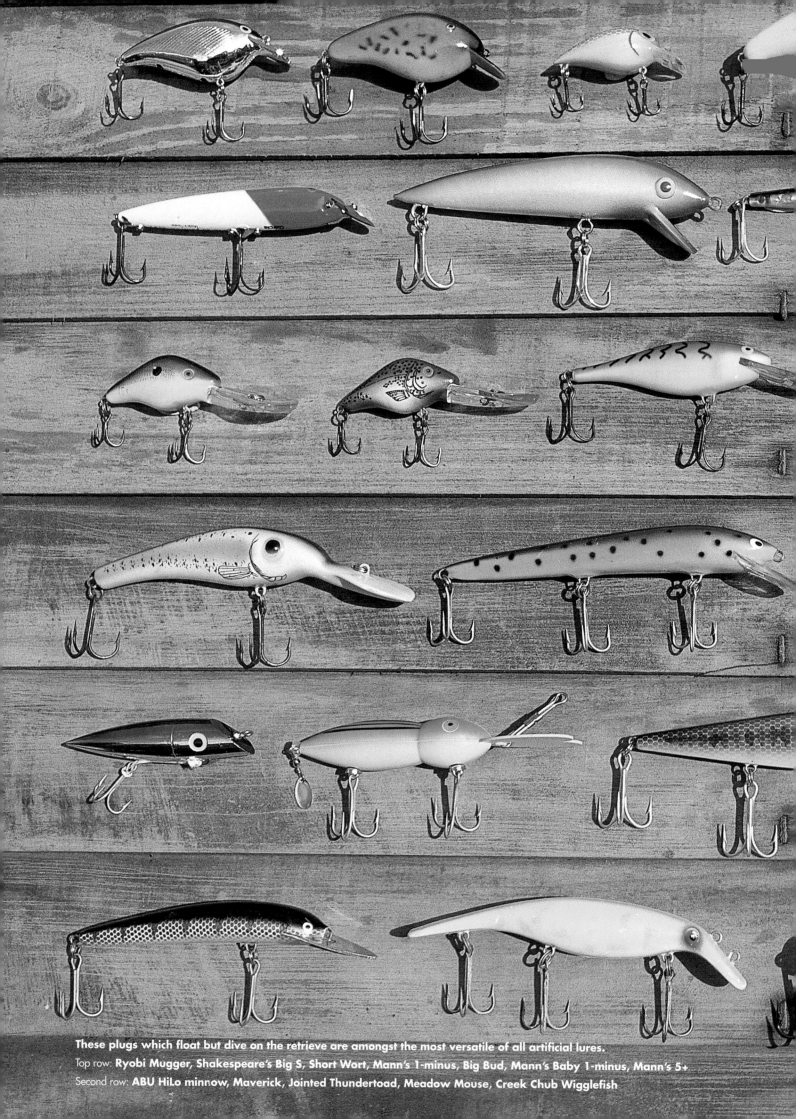

These plugs which float but dive on the retrieve are amongst the most versatile of all artificial lures.
Top row: **Ryobi Mugger, Shakespeare's Big S, Short Wort, Mann's 1-minus, Big Bud, Mann's Baby 1-minus, Mann's 5+**
Second row: **ABU HiLo minnow, Maverick, Jointed Thundertoad, Meadow Mouse, Creek Chub Wigglefish**

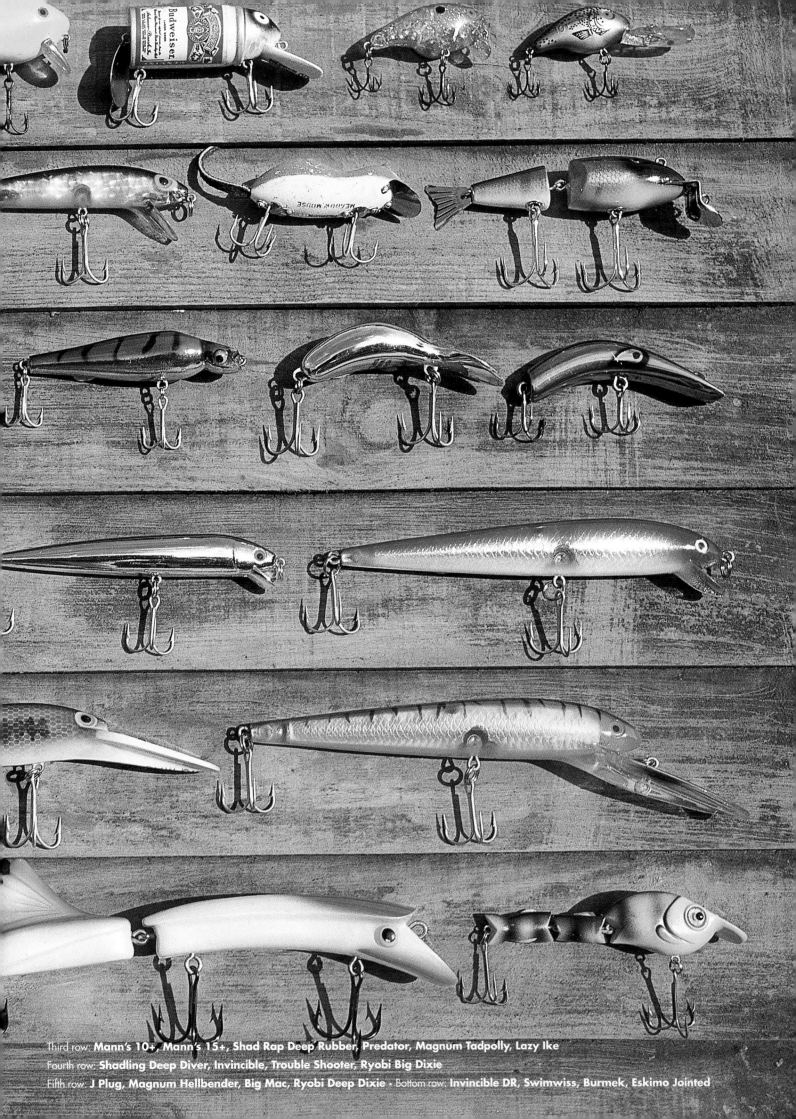

Third row: **Mann's 10+, Mann's 15+, Shad Rap Deep Rubber, Predator, Magnum Tadpolly, Lazy Ike**
Fourth row: **Shadling Deep Diver, Invincible, Trouble Shooter, Ryobi Big Dixie**
Fifth row: **J Plug, Magnum Hellbender, Big Mac, Ryobi Deep Dixie** · Bottom row: **Invincible DR, Swimwiss, Burmek, Eskimo Jointed**

rotate to churn the surface and which also act as a built-in weed-guard to the double hook. In dense surface greenery, weedless plugs are a must, and heading the list from Mann's Bait Co. is the Ghost, a highly buoyant tube of soft plastic whose large, double hook cannot hang up until a pike chomps hold. The weedless Thundertoad, complete with a plastic propeller at the front and a soft plastic body hiding a large single hook, has an extra, single 'stinger' hook in case predators are biting too early.

The Heddon Moss Boss is another weedless, surface-churning plug. It has a spoon-shaped body incorporating a large single hook and a plastic skirt, and can also be fished a few feet below the surface. The most notorious of all Heddon Lures is the Crazy Crawler, which has a built-in, flip-flop, crippled-butterfly or wounded-fish action that turns both chub and pike insane with aggression. Heddon's Zara Mouse (with a built-in weed-guard), Creek Chub Mouse (hair tail) and Throbber (with internal vibratory springs) create similar effects, as do the Dying Flutter and Torpedo, also from Heddon. These last two poppers come equipped with propellers to excite pike when they are retrieved in short, sharp bursts. Luhr Jensen's Dip I Diddle is another good propeller-rigged surface popper.

The Jitter Bug from Fred Arbogast Lures, available in both single and jointed formats, comes with an enormous up-turned lip that creates massive surface disturbance with the slightest twitch and jerk. Arbogast's Hula Popper is another favourite surface-popping lure and gains added attraction from a long plastic skirt. A similar lure, complete with a hair tail and brace of trebles, is the Trouble Maker from Gudbrod. Also worth a cast is Arbogast's Sputterbug, which has a propeller at the front and a short plastic skirt around the rear treble.

A great, jointed surface popper with big eyes, a scale finish and hair skirt, is also made by Mirror Lure. Heddon's torpedo-shaped Zara Spook has no gimmicks, simply a tantalizing action when jerked in fast while the rod tip is swung from side to side. Bass Oreno from Luhr Jensen works similarly and will zoom several inches beneath the surface if cranked in fast, in addition to gurgling and popping on the surface with a more sedate retrieve.

Floating divers

These, whether single, double or even tre-ble jointed, are the largest and most versa-tile of all the artificial lures. One can iden-tify those that dive deeply when cranked briskly by the size of their plastic or alloy lip. Big lips (or vanes) dive deep; small lips dive shallow. Some manufacturers, Mann's Bait Co. for instance, stamp each plug with the exact depth to which it will dive, and their revolutionary 'depth-plus' series in-corporates variously sized plastic lips that zoom the lure quickly down to 1ft, 5ft, 10ft, 15ft, 20ft or even a staggering 30ft after just a few cranks of the reel handle. For this reason, American lure fishermen call floating divers 'crank baits'.

Worked across the surface or in really shallow waters, in a depth band of about 1-4ft, for species like perch, chub and pike, plugs like the Ryobi Mugger, Shakespeare's Big S, Storm's Short Wart, Baby and Big Bopper, Mann's 1-Minus and Baby 1-Mi-nus, and Heddon's Big Bud, have great pul-sating actions. They also include sound chambers containing ball-bearings, which create a rattling noise.

Plugs that rely mostly on their sideways wiggle include Rapala's Shad Rap Shallow Runner, and Riplin Red Fin from Cotton Cordell, whose rippled body contours cre-ate a unique action. Cordell's Jointed Red Fin, Heddon's Hell Cat, the L Jack Min-now (which has a highly reflective body) from Yo-Zuri, ABU's Hi-lo Floating and Hi-lo Minnow, Gubrod's Maverick, Arbogast's Snooker Minnow, Magna Strike Predator and Gladiator's Bomber Long A, and Storm's Jointed Thunderstick are all excellent.

Other shallow-diving oddities with the power to excite predators include Heddon's Meadow Mouse (big chub can't resist it) and the Creek Chub Wiggle Fish, a great pike catcher.

For exploring greater depths - 6ft and deeper - you can choose from hundreds of plugs. Rapala's Rattle 'n' Fat Wrap, Shad Rap Deep Runner, Fat Rap Deep Runner and the Mini Fat Rap (a great perch, chub and trout catcher) are all absolute musts. Mann's range of 5ft, 10ft, 15ft, 20ft Deep Hog, and the incredible 30ft, also have great vibratory actions with the power to reach predators inhabiting the deepest and most irregularly bottomed gravel pits and river systems (*Artificial lure fishing - fresh-water*).

Heddon's Magnum Tadpolly, which comes in two sizes, emits massive vibra-tions even when retrieved or trolled slowly, so it works wonderfully in coloured water, as does the banana-shaped Lazy Ike and the famous Kwikfish range - all excellent trolling lures. The two 6-in long Shadlings from the Lindy Little Joe stable are strongly made and cast like rockets. Even the shal-low diver winds down to 8ft, and the deep diver reaches 20ft.

The handcrafted Invincible and Invin-cible DR balsa-wood plugs from Nilsmaster of Finland cast well and are good for 8ft plus. Lures of similar pedigree are the Hunter, the Harrier (has a great rattle) and the Kynoch Killer, a deadly salmon and pike lure possessing an exag-gerated wiggle designed to slide up the trace so that hooked fish cannot lever themselves off.

Out on its own in diving prowess is Heddon's legendary Magnum Hellbender, which zooms down to over 30ft if trolled on a long line and flips easily over irregu-lar bottom contours. Storm's Rattletot is a similar deep-diver, incorporating a loud rattle.

Though considered a neutral buoyancy plug, Smithwick's Deep Float Rattlin Rogue belongs to the floating divers be-cause its huge lip quickly zooms the plug down to 10ft where, unlike plugs that float upwards if you stop reeling in, the Rogue will hang in the water. It can then be twitched and tweaked at that depth. It ex-udes pike appeal, as does the Corado Con-queror, which is available in three sizes with potential depths of 5-12ft.

The jointed Big Bad Burmek with its deeply troughed lip is another good big-water lure guaranteed to irritate pike and trout into action with its wounded-fish wiggle. Jointed divers are not in fact fa-voured by most manufacturers, but DAM should be proud of their Eskimo Wobblers, which have a tantalizing quivering action and come in both single-jointed and dou-ble-jointed formats.

Rapala's Jointed Floating plugs also have great wiggle actions, and are available in a choice of four sizes and seven colours.

Saltwater floating divers

Super-strong models equipped for the rig-ours of casting and trolling in saltwater in-clude Rapala's range of Floating Magnums and the Diving Bang-o-B from Bagley. All have lifelike actions, with split rings and strong, galvanized treble hooks to meet the demands of tropical saltwater gamefish. The smaller models, however, work ex-tremely effectively in fresh water for big

In addition to spinners, spoons, spinner baits, buzzbaits and a variety of both surface and diving plugs, huge patterns of wet flies and buoyant deer hair imitation frogs, mice, etc., are becoming increasingly popular with artificial lure enthusiasts who wield a fly rod intentionally for pike and chub.

trout, zander and pike. From the Storm stable, the Big Mac series proves equally effective with pike and blue-water sea fish, whether you are casting or trolling.

Sinking divers

Many sinking divers can be counted down at around 1ft per second (just like a big spoon) to the desired depth band, where they then stay throughout the retrieve. Such models are Rapala's Countdown series, which come in several colours 3-5in long. The Rattlin Rapala (available in both patterned and metallic finishes) and the Rattle Spot from Cotton Cordell, are great trout and pike lures. The quickest sinking of all rattle-chamber plugs is the Vibrastar 2 from Yo Zuri, which has a translucent, big, S-shaped body full of coloured beads and really strong hooks.

The highly coloured Canadian Wiggler and Jointed Wiggler plugs, made from brass, are a great pair of deep-water divers. Rebel's sinking crayfish can also be counted down into deep lakes or weir-pools, where it quickly catches the attention of chub, trout, perch, zander and pike. A similar lure, the Flip 'n' Craw from Strike King Lures, comes with a large single hook protected by a weed-guard. It has a balanced lead head for counting down at 1ft per second and responds with a most lifelike action to a jig-and-wind retrieve.

Another great American lure is the slow-sinking, jointed Zara Gossa from Heddon, designed not to dive deeply but to dance and wiggle through the upper water layers. The Arc Minnow from Yo Zuri works almost identically.

ABU's Jointed Hi-Lo is a versatile sinker due to its adjustable, six-position diving vane. It can be wiggled or chugged at the surface over weeds or wobbled along slowly at virtually any depth.

Best known of the slow sinkers is that classic American pike lure, the Creek Chub Pikie, available in both single and jointed formats. It can be wobbled speedily just a couple of feet below the surface, or allowed to sink deep, where its tantalizing side-to-side action leaves pike no choice but to attack. Such a lure was the downfall of the UK record pike of 46lb 13oz caught by Roy Lewis from Llangdedfed Reservoir in 1992. That fish succumbed to a perch-finish Creek Chub Pikie. Other colours are Red Head, Blue Sparkel and Pike Imitation.

Completely out on its own in design is the Russelure, an unusual banana-shaped plug pressed from thick-gauge aluminium sheet and fitted with three different anchor points for slow, medium and fast retrieve. Available in 3 sizes, 4-7in in length, and with super-strong galvanized trebles, it can be used for zander and pike in addition to the heaviest of blue-water sea species. Russelures are, however, renowned in Africa for Nile perch, which find the throbbing side-to-side action irresistible.

Saltwater sinking divers

Equally effective for big pike is Rapala's Jointed Sliver, crafted from African Odom wood and patterned after the needle fish. It comes in two sizes, 5in and 9in, both fitted with super-strong split rings and trebles.

Rapala's range of Sinking Magnums, from 3in up to the giant 11in model, are among the toughest plugs made, with a throbbing side-to-side action and available in a superb range of colours. Blue mackerel and orange are hot favourites. The Yo Zuri, jointed, sinking L Jack Magnum range has a highly reflective body and comes in sizes 3-7in.

At 8in long, Rebel's single and jointed Tracdown Jaw Breakers are purpose-made for big-water trolling in the sea and in fresh water. They have tough, virtually indestructible, moulded-foam bodies, stainless diving vanes and cadmium-plated 3x strong hooks. Their unique sensor eyes catch and reflect light rays.

REDGILLS/RUBBER EELS

Redgills and Eddystone eels are the best known of these rubber eels, so effective in clear water for species like mackerel, bass, pollack, cod and coalfish. They imitate the live sand eel and come in dozens of colours, and size 3in up to 11in, holding a massive 11/0 hook. Commercial redgills come with strong, stainless-steel hooks.

To attach them, thread the line through from the head to the vent before tying on the hook, and thread the shank back into the body so that only the bend and point are visible. The smaller sizes can be fished two or three up on a trace of snoods made from blood-dropper loops (fig. 7A) as with squid. Or they can be used singly on a long trace and Eddystone boom or anti-tangle tube rig (fig. 9) in preference to a synthetic worm.

Making rubber or plastic eel lures

Basic eel-like lures can be made easily and quickly from coloured tubing. Join a hook and swivel to a split ring (fig. 10) and sleeve on a length of rubber or plastic tubing cut diagonally at the hook end.

SPINNERS

The feature that makes these lures so irritatingly attractive to predatory fish is the vibratory pulses created by a blade revolving at high speed around the wire stem or weighted bar - hence the term 'spinner'. Most famous of all are the Mepps type, which vary in size from the tiny 00 to size

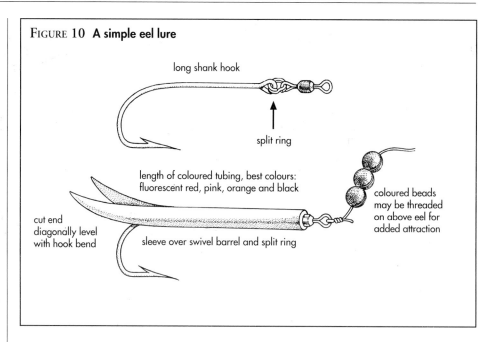

FIGURE 10 **A simple eel lure**

long shank hook

split ring

length of coloured tubing, best colours: fluorescent red, pink, orange and black

coloured beads may be threaded on above eel for added attraction

cut end diagonally level with hook bend

sleeve over swivel barrel and split ring

5. They may include coloured beads on the stem, plus the added attraction of hair, wool or synthetic strips around the treble hook. Similar spinners are made by ABU, Rublex and Landa, whose Flipz range has brilliantly coloured fluorescent blades instead of the more usual copper or chrome. Sizes 00-1 are ideal for grayling, perch, chub and trout, while sizes 2-5 are more suitable for salmon, pike and zander.

The notorious Flying Condom was originated by Kilty Lures as a salmon lure, although it is equally effective for perch, bass, pike and sea trout. In addition to the blade it has a coloured latex sheath covering the entire body, with just the treble hook exposed. A similar range, called the Flipz X, is made by Landa and is available in sizes 9-16g (¼-½oz). The Kitty Buck is of similar design, with a spray of coloured bucktail replacing the latex tube.

Most types of spinner will generally create some line twist. The answer is to incorporate an anti-kink vane, made with a short mono-trace if seeking perch, chub, trout and salmon, or from alasticum braided wire when pike and zander fishing (*Artificial lure fishing - freshwater*). There are, however, many patterns of spinners that do not create line twist. The Flying Condom range is generally kind to line and so, too, is the Voblex made by Rublex, which has a rubber head acting as a built-in anti-kink vane. The heavy head of ABU's Morrum spin and Mepps' Lusox ranges act in the same way.

An unusual way of eliminating line twist is to bend the wire at the head of the spinner upwards and at right angles, just like Eppinger's Dardeville spinner. Unfortunately, the first end of most spinners is not long enough in the wire to do this.

SPINNER BAITS

The name given to these vibratory lures, which were originally designed to catch the American black bass, is rather misleading because nothing on a spinner bait actually spins. Instead, a single or double blade fitted to the top of the V-shape sprung-wire frame vibrates. The lure is connected via the middle of the V to a snap-link trace swivel. To the lower stem is fitted a large, lead-headed single hook and a rubber skirt that folds back on the retrieve to help prevent the hook point weeding up.

The Tandem Spin from Mepps, Big Bass and the original from Blue Fox Lures, Barries Buzzer from Ryobi, Lindy Little Joe's spinner bait, are all popular patterns. They work with chub, perch and zander, and are a deadly pike lure, particularly in heavily coloured water where visibility is low, because they can be retrieved extremely slowly. When pike are coming short and not hooking up, wire a size 6 treble onto the bend of the big single with braided alasticum wire.

SPINNING JIGS

These are mini spinner baits with a much shorter frame. They consist of a vibratory blade above and a lead-headed jig below onto which plastic frogs, worms, salamanders, imitation rubber fish and so on can be sleeved. On some models the single hook is fitted with a skirt of rubber, fur, hair or marabou feathers. All are effective for catching freshwater species such as perch, chub, trout, zander and pike, plus sea species such as mackerel, pollack, coalfish and garfish.

SPOONS

The Toby lure was created in Scandinavia specifically to represent the sand eel on which both sea trout and salmon feed heavily during their life in saltwater. However, many sea species, particularly cod, pollack, bass, coalfish and mackerel, feed at some time on sand eels, and Toby-type spoons, or 'bar spoons' as they are sometimes called, prove effective the world over, not only in saltwater but with freshwater predators like perch, chub, trout, zander and pike. Toby look-alikes such as the Landa Lukki Flipz provide extra attraction by way of a 1in-long silver spoon attached to the swivel. Owing to their shape, and their availability in weights ranging from just 7g (¼oz) to over 60g (2oz), spoons are especially effective for casting long distances, and can also be trolled behind a boat for everything from brown trout to blue-water gamefish.

ABU make a comprehensive range of spoons in all sizes. The Trolling Devil, Big Wiggley, Atoms, UTOs and the Hammer range (with a highly reflective hammered finish) are great pike catchers, while the heavy-gauge Koster casts like a bullet and can be used from the shore or rocks as both *spinner* or *pirk*.

The Kilty Lure Co. also make heavy-gauge spoons in a variety of sizes, including the Heron range weighing up to 100g (3oz). The Kussamo Professor spoons have a unique tantalizing action, the 7½in model weighing 60g (2oz). Another superb range of large spoons, the Pikko Fatta Longer made by Landa, comes in three gauges and is suitable for both shallow and deep-water work.

By far the most comprehensive range of really large, heavy spoons, most suitable for trolling and casting into heavy or fast water, comes from the Dardeville stable made by the US company, Eppinger.

Excellent lures can be easily and cheaply manufactured from old spoons purchased at car-boot and jumble sales. After removing the handle with a fine-tooth hacksaw and filing down to a smooth finish, drill a hole at each end of the spoon and attach the treble hook and swivel of your choice via split rings (fig. 11). Then burnish the spoon to a bright finish with metal polish. Copper spoons, in particular, tarnish very quickly and lose that all-important flash that predators mistake for the reflective flanks of a small shoal fish.

Weedless spoons such as Eppinger's Dardeville or ABU's Toby Vass and Atom, which come fitted with wire guards that protect the hooks, are imperative for seeking predators that inhabit weedy shallows and lily beds. Choose single-hook versions in preference to trebles.

Flounder spoons

Flounder spoons vary between 2in and 3in long, and are made of either plain white plastic or chromed steel. The hook is always a small size, 1-1/0 single, attached to a sprung-wire boom so that the worm bait (rag or lugworm) is presented behind the spoon blade. When the spoon is retrieved slowly, the blade disturbs puffs of sand ahead of the worm, thus attracting flounders to it.

Fly spoon

The tiniest spoon of all, the fly spoon has a ½-¾in blade and a single hook. It is connected to a split ring and swivel so that it revolves at high speed, making it technically a spinner.

WHICH COLOUR LURE?

Artificial lures are available in such a wide range of colours and patterns that selection is never easy and always debatable. Only the predator itself can say which colours best bring out its attacking instincts on any particular day, taking prevailing water conditions into account. And on the very next day you are back to square one again. As a general rule, however, dark colours are best in low light conditions and

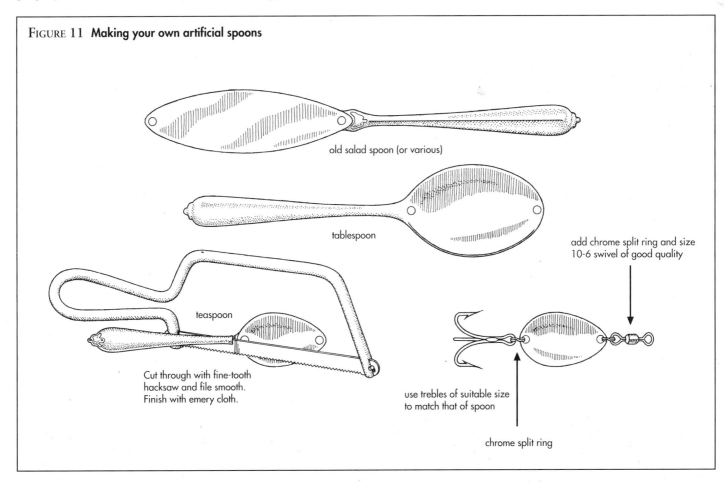

FIGURE 11 **Making your own artificial spoons**

old salad spoon (or various)

tablespoon

teaspoon

Cut through with fine-tooth hacksaw and file smooth. Finish with emery cloth.

use trebles of suitable size to match that of spoon

chrome split ring

add chrome split ring and size 10-6 swivel of good quality

The variety of spoons is enormous:

Top row: **ABU Toby, ABU Toby, ABU Toby, ABU Toby, Lukki Flipz Turbo, Lukki Flipz, ABU Big Wiggley, Weedless Atom, Atom, UTO, UTO, UTO, UTO, UTO, Koster, Copper Spoon, Silver Spoon, large Silver Spoon.**

Second row: **Kilty Mikki, Mikki, Mikki, Mikki, Heron, Heron, Large Heron, Kuusamo Professor, Professor, Landa Pikko Fatta, Pikko Fatta, Pikko Fatta, Dardevle Weedless**

Bottom row: **Dardevle, Dardevle Jack of Diamonds, Dardevle, Dardevle Wide, Dardevle, Dardevle, Dardevle, Dardevle wide, Dardevle long**

in the early morning or at dusk, when the lure is to some extent viewed in silhouette by a predator looking upwards. At midday, in bright, clear water, and especially in calm conditions, vivid, even exaggerated colours and patterns often seem to have the edge. In really green water, yellow shows up well, even at great depths, while in crystal-clear water orange and pink are tops, particularly with the pelagic, blue-water game species.

Where predators are feeding upon a particular shoal fish, imitative lure patterns often score over all others. Small wonder that perch fry patterns in freshwater and the blue mackerel for saltwater species remain high up the list.

ARTIFICIAL LURE FISHING - FRESHWATER

If there is a secret to working artificial lures, it is to remember that they are exactly that - artificial. Unless they are retrieved erratically at a speed to suit wa-

ter conditions - whether jerked, plopped or gurgled, with the odd pause, pull and lift of the rod tip - they remain pieces of wood, metal or plastic. This applies to artificials used for both saltwater and freshwater predators, be they game or coarse species. In short, artificial lures must be 'worked'.

In freshwater especially, it is very important to have an idea of a fishery's character: the depths, weed beds, snags and so on. Apart from covering the area with some sort of *fish-finder* unit, there is no better way of determining the topography of a gravel pit, for instance - by far the most irregularly bottomed of all fisheries - than to fish as you plummet, using the countdown method with a large spoon (or sinking plug).

Whether boat or bank fishing, you can break down even the largest waters into manageable areas and grid search them by allowing 1ft for every second that the spoon takes to sink to the bottom (fig. 12). A detailed sketch of a large fishery often helps, so remember to take a notebook along in

which to record your soundings.

Using this simple technique you can quickly discover the whereabouts of deep holes and troughs, shallow weedy bars and plateaux, and so on. Moreover, perch, pike, trout and zander hear the spoon's arrival and in clear water often follow its fluttering passage down until it hits bottom, whereupon the line suddenly slackens. So concentrate hard right from that first lift of the rod tip at the start of the retrieve.

Don't hold the rod completely to one side because in this position the stretch in mono-filament line could prevent the hooks getting purchase on the strike. Work the lure with the rod tip pointing almost directly at it, quickly raising the tip to bang the hooks home the moment you feel a 'hit'. A carefully pre-set clutch lets the fish take line on demand, reducing the risk of instant break-offs with big fish.

If you repeatedly lose fish (pike especially, due to their bony jaws) because the hooks fall out, seemingly for no reason, inspect the hook points as they can quickly become blunt when worked over a gravel bottom. The remedy is to carry a good-

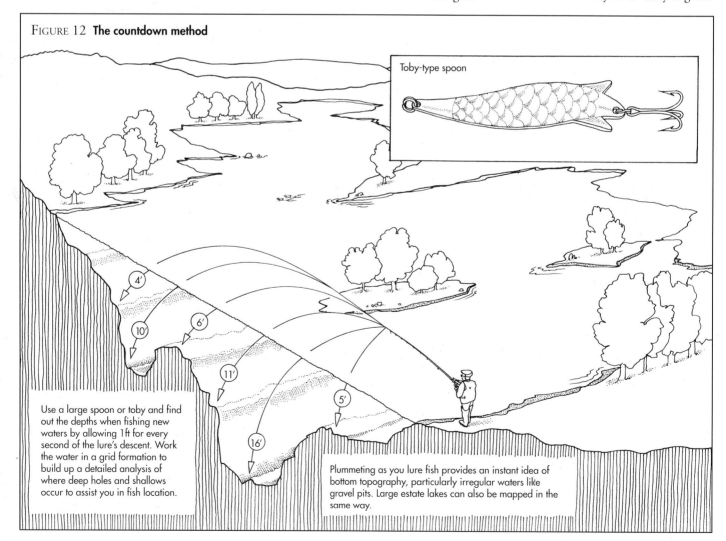

FIGURE 12 **The countdown method**

Toby-type spoon

Use a large spoon or toby and find out the depths when fishing new waters by allowing 1ft for every second of the lure's descent. Work the water in a grid formation to build up a detailed analysis of where deep holes and shallows occur to assist you in fish location.

Plummeting as you lure fish provides an instant idea of bottom topography, particularly irregular waters like gravel pits. Large estate lakes can also be mapped in the same way.

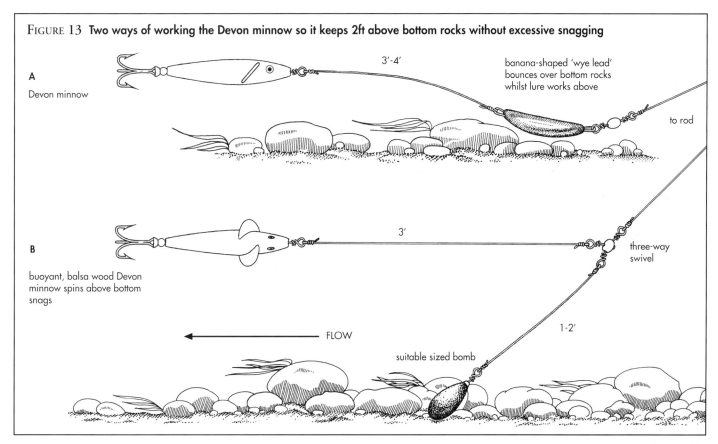

FIGURE 13 Two ways of working the Devon minnow so it keeps 2ft above bottom rocks without excessive snagging

A
Devon minnow

3'-4'

banana-shaped 'wye lead' bounces over bottom rocks whilst lure works above

to rod

B
buoyant, balsa wood Devon minnow spins above bottom snags

3'

three-way swivel

FLOW

1-2'

suitable sized bomb

quality, pocket-sized file and give each point a careful honing periodically. The hook can then be driven home with minimal force. It makes all the difference.

On really cold days fish will show more interest in artificials worked close to the bottom, while in mild, windy weather the upper water layers could prove more profitable. It is worthwhile exploring all depth bands, thereby offering every fish a snap at the artificial - just like working a wet fly in the classic 'downstream and across' technique. You can work the water in exactly the same way in pursuit of salmon and seatrout, adding a weight on the line to keep the lure close to the bottom, where fish lie in really cold conditions. Lures like the famous *Devon Minnow* (fig. 13) are best rigged either as in 13A with a 'Wye'-type weight fixed via snap-link swivels (for ease of changing) 3ft up the line; or as in 13B, for extremely fast currents, in which case the weight, usually a bomb, is tied to the end of the reel line with a separate 3-4ft lure trace connected to the middle of a three-way swivel.

Both rigs ensure that the lure works at the correct depth, right where the salmon and sea trout are lying behind boulders. Where bottom debris or rocks prove troublesome, use the buoyancy of a wooden Devon Minnow to ensure that it spins freely without snagging.

Certain lures, the Flying Condom for instance, are more successful when cast upstream and then retrieved downstream and across with the flow.

As you can see from fig. 14C, the lure is cast well upstream to between 2 and 3 o'clock (assuming the river is flowing right to left), and then retrieved down and across with the flow. This in effect gives predators a shorter period of indecision than the

John tricked this ferocious, yet handsome tiger fish from Zimbabwe's Zambezi River into striking at his trolled spinner by swapping the standard treble for a long shank single and baiting it with fish strip. A bunch of worms will also produce results, especially with members of the perch family.

'downstream and across' technique - small wonder that it is so effective with salmon and sea trout, but of course chub, perch and pike respond with similar aggression.

The most versatile lures of all are *plugs (Artificial lures)*, which fall into three categories - floaters, floating divers and sinking divers. This means that there are models to attract freshwater predators lying at all levels in the water from the surface to the depths of the deepest lake, river bed, or huge gravel pit with varying bottom contours from snaggy hideouts among reed lines to lily-clad shallows, and including vast clear areas of water in excess of 20ft deep.

In a fishery with a diverse character it is pointless, for instance, to work a *buzz bait (Artificial lures)* across the surface over 20ft of freezing cold water, because pike lying on the bottom will simply not charge upwards and grab hold of it. By the same token, a deep-diving plug cast into a bed of dense weed or lilies will become snagged and unusable in one wind of the reel handle. So before you cast, you need to think about two points: the purpose for which each artificial plug is designed, and the topography of the fishery. It helps to think of all waters as layer cakes and, taking into account elements such as barometric pressure, water clarity, depth, air temperature, evidence of shoals of bait fish, or the lack of it, explore the depth band that seems most likely to hold the predators you are after (fig. 15).

In fast-running water the current activates the lure's spoon. Take the salmon fisherman's favourite lure, the 'Toby', for instance. With it, you cast across the flow at a downstream angle of around 10 to 11 o'clock, if the river is flowing right to left (fig. 14A). Without winding in, let the current swing the lure attractively across the flow to point B, where, with little flow left to activate it, the spoon will sink to the bottom if you delay the retrieve.

To cover a certain pool or any wide stretch of river fully, take one pace downstream after every cast before working the spoon across with the flow. You can make the spoon more attractive to predators by suddenly speeding up the retrieve, pausing, speeding up again, twitching it, leaving it motionless for several seconds, and so on. Pike, especially, are roused by anything out of the ordinary, such as the movements that a wounded or dying fish might make. They often grab hold of a lure at the very last second, when it seems that their meal could be getting away, so remember to keep the retrieve going right until you lift the lure from the surface. This applies to all artificial lures, not just plugs. There are also situations, of course, when the retrieve needs to be slow and steady in order to persuade the predator to home in: fishing in deep, cold, coloured water is a prime example.

Summer plugging is different again. In addition to trout and pike, even species like chub and perch lunge across the surface to intercept floating divers and popping plugs. River chub will even attack an inert plug on the surface that is being floated down river - a deadly ruse, incidentally, for working a floating plug into all those inaccessible spots where direct casting is awkward or even impossible due to overhanging foliage. Try it.

BAITING ARTIFICIAL LURES

The addition of live or synthetic bait to the hooks of artificial lures, popular throughout North America and in many parts of Africa, also works wonders with British freshwater predators. Try adding a bunch of red worms or brandlings to the treble hook of a small spinner when you are after perch, zander or chub. Better still, swap the treble hook for a large single and, to stop the worms flying off on the cast, cut a ¼in section from a wide elastic band

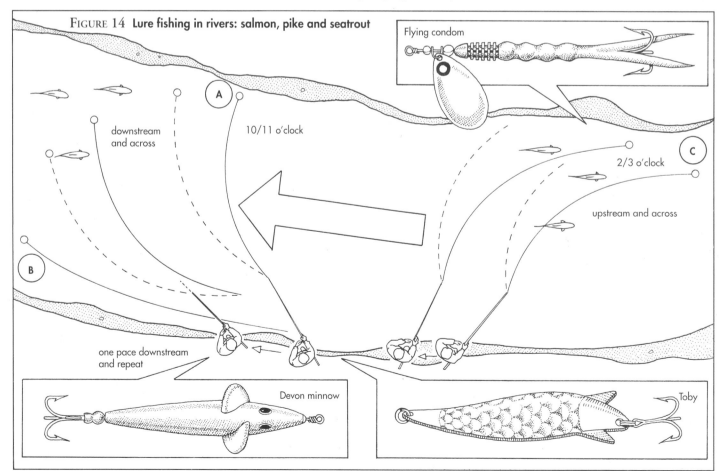

FIGURE 14 **Lure fishing in rivers: salmon, pike and seatrout**

Flying condom

downstream and across

10/11 o'clock

2/3 o'clock

upstream and across

B

A

C

one pace downstream and repeat

Devon minnow

Toby

FIGURE 15 Using the right lure when exploring each depth band

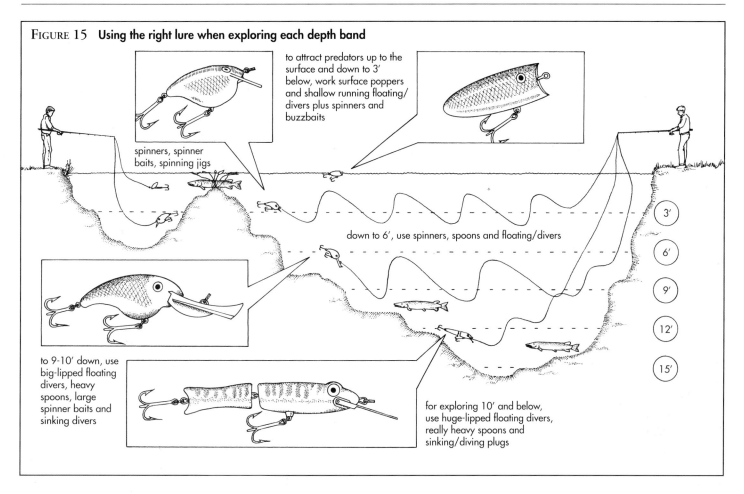

to attract predators up to the surface and down to 3' below, work surface poppers and shallow running floating/divers plus spinners and buzzbaits

spinners, spinner baits, spinning jigs

down to 6', use spinners, spoons and floating/divers

to 9-10' down, use big-lipped floating divers, heavy spoons, large spinner baits and sinking divers

for exploring 10' and below, use huge-lipped floating divers, really heavy spoons and sinking/diving plugs

3'

6'

9'

12'

15'

and slip it on over the barb.

Plastic grub tails, newts, salamanders and those long, lifelike imitation worms, available in an unbelievable array of colours, can all be sleeved onto a large single hook, as can pieces of bacon rind, strips of silvery-white fish belly (mackerel, for instance), gut segments and so on. All are exciting additions, not only for spinners and spinning jigs but even on large spoons. Simply exchange the treble hook for a single of at least two sizes larger, and ensure that the length of fish strip or gut is supported along the shank without slipping down to impair the hook-point's ability to penetrate on the strike.

For general freshwater lure fishing with pike and salmon, use a line of 9-15lb-test and a crisp-actioned, 9-10ft rod. A sloppy rod is useless for working lifelike action into lures because a soft action absorbs all your wrist movements while twitching and jerking. It also makes it impossible to drive the hook home.

The fixed-spool reel is more versatile than a small multiplier, particularly for casting really light lures a fair distance. However, those short, trigger-handled, American-style rods and baby multipliers are a joy to use when you are flipping out lead-headed spinning jigs, surface-popping

plugs and buzz or spinner baits.

You can make plastic or rubber worms really come alive (*Artificial lures - plastic worms*) using 5-6ft American bait-casting outfits, because every jerk and twitch of the rod tip is imparted to the worm. Don't bother with a wire trace for perch, trout and chub. But when pike and zander are the quarry, regardless of the type of lure always attach it via a 10in braided 10-15lb-test wire trace. These can easily be made up from a coil of alasticum with an American snap-swivel at the lure end and a size 10 swivel for the reel line (*Wire traces - freshwater*).

When specifically seeking smaller species like perch, sea trout, chub and jack pike on standard tackle, you can increase your level of enjoyment by using a light tip-actioned 7-8ft rod coupled to a fixed-spool reel holding 6-7lb-test line.

ARTIFICIAL LURE FISHING - SALTWATER

Most of the techniques for working lures in freshwater are equally effective in saltwater, but remember to rinse both lures and reels (and the rod rings) well in

cold water afterwards. Give the insides of your lure box a liberal spray of a protective aerosol lubricant as well.

Spoons, spinners, jigs and especially small to medium-sized sinking, diving plugs all work well inshore, in coastal waters wherever visibility is good for species like pollack, coalfish, mackerel and bass, plus sea trout and salmon. Even mullet will occasionally accept a small, worm-baited spinner, as will garfish. (See *Trolling*.)

For plundering the clear, deep-water marks around the coastline of the British Isles, particularly areas of very rough ground and those rusting war-time wrecks, by far the most effective technique is pirking (see *Artificial lures - pirks*). The idea is to lower the pirk down to the bottom until it makes contact with hard ground or the metalwork of a wreck, and immediately zoom it upwards in a long, exaggerated sweep of the rod. To maximize the movement at great depths, of about 100ft plus, a long 7½-8ft boat rod with a stiff action is imperative. At the top of its movement, suddenly lower the rod tip and allow the pirk to freefall down again, thus making predators such as ling, cod and pollack think it is alive.

Skippers nearly always try to drift their boats over the entire length of the wreck

(tide permitting), so you have to be ready instantly to shorten or lengthen the amount of line out, keeping the pirk just above bottom for as long as possible.

Use too short a line and your lure is yards above the fish. Have too much line out and you will pay the price of losing many more pirks than is acceptable. Incidentally, a monofilament reel line of 30-40lb test is perfect for pirking in depths up to 200ft. Beyond that, step up to a 50lb-class outfit and consider using dacron line, which stretches less, as opposed to monofilament.

The secret is to keep in touch with your pirk, so use one that is heavy enough to enable you to make at least two or three sweeps of the rod before the tide swings the pirk up and away from the wreck or bottom (fig. 16). You can then let more line out again to find bottom, or the wreck, and repeat the procedure perhaps once or twice more. After this, the pirk is not really working at the correct angle and is also far more prone to snagging. Wind in, lower the pirk down again and start afresh. It is by far the most tiring of all fishing techniques, but simply electric for hooking up with huge cod.

To catch larger fish such as the legendary halibut when drifting over deep water, such as around the Orkney and Shetland Islands, it is customary to remove the pirk's treble hook and replace it with 12in of 200lb-test monofilament (using crimps) and a 10/0 hook holding a coalfish or mackerel flapper (*Baits - sea*).

Where only small fish are encountered, use a smaller pirk than usual together with three or four snoods of feathers, squid skirts or plastic and rubber lures on single hooks, set at 18in intervals above it (fig. 7A). If you wait for other fish to grab hold after feeling the initial hits, you have a chance of hauling up a full house, sometimes with a different species on each lure. This is a regular occurrence when using a team of four to six coloured feathers for mackerel among dense shoals. By scaling everything

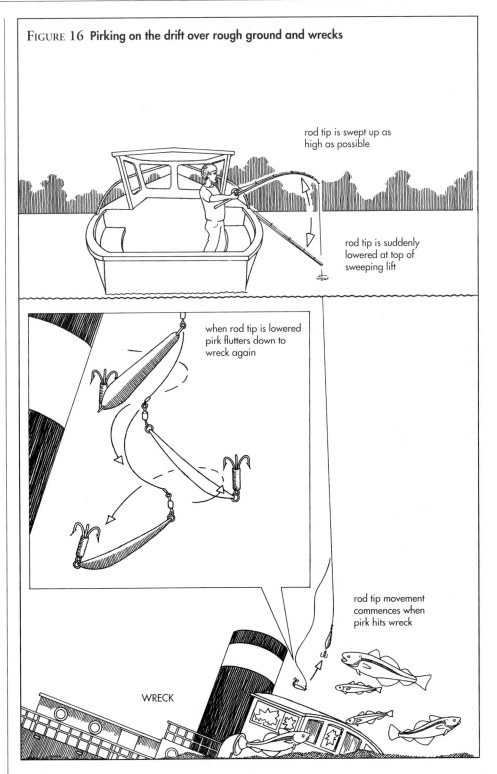

FIGURE 16 **Pirking on the drift over rough ground and wrecks**

rod tip is swept up as high as possible

rod tip is suddenly lowered at top of sweeping lift

when rod tip is lowered pirk flutters down to wreck again

rod tip movement commences when pirk hits wreck

WRECK

down to size 6 or 8 hooks with just the suggestion of a feather or thin white tubing, it is possible to catch the greater sand eel, or launce, which grows to over 1ft long and is a superb bait.

Pirking from the beach or rocks far out into clear water also catches cod, pollack and coalfish. Use a standard beach outfit with 15lb reel line, a 40lb shock leader and a 2-4oz pirk and expect hits even on the drop and before you commence the retrieve, in irregular sweeps of the rod. Step down to a lighter outfit and smaller pirks wherever the terrain and tide race permits.

When boat fishing on the drift in deep, clear water, whether over a rocky or clean bottom, plastic worms or redgill/Eddystone eels fished on light to medium tackle are deadly for cod, bass, coalfish, ling and pollack. Again, allow the lure to zoom down to the bottom on the special anti-tangle boom (fig. 9), then wind speedily upwards again. This technique is particularly attractive to big pollack and coalfish.

AVON FLOAT

See *Floats*.

Bb

BABBING

This ancient yet extremely efficient technique for catching eels, also known as 'bobbing', requires neither rod, reel nor hook. It works best at night in hot weather, when eels are on the prowl, with the angler seated comfortably in an anchored boat, or on the bank. Good locations are slow-moving rivers or tidal lakes (the Norfolk Broads, for example), where eels are prolific and where the depth does not exceed that of a long, stout bamboo cane.

Tie a length of strong cord (50lb monofilament is ideal) to the end of the cane, and to this tie the bab, which consists of several dozen lobworms carefully threaded from head to tail on to woollen yarn - worsted is best - using a baiting needle and tie them up in a clump or bunch. The yarn must be wet or the worms will burn and burst as they are sleeved on. A favourite babbing ruse is to soak the wool in fresh blood.

Sufficient weight (1-2oz bomb) is added to hold the bab on the bottom, and it is lowered down and then gently eased upwards every so often. Eels can soon be felt tugging at the worms, whereupon the bab is smoothly lifted upwards and swung onto the bank or into the boat directly over a large tub, into which the eels will drop, the simple secret being that the fine teeth of

the eel catch in the woollen yarn. Prebaiting a spot or two using a mixture of chopped worms, fresh blood, and bran to hold it all together, invariably improves the sport.

BAITS - FRESHWATER

See also *Live and dead baits - freshwater.*

BOILIES

Balls of a paste-type mixture are boiled so that they form a tough, rubbery skin that stops small nuisance species pecking away at them. Boilies are thus a super-selective bait designed originally for carp, but which tench and, to a much lesser extent, species such as barbel and chub also enjoy.

Ready-made, shelf-life boilies and frozen pre-mades are available in a huge range of colours and flavours, in diameters from 6mm minis up to giant 25mm gob-stoppers, all of which can be side-hooked or presented off the hook on a hair rig (fig. 17).

Making your own

If you cannot find suitable frozen or shelf-life pre-made boilies at your local tackle shop, try rolling your own. Virtually any combination of ingredients listed here, even the most crumbly concoction, can be kneaded into a pliable paste if it is first mixed with sufficient binders. The paste can be rolled into balls either by hand or with a bait-maker such as the Rollaball, and boiled in a deep pan until a tough skin

forms.

For high nutritional value (HNV) baits, make up the base mixture from one or two milk derivatives, such as casein, sodium casinate, calcium casinate, lactalbumen or soya isolate, plus a bulk ingredient such as soya flour or peanut meal. Then add a binder such as wheat gluten, which holds the crumbliest mixes together, plus beaten egg, which forms the skin for each batch of boilies. Make up 16oz of the base mixture, for which you will require 5-7 medium-sized eggs. Weigh all the ingredients carefully and bait-making is simple. Egg albumen can replace real eggs, together with sufficient water to knead the mix into a pliable paste.

A cheaper mixture can be made from animal or fish meal, such as trout pellets reduced to powder in a mortar and pestle; bird food and seed ingredients (Robin Red or Sluice CLO); or meal such as soya flour, semolina and maize meal - try equal parts of soya flour, semolina and maize meal. Add a binder, eggs, and 1 teaspoon each of liquid flavouring and powder colouring. Savoury, fruit and shellfish flavourings have all proved their worth, while various shades of orange and red have excellent appeal.

Many carp-bait manufacturers provide excellent recipe lists for boilies. Alternatively, you can purchase pre-formed, balanced, ready-made mixes to which you only need to add eggs plus your own choice of flavouring and colouring.

To obtain a creamy, pliable paste, always add the well-mixed ingredients a little at a time to the beaten eggs, colour and flavouring in a large bowl. Remember that the longer you knead the paste prior to rolling, the more air is squeezed out of the mixture, making it denser and ensuring that the boilies will sink.

Roll out sausage-shaped pieces of paste to the diameter you require. Cut the pieces into small segments and roll them individually on a work surface with the palm of your hand or lay them across a bait-maker. Place a few in the basket of a chip fryer,

Provided your paste is pliable without stickiness, rolling out into sausages and laying across a Gardner 'baitmaker' quickly converts it to balls ready for boiling.

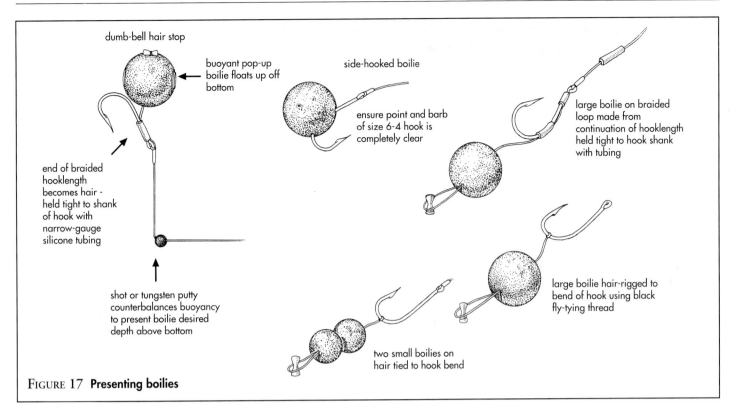

Labels in figure:
dumb-bell hair stop

buoyant pop-up boilie floats up off bottom

side-hooked boilie

ensure point and barb of size 6-4 hook is completely clear

large boilie on braided loop made from continuation of hooklength held tight to hook shank with tubing

end of braided hooklength becomes hair - held tight to shank of hook with narrow-gauge silicone tubing

large boilie hair-rigged to bend of hook using black fly-tying thread

shot or tungsten putty counterbalances buoyancy to present boilie desired depth above bottom

two small boilies on hair tied to hook bend

FIGURE 17 **Presenting boilies**

and boil them for 1-2 minutes, until the rubbery skin forms (most float when ready). Tip them onto an old towel and leave to harden off. You can then freeze your bait for the future or use them immediately.

To make pop-up boilies for surface fishing or to be suspended above the bottom, put a small portion of the paste to one side. Once you have boiled all your sinkers, roll the extra paste around small (8-10mm) polystyrene or cork balls, called 'pop-ups'. Boil these in the usual way.

BREAD

Breadcrust

While crust never stays on the hook as long as breadflake or bread paste, its buoyant quality permits you to float it above bottom weed and debris. It can also be used with a counter-balancing second bait such as sweetcorn, stewed wheat, casters, maggots or brandlings, thus turning it into a cocktail. Cut cubes or oblongs from the outside of a fresh tin loaf to match the intended hook size, and remember that crust swells to around twice its volume when saturated. Sliced loaves are ideal when using small hooks in sizes 16-10.

Floating crust can be presented at close range to species like chub and carp using simple freeline tactics, but for distances in excess of 20-25yd use the additional weight of a floating controller such as the ten pin (see *Freshwater float fishing techniques - Floating controller fishing*).

Breadflake

The fluffy dough of a white loaf is attractive to cyprinids. For quality-sized dace, rudd, roach and crucian carp, cover a size 14 to 12 hook with a piece the size of the nail of your little finger, but increase this to thumbnail size on hooks 10-6 for tench, bream, barbel, chub and carp. To ensure that after a short while you are not fishing with a bare hook because the flake came off during the cast or has disintegrated prematurely, fold a piece of flake over the hook and compress it really hard between thumb and forefinger around the shank only. Mask the point and barb with the thumb of your other hand so that penetration on the strike is not impaired.

Try a flake cocktail. Slip casters, maggots, a worm tail or two grains of sweetcorn, etc. on to the bend of the hook and then squeeze breadflake around the hook shank. A cube of crust and flake provides maximum buoyancy for fishing over dense weed.

Bread paste

With the previously mentioned species in mind, the very best bread paste is made from bread that is at least four to five days old. Remove the crusts and hold the bread under the cold tap for several seconds. Then, with clean hands, knead the sopping wet bread until all the stickiness disappears, resulting in a pliable, creamy paste. At this stage it can be wrapped in a damp cloth and used within a day or two, or popped

into a polybag and frozen for future use. A spoonful of custard powder can be added to provide colour and aroma (*Baits, freshwater - Pastes*).

Punched bread

Without question, diminutive pellets of bread punched out from a fresh white slice (*Bread punch*) are often preferred to other small baits, even maggots, by shoal species such as dace and roach, especially during the winter months when rivers run low and on the clear side. Use punched bread in conjunction with liquidized bread and introduce it on the basis of 'little and often'.

Coloured bread

To make a 2lb loaf exactly the colour of your choice - whether pink, orange, yellow or even black - obtain a 1¼lb packet of white bread-mix and some powder colouring. After dissolving a level teaspoon of the powder colouring (two spoonfuls for black) in ¾pt of hand-hot water, slowly add to the bread mix in a large bowl and stir thoroughly. Knead the dough for five minutes, and then place it in a lightly greased and floured baking tin of the appropriate size. Stretch clingfilm over the tin and leave in a warm place for 30 minutes, until the dough doubles in size. Place in the middle of a preheated oven set on 450°F/230°C/ gas mark 8 for around 45 minutes. Coloured bread, crust especially, often fools species such as chub and carp that have become wary of plain white bread.

See also *Ground baits - freshwater*.

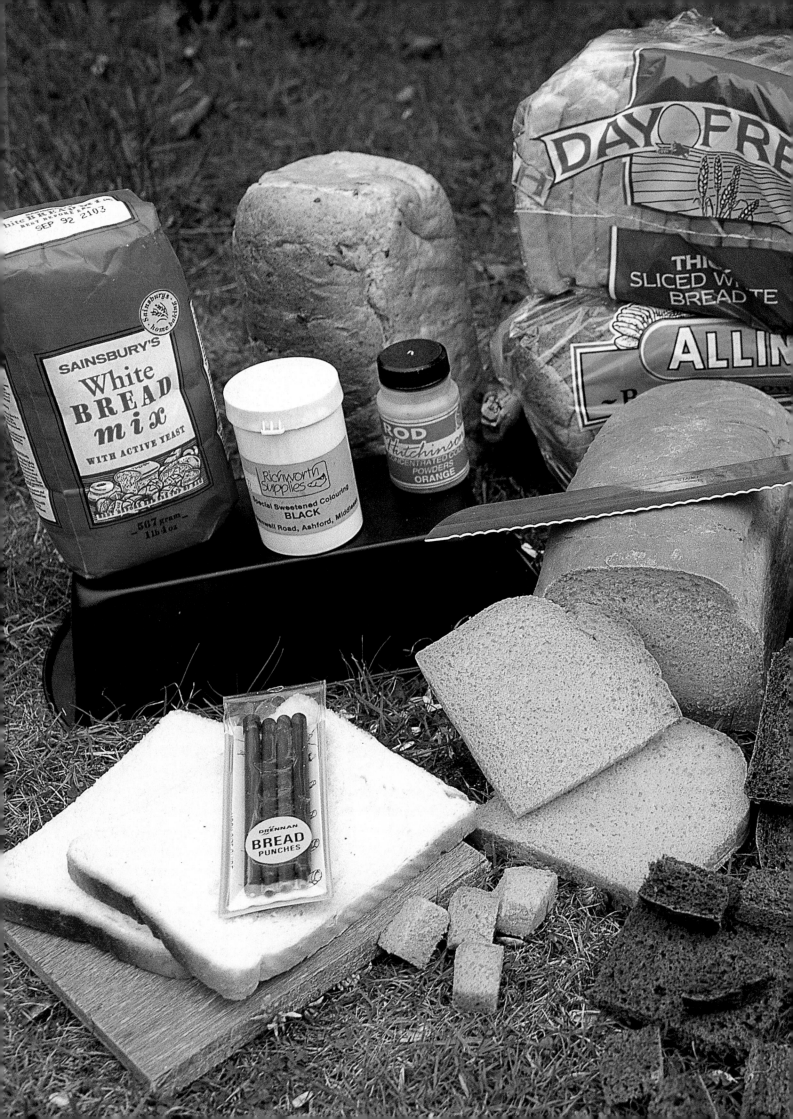

Whether used as mash or crumb for groundbait, or as hook baits of paste, crust, flake or punched into tiny pellets, the effectiveness of bread is unequalled. By adding powdered dye used in the making of carp baits to a simple baking recipe, even coloured bread is easy and often scores with those wary specimens that have become spooky of plain white bread.

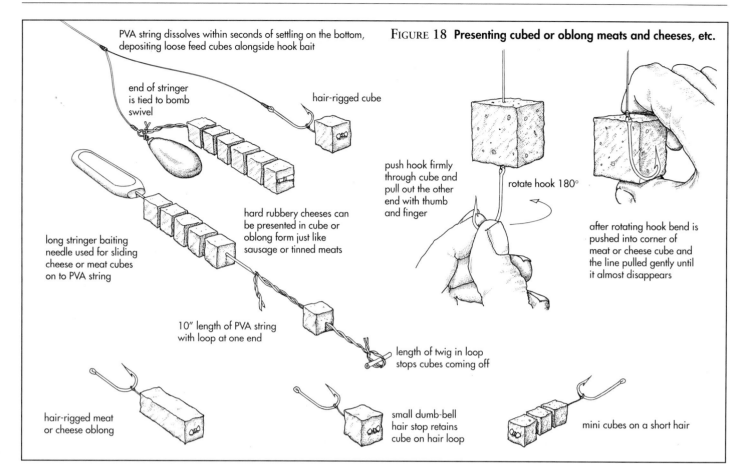

FIGURE 18 **Presenting cubed or oblong meats and cheeses, etc.**

PVA string dissolves within seconds of settling on the bottom, depositing loose feed cubes alongside hook bait

end of stringer is tied to bomb swivel

hair-rigged cube

long stringer baiting needle used for sliding cheese or meat cubes on to PVA string

hard rubbery cheeses can be presented in cube or oblong form just like sausage or tinned meats

push hook firmly through cube and pull out the other end with thumb and finger

rotate hook 180°

after rotating hook bend is pushed into corner of meat or cheese cube and the line pulled gently until it almost disappears

10" length of PVA string with loop at one end

length of twig in loop stops cubes coming off

hair-rigged meat or cheese oblong

small dumb-bell hair stop retains cube on hair loop

mini cubes on a short hair

CHEESE

While almost any cheese can be cut into cubes and presented in the same way as cubed meat (fig. 18), the rubbery cheeses - such as Edam, Gouda, Gruyère, Subenhard, Danbo, Maasdan and Emmental - best withstand the continual pecking of small, nuisance species. Plain English cheddar, however, either cubed or grated and mixed with a pliable paste (*Pastes*), is unbeatable.

FLOATING BAITS

For carp, chub, rudd and dace.

Boilies

Floating boilies can be produced by rolling the paste around a tiny cork or polystyrene ball. In addition, sinkers can be converted into floaters by baking them on a shallow tray in a pre-heated oven for 10 minutes, or by microwaving them. Timing, however, is critical when using the microwave. Test a boilie in a glass of water after just 1½-2 minutes in the microwave. Alternatively, you can get ready-made shelf-life floaters in all sizes and colours from specialist tackle shops.

Breadcrust

See *Bread* and *Coloured bread*.

Casters

See *Maggots* below; *Float-fishing techniques - Floating-controller fishing*; and fig. 19.

Marshmallows

Marshmallows are easily presented on a hair rig (fig. 19), cut into halves or quarters and used in conjunction with a controller (*Freshwater float fishing techniques - Floating controller-fishing*). They can also be freelined whole.

Paste

Add ½ teaspoon of flavouring to 12 fluid oz of water in a mixing bowl. Then, little by little, add a dry mix consisting of 8oz sodium caseinate, 2oz wheatgerm (or Bemax) plus 1 teaspoon of powder colouring. Stir firmly with a wooden spoon, then knead until pliable.

Small cat and dog biscuits

Available in a wide range of flavours, colours, shapes and sizes, these are particularly popular with carp, although chub and rudd will also succumb to these small floaters. Pedigree Chum mixers are the most popular brand and the easiest to side-hook, or thread onto a hair rig if dampened first (see *Trout pellets* below). Accepting that some will crumble during the process, it is quite possible to work an extra-sharp baiting needle or fine nut-drill gently through these dry biscuits for hair-rig presentation (fig. 19).

Sunflower seeds

These are used dry for loose feeding (carp

love them), but need to be moistened for presentation on a hair rig. Simply put a handful into a cup of hot water and leave for 10 minutes before transferring them into a polybag to retain the moisture.

Trout pellets

This great attractor (especially for carp) comes in all sizes from crumb to ½in holding pellets, and is also available in sinking form.

Floating pellets are not easy to present (*Freshwater float fishing techniques - Presenting floating baits, etc*), but can be threaded on to a hair rig, in conjunction with a cube of brown crust to aid buoyancy, if they are first made rubbery by splashing them with a handful of water and placing in a polybag for 20 minutes until they have absorbed all the moisture.

Alternatively, mould two or three pellets together with transparent bait adhesive such as Bogey, made by Kryston, and sleeve onto a hair. Another ruse is to sleeve a slither of breadcrust on to the hair and cover it with trout-pellet paste; or simply attract with floating pellets and present a small, similar-looking bait on the hair.

Making your own floaters

To make floaters guaranteed to float, add at least double the number of eggs to your favourite home-made boilie mix, and whisk

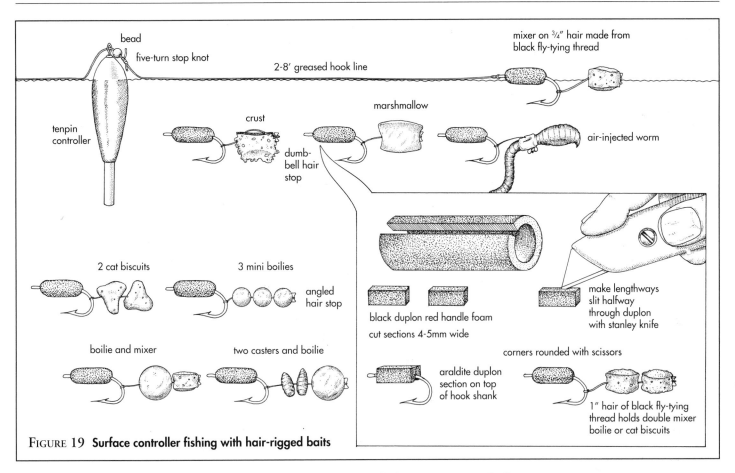

FIGURE 19 Surface controller fishing with hair-rigged baits

until you have a soupy consistency - which will produce the desired rubbery floating cake. Pour the mixture into a well-greased, shallow baking-tin to a depth of around ¾in and smooth the top with a fork before popping into the middle of a pre-heated oven set to 350°F/180°C/gas mark 4 for around 30 minutes. Tip out the cake, allow it to cool, and either pop it into the freezer for future use or use it immediately by cutting into cubes or oblongs of the desired size with a sharp, long-bladed knife. Present either directly on the hook or on a hair rig (*Freshwater float fishing techniques - Floating-controller fishing*).

Try any variation of the following recipe, which fits perfectly into a 7x11x1½in deep baking-tray:

2oz sodium caseinate
4oz powdered trout pellets, powdered cat biscuits, Sluis CLO bird floor or Robin Red
3oz maize meal, semolina, soya flour or peanut meal
1oz wheat gluten
1oz baking powder
1 teaspoon powder colouring (yellow or orange)
1 teaspoon liquid flavouring (to suit base ingredient)
12 eggs

MAGGOTS

The most commonly used freshwater bait in the UK, and available from all tackle shops, maggots originate from four different flies.

Gozzers

These are softer than standard, shop-bought maggots (see below) and originate from the common European bluebottle, which does not breed indoors. It is, therefore, a commercial rarity bred only by specialist match fishermen, who prefer its succulent skin when tempting bream from difficult waters.

Pinkies

These small maggots come from the shiny-backed greenbottle, and are not really pink. They get their name from a pinkish tinge that occurs within hours of their being taken away from their feed.

They can, like all maggots, be easily coloured pink, yellow, red or bronze by riddling off any sawdust and adding a capful of Spectra liquid dye to each ½gal. After 30 minutes the dye will be evenly distributed over each maggot by their movement. At this point add ½pt of maize meal for each pint of maggots. Pinkies make a fine hook-bait when used with light tackle in clear, cold-water conditions and as loose feed.

Squatts

Bred from the common housefly, this tiny maggot is a favourite of bream fishermen, who mix it in with their groundbait because it barely moves and will not burrow into a silty bottom. It is a good hook-bait for tiny fish when used with extra-fine terminal tackle (size 22-26 hooks) in waters where bloodworms are banned.

Standard hook-bait maggots

Available ready-coloured in red, yellow or bronze, in mixed colours or plain white, these are bred from the second most common European bluebottle, and last noticeably longer when kept chilled, preferably in an old fridge or on the concrete floor of the garage. Keep only 1pt of maggots in a 2pt box, plus ½pt of maize meal. Two pints of maggots crammed into a 2pt box at the tackle dealers to avoid buying another box is false economy. Present maggots on small hooks, and to hook them without breaking the skin and releasing the juices, nick the hook point through the blunt end only, between the two tiny dots. The black moving line through the middle of the body is the feed line and signifies that a maggot is fresh off the carcass on which it was fed at the maggot farm. Old maggots slow down noticeably during the initial stage of metamorphosis, as they turn into a chrysalis or pupa called a *caster* (below) by anglers.

For chub, barbel, tench, carp, catfish and eels, all kinds of processed meats and cheeses will prove effective due to their strong aroma. Whether tinned, in skins or in blocks, each may be cubed, oblonged or even triangled with a sharp knife and offered either on or off the hook using hair rig presentation for wary fish. For loose feed, dice the same into mini-particles or try sinking trout pellets in granular form, also called trout fly crumb. Stewed hempseed is also an excellent attractor loose feed, especially when used in conjunction with meat cubes.

Casters

To obtain fresh (sinking) casters that are yellowy-gold in colour, put slow maggots through an 1/8in-mesh riddle (every few hours during the summer months) into a chilled, plastic bait-box. Cover them with a piece of damp towelling and store in the coldest part of the fridge, which will greatly retard metamorphosis. Add further batches of riddled casters as they come off. Alternatively, put them straight from the riddle into a bucket of water and skim off any floaters. Transfer the sinkers into a polybag and put straight into the fridge, where they have a life of 3 or 4 days and should be used before starting to stink. Putting them into water obviously terminates metamorphosis by killing the maturing insect.

Casters are an excellent alternative hook-bait to maggots, and an unbeatable addition to cereal-based groundbaits, especially for bream and tench. They can produce staggering results with roach, dace, chub and barbel, even from clear-flowing rivers, when used in conjunction with hempseed that is either loose-fed or deposited via a block-end feeder. Cocktails of casters in conjunction with brandlings, bread, sweetcorn or maggots are very effective for fishing over weed beds due to the inherent buoyancy of dark (floating) casters.

Floating casters

Simply allow these to turn dark brown before riddling them off, and present them on a flat float rig or with a tenpin floating controller (*Freshwater float fishing techniques - Floating-controller fishing*). Catapult loose feed well upwind and wait for species like dace, rudd, chub and carp to suck them down.

MEAT

Dog treats

Pelleted dog food - the type with a hole through the middle - and meaty-type dog treats 3/4in long and 3/8in thick, make wonderful baits for species like carp when presented on a hair rig.

Raw meat

For catfish and eels especially, plus carp and even tench, strips or chunks of raw steak or liver can prove an effective alternative bait owing to the high blood content.

Sausage-type meat

As any visit to the chilled-meat counter at the local delicatessen or supermarket will instantly confirm, there is an almost endless choice of superb bait for species such as tench, barbel, catfish, carp and chub, all conveniently wrapped in sausage-type skins.

Pre-cooked chipolatas are available in tins, as are mini cocktail sausages. Larger sausages such as black pudding, salami, saveloys, garlic-flavoured German sausages, smoked sausages, pepperami, and even plain or spiced pork or beef bangers (cooked and left to cool), can all be cut into cubes or oblongs and presented either straight on the hook or threaded onto a hair rig for super-wary fish (fig. 18).

Tinned meat

For the previously mentioned species, tinned meats such as luncheon meat, chopped pork roll, tinned ham and bacon grill, should be presented in the same way as sausage-type baits. Some brands contain more fat than others, and are thus more buoyant (handy for fishing over dense weed beds), while other brands are heavier and more solid and therefore stay on the hook longer (fig. 18).

A tin or two should have a permanent home in the bottom of your tackle bag. Both sausage-type and tin red-meat cubes or oblongs are most effectively presented in conjunction with a loose-feed attractor such as hempseed, stewed wheat, tares, red dari seeds (*Particle baits* below) or sinking trout pellets in granular form, also called fry crumb (*Pastes: Trout pellets* below).

NATURAL BAITS

Beetle larvae

Found in the rotten, pithy wood of fallen trees, particularly silver birch, oak, ash and elm, the huge, fat, half-curled grubs of the stag beetle make fine baits for chub and carp. Only slightly smaller and just as effective are the grubs of the cockchafer beetle, which are commonly found by digging over the garden.

Bloodworms

Most cyprinids consume vast quantities of midge larvae (*Buzzers*) daily, the most recognizable of all being the bloodworm, which is bright red and derives its name from the haemoglobin in its blood. While the larvae of many midge species are a drab grey or green and live in home-made protective tubes, bloodworms are free-swimming and live amongst the bottom silt, where match fishermen, especially, gather them using a thin, flat steel blade lashed on to a broomstick.

It is far less trouble, however, to purchase them by the pint from specialist tackle centres. So that they do not disintegrate, use fine-wire hooks in sizes 20-26.

A smaller species of midge larvae, known as 'jokers', harvested from semi-polluted streams below sewage outfalls, are used as loose feed when bloodworms are offered on the hook.

Brandlings

Most commonly found in manure heaps, brandlings are a great bait for species such as bream, tench, rudd and crucian carp. They are easily recognizable by their gyrating movements, yellowy-orange rings around the tail and the pungent yellow fluid that leaks out when they are hooked. Present one on a size 14, two up on a 12, or in bunches on sizes 10 and 8.

Caddis grubs

Always present on the river bed, crawling slowly about in their protective cases constructed from pieces of wood or sand and gravel particles, the maggot-like caddis grub is a fine natural bait adored by dace, roach, chub and rudd. Remove the grub by pinching its tail while easing its head and legs out from the front of the case with thumb and forefinger. Present two up on a size 12 hook.

Cockles

Though tiny orbshell and peashell cockles are common in both still and running freshwater and figure in the diets of all cyprinid species, which crunch them into pulp with their pharyngeal teeth, it is not worth obtaining them for bait. Sea cockles, available from fishmongers in bulk, deshelled and boiled, and ready for use, are wolfed down by tench, chub, bream, carp and barbel. You can easily dye cockles the colour of your choice by adding 1 teaspoon of powder dye to a cup of boiling water, and stirring them around in this in a plastic tub for a couple of minutes before straining off the excess fluid. They can then be frozen for future use or freelined, ledgered or float-fished straight away.

Crayfish

The indigenous crayfish, the largest British freshwater crustacean, is now nearly extinct in some areas of the country. Pollution and a gradual change in the make up of river water due to excessive concentrations of farming chemicals are partly to blame, along with the accidental introduction throughout many river systems of the larger, American signal crayfish. This unfortunately carries a disease that has wiped out entire colonies of indigenous crayfish.

FIGURE 20 Mounting shrimps and prawns

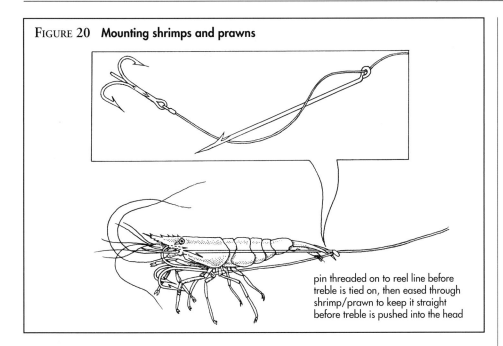

pin threaded on to reel line before
treble is tied on, then eased through
shrimp/prawn to keep it straight
before treble is pushed into the head

Dendrobenas

Available pre-packed in cartons from specialist tackle shops, this very large, red worm, which comes from Holland, fits nicely onto a size 8 hook. All cyprinids love them.

Freshwater shrimps, sea shrimps and prawns

Freshwater shrimps are so active that it is not easy to present them live. However, a size 14 hook holds a pair nicely and is appreciated by dace, roach, grayling and chub. Shrimps and prawns from the sea also make fine baits for freshwater species. Both can be used for trout, chub or barbel in their natural grey-green state, or boiled, which turns them pink. Salmon fishermen rely on this superb bait when all else fails or whenever river conditions are not conducive to fly fishing, and both are available in their natural state, or dyed a variety of colours. A special shrimping/prawning pin, 1½-2½in long, is threaded onto the

Long trotting for salmon using a centre pin reel and a shrimp presented attractively beneath a float, will take fish from awkward lies that are impossible to fly fish.

Far less widespread, though nevertheless now living in certain southern river systems, is a Mediterranean species from Turkey.

While both alien species were originally imported for food and stocked into still-waters only, their migration into running water means the eventual extinction of the indigenous crayfish, now on the endangered species list, and subsequently protected.

This means that no longer can the indigenous crayfish be used to catch chub, which would greedily wolf down those in the 1½-4in range when freelined on a size 4 hook to 6lb test. There is nothing to stop you from presenting young imported crayfish.

line above a treble hook and sleeved through the bait to keep it straight (fig. 20).

Most freshwater species - carp, tench, chub and barbel in particular - succumb to ready-boiled and peeled shrimps and prawns, used whole or in pieces. Loose-feed with small fragments of same.

Grasshoppers, locusts and house crickets

Catch your own grasshoppers, or visit a pet shop, where you will probably find crickets and locusts for feeding to lizards, frogs, birds and spiders. All make fabulous chub baits (*Freshwater float fishing techniques - Floating-controller fishing*).

Grubs and caterpillars

Any sizable caterpillar or grub, such as leatherjackets (larvae of the crane fly or daddy longlegs) can also be used to catch chub. Better still, catch a supply of live 'daddies' when they hatch by the million in the autumn, and carefully mount them on size 12 or 14 hooks.

Lobworms

Whether they are collected by digging over the garden or picked off the lawn by torchlight during the hours of darkness following prolonged rain (the local cricket pitch is favourite), lobworms are much loved by all cyprinid species, particularly perch, chub, carp, tench and barbel. To present one enticingly over weed, inject the head with a little air from a hypodermic syringe and pinch two swan shots onto the line (to counteract the worm's buoyancy) at exactly the distance above the hook that you wish

FIGURE 21 **Presenting air-injected lobworms above bottom weed**

gently inject air from hypodermic syringe into worm's head

size 6-4 hook

two swan shots on line counterbalance worm's buoyancy so it floats just above bottom weed

the lob to be seen above the bottom (fig. 21).

When freelining a lobworm among lily pads for carp or tench, or drifting one downstream for chub lying beneath low, overhanging branches in an overgrown river, inject a little air into it to encourage it to gyrate attractively as well as to make it float.

Lugworms and ragworms

Both worms, which burrow in the mud and sand beneath the sea, are attractive to the larger freshwater species such as barbel, bream, tench and carp. Hook lugworms as you would a lobworm, but cut large, king ragworms into 1-2in sections so that you can thread them onto the hook easily.

Mayfly nymphs

Distinctively creamy in colour with brown markings and three tails, the mayfly nymph is a fabulous natural early-season bait for dace, roach, chub and grayling. Collect them from silty margins beside clumps of reed or rush stems using an Aquarium-type net and long-trot on a size 14 hook.

Meal worms

Available from all good pet stores and specialist tackle shops, in four sizes from minis (pinkie sized) to super giants (1½in long), meal worms attract all cyprinid species caught on maggots but last three times as long without refrigeration.

Mussels

Freshwater mussels, especially the large swan mussel, contain a voluminous amount of orangey meat, adored by catfish, eels, tench and carp. Sever the hinges and open the shell with a thin-bladed knife, and ledger or' freeline the whole piece of flesh on a size 4 hook while loose-feeding chopped mussel fragments around the hook-bait. Most lakes and gravel pit complexes contain mussels. Wade in and pick mussels from among the bottom silt, or use a long-handled garden rake to pull them up.

Redworms

Found in compost heaps of rotting leaves rather than manure, this short, slow-moving worm is a favourite with all cyprinid species, as well as with grayling and perch.

Slugs

Although dace, barbel and even the odd roach may peck at a small slug, this particular bait belongs to the insatiable chub. To the stealthy, wandering, summer chub-stalker there is no finer bait than a large

slug. The plop as the slug hits the surface (freelined on a size 6 or 4 hook) brings chub out from the most impenetrable, jungle-type habitats. Black slugs are most favoured, red-brown next, followed by the great grey slug. Each averages 2-3in long.

Snails

Little more than a small slug in a shell, snails can be removed from their shells and presented two or even three up on a size 6 hook, providing similar casting weight to a large slug. They are a good standby bait when slugs are difficult to find.

Squid

A bait from the sea that pike, eels and catfish adore, squid can be used in strip form, or small, whole squid (4-6in long for eels and catfish, 6-8in long for pike) can be presented individually. Carp also love squid, as many a surprised angler with his thoughts on catfish has discovered.

Tebos

Larger than the biggest meal worm, these moth larvae from Chile are loved by chub, especially, whether long-trotted or ledgered. Loose-feed with maggots.

Wasp grubs and nests

Procured during the summer months from fruit farmers or the local council pest controller, both of whom destroy wasp nests, the sweet-smelling cakes and succulent, soft, white grubs inside can turn chub absolutely wild. They are also good for dace and roach. Long-trot the grubs or, for chub alone, freeline a 50p-sized chunk of floating cake (*Freshwater floatfishing techniques - Presenting floating baits, etc.*).

Waxworms

This white, juicy, fat and extremely buoyant grub, the larva of the wax moth that infests beehives, is available from pet shops and comes prepacked in a tub. It is a great hook-bait substitute for chub and grayling when wasp grubs are in short supply.

Whitebait

These tiny sea fish (a sardine), available from delicatessens and wet-fish shops, may seem a strange bait for freshwaters. They can be used as loose feed when you are ledgering deadbaits for eels, pike, catfish, perch or zander. Or they can be presented individually on a size 6 hook (2 on a size 4) and ledgered for chub or barbel.

PARTICLE BAITS

Particle baits that are available in tins - sweetcorn, borlotti beans, red kidney beans, baked beans and butter beans - are pre-

cooked and ready to use. All seeds, dried pulses and beans must be softened by soaking in water, so that they do not swell inside the fish's stomach and cause problems. Place the bait in a large plastic tub and cover with several inches of boiling water to allow for the baits' expansion. Press the lid on and leave for two days.

To prepare peanuts, hempseed, tares, tick beans, maple peas, blue peas, black-eyed beans and black beans: an initial soaking in cold water for 48 hours helps preparation. Should you wish to colour them, add a teaspoon of powder dye to the boiling water and stir thoroughly.

To prepare wheat, buckwheat, mung beans, chick-peas, soya beans, red dari seeds, malting barley, pearl barley and rice

All these particles can be effectively used for tench, chub, barbel and carp, once properly prepared.

(which cannot be hooked but is a wonderful loose feed: cover each with twice its own volume of water in a large old saucepan and bring to the boil.

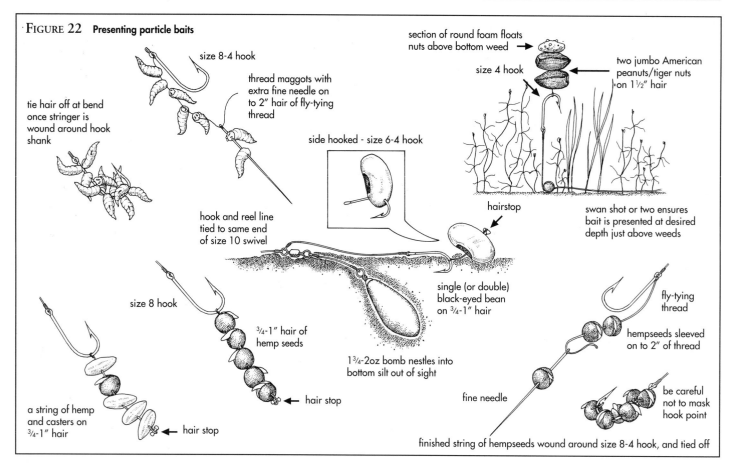

FIGURE 22   Presenting particle baits

tie hair off at bend once stringer is wound around hook shank

size 8-4 hook

thread maggots with extra fine needle on to 2" hair of fly-tying thread

section of round foam floats nuts above bottom weed

size 4 hook

two jumbo American peanuts/tiger nuts on 1½" hair

side hooked - size 6-4 hook

hairstop

swan shot or two ensures bait is presented at desired depth just above weeds

hook and reel line tied to same end of size 10 swivel

size 8 hook

¾-1" hair of hemp seeds

single (or double) black-eyed bean on ¾-1" hair

fly-tying thread

hempseeds sleeved on to 2" of thread

a string of hemp and casters on ¾-1" hair

hair stop

1¾-2oz bomb nestles into bottom silt out of sight

hair stop

fine needle

be careful not to mask hook point

finished string of hempseeds wound around size 8-4 hook, and tied off

Leave to simmer for 10-20 minutes then turn off the heat, put the lid on the saucepan, and leave the bait to stew for 24 hours. If you wish to colour light particles such as wheat or soya beans, add a spoonful of powder dye to the water.

To prepare really hard particles such as tiger nuts and maize: soak for two days in cold water; then put into a pressure cooker for 20 minutes.

Small batches (½pt) can be prepared in the microwave. Soak the bait for two days, put into a cereal bowl, just cover with water, and leave for 15 minutes on the 'high' setting.

Elderberries

Picked fresh during the late summer and early autumn, elderberries catch dace, roach and chub and are particularly effective used in conjunction with loose-fed hempseed. Harvest them before they become over-ripe and preserve them in glycerine or a diluted solution of formulin for use during the winter months.

Hooking particle baits

Most particles can be side-hooked, one, two, three or four grains up, or presented on a hair rig (fig. 22). While roach, rudd and bream love the softer particles such as sweetcorn and stewed wheat, bottom-feeding species such as carp, tench, chub and

barbel have enormous crunching power in their pharyngeal (throat) teeth. And because they are used to hoovering up countless individual food items on a daily basis, they are far less wary of particles than of large, single hook-baits.

PASTES

Bird-food paste

Into a mixing bowl put 2 cups of any of the cereal-based bird foods available from a pet store. Add 3 raw eggs and knead into a creamy paste, adding a teaspoonful of colouring and flavouring if required.

Cat-food paste

Tinned cat food makes great baits for catfish, eels, carp and tench. Mix it with a stiff binder such as plain flour or, better still, cornflour and wheatgerm, until of a stiff but pliable consistency. Egg albumin, boilie gel and wheat gluten are alternative binders worth trying. Add 1 spoon of powder colouring if you wish to change the colour.

Cheese paste

To plain bread paste add equal parts of finely grated cheddar, Danish Blue or Gorgonzola for a marvellous paste that carp, tench, barbel and chub adore. You can add 1 teaspoon of turmeric to make the paste more yellow, or flavourings such

as Marmite, Bovril or even curry powder, and then knead thoroughly until the mixture has a creamy consistency. Wrap the ball of paste in a clean cloth or store it in the freezer in a polybag for future use. Incidentally, all of the following pastes can be stored in the freezer.

Flour-and-water paste

This, the simplest of paste baits (great for roach, chub and bream), relies on the natural gluten of wheat flour to stop it coming off the hook. To make a large ball, put three cups of plain flour in a bowl and knead while you slowly add water - plus, if you desire a coloured paste, 1 spoon of either blancmange (pink) or custard powder. A distinct deep yellow colour is achieved by adding a spoonful of turmeric.

Protein paste

Both the dry, milk-based, protein ingredients and the recipes used in the manufacture of *boilies* (above) can be used should you require a simple creamy paste. Add water, plus a teaspoon each of liquid flavouring and powder colouring, and knead thoroughly. To make a really buoyant paste that comes to rest gently on top of weeds, add 2oz of sodium caseinate to the base mix.

A soft, rubbery paste (to withstand the attentions of nuisance species when you are after tench and carp) can be made by kneading together 1 part calcium caseinate to 2 parts of wheatgerm, plus water and your favourite flavouring and powder colouring.

Sadza paste

Although this particular paste is made from white maize meal throughout southern Central Africa, yellow maize meal, easily obtainable in the UK is fine. To a pan containing 1½pts of boiling water, add 3 cups of maize meal, 1 cup of plain flour, plus a powder colouring of your choice (1 teaspoon) and two beaten eggs. Reduce the heat to a slow boil while stirring the mixture firmly with a wooden spoon, until it reaches a smooth, rubbery consistency. You can add curry powder, crushed oxo cube, liver powder and so on in order to spice up the paste, which stays on the hook well and attracts all cyprinid species.

Sausage-meat paste

To plain beef or pork sausagemeat, add cornflour, plus 1 teaspoon of liquid or powder colouring (should you so wish) and knead into a smooth, creamy consistency.

Semolina paste

Any powder colouring or flavouring should be added to the dry semolina. Add 2 cups of semolina to a large saucepan containing 2 cups of boiling water. Stir quickly for 20-30 seconds and you have a coconut-sized ball of decidedly rubbery paste loved by all cyprinids.

Trout-pellet paste

Available in several sizes from tiny fry crumb to ½in diameter holding pellets, this commercial fish food is a mixture of oil, fish meals and binders, and comes in both floating and sinking form.

Splash heavily with hot water (without over-soaking) and leave for 30 minutes for the water to be absorbed. Knead the mixture into a creamy paste, adding cornflour to blot up any excess water.

Knead 2 raw eggs into the mixture for an extra-creamy paste. For extra attracting power, add Phillips yeast mixture (a bird tonic), Marmite, Bovril or even a couple of beef stock cubes. A teaspoonful or two of dark brown colouring can be mixed in for a really dark paste.

Floating trout pellets are an effective surface attractor (*Floating baits* above) for carp, while the sinking pellets - particularly trout-fry crumbs - are a super loose feed for carp, barbel, tench and chub when you are presenting cubes of meat, cheese, boilies or seed and nut particle baits on the hook.

Collecting fresh sea bait at low tide from beneath weed and the rocks is not only free, it can prove great fun, as east coast skipper John Rawle and the author illustrated during the filming of a 'Go Fishing' programme, with a bucket full of peeler crabs.

BAITS - SEA

ARTIFICIALS

The list of artificial baits useful in the sea is endless; plugs, spinners, spoons, rubber eels, feathers, muppets and so on all work for certain species when used in the right place. The point to bear in mind is that only a limited number of UK saltwater species readily take lures. These include mackerel, bass, pollack, coalfish and cod. Others, such as wrasse, mullet, ling and garfish, can be caught on lures on occasions, especially if the lure is baited. A selection of lures is a worthwhile addition to any sea angler's tackle box.

See also *Artificial Lures*

CRABS

Common shore crab

The common shore crab makes an excellent all-round bait when used at the peeling stage. To grow, the crab first develops an entire new skin beneath its existing shell. The crab then draws in water and the old shell splits, revealing the soft, jelly-like new skin beneath. This 'peeler' is extremely vulnerable to predatory fish.

Peeler crab makes a fine bait for many species, notably bass, cod, smooth hounds and flatfish. They keep well if kept cool and moist and can be used either whole or cut into pieces. Hard crabs, that is, crabs not in the peeling state, are really only useful for wrasse and smooth hounds.

Edible crabs

Edible crabs are not as widely available as the common shore crabs, but they, too, make a wonderful bait when used at the peeling stage. Edible crabs tend to populate the open shoreline rather than creeks and estuaries. Low water on the largest tides is usually the best time to collect them.

The refrigerator is the ideal place for keeping sea bait fresh and in good order, particularly razor fish, lugworms, ragworms and peeler crabs shown here.

Edible crabs are a commercial shellfish species, and as such there is a strictly enforced minimum size limit. This varies from area to area, the minimum being 115mm in the Solway Firth and the maximum being 160mm for males in Cornwall.

Hermit crabs

The hermit crab does not grow a hard shell, but takes over an empty whelk shell. It can be collected very easily using a baited drop net, which is just one of the reasons why it is such a popular bait. In order to use it, a hermit must first be removed from the shell, either by carefully cracking the shell away or leaving it in a bucket of water until the crab crawls free, usually within an hour or so of capture. Hermit crabs are an excellent all-round bait, but are particularly noted for smooth hounds and rays.

Velvet swimming crabs

Another species that, like the common and edible crabs, makes a fine bait when used at the peeling stage is the velvet swimming, or fiddler, crab. Again, this species tends to favour the more exposed shorelines, and low water on the largest tides is the best time to collect them. Used at the peeling stage, velvets are rated by many specialist bass anglers as being the top crab bait for the species. They are also one of the most aggressive species of crab, and should be handled with care.

CUTTLEFISH

Similar in looks to squid, but with noticeably shorter tentacles, cuttlefish have become a very popular bait in recent years,

particularly with conger anglers. Cuttlefish can be caught on occasions on mackerel feathers and other lures, usually in the summer. However, the most reliable way to obtain some is to buy them direct from commercial fishermen, who catch them as a by-product in their nets. Cuttlefish freeze well.

For conger and larger fish, first remove the familiar flat backbone using a sharp filleting knife. Then cut the fish to the required size. Long, thin strips of cuttle flesh are superb for bream and flatfish. Many big bass have also fallen to a cuttlefish bait.

FISH

Herring

Although not as widely available as mackerel, fresh herring ranks a close second in popularity with sea anglers. Herring is a very oily fish and has tremendous appeal for a similarly wide variety of species. Many anglers consider herring a superior bait to mackerel for certain species of fish, notably rays and whiting.

Mackerel

Mackerel is, without question, one of the most popular baits with sea anglers. Throughout the summer fresh mackerel can be readily caught off many UK ports, but unfortunately not in the numbers that they used to be.

A fresh fillet, or cone, of mackerel takes

For species like ling, tope, conger eels, and big rays, few baits can compete with fresh mackerel, particularly when used in cones or cut as flappers.

To tempt large flatfish, a side of fresh sand eel adorns the hook of this attractor spoon rig, together with a string of coloured beads.

a lot of beating for many species of fish. Mackerel can be used in all shapes and sizes, from the thinnest slither of flesh for bream or flatfish, through to a whole live mackerel, which is deadly for bass or sharks. A mackerel head and sides, with the entire backbone and tail removed - known as a flapper because the sides flap attractively in the tide - is a superb bait for conger, tope, ling and more. Frozen mackerel is a useful bait when supplies of fresh mackerel are limited.

Sand eels

There are two types of sand eels of interest

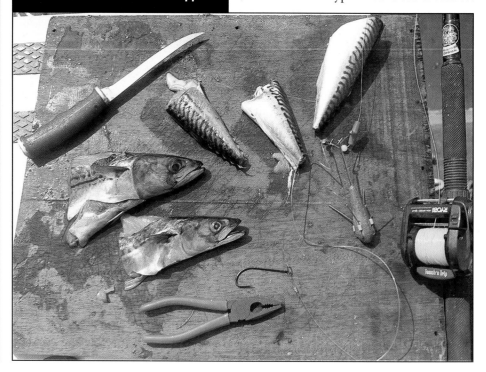

to sea anglers, the lesser sand eel and the larger, greater sand eel, or launce. The lesser sand eels are widely available through tackle shops in blast-frozen packets. They are a deadly bait for many species of fish, bass, rays and turbot in particular. When they are available live, through some coastal tackle shops, they are without question one of the finest baits of all for bass and pollack, fished on a long, flowing trace.

Greater sand eels are often caught on feathers by anglers trying to catch mackerel or herring. They, too, make a wonderful bait for bass, pollack and turbot when fished live, but a long fillet from the side of a greater sand eel is an excellent bait for many species of fish.

Sprats

Not a bait that is widely used, sprats are another very oily fish and make a useful substitute when mackerel and herring are unavailable. Sprat flesh is very soft and requires careful presentation to keep it on the hook. However, a long, thin fillet from the flank of a sprat is a superb bait for dabs, plaice and whiting.

SHELLFISH

Clams

Clams live on the extreme low water line of open beaches, as well as within estuaries. They are located by looking for their large blow holes, and then dug using a fork or spade. Fresh clams are an excellent bait for bass and flatfish.

Cockles

This is an excellent bait, particularly the larger queen cockle. A few can often be dug when digging worms on sandy beaches or near the mouth of estuaries. Shop-bought cockles tend to be cooked, but can be useful for mullet and flatfish.

Limpets

Widely available, limpets are not rated as an effective bait by most anglers. The only fish that are regularly caught using limpets are wrasse, but occasionally bass, flatfish and pollack are taken on them. They are useful for bulking out other baits that are in very short supply.

Mussels

Mussels are a very good bait when they can be obtained, and are very popular in the north of England and Scotland. They are nearly always used fresh and alive, and make an excellent bait for cod and various species of flatfish. However, the flesh is very soft and requires careful presentation using fine elastic thread if it is to remain intact

on the hook during casting.

Prawns

Live prawns are probably one of the most under-used and underestimated baits available to the sea angler. UK tackle shops do not sell them, so the angler has to put the time in to catch his own. A float-fished live prawn can be nothing short of devastating for bass, wrasse, pollack and many other species.

Razorfish

Empty razorfish shells are a familiar sight along the highwater mark on many beaches, yet few people ever see the live animal fresh out of the sand. Razorfish live in deep vertical burrows on the extreme low water mark on sandy beaches. They can either be dug using a fork or spade, or salted. Salting involves pouring either dry table salt or a heavily concentrated saline solution down the burrow, which forces the razorfish to evacuate its burrow.

Silver eels

A section of silver eel is an extremely selective bait. They were first used on a regular basis in and around the Thames estuary for tope, but some large bass have also been caught by anglers using eel chunks. Frozen eel baits can also work well.

SQUID

There are many species of squid worldwide, and several that live in British waters. However, it is the frozen Californian calamari squid that is of most interest to anglers. Calamari squid are widely available through tackle shops and fishmongers, usually sold in 1lb or 5lb boxes. The best squid to use for bait are those that are still pearly white. If the squid has started to thaw and then been refrozen, it develops a pinkish tinge and makes an inferior bait.

As a bait, squid has many applications. It can either be fished whole, making an excellent offering for bass, conger and cod, or it can be cut into strips and used either singularly or as part of a cocktail. Squid is a bait that few fish will ignore, and being so readily available and cheap it is popular with many anglers.

WORM BAITS

Black lugworm

Black lug are the largest of the two common species of lugworm, the other being the blow lugworm. They are dug or pumped using bait pumps at low water on spring tides. They are much larger and tougher than blow lug, and are one of the

most effective baits for cod and many other species. Unlike the more delicate blow lug, black lug freeze very well and are a noted bait for several species of flatfish, notably dabs and plaice.

Blow lugworm

Blow lug are by far the commonest lugworm available in the UK, and their presence is usually given away by the typical sand coils and blow holes that can be clearly visible on a beach.

Blow lug are a very good all-round bait and will catch most of the popular species of fish, notably flatfish, cod, bass and rays. They can be dug using either a spade or fork, either individually or, when they are thick on the ground, by trenching through the area of greatest concentration.

Ragworm

Several species of ragworm are used by sea anglers.

Harbour rag

Harbour ragworm, or maddies, are the smallest variety of ragworm in common use, and as their name suggests they are found in and around harbours or tidal estuaries, usually living in thick grey mud. They are a very delicate worm, usually fished in bunches on fine-wire hooks for flatfish, eels and mullet.

King rag

These are the commonest species of ragworm and are available from 2in long to 1ft. They are a very good all-round bait, and are relatively easy to keep for several days. King rag are dug from a variety of different types of beaches, those consisting of mud and shale tending to be the best.

King rag can be used in several ways. They can be threaded, either whole or in sections, onto the hook in the standard way, or they can be lightly nicked through the head with the hook and fished live on a long, flowing trace - deadly for pollack, wrasse, bass and coalfish. Commercially farmed ragworm are now available through many tackle shops and these appear to be of comparable quality to natural worms.

White rag

White rag are a very popular bait with keen match anglers, who will travel long distances in order to acquire a supply. White rag are dug from clean beaches consisting of coral sand. They are usually cut into pieces and used to tip cocktail baits, but are equally effective if fished whole. This is another bait that will keep well if kept cool and moist. Use on fine wire hooks.

BAIT-DROPPERS

Bait droppers are unbeatable for depositing small seed baits such as hemp and tares, or maggots or casters, accurately on the bottom of a river in the strongest currents.

Most freshwater bait-droppers are 'frying-pan' shaped, like the famous Thamesley, and are constructed from plastic or wire mesh. They have hinged lids incorporating a simple release catch on a lead-weighted stem. When the weight touches bottom the lid flaps open, releasing the load instantly. Smaller models suitable for releasing bloodworms, pinkies or squatts when pole fishing, like the ZLT, work most effectively in canals and still waters for getting the loose feed down through shoals of small fish to the bottom.

For sea fishing in weak tides, canister-type, home-made droppers are simple to construct, but the cheapest of all, and one which works with devastating accuracy in the strongest of tides, is the 'carrier-bag dropper'. Thread the line (40-50lb is ideal) of a spare outfit through the bottom of a heavy plastic carrier-bag. Tie sufficient lead onto the line to reach bottom quickly, and tie the bottom of the bag around the weight with strong cord.

Pour your rubby-dubby of finely chopped fish pieces, guts, oil and bran into the bag and lower it over the side of the boat until it hits bottom. The water pressure forces the sides of the bag tightly together, ensuring that the bait is released only on the sea bed, at which point you give a hefty jerk to invert the bag. This method is simple yet effective for sharks, rays and all bottom-feeders.

BARBEL
(Barbus barbus)

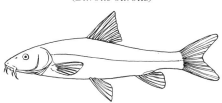

Average size: 3-5lbs
Mega specimen: over 10-12lb
British record: 16lb 2oz (7kg 314g)

An elongated, powerfully built freshwater species, the barbel is capable of holding its position close to the bottom in the strongest currents, hence its flat belly and huge suction-type pectoral fins. All its fins are large, and the deeply forked tail has a pointed upper lobe while the lower lobe is noticeably rounded. Small, deeply embedded scales cover the wiry body, which is olive-brown along the back fusing into muted brass down the flanks. All fins are evenly coloured a warm - sometimes orangey - red.

The snout is pointed and overlaps the lower jaw. No less than four long, sensory barbels or whiskers provide good locational sensitivity to the semi-protrusible, hoover-like mouth. Incidentally, the gudgeon has just two barbels, while loach have six.

It feeds on shrimps, crayfish, snails, caddis, and so on, plus small fish, all of which are crushed to a pulp prior to swallowing by its immensely strong pharyngeal teeth, set in the back of its throat.

Reproduction takes place in the late spring or early summer on the fast, gravelly shallows, where several males may compete to spray a cloud of milt over the eggs shed by one swollen-bellied female. The eggs lodge between gravel particles and hatch around two weeks later.

HABITAT AND DISTRIBUTION

Barbel always prefer to occupy the fastest, most well-oxygenized water over a clean sand or gravel bottom, especially where long, flowing weed beds or overhanging willows provide shade. They are found in England, and in just one river - the Wye - in Wales, where they are slowly spreading after being introduced. They are most prolific in fast-flowing rivers such as the Hampshire Avon, Dorset Stour, Kennet and Severn, but the Thames and Great Ouse and their tributaries also contain good concentrations.

TECHNIQUES

Freshwater float fishing techniques - Waggler fishing in rivers; Long trotting; Ledgering techniques - Quivertipping.

BARRACUDINA
(Paralepis coregonoides)

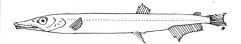

British record: 1oz 14dr (54g)

This long, slim, rarely caught, very small sea species generally inhabits deep waters, feeding upon small fish and plankton. Brownish in colour with lighter undersides, it has a pointed snout and large eye and a very conspicuous lateral line. Its dorsal fin starts beyond the middle of the body, and it has a tiny adipose fin in front of its pointed tail, and a long anal fin. Its jaws are well armed with teeth - a barracuda in miniature.

Migration

Spawning

BARBEL

Following an exciting battle amongst the clear, weedy and fast-flowing waters of the beautiful Dorset Stour downstream from Throop Mill, John Wilson looks justifiably happy with this muscle-packed 8lb barbel. The winning combination was a cube of luncheon meat hair rigged to a size 10 hook, presented on a three swan shot rig, quivertipped in a narrow gravel run between beds of bullrushes.

BASS

(Dicentrachus labrax)

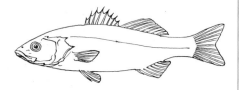

Average size: 3-8lb
Mega specimen: over 12lb
British record: 19lb 9¼oz (8kg 876g)

This valuable, commercial food fish is highly prized by sea fishermen. It is distinctly perch-like in appearance with two dorsal fins, the first spiked, the second having soft rays. It has a streamlined body with large fins and a forked tail.

Colouration is a metallic greeny-blue along the back, fusing into sides of bright silver, with a silvery white belly. The fins are all light grey. There are extra spines to the leading edge of the anal fin and around the gill plate, and the large, expandable mouth has thick-rimmed lips.

A double-figure bass is every fisherman's dream. John's dream came true whilst tope fishing in the Thames estuary using eel section for bait, with this 11¼-pounder, whilst aboard *Donna Mary* skippered by John Rawle. A complete fluke - but don't we all need a little luck now and again?

Bass spawn in the late spring around inshore waters, the eggs and young drifting with the tides. It preys upon small shoal fish such as sprats and sand eels plus worms, prawns, squid and crabs.

Spawning

Immature fish

BASS

FIGURE 23 Beachcasting using the pendulum cast

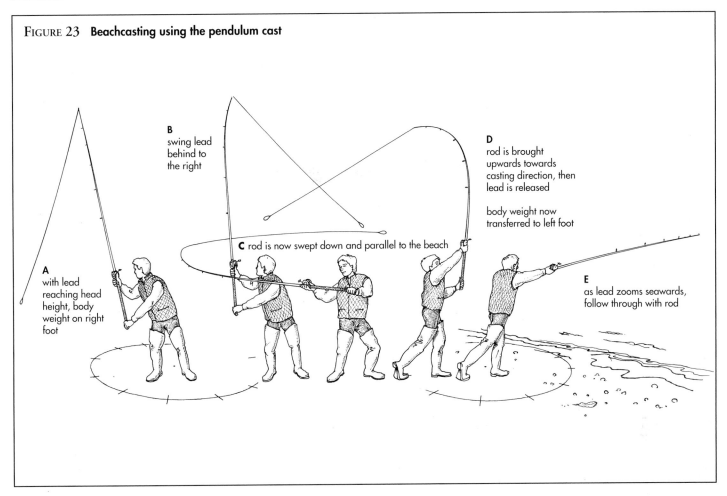

B swing lead behind to the right

D rod is brought upwards towards casting direction, then lead is released

body weight now transferred to left foot

C rod is now swept down and parallel to the beach

A with lead reaching head height, body weight on right foot

E as lead zooms seawards, follow through with rod

HABITAT AND DISTRIBUTION

It is widespread around the Irish coastline, Wales and southern England. Bass are common in and around the mouths of large estuaries, particularly the Thames Estuary, and in certain areas they even penetrate high upstream into completely freshwater. Adult bass love feature feeding-grounds such as surf beaches, off-shore reefs and sand banks.

TECHNIQUES

Artificial lure fishing techniques - sea; Beach-casting; Downtide boat fishing; Floatfishing in harbours and off the rocks; Trolling; Uptide boat fishing.

BEACHCASTING

Sometimes fish are working close in, sometimes not. Sometimes a 50yd flick will put your bait in front of bass or cod feeding beneath the third or fourth breaker out; and sometimes you won't get a bite unless you place the bait way out beyond the sand banks or into deeper water. Long-distance casting and the ability to place a lead plus bait 100-150yd out are essential skills for consistent re-sults, whether you are match or pleasure fishing. And there is no easier or more effective cast for this than the pendulum.

PENDULUM CASTING

To protect other fishermen along the beach, ensure that the shock leader is correctly knotted to the main line (*Knots*) and strong enough to alleviate sudden break offs from a 5-6oz grip lead - 50-60lb test is ideal - whether using a fixed-spool or multiplier reel.

Imagine that you are standing on a clockface, facing 4 o'clock. If you are right-handed, position your left foot at around three o'clock and your right foot at five o'clock. Concentrate your weight on your right foot and swing the lead (on an 8ft drop) directly away from you up the beach so it reaches head height at about 7 o'clock (fig. 23A). As the pendulum motion brings the lead back towards you, push down on the butt grip with your left hand, and bring the right hand, gripping the reel slightly, to the right so that the lead passes behind you to the right (fig. 23B).

When the lead reaches the very top of the swing above the rod tip, behind and way above your right ear, *now* and only now is the time to start the power part of the cast: increase your arm speed while drawing the lead downwards, simultaneously bending the legs slightly as your whole body turns towards the sea, and sweep the rod parallel to the beach (fig. 23C). Watch an athlete throw the discus to get a good idea of the action. As compression builds up in the rod, really winding up the rod tip, bring it upwards towards the casting direction, and simultaneously pull down with the left hand while pushing strongly with the right (fig. 23D).

Your body weight will now have been fully transferred from back to front foot as you face the sea head on and release the lead, following through with the rod to allow the line a friction-free passage (fig. 23E).

Remember that only rapid-taper beachcasting rods permit the pendulum cast to send leads out truly great distances. Soft, all-through-action rods absorb too much of the power built up in the cast to do this. By the same token, because of their manoeuvrability and the fact that such a rod can be brought round faster, 11½-12 ft models perform best. Longer rods, therefore, do not produce longer casts.

Note also, from fig. 24A, that the cast should be made well up tide when a strong

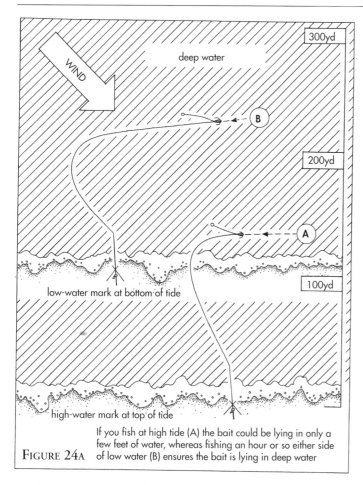

300yd

deep water

WIND

200yd

B

100yd

A

low-water mark at bottom of tide

high-water mark at top of tide

If you fish at high tide (A) the bait could be lying in only a few feet of water, whereas fishing an hour or so either side of low water (B) ensures the bait is lying in deep water

FIGURE 24A

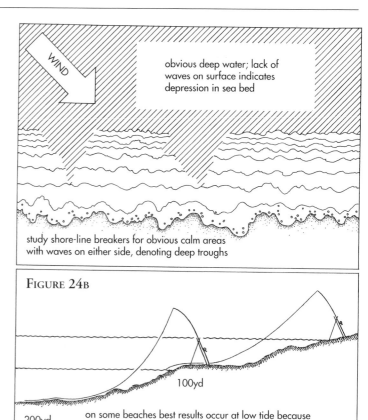

WIND

obvious deep water; lack of waves on surface indicates depression in sea bed

study shore-line breakers for obvious calm areas with waves on either side, denoting deep troughs

FIGURE 24B

100yd

200yd

on some beaches best results occur at low tide because deep water is reached with just a modest cast

sea is running. Walk as far as 50yd along the beach and then pay out plenty of free line to form a huge bow, while the lead digs in firmly, before walking back and putting the rod in its rest. A cast straight out is an invitation to the tide to wash the terminal rig straight back up the beach. To alleviate water pressure against the line, use as light a reel line as you can safely get away with and keep terminal rigs simple. A reel line of about 15lb test not only allows you to cast further - because more 15lb-test than 20lb-test line fits on to the spool - but its reduced diameter, and therefore reduced water resistance, permits the use of lighter leads.

Exactly where to fish is the greatest puzzle facing the majority of sea fishermen when one stretch of beach looks very much like the rest, but there are pointers to consider. A stroll along the beach with binoculars, studying tide direction, surface displacement and wave patterns, will provide an enormous amount of valuable information about what lies on the sea bed. Noticeably calmer areas of flatter sea, for

instance, indicate that the water is too deep for breakers to build up over it, while surf-topped waves and heavily coloured water suggest shallow sand bars.

Flat beaches that suddenly drop away into deep water invariably fish best at low tide. Even a really long cast made when the tide is right in could place the bait in mere inches of water - precisely the place

where you would stand at low tide (fig. 24B).

Study your beach when all is revealed, and there is no better time than at the very bottom of a low spring tide. Features such as gullies, rocky areas, old wooden groynes, weed, shellfish beds, even the snags, will all be revealed and the sea won't look so uninviting after all.

UKSF casting guru Paul Kerry, who has done more to popularize the pendulum cast than anyone, slowly winds a cod through the surf on Great Yarmouth's south beach.

BITE INDICATORS AND ACCESSORIES

BOBBIN INDICATORS

These indicators, which clip onto the line between butt ring and reel and are retained by a dacron or fly-line cord fixed to the front rod rest, are an indispensable item in the ledger fisherman's kit. They are available in easy-to-see, daytime colours. The tenpin bobbin, for example, is fluorescent red and comes ready fitted with a dacron retaining cord. There are also special night-time models. The famous 'glo bobbin' contains a 300-microlambert, luminous betalight element set into a transparent body. It will last for many years and provides round-the-clock bite indication. Bobbins are especially effective for use in slow-moving rivers and all still waters, particularly when ledgering at a distance. Between one and three swan shots can be pinched onto the retaining cord immediately below the bobbin to prevent sub-surface tow or cross winds slowly pulling it up.

BUTT-BITE INDICATOR

This most effective indicator looks rather like a swing tip except that it has a terry clip at one end instead of the customary thread. It is clipped over the rod or reel handle a couple of inches in front of the reel, with the line threaded through the ring at the bottom. Once the slack is taken up after casting, the indicator hangs down at an angle of around 45 degrees, registering both forward and backward movements of

For the huge tench of famous Sywell reservoir in Northamptonshire, John ledgers a fixed paternoster, open-end feeder rig baited with lobtail, and concentrates on the bobbin indicator clipped on between reel and bite alarm.

the line. The length varies from 7in to 9in depending on the make. Once you have become accustomed to its presence on the rod, casting is not affected.

A handy indicator to have in exceptionally windy weather, it is also particularly useful to anglers with failing eyesight.

COIL INDICATORS

Simple coil indicators are used when baits are being ledgered or freelined at close range for species such as eels, tench, carp and catfish. You can fold a piece of kitchen foil in half and roll it into a coil (it has a lovely 'rustle'), or make a range of coil

indicators from 1½in diameter plastic piping in a variety of weights (fig. 25) by cutting each a little longer than the previous one. Coils from 1in to 2in long in ¼in increments gives five different sizes.

Coil indicators are easily attached between reel and butt ring, easily seen, and indicate both forward and drop-back bites. What is more, they usually fly off conveniently when you strike hard.

DROP-OFF/DROP-ARM INDICATORS: MANUAL AND ELECTRONIC

The simple drop-off or drop-arm indicator provides great visual indication of a bite when you are ledgering for predators like zander and pike. If the fish moves off and directly away with the bait, the line pulls freely from the clip, letting the arm fall down. And if the fish swims directly towards the rod, the arm slowly falls backwards. There is therefore no possible chance of a deeply hooked fish.

The basic unit consists of a plastic-covered steel needle with a flexible junction of silicone tubing; plus a terry clip at one end for fixing to the rear rod rest and to the rear of the reel; plus a 1½in-diameter fluorescent orange polyball and a functional line clip at the other end. After casting and tightening up the line, open the bale arm and fix the line in the line clip.

The ET Backbiter range combines a drop-arm indicator with a simple buzzer plus an LED. The deluxe version even has

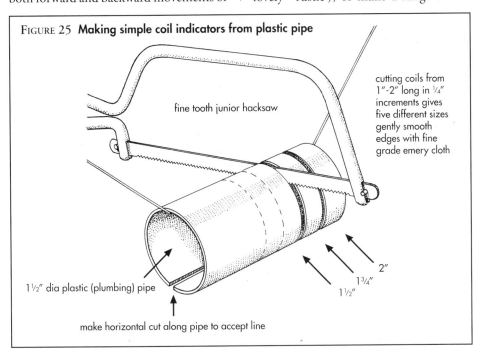

FIGURE 25 **Making simple coil indicators from plastic pipe**

fine tooth junior hacksaw

cutting coils from 1"-2" long in ¼" increments gives five different sizes gently smooth edges with fine grade emery cloth

1½" dia plastic (plumbing) pipe

2"

1¾"

1½"

make horizontal cut along pipe to accept line

volume control, and both are available in either single or double formats.

ELECTRONIC, ANTENNA-TYPE BUZZER/BITE ALARMS

Now superseded by alarms that operate through magnetic reed switches and photo-electric cells, antenna-type buzzers - the first electronic bite alarms ever marketed - are still popular because they are inexpensive. They work on the contact-breaker principle: when the line is pulled across the antenna, to which a breaker point is joined, the circuit is completed and the buzzer sounds. A light-emitting diode also gives a visual warning (fig. 26).

You can increase or decrease the pressure on the antenna as required to counteract sub-surface tow or to register any kind of forward bite, from twitches to steady pulls. Drop-back bites, however, are not registered.

MONKEY CLIMBERS

The monkey climber is a bobbin on a stick, the stick stopping it blowing about in the wind. It is mainly used by carp fishermen, but is also effective for ledgering in still-waters for other species. Monkeys that run up and down effortlessly on a black (PTFE-coated) stainless-steel rod, aptly called 'grease monkeys', are excellent because they create minimal resistance to shy-biting fish, so twitches can be identified and confidently struck.

The plastic monkey is sleeved on from the bottom of the rod and cannot fly off when you strike because the rod flattens out at the top. For bolt-rig techniques, special PTFE-lined, high-density, heavy-plastic monkeys are used to counteract sub-surface tow and to indicate drop-back bites. They are available in a variety of see-through, fluorescent colours and take a betalight luminous element for night fishing.

PHOTO-ELECTRIC CELL AND MAGNETIC REED-SWITCH ELECTRONIC BITE ALARMS

In 1978 the first optonic bite indicator was made available to British anglers, opening up a completely new concept in electronic wizardry, and it is now considered standard equipment by the majority of carp fishermen.

The secret of optonic-type indicators lies in the way in which line travels effortlessly across a sensitive wheel, giving a single bleep-tone, plus a warning light from an LED (light-emitting diode) for every ³⁄₄in

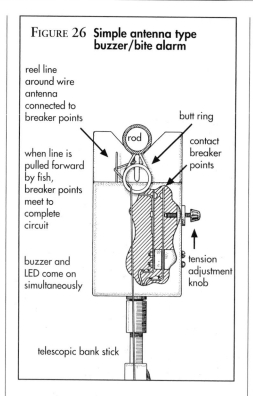

FIGURE 26 Simple antenna type buzzer/bite alarm

reel line around wire antenna connected to breaker points

butt ring

rod

contact breaker points

when line is pulled forward by fish, breaker points meet to complete circuit

buzzer and LED come on simultaneously

tension adjustment knob

telescopic bank stick

of line being taken; or, in the case of drop backs, dropping back towards the rod. This tells you instantly whether the bite is a mere twitch, a slow run, or a really fast run (fig. 27). When the line rotates the frictionless wheel, a tiny fan-blade interrupts the light beam of a mini photo-electric cell. Another

system, used in the Optonic Magnetonic and several other commercial units, operates via a magnetic reed-switch, which replaces the photo-electric cell - models like the Fox Micron and the AVA.

Systems such as the optonic are available in various self-contained, cordless, compact models, with or without volume and tone control and with sensors (or heads) connected by wires to a separate 'sounder' unit. This can be positioned several yards away inside a bivvi, where it effectively becomes an alarm clock during the hours of darkness. Another feature of many heads is a latching LED that remains on for several seconds after the bite, or line bite, has occurred, indicating on which rod the action happened should you be looking elsewhere at the time.

QUIVER TIP

Screw-in, commercially made quiver tips are available in different tapers, and are subsequently rated in test curves of 1-4oz rather like rods. A delicate 1oz tip provides visible bite indications from roach and dace living in a slow-moving canal, or from bream and tench in stillwaters, while a 3-3½oz tip is required for ledgering in fast rivers for barbel and chub.

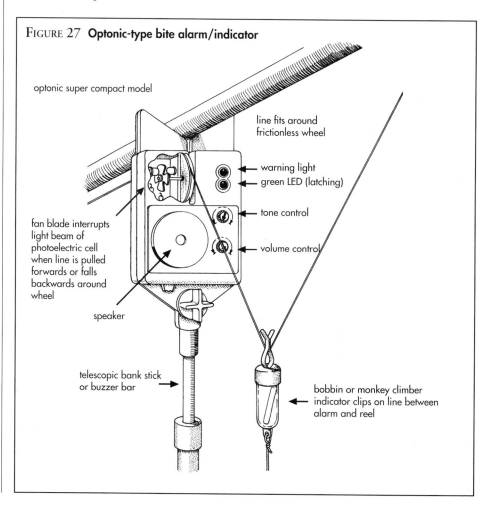

FIGURE 27 Optonic-type bite alarm/indicator

optonic super compact model

line fits around frictionless wheel

warning light

green LED (latching)

tone control

volume control

fan blade interrupts light beam of photoelectric cell when line is pulled forwards or falls backwards around wheel

speaker

telescopic bank stick or buzzer bar

bobbin or monkey climber indicator clips on line between alarm and reel

For ledgering with up to four rod set-ups in large still waters, particularly in ex-gravel workings or reservoirs where the banks are hard, alloy or stainless steel rod pods are the answer. These rigid ground frames combine bank sticks, buzzerbars, back rests, alarms and either swinger or monkey climber indicators.

All are available with fluorescent coloured tips. Many anglers, however, find that plain, matt white shows up best against varying backgrounds, particularly in low-light conditions. And when you shine a torch on it while fishing after dark, it is easy to see.

It pays to whip on an additional ring halfway between the thread and tip ring on commercially produced quiver tips so that the line is fully supported and follows the curve of the tip under full pressure.

SPRING TIP

This ingenious indicator is a solid-glass, rapid-taper quiver tip, the thick end of which passes through the middle of a 2in-long spring. The spring is joined to a moulded rubber sleeve fitted with a threaded end, and this in turn screws into the tip ring of your ledger rod. It can be used as a powerful quiver tip, or, if pulled gently from the moulding so that only the very end is gripped by the spring, as a hinged quiver tip that registers the tiniest of bites. It is therefore most suitable for shy-biting dace, roach and bream in running water.

SWING TIP

When ledgering for species like rudd, roach and bream in stillwaters or very slow-moving rivers, a swing tip of 10-12in that hangs down and provides valuable slack to a biting fish, offers the most sensitive bite indi-

cation. They are made from cane or fibreglass and screw into the threaded end ring of a ledger rod via a silicone rubber junction that should be pliable but not floppy, otherwise casting is impaired.

For slow-moving rivers, a loaded swing tip will be necessary. This has lead wire wound around the tip next to the top ring.

If the current pressure forces this upwards, thus minimizing its effect, switch over to the extra tension provided by either the spring tip or quiver tip.

Once you have made a cast and placed the rod on two rod rests parallel to the water for smooth, sideways striking, you can detect bites most easily by positioning a simple target board immediately behind the swing tip. Fig. 28 describes how to make one.

SWINGERS

These arm-type indicators, designed by Fox Tackle, incorporate a housing for a luminous betalight element for night fishing; clamp onto the front rod rest or bank stick immediately below the bite alarm; and fix easily to the line via a sensitive clip. Models of similar design, called Pendulator and Sensoriser, have articulated joints to minimize resistance from a biting fish. All have been evolved as accessories to the designer world of carp fishing and are really sophisticated bobbins.

BANK STICKS AND ROD PODS TO ACCOMMODATE ELECTRONIC BITE ALARMS

Electronic bite alarms become the front rod rests, for which the buzzer bar was invented. Available in alloy or stainless steel, buzzer bars take two, three or even four rod set-ups and screw into the standard ⅜in BSF

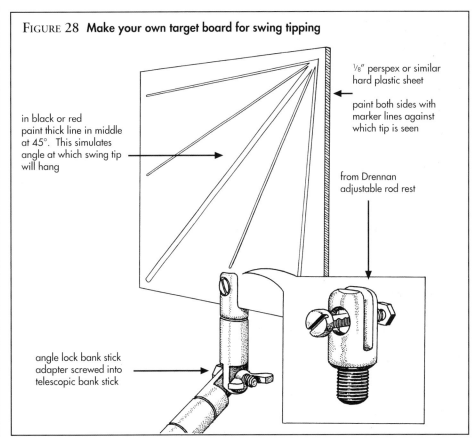

FIGURE 28 **Make your own target board for swing tipping**

⅛" perspex or similar hard plastic sheet

paint both sides with marker lines against which tip is seen

in black or red paint thick line in middle at 45°. This simulates angle at which swing tip will hang

from Drennan adjustable rod rest

angle lock bank stick adapter screwed into telescopic bank stick bank-stick thread. For both front and back rests (separate U-type screw-in heads take the rod butts) invest in a pair of telescopic bank sticks to allow for a variety of margin depths. Stainless steel lasts longer than alloy.

For really tough banking, as found on some gravel pits, reservoirs and the like, the rod pod is the answer. This is a complete rod set-up with a ground frame combining bank sticks, a twin or three-unit buzzer bar, with an aerial bar in the middle to take monkey-climber indicators. Rod pods are available in coated alloy and in stainless steel. Mini tripods, useful on places such as hard ground, concrete banks and stagings, are also available.

BITTERLING
(*Rhodeus sericeus*)

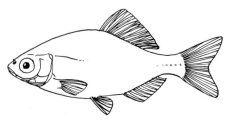

British record: none

This silvery, freshwater species, rarely exceeding 3in long, has the deep-bodied appearance of a microscopic silver bream. It is very rarely caught by anglers, though it lives in ponds, lakes and lowland river systems throughout England and Europe, feeding on planktonic crustaceans and minute, aquatic insect larvae. It has a unique reproduction cycle in that the female deposits her eggs via a long tube extending from the vent, which she places into the gill chamber of the freshwater mussel. About 10-20 eggs are deposited in each mussel. To add insult to injury, the male bitterling then squirts sperm into the mussel's breathing tube to fertilize the eggs.

The young hatch after 3-4 weeks and leave their host within a few days. The bitterling then reciprocates by playing host to the mussel's parasitic larvae, which attach themselves to the fish's fins. In this way, they are distributed further afield.

BIVVIES

Gleaned from the wartime word 'bivouac', the modern bivvi is in fact nothing more than a sophisticated, *specialized tent designed for anglers wishing to fish overnight or through exceptionally bad weather.*

Bivvies are available in various grades of waterproof reinforced nylon and proofed canvas. Though durable, they are exceptionally heavy to carry, particularly when wet. Most are designed to fit over angling umbrellas and are therefore available in 45in, 50in and even 60in sizes, converting the brolly into a sizeable igloo-type tent.

The standard bivvi converts the brolly into an upright tent. The overwrap bivvi is used in conjunction with a special 'nu brolly' umbrella, the pole of which can be unscrewed once the bivvi is erect. To make a strong door-frame, storm rods (specialized bank sticks) are sleeved into the bivvi's vertical hems prior to the centre pole being taken away. A waterproof ground sheet is then laid for the base, and the edges of the bivvi secured down with camping pegs. Specialized oval brollies, with oval bivvies to match, are also available.

Storm sides that can be attached with velcro edging (or sewn in place) convert any standard umbrella into a part shelter or full bivvi. Many specialized bivvies have see-through doors, windows, even mosquito doors, while some are double skinned to alleviate condensation.

A new generation of one and two man bivouacs, called Pop-up bivvies, such as the Relum 'Broddie' are fitted with tension poles. They can be erected within seconds and are completely self-contained, so an umbrella is not required. The models made by Gardner and by ET Tackle even have built-in ground sheets.

BLACKFISH
(*Centrolophus niger*)

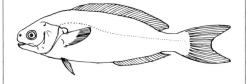

British record: 4lb 9oz (2kg 69g)

This oceanic species occasionally strays into shallow water around the UK's southern coastline. It has a slender, very deep brown body, often flecked with silver, and equally dark fins. The tail is forked and the snout rather blunt. It averages around 18in long but can grow to double that size. It is extremely rare and is only occasionally caught by anglers.

Its natural diet consists of jellyfish, small fish and crustaceans, plus weed growing on rocks.

BLACKFISH, CORNISH
(*Schedophilus medusophagus*)

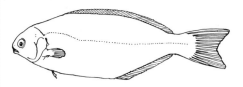

British record: 8¼oz (233g)

Noticeably deeper in the body than the oceanic blackfish, the Cornish blackfish is just as rare around the coasts of the British Isles. It has a deep, compressed body, a forked tail, a noticeably blunt snout and a small head. It is brown all over with a violet, or sometimes green, hue. Adults can reach 2ft in length and a weight of several pounds.

It feeds on jellyfish, crustaceans and small fish.

BLEAK
(*Albernus alburnus*)

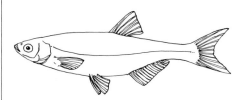

British record: 4¼oz (120g)

The bleak is by far the smallest British freshwater fish that anglers specifically set out to catch. Match anglers love its willingness to bite and the fact that it masses in huge shoals, while the predator-hunter knows full well that the silvery bleak makes a fabulous livebait for trout, big perch, zander, chub and pike.

In cross-section the bleak is extremely thin and flat-sided, with a large eye and a distinctly turned-up, herring-like mouth, denoting its preference for feeding close to the surface. Its large scales, which are easily dislodged, are used in the manufacture of imitation pearls in parts of Europe. The fins are a transparent yellowy grey and the tail is deeply forked. Its colour varies along the back from a metallic greeny-blue to sides of shimmering silver.

Spawning takes place in the late spring. Its diet consists of aquatic insect larvae and the resulting flies as they hatch.

HABITAT AND DISTRIBUTION

The bleak is limited to some English river systems, but is also found along the eastern edge of Wales in the River Wye and its tributaries. It is absent from Scotland and Ireland. It prefers slow-moving, lowland river systems, where it forms huge shoals, and it always occupies the upper third of the river unless temperatures are exceedingly low.

TECHNIQUES

Freshwater float fishing techniques; Pole fishing.

BLENNY, BUTTERFLY

(*Blennius ocellaris*)

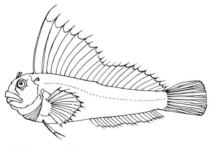

British record: 1¼oz (32g)

The butterfly blenny is one of the tiniest of fish the sea fisherman is ever likely to catch - it seldom exceeds 6in - and the strangest-looking of all blennies. It has a chunky, olive-brown body with darker bars across the back and flanks. There is a conspicuous eye spot on the double dorsal fin, which has a long leading edge. Immediately above the raised eyes sits a pair of tentacles, and there are appendages at the base of both the first dorsal and pectoral fin rays. It also sports a pair of feelers immediately beneath the pelvic fins.

Reproduction occurs in the late spring, and the eggs are guarded by the male. The butterfly blenny's diet consists of worms, small fish and crustaceans.

BLENNY, TOMPOT

(*Parablennius gattorugine*)

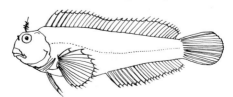

British record: 5½oz (156g)

Generally frequenting southern shorelines

of the British Isles, the spiny tompot blenny seldom reaches 10in and has an array of fins similar to those of the freshwater ruffe. The first half of its dorsal is heavily spiked and the second half consists of soft rays. It also has large fan-like pectoral fins with a pair of feelers immediately beneath them. Above its weird raised eyes are two branched tentacles. It is coloured a yellow-brown with several dark bars running across the flanks.

Reproduction takes place in the spring and the eggs are guarded by the male. Its diet consists of worms and crustaceans.

BLENNY, VIVIPAROUS

(*Zoarces viviparus*)

British record: 13oz (368g)

Commonly referred to by sea fishermen as the 'eelpout', this wiry, slippery little fish has a bulbous head with a cavernous mouth and thick lips, huge fan-like pectoral fins, plus a long, tapering body with dorsal, tail and anal fins combined in one continuous fin. There is an unmistakable indentation in this fin close to the tail. The viviparous blenny averages 10-12in in length and frequents rocky shorelines. It lives beneath large stones, where it is suitably camouflaged being olive-brown along the back and dirty yellow underneath.

Mating occurs in the late summer, and the eggs develop inside the female. By Christmas the young are born, fully formed and ready to fend for themselves. Its diet consists of small crustaceans, molluscs, fish and worms.

BLENNY, YARRELLS

(*Chirolophis ascanii*)

British record: 2¾oz (80g)

This tiny, brownish-mottled saltwater rock-dweller has a long but deeply compressed body, and exceedingly long dorsal and anal fins that almost butt on to its small, rounded tail. It has a strange, fringed tentacle above each eye, and small appendages

at the back of the head and on the first dorsal spines.

Reproduction takes place during early winter, and the resulting fry drift with the plankton. Its diet consists of small worms and molluscs.

BLOCK-END FEEDER

See *Swimfeeders.*

BLUEMOUTH

(*Helicolenus dactylopterus*)

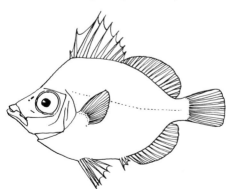

British record: 3lb 2½oz (1kg 431g)

This strongly spined member of the scorpion family has a large mouth, with expanding jaws, and the mouth and gill cavity are indeed dark blue. Its overall colouration, however, is red, fusing into rose pink underneath. It has huge eyes, large perch-like pectoral fins and a double dorsal fin, the first of which is heavily spined. There are more spines on the leading edge of the anal fin, and the tail is squared.

The bluemouth's diet consists of small fish and crustaceans.

BOAR FISH

(*Capros aper*)

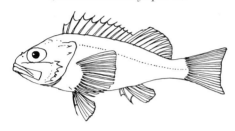

British record: 3oz (85g)

This strangely coloured, tropical reef fish is sometimes found along the south-western shorelines of the British Isles. It has a deep, compressed body with flattened sides, a small head, huge eye and pointed snout with protrusible, bony jaws, and rarely exceeds 6-7in. Its overall colouration is deep red with yellowy irregular markings. The erect dorsal fin consists of several large, strong spines. There is also a strong spine to the leading edge of the pelvic fin. It has a dietary preference for small crustaceans, shrimps in particular.

BOBBIN LEDGERING

See *Ledgering techniques.*

BOGUE

(*Boops boops*)

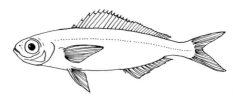

British record: 1lb 15¼oz (885g)

This rather slim sea bream is a shoaling species most commonly found in the Mediterranean, but it is occasionally caught from the southern coastal waters around the British Isles. It has a streamlined body, oval in cross-section, with the characteristically large eye and long, double dorsal fin of the sea bream family. The first dorsal fin is spiked, and the second has soft rays. It has a small mouth holding visible teeth. Colouration is grey to greeny-blue along the back, fusing into lighter flanks with a dark spot at the base of the pectoral fins. It rarely exceeds 18in, and is more commonly caught between 10-12in.

It enjoys a diet of molluscs, sea weed and crustaceans from rocks.

BOILIES

See *Baits - freshwater.*

BOLT-RIG LEDGERING

See *Ledgering techniques.*

BREAD

See *Baits - freshwater.*

Bread punches are available in head sizes from 1.5-5mm for delicately presenting compressed bread pellets.

BREAD PUNCH

When shoal species such as dace, roach, bream and chub become shy of maggots or casters, small pellets of punched bread that swell attractively in the water will produce the action in both still and running water, especially during the winter months.

Pen-type punches, such as the Seymo unit, have four interchangeable brass heads offering a choice of compressed bread pellets 2.5-5mm in size. The Seymo bait punch has an eject button and makes even larger pellets, not only from bread but also from meat and cheese. Also available from Seymo is a set of two bread punches that float, with brass heads (2.5-5mm) and coloured bodies.

Drennan's set of four plastic, disgorger-sized punches have heads ranging from 2mm to 5mm with extra-shallow bowls that really compress thick-sliced bread but only lightly compress thin slices - a feature that allows control of the rate at which the pressed pellet descends. Because they are chamferred below the hook slot, the hook point does not touch the bowl and quickly lose its edge.

For canal fishing, which dictates tiny pellets, the individual punches in a set of five made by Heaver Angling Products have brass, slotted ends that turn out 1.5-4mm pellets. The secret when punching bread is to put the slice on a hard surface, such as a piece of plywood, and firmly press the punch straight down onto it. The hook point is inserted through the middle of the pellet, which is then carefully eased out. Loose-feed with liquidized bread when you are using bread pellets on the hook. (*Groundbaits - freshwater.*)

BREAM, BLACK - SEA

(*Spondyliosoma cantharus*)

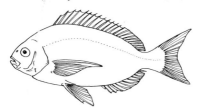

Average size: 2-3lb
Mega specimen: over 4lb
British record: 6lb 14¼oz (3kg 125g)

The black bream is indeed well named, for it has charcoal-grey sides with several dark, vertical bars, and dark greyish fins, although a silvery sheen is often noticeable along the flanks. It has a typical, deep bream shape with a long, spiked dorsal fin and forked tail. The head and jaws are small, and the upper jaw holds many curved, needle-like teeth inside the outer row. Reproduction occurs in the spring, when the female lays eggs in a depression in the sandy sea bed excavated by the male and guarded by him until the eggs hatch. Its diet consists of crustaceans, small fish and seaweed.

HABITAT AND DISTRIBUTION

The black bream loves broken ground, rocky outcrops and wrecks, where it masses in large shoals. It is most common in the Mediterranean, but there are localized concentrations around the British Isles, mainly in south and south-western offshore waters.

TECHNIQUES

Downtide boat fishing; Drift fishing at sea.

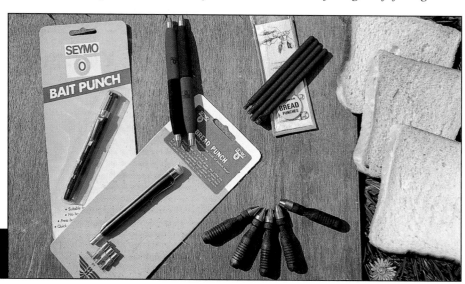

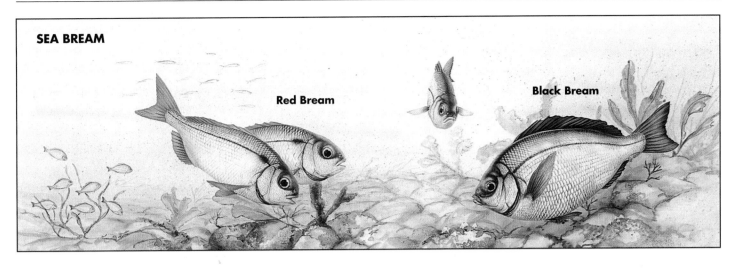

SEA BREAM

Red Bream

Black Bream

BREAM, RED - SEA

(Pagellus bogaraveo)

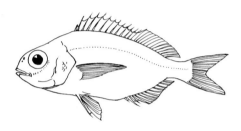

Average size: 1½-2½lb
Mega specimen: Over 5lb
British record: 9lb 8¾oz (4kg 330g)

This saltwater bream has the classic, deep-bodied bream shape with a noticeably large eye, denoting its affinity for deep water. It has a small head, strong, teeth-laden jaws, and a dark spot on the shoulders behind the gill cover. It has long dorsal and anal fins, a strikingly long pectoral fin and a forked tail. Colouration varies from reddish-pink along the back and flanks, fusing into silver lower down. All the fins are a warm grey. No confusion whatsoever with the black bream.

It reproduces in the late summer in warmer seas to the south-west of the British Isles, and enjoys a diet mainly of small fish, crustaceans and squid.

HABITAT AND DISTRIBUTION

Found over deep, rough ground, rocks and around wrecks, the red bream is present all around the British Isles in deep waters, but is most common to the south-west and throughout the Mediterranean.

TECHNIQUES

The red bream is not specifically angled for, but is caught as a bonus species from southern charter boats working well off-shore around wrecks.

BREAM, COMMON -

FRESHWATER

(Abramis brama)

Average size: 2-3lb
Mega specimen: Over 10lb
British record: 16lb 9oz (7kg 519g)

The common, or bronze, bream is easily recognizable from its deep, compressed body, which is heavily covered in protective slime, its large fins, which include a long anal fin and a deeply forked tail, and its fully protrusible mouth. Colouration varies enormously from the silvery-sided young bream (often called tin plates), to the pale flanks and dark grey backs of the adult. Bream that live in clear water have decidedly golden flanks and backs of deep bronze.

Spawning takes place over warm, weedy shallows in late spring. The males become noticeably aggressive and sport knobbly, white tubercles over their heads and shoulders, like all cyprinid species. The pale-yellow eggs are distributed over soft weeds, and hatch within 8-12 days.

Bream feed on a diet of annelid worms and aquatic insect larvae. A noticeable change in water colour often takes place when bream are browsing in large shoals through deep silt due to the disturbed silts.

HABITAT AND DISTRIBUTION

Bream live in large shoals in the deepest areas of both still and slow-moving, coloured waters such as broads, meres, lakes, canals, drains and tidal waterways. It also fares well in rich, clear-flowing river systems, where it is especially attracted to weir-pools. It reaches optimum size in weedy gravel-pit complexes and reservoirs.

Bream are common throughout the British Isles, and are particularly prolific in southern Ireland, in lakeland and river systems both small and large, but their distribution in Scotland is limited to a few lochs only.

TECHNIQUES

Freshwater floatfishing techniques; Freelining; Ledgering techniques - Quivertipping, Bobbin ledgering in stillwaters; Pole fishing.

BREAM, SILVER -

FRESHWATER

(Blicca bjoerkna)

Average size: 3-5oz
Mega specimen: over 10oz
British record: 15oz (425g)

This delicate, virtually slimeless little bream has a large eye, noticeably large scales and pink fins. It has a small head, and its mouth is not fully protrusible like that of the common bream. Overall colouration is pale silver. When erect, the dorsal fin is unusually high and the large tail is deeply forked.

Silver bream spawn in the late spring. The yellow eggs are distributed over soft weeds and hatch quickly within 4-6 days.

Spawning

Juveniles

BREAM

Its natural food consists of plant tissue, aquatic insect larvae, crustaceans and micro molluscs.

HABITAT AND DISTRIBUTION

A lover of lowland river systems, ponds and lakes, the silver bream has unfortunately become almost extinct within the British Isles, although there are still isolated populations in East Anglia. Because they are silvery along the flanks when young, small common bream are taken for silver bream by anglers, but the silver bream is in fact quite rare. In Europe, France especially, it is a common river species.

TECHNIQUES

The silver bream is occasionally caught by accident by anglers float-fishing for rudd, roach or bream.

BREAM HYBRIDS

When either roach or rudd gather in the same areas of shallow weedy water that bream use for spawning, hybridization will occur.

BREAM/RUDD HYBRID

These thick-set, immensely powerful hybrids are blessed with the rudd's colouration, though nowhere near so bright, and the bream's deep flanks, and they can average 2½-3½lb in weight. Rarely caught in English waters (due to the

Though bream reach weights in excess of 16lb, double figure specimens are rare. Small wonder John's fishing buddy, Len Head, from Sudbury is pleased with these 11lb and 12lb monsters caught on lobtails from a Norfolk lake.

scarcity of rudd), they are extremely common throughout southern Ireland, where they are highly prized for their fighting qualities.

BREAM/ROACH HYBRID

The most noticeable features of this hybrid are the lack of warm (roach-like) pigmentation in the fins, and the fact that the scales are larger than those of the bream but smaller than those of the true roach. Some hybrids appear more bream-like, with semi-protrusible mouths, while others are distinctly roach-shaped but drab in colour and have unnaturally long anal fins. The dorsal and anal fins often have a dark outer rim, a peculiarity that is more pronounced in low water temperatures.

Bream/roach hybrids generally run on the small side, around 1½-3lb in weight, but isolated specimens of over 7lb have been recorded.

BRILL
(*Scophthalmus rhombus*)

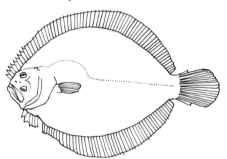

Average size: 3-4lb
Mega specimen: over 10lb
British record: 16lb (7kg 257g)

This thick-set, left-sided (both eyes on the left of its head) flatfish is not as wide as its cousin, the turbot, and they are easily told apart by the fact that the first rays of the brill's long dorsal fin are free of the normal membrane. Also, unlike the turbot, the brill does not have tubercles along its back. The mouth is curved and the head large. Colouration is an overall light sandy brown overlaid with both light spots and noticeably darker flecks. Unlike the turbot, these spots do not occur on the tail. Underneath, the brill is a creamy white.

It feeds upon small flatfish, crustaceans, squid, sand eels and so on. Reproduction takes place in the late spring or summer, and the resulting eggs and fry remain floating in the surface layers until they mature, at which point they descend to a life on the ocean floor.

HABITAT AND DISTRIBUTION

The brill is most commonly found over sandy banks and sometimes over gravel and mud. Although they are caught from similar areas, the brill is often found in faster, shallower water than is the turbot, and it is particularly attracted to the tops of banks. Its distribution is limited to choice areas of sand and gravel banks off England's south coast and off western and northern Ireland.

TECHNIQUES

Downtide boat fishing; Drift fishing, at sea; Uptide boat fishing.

BUILT CANE

Built cane was once the standard rod-building material throughout the world, prior to the advent of fibreglass and carbon fibre, but only a few British manufacturers still produce hand-crafted rods of built cane (mostly fly rods). Each rod section consists of six strips of tonkin cane, triangular in cross section, which are glued together. This forms an incredibly strong all-through-action, fishing-rod blank that can be made in various tapers to suit most fishing situations. The joints are fitted together with brass-splint end ferrules. Hollow built cane, whereby the inner section of each triangular length is removed prior to the blank being glued together, creates a noticeably lighter rod.

BULLHEAD
(*Cottus gobio*)

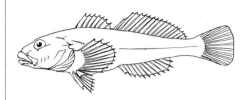

British record: 1oz (28g)

Averaging 2-4in long and nicknamed miller's thumb because of its wide, flattened head, the bullhead spends much of its life beneath large stones on the river bed, feeding on shrimps, aquatic insects and fish eggs. It has noticeably large pectoral fins, a rapidly tapering body, and prefers swift, clean-flowing streams where it darts quickly from one hide-out to another, although it will tolerate sluggish ditches. The bullhead spawns in the spring and the sticky eggs, which adhere to the undersides of stones, are guarded by the male until the fry emerge three weeks later. It is common throughout England and Wales but absent from Scotland and Ireland.

TECHNIQUES

The bullhead is rarely caught by anglers but, if specifically captured in a hand-net, it makes a fine bait for trout, chub and perch.

BRILL

BULLHUSS

(Scyliorhinus stellaris)

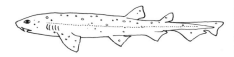

Average size: 5-10lb
Mega specimen: over 12-14lb
British record: 22lb 4oz (10kg 92g)

Also called nursehound and greater spot-ted dogfish, the bullhuss can easily be told apart from the lesser-spotted dogfish by its broad nasal flap, which covers each nos-tril, and by its first dorsal fin, which is set further forward than that of the lesser-spot-ted dogfish. A vertical line can be drawn from the leading edge of its first dorsal to the base of its pelvic fin. The pectoral fins are large and powerful. It has a dark-shark appearance and coarse-sandpapery, warm-brown skin overlaid with dark spots of varying size.

The reproductive cycle starts in the late spring, when the female deposits egg-cases in shallow water. The eggs are fertilized in-side the female by the male. They then be-come encased in a smooth-sided, 4-5in long sac (called a mermaid's purse) supplied at all four corners with long, curled ten-drils that attach it to weeds. Some eight to nine months later, the young bullhuss, now 6-7in long, hatches from its protective home. Bullhuss are a bottom-living shark, and consume a varied diet of small flat-fish, molluscs and crustaceans, especially crabs.

HABITAT AND DISTRIBUTION

Although generally regarded as a deep-wa-ter species, the bullhuss will hunt in shal-low areas where the ground is rough or very rocky and in harbours with prolific colo-nies of crustaceans. It is widely distributed around the British Isles, the largest con-centrations being found off the south and south-west coasts.

TECHNIQUES

Downtide boat fishing; Uptide boat fishing.

BURBOT

(Lota lota)

British record: none

Unique for being the only freshwater rep-resentative of the cod family, this dark, mottled, nocturnal bottom-dweller is now assumed to be extinct in freshwater fisher-ies within the British Isles. It was well dis-tributed over 100 years ago, particularly in East Anglia, and was eaten for its delicious flesh. It does not tolerate the slightest pol-lution, however, and now thrives only in cold, clear-flowing rivers in Europe and in North America, where it averages 4-8lb, occasionally topping 20lb.

BUTTERFISH

(Pholis gunnellus)

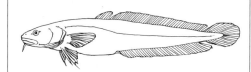

British record: 1⅛oz (32g)

This long, blenny-type sea fish has a deeply compressed body and upturned mouth. Its long dorsal fin stretches from immediately behind the head to the junction of the small, rounded tail, and its anal fin is roughly half the size. It is greeny brown in colour with a dozen or so white-ringed spots along the base of the dorsal fin. A dark line runs through the eye to the corner

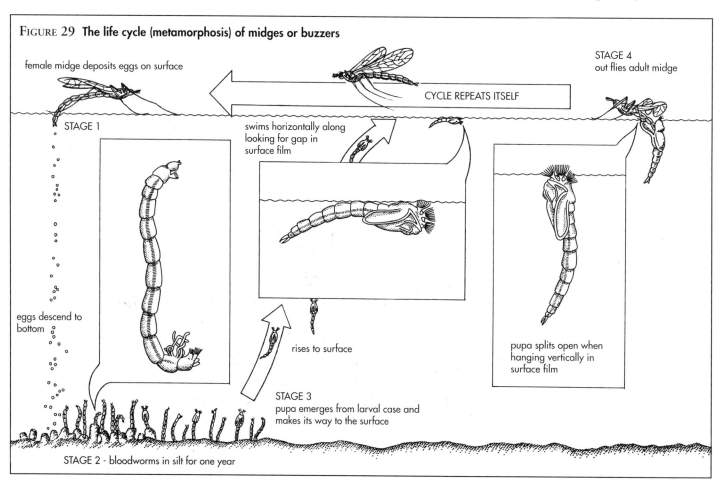

FIGURE 29 **The life cycle (metamorphosis) of midges or buzzers**

female midge deposits eggs on surface

STAGE 4
out flies adult midge

CYCLE REPEATS ITSELF

STAGE 1

swims horizontally along looking for gap in surface film

eggs descend to bottom

rises to surface

pupa splits open when hanging vertically in surface film

STAGE 3
pupa emerges from larval case and makes its way to the surface

STAGE 2 - bloodworms in silt for one year

Cc

CRUCIAN CARP

Larvae

of the mouth.

It averages 6-8in long and lives along rocky sea shores all around the British Isles, feeding on worms, micro molluscs and tiny crustaceans. Owing to its tiny size, the butterfish is rarely caught on rod and line.

BUZZERS
(Chironomidae)

The correct name for this enormous family of terrestrial and aquatic flies is the 'midge'. It is affectionately called the 'buzzer' by fishermen because, when clouds of egg-laying females hover over the water prior to shedding their loads, they make a loud, distinct buzzing sound.

There are over 400 different species of midges, some of which provide a valuable and abundant food source in both still and running water for many species of freshwater fish, particularly trout, tench, bream and carp. Their life story is fascinating and, like that of most aquatic flies, is based on a yearly cycle from egg to fly, although many species produce two or three generations during a season.

There are four distinct stages of midge metamorphosis (fig. 29). The egg, the larva (better known as the bloodworm or joker by match fishermen), the pupa and lastly the winged midge, an egg-laying insect that dies shortly after fulfilling its purpose.

1. The adult female dips down over the water to oviposit (lay), and her tiny eggs then sink to the bottom and hatch into larvae.

2. The thin, maggot-like larvae vary in colour according to their species. Best known of all is the bloodworm, which has haemoglobin in its blood and is among the largest of the midge species. Most midge larvae, however, are either dull brown or green. Up to 1in long, some larvae are free moving among the bottom silt, while others build protective tubes in which they remain for a year. Species such as bream, tench and carp, especially, gorge themselves on midge larvae when they can. Bubbles from disturbed gases in the silt and those emitted through a fish's gills as it chews rise in clouds to the surface.

3. The pupal stage comes next and develops within a few days, during which time the insect rapidly changes colour and shape inside its larval case. When ready, the case splits open to reveal the mature pupa, which rises to the surface ready for the final stage. From this point on, midges are fair game for trout and other upper-water feeders such as rudd and dace.

4. With its external, white, breathing tubes clearly visible on top of its bulbous head, the pupa swims slowly along in a horizontal position trying to break through the surface film. Once it has accomplished this, it hangs vertically in the water and soon splits open, enabling the perfectly winged adult midge to emerge. The miracle of metamorphosis complete, the midge flies up into the air, where it mates. The females lay their eggs and the entire cycle begins again.

CAGE FEEDER

See *Swimfeeder*.

CARP, CRUCIAN
(Carassius carassius)

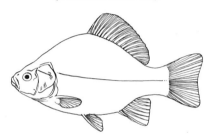

Average size: 8oz-1¼lb
Mega specimen: over 3lb
British record: 5lb 10½oz (2kg 565g)

Deep bodied and nicely rounded, with a small head and slightly upturned mouth (without barbels), the crucian has a distinct and even scale pattern and is coloured an overall buttery-bronze. Its fins are also rounded and are an even, warm grey. Crucians tend to shoal according to their size and feed on a diet of aquatic insect larvae, soft plant tissue and crustaceans. Their distinctive, tiny feeding bubbles can be seen on the surface in small clusters. Reproduction takes place in the late spring/early summer, and the yellow eggs, which are spread over soft weeds and around marginal grasses, hatch one week later.

HABITAT AND DISTRIBUTION

This little carp fares best in small, coloured or weedy stillwaters - farm ponds, lily-clad lakes and pits. It is common throughout England, particularly in East Anglia, but absent from Scotland and Ireland.

TECHNIQUES

Freshwater floatfishing techniques - The lift method; Waggler fishing in rivers; Pole fishing.

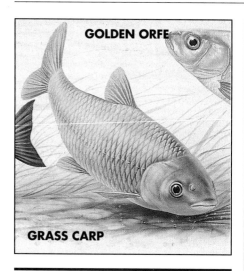

GOLDEN ORFE

GRASS CARP

CARP, GRASS

(*Ctenopharynagodon idella*)

Average size: 3-6lb
Mega specimen: over 12-15lb
British record: 25lb 4oz (11kg 453g)

Looking very much like the chub, this Asian import can easily be distinguished from it despite its torpedo-shaped, chub-like body and regular scale pattern. Its best distinguishing feature is the low-set eye - almost level with its mouth - and the mouth is noticeably mullet-like and smaller than the chub's. It also has a larger tail, which is deeply forked, and a lack of red pigment in its fins, all of which are an even grey. It is dark grey to brown along the back, fusing into flanks that vary from pale to brassy-pewter. It characteristically hovers just beneath the surface with its head angled upwards, and is an enthusiastic surface to mid-water feeder. It consumes vast quantities of soft plant tissue, including algae, but also takes fishermen's baits,

including bread, maggots, sweetcorn and pastes, from the bottom. It is a deliberate feeder, and becomes noticeably more aggressive in really warm water.

Grass carp cannot spawn in the wild in our temperate climate. Indigenous to the Amur river system in China, their eggs, which are laid in the spring, need to drift in warm, running water (above 65°F) for many miles prior to hatching.

HABITAT AND DISTRIBUTION

Grass carp fare well in most small stillwaters, particularly those rich in aquatic plants. Its distribution within the British Isles is limited to isolated pits, ponds, lakes and irrigation channels in England and Wales, where it has been stocked. It is absent from Ireland and Scotland.

TECHNIQUES

Freshwater floatfishing - laying on, the lift method, Surface controller fishing, Waggler fishing in rivers, Freelining; Ledgering techniques - Bobbin ledgering in stillwaters.

CARP, HYBRIDS

CRUCIAN CARP/WILD OR KING CARP CROSSES

When crucian and wild or king carp share the same spawning site, spreading their eggs over marginal grasses and across soft-rooted weeds, hybridization between the species is liable to occur. This results in carp that appear decidedly different from each of their parents.

Unfortunately, the exact parentage of these hybrids is not easy to distinguish, although there are pointers. For instance, as both wild and king carp have four long barbels protruding from the corners of their mouths, and crucian carp do not, be immediately suspicious of any odd-looking carp that has considerably smaller barbels

than a true wild or king carp of the same size would have.

In the case of hybridization between wild carp and crucians, their offspring, apart from sporting only tiny barbels, have noticeably different scales, with next to little edging between each. Colouration on these hybrids is also noticeably more even overall than on either a wild or king carp.

CRUCIAN CARP/GOLDFISH OR SHUBUNKIN CROSSES

Should someone inadvertently introduce shubunkins or goldfish into a small, heavily overstocked pond or pit full of crucian carp, some very strange-looking hybrids could result: seemingly 'passable' crucians with huge fan-like tails; part-coloured crucians; and throwbacks to the original uncoloured goldfish, which are dark pewter all over and lack any hint of the crucian's lovely golden-bronze colouration. If a crucian does not look exactly how it should, with golden-bronze rounded body and fins, call it a hybrid.

CARP, KING

(*Cyprinus carpio*)

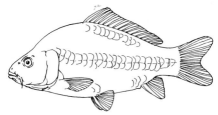

Average size: 5-12lb
Mega specimen: over 30lb
British record: 51lb 8oz (23kg 358g)

The vast majority of carp caught within the British Isles are various strains of king carp. These differ from the original, fully-scaled wild strain in that, through selective breeding by European fish-farmers, they have become much quicker growing,

CARP

Metallic male common carp

Eggs

Coloured and metallic carp crosses

Female metallic carp

King carp scaleage varies enormously. John caught this duo of 20lb-plus 'plated mirrors' from Hampshire's River Test.

much thicker set and considerably deeper in the body, often with a distinct, humped back rising at the shoulders.

In addition, the scalage of king carp strains varies enormously, from fully-scaled commons to completely scaleless, leather carp. Mirror carp are so called because they have just a few large, reflective scales covering small sections of their bodies, while linear-scaled king carp have one continuous row of scales along their lateral line. Fully-scaled mirror carp are entirely covered with irregularly shaped scales, and starburst mirror carp have an explosion of variously sized scales, mostly tiny plus one or two large ones.

Exact categorization is virtually impossible because the scalage permutations are endless and as varied as body colours. The back can vary from brown to blue-grey or pale bronze to sandy-beige, with flanks of beige, pewter, golden bronze, pale grey, or even a warm, yellowy tinge.

The fins, and especially the tail, are large, and are tinted various shades of grey with a touch of warmth. Sometimes there is even an orangey hue in both the lower half of the tail and the anal fin. The mouth is semi-protrusible, with a pair of sensory barbels situated at the corner of each jaw-hinge. At the extreme tip of each barbel or feeler is a taste pad. These help the carp locate its food, which consists of annelid worms, aquatic insect larvae and crustaceans, all of which it chews between its powerful pharyngeal teeth, situated in the back of the throat.

Reproduction occurs in the late spring or early summer. The eggs are distributed over soft, rooted weeds, lily-pads, submerged tree roots and marginal grasses. The resulting fry hatch some 6-10 days later.

HABITAT AND DISTRIBUTION

Originally it was thought that king carp flourished only in stillwaters such as ponds, pits, estate lakes and reservoirs. However, they are now common, and in many cases breeding, in numerous lowland river systems in England, particularly throughout the Midlands, East Anglia and southern England. King carp prefer, and grow to their maximum size in, extremely rich stillwaters, but will tolerate and quickly adapt to almost any situation. They are the most durable, and owing to their potential size the most widely stocked, freshwater sport fish within the British Isles, although they are still rare in Scotland and Ireland.

TECHNIQUES
Freshwater floatfishing techniques - Laying on, The lift method, Surface-controller fishing; Flyfishing; Freelining; Ledgering techniques - Bobbin ledgering in stillwaters, Bolt rig ledgering.

CARP, KING - VARIANTS
(*Cyprinus carpio*)

The original wild carp, the king carp variants and the coloured koi carp all share the same Latin classification.

We have the Japanese to thank for cultivating the first coloured carp (*koi* is Japanese for 'coloured'), which date back to AD700 during the Hei-an period. By the Middle Ages, during the Momyama Era (1582-98), the culture of koi carp was popular throughout Japan. And today its popularity is world wide.

The best, most exquisitely coloured brood fish are still in Japan, but koi of excellent colour and durability are now bred in countries such as America, Israel and France, and imported for distribution throughout the British Isles, not only for the pond-fish trade but as a target fish for anglers.

Fishery owners and managers generally choose coloured king carp in muted shades so that they do not look too out of place in a wild environment. The most popular variant is the 'metallic', and it is often sold at water-garden centres under the name 'Ghost Koi' because the etching across the skull and along the back is the first thing you see of the carp underwater.

This durable, fast-growing fish, the result of crossing a white Japanese male ogon koi with a naturally coloured German-type female king carp of mirror or common scalage, may have etching on the scales in various shades of silver, gold, beige or bronze.

A small percentage of the offspring will be almost as white as the male ogon parent, while a large percentage will appear to have little etching at all, save perhaps for a pearly-silver tint on their pectoral and pelvic fins. A certain number will have the beauty of both brood parents, with noticeable metallic etching across the skull, back, flanks and fins. The permutations available from crossing koi with naturally coloured king carp, taking the number of

scale patterns into consideration, is quite staggering and provides enormous scope for stillwater fisheries in the future.

CARP, WILD
(*Cyprinus carpio*)

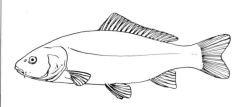

Average size: 2-3lb
Mega specimen: over 8-9lb
British record: none, due to the difficulty in establishing true wild carp

As there is no genetic difference between a thin, fully-scaled king carp and a well-proportioned wild carp (wildie), it is impossible to distinguish between the two in the case of fish caught from the vast majority of carp waters within the British Isles. The exceptions are those from ponds and estate lakes where only the original form of wild carp were ever stocked, and where to this day only fully-scaled common carp are ever caught. Then, and only then, could the water possibly contain true wild carp.

Introduced into the British Isles during the Middle Ages, the original wild carp is a fully-scaled, long, streamlined fish with four sensory barbels and a semi-protrusible mouth, just like the king carp strains that evolved from it. Colouration, reproduction and dietary requirements are the same as for king carp.

Wild carp are most prolific in farm ponds and bite eagerly, providing youngsters with wonderful sport.

WILD CARP

HABITAT AND DISTRIBUTION

The wild carp fares best in warm, shallow, heavily coloured ponds and lakes. However, owing to the widespread introduction of king carp strains, there are few 'wildie-only' fisheries within the British Isles.

TECHNIQUES

As for *King carp*.

CASTERS

See *Baits, Freshwater - Maggots*.

CASTING

See *Beachcasting; Fly casting*.

CATAPULT

Specialized fishing catapults with pouches in a range of sizes are indispensable for placing loose-feed baits, such as casters, hemp seed, maggots and boilies, accurately over distances in excess of a few yards and for feeding into the wind.

Most catapults have half-circle frames and moulded-plastic hand grips. On some, silicone rubber elastic is joined to the frame with snap-swivels and split rings so that it does not twist or tangle between shots. On other models, hollow silicone elastic is fitted to the frame via a revolving spigot. The most foolproof range of catapults - 'Reddicat', manufactured by Wychwood Tackle - has silicone elastic threaded right through the frame to eliminate all weak spots and tangles. For maggots, casters and all seed and bean particle baits, a simple vinyl pouch fitted with thin-gauge elastic is ideal.

For propelling groundbait balls, the pouch should be rigid so that it doesn't distort or crumble the ball when the elastic is pulled back. Most groundbait catapults are fitted with strong, surgical elastic and have wide frames. In order to propel boilies accurately over great distances, commercial carp catapults are fitted with small, moulded, cup-like pouches and super-strong, surgical elastic. Wrist-rocket catapults, which have a wrist brace to ensure rigidity during firing, are much favoured by carp fishermen.

As most tackle dealers stock spare elastic and pouches, you can make a catapult to suit your own requirements using plywood, alloy-rod, high-density plastic or aluminium-sheet frame.

See also *Throwing stick*.

CATFISH, ARISTOTLES
(*Silurus aristotelis*)

British record: none

Related to the wels catfish, and almost identical to it, the Aristotles catfish can be distinguished by the two barbels sprouting from beneath its chin, whereas the wels has four. The Aristotles catfish has extremely limited distribution, being found only in Greece, within the Akheloos river system. Individual fish do, however, travel throughout Europe and the British Isles via the ornamental pond-fish trade.

Whether loose feeding small particle baits like casters, maggots or sweetcorn at close range, or propelling heavy balls of groundbait great distances, it is essential to obtain the correct catapult for the job.

CATFISH, BULLHEAD
(Ictalurus melas)

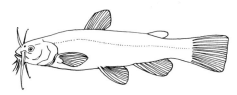

British record: 2oz (85g)

This blackish, smooth-bodied, thick-set aggressive little catfish rarely exceeds 12in in length. It has a broad head and a wide mouth sporting eight barbels in all, four on its snout and four beneath the protruding lower jaw. It has a tiny adipose fin and a large, squared-off tail. Bullhead catfish spawn in summer, and the resulting fry, which hatch in 5-6 days, are guarded by one of the parents. It feeds on crustaceans, molluscs, small fish and amphibians, and exists only in very localized waters in England. It is widespread in Europe, especially France.

CATFISH, CHANNEL
(Ictalurus punctatus)

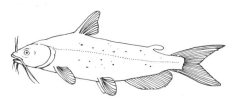

Average size: 3-6lb
Mega specimen: 10-15lb plus
British record: none at present. Channel cats regularly attain weights in excess of 30lb in North America, where the record is in excess of 50lb (22.7kg)

The channel catfish has a thick-set, smooth, scaleless, pale grey body with a wide, flattish head and a cavernous mouth containing bristle-like gripping pads inside both the upper and lower jaws. The snout overhangs the lower jaw and sports a long, thick barbel at each corner. Two erect barbels sprout from the middle of its skull, and there are four slightly longer ones immediately below the chin, making eight in all. Its fins are dark grey, large and powerful, and the tail is deeply forked. There is a strong spine to the leading edge of both dorsal and pectoral fins, and a tiny, rubbery adipose fin. It feeds on other fish, crustaceans and molluscs, and spawns in late spring or early summer.

HABITAT AND DISTRIBUTION
The channel catfish prefers coloured lakes and river systems and is present only in isolated waters in southern England, having been introduced originally by the ornamental and pond-fish trade.

TECHNIQUES
Usually caught by accident on meat and fresh fish bait, it is liable to suck up any food presented on the bottom. It fights extremely hard.

CATFISH, WELS
(Silurus glanis)

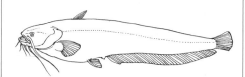

Average size: 5-15lb
Mega specimen: over 30-35lb
British record: 49lb 14oz (22kg 623g)

By far the longest and potentially the largest of all British freshwater species, the wels catfish reaches weights in excess of 300-400lb in Eastern Europe. It has a smooth, scaleless body, mottled in olive, brown and sometimes shades of mauve, and tapering rapidly, tadpole-fashion, from its large flattened head to its tail. Its wide cavernous mouth contains bristle-pads of fine teeth just inside both the top and lower jaws. There are four short sensory barbels under the chin and one extremely long feeler situated in front of each eye, close to each jaw hinge, making six in all.

The dorsal fin is quite tiny and stands erect. The pectoral fins are large and fan-like, and the pelvics are small. The anal fin is long and almost joins the small, squared-off tail.

The wels spawns during the summer. Eggs are deposited by the female into a nest on the bottom prepared by the male, who stands guard until they hatch.

The wels feeds on fish, amphibians, and even small swimming rodents. Adult wels occasionally suck down waterfowl from the surface, although generally speaking they scavenge from the bottom, and are largely nocturnal feeders.

HABITAT AND DISTRIBUTION
The wels loves snaggy, weedy, undercut bank caverns and hide-outs in stillwaters that are prolific in shoal species such as roach, rudd and bream. It fares well in heavily coloured ponds, lakes and pits throughout the Midlands, East Anglia and southern England, where it has been introduced. It is still comparatively rare, however, and is absent from Scotland and Ireland.

TECHNIQUES
Freelining; Ledgering techniques - Livebaits and deadbaits.

WELS CATFISH

Wels catfish have yet to reach monstrous proportions in British fisheries, which is why enthusiasts like Keith Lambert from Hertfordshire regularly travel across the Channel to Europe. This 86lb beauty came from the Rio Segre in Spain.

CHARR, ARCTIC

(*Salvelinus alpinus*)

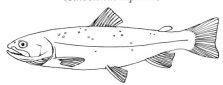

Average size: 8oz-1¼lb
Mega specimen: over 3lb
British record: 7lb 7oz (3kg 373g)

The Arctic Charr is the most exquisitely coloured of all the salmonids. It has the classic trout shape with a forked tail and a noticeable white edge to the pectoral, pelvic and anal fins, which have a warm, pinkish hue. The tail and dorsal fin are dark grey. The back is either greeny-blue or pewter, fusing into flanks of pale orange scattered with white and orange spots. Males are covered in an intense orange-red pattern, which is particularly vivid during the spawning season between December and April. The hen fish excavates a depression in the gravel beds of mountain streams, or the lake bed, in which to lay, and the eggs take several weeks to hatch.

Charr feed on plankton, aquatic insect larvae, crustaceans, molluscs and small shoal fish.

HABITAT AND DISTRIBUTION

The charr prefers the pure, clear, deep water of lochs and lakes, where it resides at great depths, except during its reproduction cycle when it enters rivers and mountain streams. It is found in the Lake District, Scotland, Wales and Ireland, though each strain of charr various enormously.

TECHNIQUES

Artificial lure fishing - freshwater; Fly fishing - Loch-style; Trolling.

CHARTER BOATS

Charter boats provide many anglers with their only access to offshore fishing. British charter boats tend to be purpose-built for angling and generally carry up to twelve anglers.

Elsewhere in Europe, redundant commercial boats are pressed into service for angling, often with limited space and facilities. Most UK ports have at least one regular charter boat; some, such as Plymouth, Whitby or Swansea, play host to several dozen.

When a group of anglers charter a boat they are paying not just for a boat to take

CHARR

POWAN

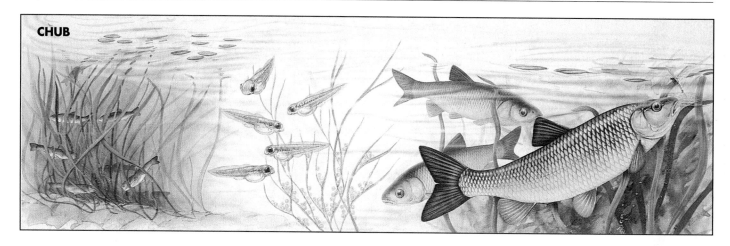

CHUB

them to sea, but also for the skipper's local knowledge. A good charter skipper will be on hand throughout the day to offer advice, assist the novice, land fish, sort out the inevitable tangles and generally ensure the well-being of his party. In the event of bad weather, it is the skipper's responsibility to ensure that the boat and anglers get safely back to port at the end of the day.

When booking a charter boat, it is wise to seek the skipper's advice at an early stage. Tell him what you would like to catch, and be sure to tell him the level of experience of the anglers. Let him recommend a suitable date and heed his advice regarding the best baits, tackle and methods to use. Avoid unregistered charter boats, which will invariably not be equipped to the same standards as registered boats.

Chub
(Leuciscus cephalus)

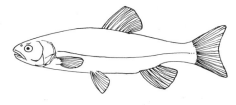

Average size: 1½-3lb
Mega specimen: over 5lb
British record: 8lb 4oz (3kg 743g)

Chub are an aggressive shoal fish and one of the wariest, yet greediest, of all British freshwater species. The body is torpedo-shaped and the head rather blunt, with a large mouth and thick-rimmed lips. At the back of the throat are a pair of powerful pharyngeal teeth, which the chub uses to crush small fish and crustaceans into pulp before swallowing. Colouration is dark grey-brown along the back fusing into brass down the flanks, with a creamy belly. The

dorsal fin and slightly pointed tail are dark grey, while the pelvic and anal fins have a tint of pale orange. Both the dorsal and anal fins are nicely rounded compared to those of the dace, which are concave, the easiest way of separating the two species.

The chub's diet consists of aquatic insect larvae, small fish, crustaceans such as shrimps and crayfish, plus small molluscs. Spawning takes place on the fast, gravelly shallows in late spring or early summer. The females distribute their eggs over willow moss and among the gravel, while the males spray milt to fertilize them. Incubation takes around 10 days.

HABITAT AND DISTRIBUTION

Above all, chub love hide-outs and a roof over their heads. First and foremost a river species preferring feature habitats beneath which they can retreat - flowing weed beds, overhanging willows, undercut banks, weir-pools, bridge arches and so on - they also fare well and pack on weight to specimen proportions in stillwaters, pits and lakes especially. Chub are prolific throughout most lowland river systems in England,

but are absent from Ireland. They are rare in Wales except for the River Wye and its tributaries, and exist in a handful of the rivers in southern Scotland, the Annan being famous for producing specimen chub.

TECHNIQUES

Artificial lure fishing - freshwater; Fly fishing; Freshwater float fishing techniques - Long trotting, Stick-float fishing, Stretpegging, Surface-controller fishing, Waggler fishing in rivers; Freelining; Ledgering techniques - Live baits and deadbaits, Quivertipping.

Coalfish
(Pollachius virens)

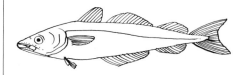

Average size: 4-8lb
Mega specimen: over 20lb
British record: 37lb 5oz (16kg 923g)

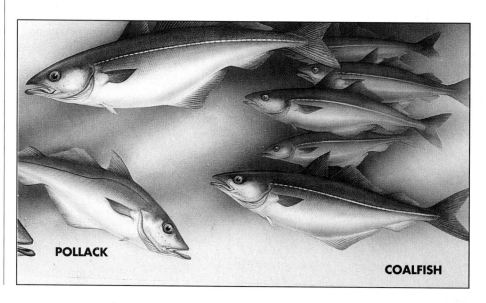

POLLACK

COALFISH

As Norfolk angler Terry Houseago knows only too well, chub are amongst the most obliging of British freshwater fishes. During the winter months when temperatures are low he regularly accounts for superbly conditioned specimens like this four-pounder on quivertipped breadflake or cheese paste from his local River Wensum.

Though shore fishermen think of cod as a winter quarry, John shared this fine haul of prime specimens with Mel Russ, editor of *Sea Angler* magazine, whilst working pirks and rubber eels on light tackle over a deep water wartime wreck some 20 miles out from Hastings during the month of June.

Also known as the 'saithe' and the 'coley', the coalfish is a shoaling member of the cod family and has tiny scales, extremely smooth skin and fins that lack spines. Coalfish are similar to, and often confused with, the pollack, which also has three dorsal fins, a pointed tail, a tiny pair of secondary pectoral fins and two long anal fins. But while the pollack has a curved lateral line, that of the coalfish is straight and cream coloured. The coalfish's lower jaw protrudes slightly, but is nowhere near as prominent as the pollack's.

Colouration is dark grey-green along the back fusing into muted silver along the flanks and belly. Its food consists of sprats, sand eels, herring, mackerel and crustaceans. Reproduction occurs between January and April. The fry float close to the surface and are carried inshore from the deep-water spawning grounds.

HABITAT AND DISTRIBUTION

Young 'schoolies' are commonly found around harbour walls and over rocky outcrops, while adult coalfish much prefer deep-water marks around wrecks or over really rough ground. Widely distributed in the northern Atlantic, and consequently most common in Scottish waters, specimen-sized coalfish are also caught regularly from southern and south-western off-shore marks.

TECHNIQUES

Artificial lure fishing - sea, Downtide boat fishing; Drift fishing at sea; Floatfishing in harbours and off the rocks; Wreck fishing.

COD

(Gadus Morhua)

Average size: 5-15lb
Mega specimen: over 30lb
British record: 53lb (24kg 39g)

The most popular and most commonly caught of all British sea fish during the winter months, the cod can reach weights well in excess of 100lb. The cod is a shoaling species possessing a thick-set body and a large head with a voluminous mouth lined with fine teeth. The upper jaw overhangs the lower, from which sprouts a single, long

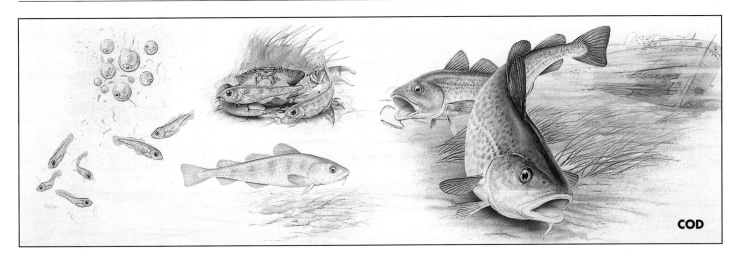

COD

barbel. The lateral line is curved above the pectoral fin, below which are much smaller secondary pectorals. There are three dorsal and two anal fins, all having soft rays, and a rounded tail.

Colouration varies according to the environment, but generally the back is a sandy brown, with distinct mottling along the flanks and an off-white belly. Cod living over rocks in clear water are the most distinctly marked, sometimes being a reddish-brown.

The cod's diet consists of worms, crustaceans, sprats, herrings, sand eels and so on. Spawning occurs between February and April in deep water. The eggs then rise to the surface and hatch within 2-4 weeks.

HABITAT AND DISTRIBUTION

During the summer months cod are mostly confined to deep-water, offshore marks around the British coastline, particularly over rough ground and around wrecks. From September onwards, however, they move inshore, often in massive shoals.

TECHNIQUES

Artificial lure fishing - sea; Beachcasting; Downtide boat fishing; Drift fishing at sea; Feathering; Uptide boat fishing.

COMBER
(Serranus cabrilla)

British record: 1lb 13oz (822g)

This small fish is a member of the sea perch family, and is of Mediterranean origin, although it is occasionally caught offshore from British south-western waters. It has a brownish back and flanks overlaid with several dark, perch-like vertical bars, and greeny-blue stripes under its chin and

across the gill plates. The first part of the double dorsal fin has strong spines, and there are more spines at the start of the anal fin. It has a large mouth with bony lips, and there are three flat spines on the gill cover.

The comber feeds on crustaceans, squid and small fish, and breeds during the summer.

COMPASS

See *Navigation at Sea.*

CONFLUENCES

Areas where two large rivers meet, or where feeder streams and carriers join the main flow of the mother river, provide wonderful hotspots where numerous species meet or pass through. Salmon and sea trout, for instance, often gather at these junctions before continuing their upstream migrations.

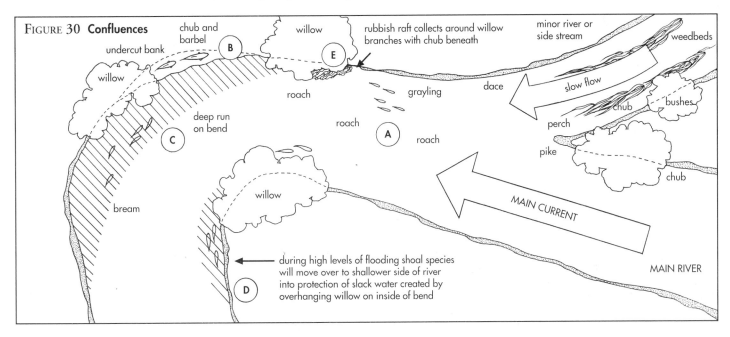

FIGURE 30 **Confluences**

chub and barbel
willow
rubbish raft collects around willow branches with chub beneath
minor river or side stream
weedbeds
undercut bank
B
E
willow
deep run on bend
roach
grayling
dace
slow flow
chub
bushes
roach
perch
C
A
roach
pike
chub
bream
willow
D
MAIN CURRENT
MAIN RIVER
during high levels of flooding shoal species will move over to shallower side of river into protection of slack water created by overhanging willow on inside of bend

If one river carries colour while the other runs clear, shoal species like dace, roach and chub will edge into the former, where they feel less vulnerable to predators. Predators such as perch and pike love to lie in wait in the V of the confluence for shoal species to pass by.

In small river systems, confluences are usually easy to read in that shoal species such as dace, grayling or roach like to occupy the steady, filter lane of water immediately to the side of the main junction, a run that is always well scoured but through which a constant stream of food particles is brought down. In large confluences, however, a careful study of surface currents is imperative for success. There will be several different current channels, often of varying speeds, which all intermingle to create large areas of tumbling water where vortexes spiral up from the bottom and break on the surface. Obviously these areas are to be avoided as fish close to the river bed do not like changing direction every few seconds or having to chase every

food item. In fast currents, the smoother water is often at the very end of the junction where the two flows converge, and this is where shoal species will take up residence (fig. 30A).

If the river bends immediately downstream from the confluence there is bound to be a long, deep run on the outside of the bend, created by the extra push of water - another great hotspot for many species. In the deepest part of the run there could be a shoal of bream or quality roach (fig. 30), while beneath the bank where it is well supported by a mass of willow roots (fig. 30B) chub or barbel could be lying in an undercut carved out over many years by the constant push of water.

During high flood levels many of these species, particularly roach and bream, will move to the shallower side of the river, into the protection of a large slack created by the overhanging willow on the inside of the bend (fig. 30D), a spot completely devoid of fish under normal conditions except for minnows and the occasional pike.

Confluences of wide, lowland rivers create hot spots for species like roach, bream, pike and zander. The middle river here is the Great Ouse which empties into the 100ft drain (right) to become the tidal Great Ouse and into the Great Ouse Relief Channel via the massive sluices at Denver. Entering the Relief Channel on the left is the renowned Cut Off Channel.

Bankside features such as overhanging willows or alders have immense attraction to chub, particularly when low-hanging branches collect rafts of rubbish (fig. 30E). Barbel also love rafts because they provide shelter from daylight, particularly in swims where the bottom is clean gravel or sand. Bushes that overhang the water provide shade to barbel, chub and pike. The stealthy fisherman can easily observe these species through polaroid glasses when the rivers run crystal clear during the summer months, and can often catch them using simple *freeline* tactics.

Dd

COUCH'S SEA BREAM
(Sparus pagrus)

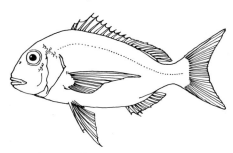

British record: 1lb 1¾oz (501g)

This typical, Mediterranean-type, shoaling sea bream is occasionally caught from southern and south-western waters around the British Isles. It has a deep, pinky-silver body with a high forehead, strong jaws laden with curved teeth in front and flat, crushing teeth at the back. The front half of the long, continuous dorsal fin is spiked, while the rear half has soft rays. The anal fin is spiked and the tail forked. All the fins are translucent pink.

It feeds on molluscs and crustaceans, as its formidable array of teeth suggest.

CRAB

See *Baits - sea.*

CRAYFISH

See *Baits - freshwater.*

CRUSTACEANS

This term covers a huge range of aquatic creatures possessing a hard, shell-like outer skin - from tiny freshwater shrimps and crayfish to the shrimps, prawns, crabs and lobsters of salt water.

CUTTLEFISH

See *Baits - sea.*

CYPRINIDS

Members of the Cyprinidae or carp-like family of freshwater fish, which includes all carp, barbel, bream, chub, tench, roach, rudd and dace down to the humble minnow, have one feature in common. All lack teeth in their jaws, but are equipped with a pair of powerful pharyngeal teeth in their throats with which they chew food. Another characteristic is that during the spawning season male cyprinids grow tiny white tubercles over their bodies. These are particularly noticeable across the head and shoulders and are used for bumping into the swollen bellies of females to stimulate them into releasing their eggs. Small species such as dace and golden orfe are easily sexed during the spring simply by handling them. The males feel decidedly rough to the touch.

DAB
(Limanda limanda)

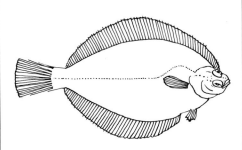

Average size: 3-12oz
Mega specimen: over 1½lb
British record: 2lb 12¼oz (1kg 254g)

This, the smallest of the Pleuronectidae family of flatfish, which have both eyes on the right side of the body (left-sided dabs are very occasionally caught), has a sandy-brown back overlaid with dark freckles and a translucent white underside. It is immediately recognizable by its coarse skin, caused by tiny saw-like teeth along the edge of each scale on its back. The lateral line is noticeably curved around the pectoral fin. The dab has a small, upturned mouth and feeds on crustaceans, small molluscs and worms.

Reproduction takes place in the late spring or early summer. The eggs float near the surface, and the fry, or post larva, that emerge from them undergo metamorphosis as the left eye moves over to the right side of the head. Once this is complete, the mini dabs sink to the sea floor and start their sedentary life as flatfish.

HABITAT AND DISTRIBUTION
A prolific, shallow-water flatfish, the dab is distributed all around the British Isles, and is most commonly found over a sandy or mud bottom.

TECHNIQUES
Beachcasting; Downtide boat fishing; Uptide boat fishing.

DACE
(Leuciscus leuciscus)

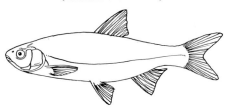

Average size: 2-6oz
Mega specimen: over 12-14oz
British record: 1lb 4¼oz (574g)

The dace has a slim, smooth, rounded body with an even pattern of silvery, highly reflective scales along its flanks and belly. The back is olive-grey. The head is small and neat, and the fins translucent. The tail is grey and deeply forked. The dorsal and anal fins curve inwards, in complete contrast to those of the chub, which are rounded - this is the most efficient way of distinguishing between the two species. The pectoral and anal fins of adult dace often show a tinge of yellowy-pink.

The dace's diet consists of aquatic insect larva and small crustaceans. Spawning usually occurs during the hours of darkness in early spring, at which time the males are easily distinguishable from the smooth, pigeon-chested females by their rough skin.

HABITAT AND DISTRIBUTION
Although dace congregate in huge shoals in coloured lowland rivers, even in wide tidal rivers, they are the darting lifeblood of shallow sparkling brooks and streams that run crystal-clear over clean gravel beds. Long runs at the tail-end of weir-pools or runs between long flowing beds of rooted weeds are their favourite homes. Dace are common throughout English river systems and in selected Irish rivers, where they have been stocked. They are prolific in the Welsh Dee and in the Wye and its tributaries, but rare in Scotland.

Juveniles

Spawning

DACE

TECHNIQUES

Freshwater floatfishing techniques - Stick-float fishing, Stretpegging, Waggler fishing in rivers; Fly fishing; Freelining; Ledgering techniques - Quivertipping; Pole fishing.

DAPPING

See *Fly fishing.*

DETRITUS

This is the top layer of bottom debris, consisting of organic waste in the process of being broken down - fallen leaves, plant tissue, dead micro-organisms and so on are all reduced to a rich, organic silt. When fish such as tench and carp root through detritus in search of annelid worms, midge larvae and shrimps, gasses are released from the detritus that stream upwards and bubble through the surface film. Hence the theory that fish responsible for bubbles rising to the surface are feeding fish. Not all feeding bubbles come from gasses locked up in the bottom detritus, however. They are also produced by the fish themselves, spewing from the gill slits while fish are chewing food with their *pharyngeal teeth.*

DINGHY FISHING IN FRESHWATER

There are numerous situations in which fishing from a boat greatly enhances the chances of success. In tidal river systems, on waterways that are densely lined with reeds, and on marshes where fishing from the bank is impossible (the Norfolk Broads, for instance), access to a dinghy makes all the difference between success and failure.

From the comparative luxury of a wide, flat-bottomed punt, John nets a bream during a session shared with Len Head. To keep the craft anchored steady, heavy mudweights are imperative.

You need to be well organized and own or acquire a pair of heavy *mudweights* on long ropes for keeping the boat anchored in windy conditions. As sound carries easily through water, the addition of an old piece of carpet on top of the floorboards will minimize vibrations. Endeavour to position the dinghy sideways on to the wind (with a mudweight at each end) so you can fish straight downwind.

On stillwaters it is always better to fish from further away to begin with, because you then have the option of moving closer in rather than anchoring too close initially and scaring the fish. Remember, also, that when afloat, the temperature and wind chill factor are noticeably lower so take adequate warm clothing and waterproofs. Keep a few plastic bin-liners handy in your tackle bag to protect items like the camera bag should the heavens really open.

When anchoring in rivers, anchor bows-on to the current. First lower the bows mudweight plus several extra yards of rope, and when the boat settles, lower the stern weight on a fairly tight rope.

Take time to make up the rods and arrange all large items neatly in the boat, preferably before you set off so that once the mudweights have been lowered there is minimal disturbance in the boat. Several hours in a boat encourages fidgeting, so take along a comfortable folding chair, which, if you are float fishing, will allow you to control the tackle more effectively by dipping the rod tip below the surface to sink the line and counteract surface drift.

In deep waters *fish-finders* are a great help, but when exploring fisheries of just 4-5ft deep or less, don't expect the fish to allow your dinghy to pass over them - they will be long gone. In really clear water, even shoal fish living in depths of 8-12ft might vacate the area prior to your boat passing over (*Drift fishing in freshwater*).

DINGHY FISHING AT SEA

If you are new to dinghy fishing you will not have the experience to assess the performance of a boat, and it is good advice to take someone along who has a sound knowledge of small boats; preferably someone with a few years experience of fishing the same area as you.

Remember that the ideal boat does not, and probably never will, exist and it is normally necessary to make compromises. The trick is to buy the boat that most suits your style of angling, and never compromise in any way on safety.

The boat should have a good freeboard, or high gunwhales or sides. Knee height should be considered the minimum amount of acceptable freeboard. Gunwhale rails will improve onboard safety by minimizing the risk of anyone falling overboard, but they add nothing to the boat's seaworthiness. Look for a boat with a lot of free deck space from which to fish, allowing for the addition of petrol tanks, anchor, fish boxes and fishing tackle.

Plenty of dry storage space for tackle and equipment is also useful. There is nothing worse or more dangerous than fishing from an untidy and cluttered boat. Essential items of equipment that are not required for regular use should always be kept close at hand - flares, first aid kit, fire extinguishers and so on (*Safety afloat*).

A boat with a sump or bilge built into the deck to collect spray and rain water will help to keep the deck dry. This is also the ideal place to install the pick-up tube for a bilge pump. Such positions are also the ideal site for the transducer for a fish-finder.

Give a lot of thought to the choice of engine. Many boat/engine packages are now available, but there will always be the dealer who recommends an engine that either overpowers or underpowers a particular boat simply because he has that engine in stock. All boats will have a recommended power range, and the most powerful engine recommended for use on that boat is preferable to underpowering it with a smaller engine. That way, when the boat is fully kitted out it should still give a fair degree of performance. Never overpower any boat - the results could be fatal. If in doubt, seek advice from the boat's manufacturer.

A trailer is often the part of the package that people give least thought to. Many people do not find out whether they have bought a suitable trailer until the first time that they launch and retrieve the boat. The overwhelming amount of damage caused to trailered boats occurs at the launch site, and a high percentage of these accidents can be prevented by using a decent trailer. Look for one that gives the hull plenty of support, and with efficient rollers to assist launch and retrieve.

The purchase of secondhand boats, engines and trailers entails a certain amount of risk. There are bargains about, but more than a few are rubbish. Again, if you are inexperienced with boats, it is imperative that you take someone along with you who knows small boats inside out.

Secondhand engines are always a gamble. If possible, buy a secondhand boat and trailer, but try to buy a new engine. Any secondhand engine should immediately receive a full service from a qualified marine mechanic who will have the knowledge, experience and specialist tools to service it.

Why not suggest that before you buy an engine, you have it examined. Explain that you will gladly pay for the cost of a mechanic to give the engine a good once-over should the result prove satisfactory. If the person selling the engine is genuine, he will not object; if he does object, look elsewhere.

DISGORGERS - FRESHWATER

For removing small hooks, whether spade end or eyed, in sizes up to a 14 or 12, the simple barrel-nosed disgorger, through which the line fits via a slit, is unbeatable.

Barrel disgorgers are available in aluminium and plastic, and come in three 'head' sizes, accommodating really tiny to quite large hooks (a size 12 or 10). To use one, ease the line into the head slot, twist it round the barrel a couple of times, and then gently slide the disgorger into the fish's mouth until the hook fits into the slot. Give a gentle push and out pops the hook.

When a pike is deeply hooked, forceps can be inserted carefully through the gill opening and the hooks removed from throat tissue without harm to either pike or the angler's fingers.

The 17in-long, deep-throat, treble-hook disgorger provides an alternative way of removing hooks from toothy predators. The cone situated on the business end covers the claws of the treble when it is pushed inwards and instantly releases the hook points and barbs.

Old-fashioned disgorgers with fork-like ends should never be used. Their points can pierce soft throat tissue with devastating effect, often resulting in the premature death of delicate species.

See also *Artery forceps*.

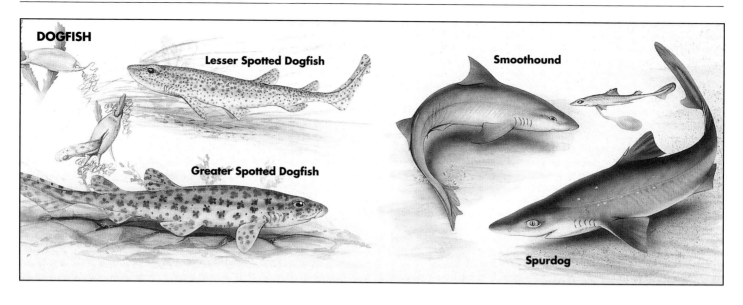

DOGFISH

Lesser Spotted Dogfish

Greater Spotted Dogfish

Smoothhound

Spurdog

DISGORGERS - SEA

T-BAR

The T-bar is probably the most useful un-hooking device ever designed for sea anglers. As the name suggests, it is T-shaped, comprising a handle and a shank, generally 6-10in long. The bottom ½in of the shank is bent back on itself to form a U shape. Success with the T-bar requires a certain knack, but fish can be swiftly dealt with once the technique has been mastered.

Hold the T-bar in your right hand and the hook length in your left (vice versa if you are left-handed). Place the hook length in the U at the end of the T-bar shank, and slide the T-bar towards the hook. Try to manipulate it so that it slides onto the hook shank. Then lower the hook length in the left hand, while raising the right. This action allows the fish's own body weight to pull the hook out. Sometimes a slight twist and a firm jerk will be necessary to remove the hook. Never hold the fish or try to use the T-bar as a conventional disgorger.

PLIERS

Many sea anglers use a pair of pliers to remove hooks, and in many circumstances they are ideal for the job, especially when the hook can be seen. Care is needed to prevent damage to both the fish and the hook.

Standard engineering pliers are usually used, but saltwater very quickly ruins them if they are not regularly oiled. A few tackle companies manufacture stainless-steel pliers designed for the task, but these tend to be expensive. Avoid chromed pliers, which have a greater tendency to corrode and seize up.

WIRE-CUTTERS

Wire-cutters are being used more and more afloat as the emphasis on catch-and-release increases. Many species, such as conger eels, tope and the larger sharks, will almost certainly be damaged if swung inboard for unhooking. If you cannot remove the hook easily with the fish outside the boat, use a decent pair of wire-cutters to cut the trace with the fish still in the water, leaving as short a length of wire as possible in the fish. Provided that the hook is bronze, both the trace and the hook will quickly corrode and fall free.

FORCEPS

Forceps are widely used by freshwater anglers for removing hooks from fish, but they have limited application at sea. They are useful for unhooking small species of fish, and for removing treble hooks from larger specimens. The best type are forceps intended for medical use, made from stainless steel and with a very strong locking grip.

DOGFISH, BLACK-MOUTHED

(*Galeus nelastromus*)

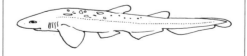

British record: 2lb 13½oz (1kg 288g)

A member of the Scyliorhinidae family of sharks, of which there are over fifty species, the black-mouthed dogfish is rarely taken on rod and line due to its preference

for exceedingly deep water. It has a broad, flattened snout with wide-apart nasal flaps, and a ridge of denticles along the back of the tail. Together with a black stain inside the mouth, these are its most recognizable features. The body is a warm brown along the back, overlaid with dark rounded blotches, fusing into sandy flanks and a creamy belly. It feeds on crustaceans and small fish, and reproduces in the summer. The eggs are fertilized inside the female by the male, and then laid in individual protective cases by the female, in a similar way to both the lesser-spotted dogfish and the bullhuss.

DOGFISH, GREATER-SPOTTED

See *Bullhuss.*

DOGFISH, LESSER-SPOTTED

(*Scyliorhinus canicula*)

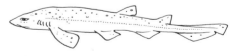

British record: 4lb 15¼oz (2kg 244g)

The lesser-spotted dogfish is by far the most regularly caught of all British sharks. Like both the black-mouthed dogfish and the bullhuss, it has two dorsal fins, and its nostrils are covered with broad flaps with just a small gap between them. The inner nasal flap is pointed. It has coarse skin, sandy-brown in colour, overlaid with small dark spots. The belly is a dirty cream colour.

An aggressive bottom-feeder, particularly partial to crustaceans and molluscs, it also takes worms and small fish. It has a similar reproduction cycle to that of the *bullhuss,* the female depositing individual egg-cases, but in pairs (once the male has fertilized her eggs internally), during the winter and spring. The young dogfish emerge from these several months later, perfectly formed.

HABITAT AND DISTRIBUTION

Commonly distributed around the British Isles, this dogfish prefers a clean, sandy or gravel bottom.

TECHNIQUES

Beachcasting; Downtide boat fishing; Uptide boat fishing.

DOGFISH, SPURDOG

(*Squalus acanthias*)

Average size:	6-10lb
Mega specimen:	14-15lb
British record:	21lb 3½oz (9kg 622g)

This is a member of the spiny shark family, and for good reason. In front of each of its two dorsal fins is a strong, extremely sharp spine. The spurdog has a streamlined body shape and pointed tope-like snout. It is dark grey along the back and sides, dotted with small white spots fusing into a dull creamy belly. Its teeth are flattish, mosaic-like and designed for crushing sprats, sand eels, squid and crustaceans.

The spurdog is oviparous, giving birth to up to a dozen or so live young, following an extremely long gestation period of up to 20 months.

HABITAT AND DISTRIBUTION

The spurdog is found over a sandy or muddy bottom in localized areas around the British Isles. It has suffered considerably from commercial fishing.

TECHNIQUES

Beachcasting; Downtide boat fishing; Uptide boat fishing.

DOWNTIDE BOAT FISHING

Downtiding has always been the traditional method of presenting a bait on the sea bed when boat fishing at anchor, as opposed to the comparatively modern technique of uptide boat fishing.

When several rods are being fished, it makes sense to vary the weight of leads being used to hold bottom in the tide flow (fig. 31). If the baits are spread out downtide, far fewer tangles will occur than if everyone uses the same-sized lead within a small area. Even in very weak tide flows, the bait can be worked a long way downtide from the boat using minimal lead, thus exploring a large area of the sea bed.

A multiplier reel is imperative for boat fishing (*Reels - Multiplier*). Allow the flow to take the rig downtide until the lead touches bottom, using gentle thumb pressure on the spool to stop it from overrunning. Then lift the rod tip smartly, causing the lead to bounce a few yards further downtide. The bait can be made to work progressively further away from the boat in this way, which is an excellent method of contacting species like bass, pollack or coalfish. Alternatively, it can be anchored in one spot by paying out several yards of line to form a huge bow (fig. 31C).

With several baits already placed, covering areas immediately downtide of the anchored boat, this angler employs a light lead to search the sea bed further downtide by gently working his bait along in the flow.

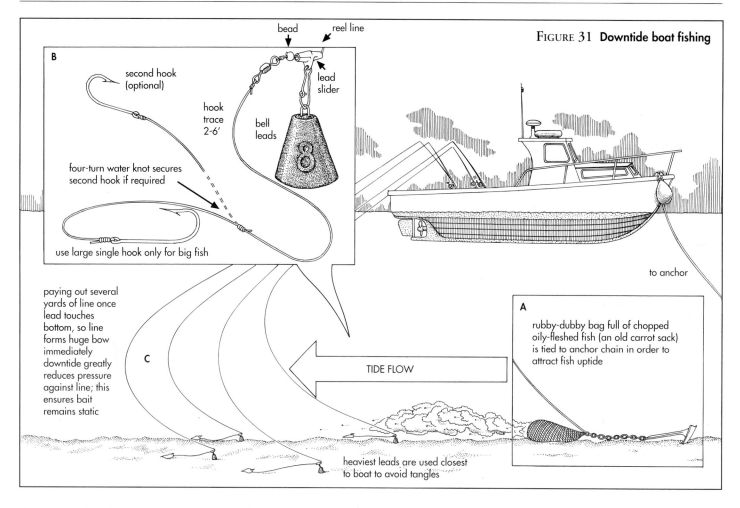

FIGURE 31 **Downtide boat fishing**

B — second hook (optional); hook trace 2-6'; four-turn water knot secures second hook if required; use large single hook only for big fish

bead; reel line; lead slider; bell leads

paying out several yards of line once lead touches bottom, so line forms huge bow immediately downtide greatly reduces pressure against line; this ensures bait remains static

C

TIDE FLOW

A — rubby-dubby bag full of chopped oily-fleshed fish (an old carrot sack) is tied to anchor chain in order to attract fish uptide

to anchor

heaviest leads are used closest to boat to avoid tangles

Owing to reduced current pressure against the line, the lead will then hold the bait static. If it fails to do this, pay out still more line until it does, or change to a heavier lead. Only at slack tide can the lead be expected to hold bottom without paying out line and creating a bow.

Many bottom-feeding species such as rays, tope, smoothhounds, pouting, whiting, cod, ling and conger eel can only be induced to bite once the bait is static, especially if the sea is heavily coloured. Rays, in particular, use their entire body to smother the bait while centralizing it beneath their mouth, so if you move the bait or strike prematurely you will lose the fish. After giving a gentle nod or two on the rod tip, the ray will usually move off with the bait well inside its mouth, at which point the strike can be made.

To induce bottom-feeders to move uptide towards ledgered baits, a rubby-dubby bag (an old carrot sack) full of minced or chopped, oily-fleshed fish can be tied to the anchor rope immediately above the chain (fig. 00A).

Terminal rigs are best kept as simple as possible (fig. 00B), with a lead slider threaded on to the reel line and stopped against the hook-trace swivel with a plas-

tic bead. Leads can then be changed quickly to suit various states of the tide.

The hook trace can vary from 2ft to 6ft depending on whether the bait is required to move about in the flow or lie perfectly still. Single hook traces are advisable where sizable fish like big cod, turbot, tope and rays are expected, but when using worms for small species such as flatties and whiting you can add a second hook to the trace on a 6in snood using a *four-turn water knot* (*Knots*).

When setting out specifically for conger eels, use a 50lb-class outfit and mount a whole fresh bait such as a sizeable squid or cuttlefish or a whole fresh mackerel on a size 8/0 or 10/0 hook to 24in of 150lb monofilament. Mackerel flappers (with the backbone and tail segment removed) allow more of the scent to permeate in the water, but are liable to be sucked to pieces by the ever-hungry pouting. It all depends on the density of small shoal fish around the wreck. Either way, change the bait at least every twenty minutes.

Conger bites are frequently nothing more than a gentle nod or two on the rod tip, followed by a yard or two of line being taken. Strike immediately and haul hard, prising the eel upwards and away from the

rusting ironwork. Tighten the reel's drag right down for these early stages of the fight, and only slacken off to allow the occasional crash dive or two (as conger do) when the eel is well off bottom and away from the wreck.

It is not uncommon, when presenting a large fresh squid or fish bait with conger in mind, for a really big cod or pollack, or even a turbot, to swallow it.

DRAGONET
(*Callionymus lyra*)

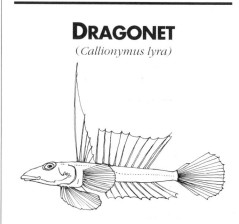

British record: 5½oz (155g)

This small species, with a flattened, triangular head and eyes set into the very top of the skull, resembles the gurnard. It has two dorsal fins, the first quite short with a long leading ray; the second dorsal has soft rays.

A similar-sized anal fin is positioned immediately below the dorsals and the tail is rounded. It is pale brown, with several dark markings along the flanks. Males have exaggerated fin rays and blue and yellow stripes. It feeds on worms, molluscs and crustaceans, and reproduces in the early spring.

The dragonet prefers a muddy or sandy bottom in relatively deep water, and is distributed in isolated pockets around the British Isles.

DRIFT FISHING IN FRESHWATER

Apart from loch-style fishing for trout (see Fly fishing) there is little scope for drift fishing on huge stillwaters, except when fishing for pike, and to a much lesser extent for perch and zander. Ideal waters for drift fishing are large reservoirs, lakes and lochs, and even wide sluggish rivers, and results often rely on covering as much water as possible. And when pike have been located, a mudweight can be lowered for a more thorough search of the entire area (see Dinghy fishing in freshwater).

Drift fishing is a matter of using the wind to your best advantage, so take into account its strength and direction. Choose long areas, either through the centre channel, or parallel with the shoreline so that at least one angler (if two are sharing the boat) has features such as dense reed lines, promontories, sunken trees, dykes, or river entrances to cast to. Row or motor to the furthest point upwind and turn the boat side-on to the wind. Then put out a drogue, which will slow down the boat's passage to a fishable speed. A couple of old keepnets put out over the side will achieve similar results, but it pays to invest in a proper drogue.

You then have a choice of casting out floatfished livebaits or deadbaits from each end of the boat (see *Drift-float fishing in freshwater; Sliding-float fishing for predators*), while working the water in front of the boat with artificial lures or with *wobbled deadbaits*.

Alternatively, livebaits or deadbaits presented on float rigs can be trolled slowly behind the boat while lures or wobbled deadbaits are worked from the front and sides of the boat. There is, indeed, plenty of scope to be as thorough or as relaxed as the mood and weather conditions dictate (fig. 32).

DRIFT FISHING AT SEA

Fishing from a drifting boat is an excellent method of presenting a bait or lure when you need to cover as much ground as possible in order to locate isolated pockets of feeding fish. Drifting over clean ground can look deceptively easy, but the angler must ensure that he maintains contact with the bottom at all times.

The vast majority of British species are bottom-feeders and baits trailing in mid-water will catch few fish.

It is generally possible to use light tackle when drifting. Tackle heavier than 12lb or 20lb-class is rarely required, but if big rays or turbot are on the cards, or if the tidal strength and water depth dictate it, increase the tackle accordingly.

The ideal end rig is a simple running ledger with a hook length of up to 6ft; often longer when drifting for plaice. A boom

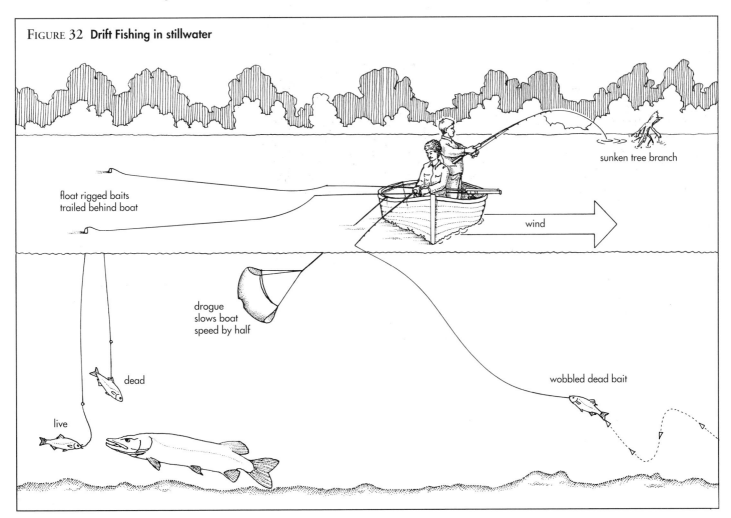

FIGURE 32 **Drift Fishing in stillwater**

float rigged baits trailed behind boat

sunken tree branch

wind

drogue slows boat speed by half

dead

wobbled dead bait

live

Whether working artificial lures above the rusting ironwork of a wartime wreck, or gently bumping a baited spoon rig behind the boat, drift fishing is amongst the most productive of all techniques.

lead tap on the bottom, do not immediately re-engage the reel, but use your thumb to check the line running off the spool. A small multiplier is a far better choice than a fixed-spool for this sort of fishing. Release a little more line. Then, with the spool checked, slightly raise the rod tip and lower it to reconfirm that the bait is still on the bottom. If not, release a little more line. Repeat this process continually throughout the drift with the baited rig getting further and further behind the boat. When the boat is drifting really slowly over an exceptionally clean bottom of sand or mud, you can put the reel into gear once the rig is a fair way back from the boat and allow the bait to bump gently along the ocean floor. But be ready to react to the slightest knock on the rod tip. If you feel a bite, do not strike; release a few yards of line to avoid moving the baited hook away from the fish. After about a minute, check the line leaving the spool. If a fish is there, either you should feel a rattle on the rod tip or the rod will slowly bend over against the resistance caused by the weight of the fish. Re-engage the spool, wind in any slack and with one steady movement raise the rod, winding the reel at the same time to set the hook.

Drifting over rough ground is far more demanding. In general, the angler will require heavier tackle - to cope with the snaggy conditions, not with the fish. Even so, a 20lb- or 30lb-class rig will cope with the majority of conditions, but 50lb-class might well be required over the roughest marks, or in very deep water or strong tide situations that demand heavier leads. The running ledger rig is useful over rough ground, but a paternoster with the baits above the weight can be a better choice (fig. 33B). When using the paternoster, it is a good idea to fish the lead off a weak link, which should minimize tackle losses to just the lead. Shorter hook snoods will reduce snag-ups

The prime consideration when drifting over rough ground is to avoid having baits trailing behind the boat so as to prevent them getting dragged into snags. It is therefore important to maintain as vertical a line between rod tip and end rig as possible, and this often requires the use of an extra couple of ounces of lead.

When after sharks it is preferable to drift with the bait presented somewhere between 20ft below the surface and 100ft down. To attract sharks up to the drifting

of about 4in will help to keep the rig tangle-free and assist bait presentation. A small bead to protect the knot and a small swivel completes the trace (fig. 33A). The breaking strain of the nylon should depend on the species you expect. Consider 20lb bs as the minimum, but step up to 40lb or 50lb if you anticipate rays or big turbot.

The choice and size of lead is very important. You will need just enough weight to keep the rig on the bottom, but not so much that you overload the rod. The old-fashioned, circular, studded watch leads are ideal. Some anglers claim that these kick

up little puffs of sand as they drag across the bottom, attracting fish. The addition of an attractor spoon on the hook length about 6in from the baited hook is popular when fishing for plaice and other species of flatfish.

With practice, it is easy to keep the bait on the bottom. Facing away from the direction of the drift to avoid the line dragging back under the boat's keel, lower the bait over the side and down to the bottom slowly to prevent the long hook-length spinning back around the main line (this is where a boom helps). When you feel the

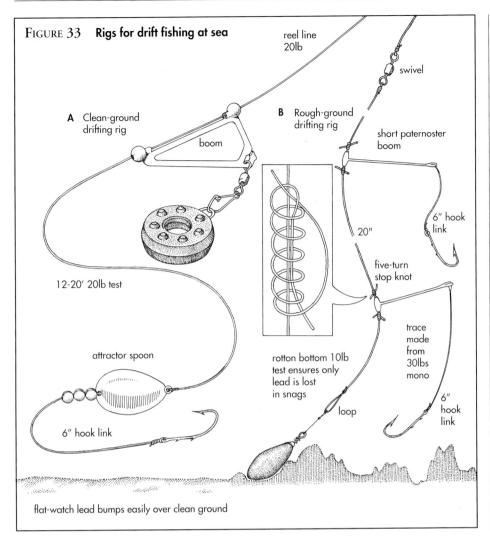

FIGURE 33   **Rigs for drift fishing at sea**

A   Clean-ground drifting rig

boom

reel line 20lb

swivel

B   Rough-ground drifting rig

short paternoster boom

12-20' 20lb test

20"

6" hook link

five-turn stop knot

attractor spoon

6" hook link

rotton bottom 10lb test ensures only lead is lost in snags

loop

trace made from 30lbs mono

6" hook link

flat-watch lead bumps easily over clean ground

boat, a rubby-dubby bag is made up and hung over the side at water level. The motion of the boat slaps it down on the water surface every few seconds, releasing a steady stream of groundbait particles and an oily slick (see *Groundbaits - Sea* and fig.34). Tackle consists of 50lb- or 80lb-class outfits with 6/0 or 9/0 multipliers respectively, loaded with fresh monofilament. Traces are made from two 8ft lengths of 250lb cable-laid, stainless-steel wire joined in the middle with a Berkeley 3/0 swivel. Crimped on to the reel end of the trace is another swivel, and on to the business end a pair of 10/0 or 12/0 sea-master hooks set 5in apart presenting a pair of fresh mackerel flappers or one large mackerel.

To drift the baits downtide from the boat, a partially inflated balloon is tied to the reel line with a short length of 4lb monofilament using a *five-turn stop knot (Knots)*. When a shark engulfs and makes off with the bait, either the balloon or 4lb-test, or both, will burst leaving no resistance. Up to four rods are usually fished, each with the bait set at a different depth below the surface, from 20ft down and at varying distances behind the boat (say, 20yd, 40yd, 60yd and 80yd) to maximize the chance of a run and to help prevent tangles.

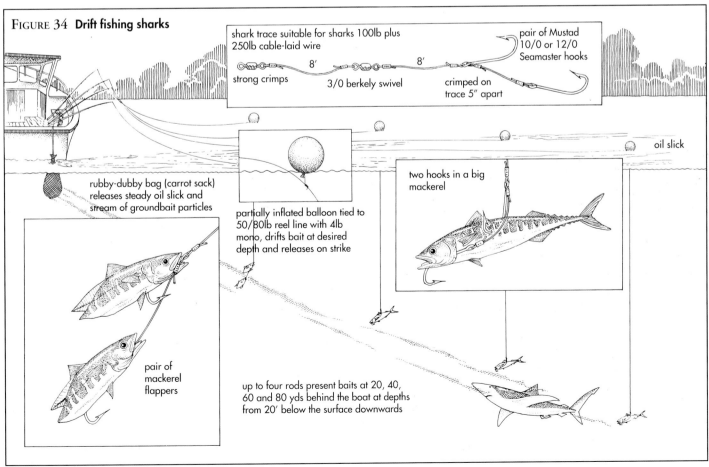

FIGURE 34   **Drift fishing sharks**

shark trace suitable for sharks 100lb plus 250lb cable-laid wire

pair of Mustad 10/0 or 12/0 Seamaster hooks

strong crimps

3/0 berkely swivel

8'

8'

crimped on trace 5" apart

oil slick

rubby-dubby bag (carrot sack) releases steady oil slick and stream of groundbait particles

partially inflated balloon tied to 50/80lb reel line with 4lb mono, drifts bait at desired depth and releases on strike

two hooks in a big mackerel

pair of mackerel flappers

up to four rods present baits at 20, 40, 60 and 80 yds behind the boat at depths from 20' below the surface downwards

The reel should be left out of gear with the clutch pre-set on a firm drag (to help nail the hooks home) and the rachet on. Once a shark screams off with the bait, flick the rachet off and thumb the spool to stop it from over-running, while simultaneously pointing the rod at the fish. If the run is rather jerky and stops every few feet, the shark is probably working the bait into a swallowing position, or it could simply be a small fish, so wait until line pours steadily from the reel before flicking over the clutch lever and putting the reel into gear. Don't try to strike immediately. Wait until the line pulls really tight, taken up by the shark's full weight - then and only then, heave back into it so that the hooks find purchase. And hang on.

When only small to medium-sized blue sharks or tope are on the cards, step down to a 30lb outfit and have some fun. Hauling them in on heavy shark gear more suitable for porbeagles or a mako provides no contest. A much lighter trace with a single 8/0 can also be used. Join 6ft of 100lb, cable-laid wire with a 1/0 swivel to 6ft of 60lb monofilament, and join it to the 30lb reel line with another swivel.

DRIFT-FLOAT FISHING

See *Freshwater floatfishing techniques.*

DROGUES

Drogues are shaped like, and indeed work on the same principle as, a parachute. They are used to slow down the passage of a boat as it is pushed along by the wind, enabling fishing to be done in a more controlled manner.

Usually constructed from rot-proof nylon or canvas, drogues are attached to the boat by about 30yd of rope or strong cord, and sometimes has a short length of chain tied into it to make it fish deeper.

In loch-style fishing, where the boat drifts side-on and anglers sit side by side, casting in front of the boat, the drogue is most commonly attached midway along the rear gunwale and usually off the rowlock. If the drogue is moved slightly off-centre towards the bows or stern, by means of a G-clamp, this will make the boat crab across the wind, enabling it to run along a shoreline rather than straight onto it.

Boat anglers fishing with lures on sunk lines position the drogue off the stern. Then, positioned one behind the other,

they cast across the wind at right angles to the boat - one casting to the left, the other to the right to avoid tangles and to search more water. The continued movement of the boat downwind causes the lines to pull round into a wide curve, and takes often come as the retrieved lure begins to accelerate round the tightening arc.

In recent years pike anglers afloat have begun to appreciate the advantages of controlling the drifting speed of the boat with a drogue. It can be used either when lures are being cast and retrieved, or when baits are fished beneath floats, and allows the water to be covered much more effectively.

DROP NETS

Piers, harbour walls, breakwaters and many rock marks provide excellent angling platforms for the sea angler. But landing sizeable fish from a position many yards above the water level, especially fish that are only lightly hooked, can be nigh-on impossible where there is no safe, low-level access unless a drop net is used.

A drop net consists of a large circular frame - old cycle wheels were used - with netting attached. Ideally the frame is weighted, or a stone is placed in the mesh to provide stability in windy conditions. A long length of rope is attached to the frame to lower and position the net and to retrieve the fish. Several companies now produce excellent drop nets.

Landing fish using a drop net is an art in itself. It is important that the fish is well beaten first, not wildly thrashing about on the surface. The net should be positioned just below the water surface and the fish should be guided over the rim; do not take the net to the fish as this can cause it to panic. A deep-mesh netting will prevent fish jumping free. Always take great care to make sure that your line doesn't tangle around the drop net, and that the net doesn't foul around pier supports or other obstructions. The assistance of another angler to net a fish will be a big help.

DROP-ARM INDICATOR

See *Bite indicators and accessories.*

DRY-FLY FISHING

See *Fly fishing.*

ECHO-SOUNDER

See *Fish-finders.*

EEL, CONGER

(*Conger conger*)

Average size: 15-30lb
Mega specimen: over 70lb
British record: 112lb 8oz (51kg 30g)

The conger has a long, immensely powerful, scaleless, rounded, grey-brown body with a pale creamy belly. Like the freshwater eel, its dorsal, tail and anal fins form one continuous frill that starts immediately behind the prominent, pointed pectoral fins and finishes behind the vent half way along the underside of the body. The same frill starts considerably further back on freshwater eels, which have protruding lower jaws, whereas the conger's upper jaw slightly overhangs the lower. The eye is oval and large and the jaws are very strong. It is a voracious feeder, preying on squid, octopus, shoal fish species and crustaceans.

The conger breed at great depths in the Atlantic Ocean. Its off-spring metamorphose from leaf-shaped, transparent larvae, called leptocephalus, into young conger eels.

HABITAT AND DISTRIBUTION

It has a preference for the dark hide-outs found along rocky shorelines, in the crevices of deep water, harbour walls and jetties, the rough ground of deep offshore marks and especially among the rusting ironwork of deep-water wrecks. Conger are found wherever the habitat is suitable around the British Isles, with the largest concentrations inhabiting the wartime wrecks lying in deep water off the southern and south-western coastline.

TECHNIQUES

Beachcasting; Downtide boat fishing; Floatfishing in harbours and off the rocks; Wreck fishing.

Extracted from a wreck lying 130ft down some 30 miles off the Sussex coast, this 76lb conger eel gobbled up a mackerel 'flapper' to provide John with some gut-busting action.

Ee

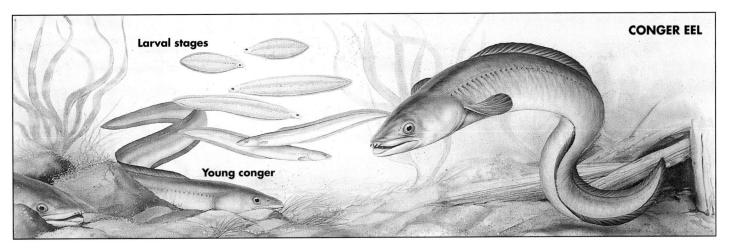

Larval stages

Young conger

CONGER EEL

EEL, FRESHWATER
(*Anguilla anguilla*)

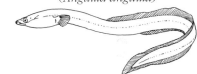

Average size: 8oz - 1½lb
Mega specimen: over 5-6lb
British record: 11lb 2oz (5kg 46g)

The eel's long, supple, slippery body is round in cross-section and covered in a heavy coating of protective mucus, making confusion with any other species impossible. It has a small, neat head and strong jaws lined with microscopic, whisker-like teeth. The lower jaw protrudes. The dorsal fin starts one-third of the way along the back and continues around the laterally compressed tail, finishing just in front of the vent half way along the belly. Colouration is a yellowy-brown, but changes to a striking, metallic, silvery bronze prior to an eel's migration to sea to breed. The snout then becomes more pointed, the eyes glass over, and the body's fat content increases in readiness for the monumental journey ahead.

Mass migration of these silver eels occurs throughout the late summer and autumn, when, after several years in freshwater, they feel the urge to reproduce. Even eels living in tiny ponds or pits miles from the nearest river system find running water and travel downstream. Once at sea they cross the North Atlantic, to the depths of the Sargasso Sea, where they spawn. The resulting fry, which are extremely thin and leaf-shaped, spend up to three years drifting

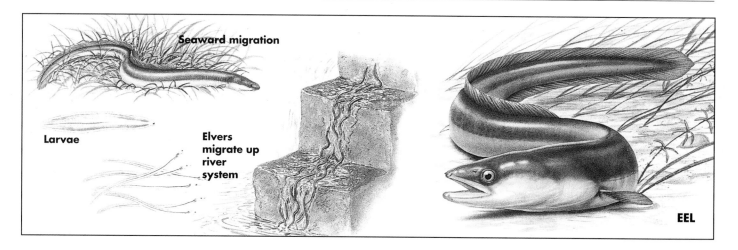

Seaward migration

Larvae

Elvers migrate up river system

EEL

with the Gulf Stream currents towards Europe. They shrink into 'glass eels' or elvers immediately prior to migrating by the

Who would have thought this eel started its life in the Sargasso sea

million up into freshwater during the late spring and summer. Some travel far inland across wet meadowlands by night during heavy rain to reach the most remote of farm ponds. Some stay in running water. And a percentage never enter freshwater, preferring to stay in wide estuaries or even in the sea. And when they feel the urge to reproduce, their entire fascinating life cycle repeats itself.

Eels feed upon all kinds of aquatic insect life, crustaceans, amphibians, small fish and so on. They become noticeably more aggressive during the hours of darkness, and thundery weather finds them particularly active.

HABITAT AND DISTRIBUTION

There is scarcely a waterway in the British Isles that does not contain at least a small population of freshwater eels. Throughout most river systems they are the most common of all bottom-feeders, preferring to remain hidden in the thick bottom silt around weed beds, beneath bridge arches, in weir-pools, among the roots of overhanging trees, within the cracked masonry of lock cuttings and old boat-houses, and so on.

TECHNIQUES

Babbing; Freelining; Ledgering techniques - Bobbin ledgering in stillwaters.

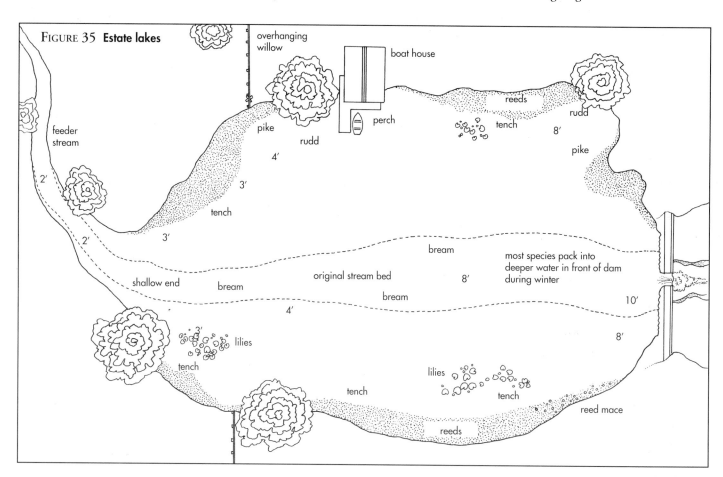

FIGURE 35 **Estate lakes**

overhanging willow

boat house

feeder stream

pike

rudd

perch

reeds

tench

rudd

pike

8'

4'

3'

tench

2'

2'

3'

shallow end

bream

original stream bed

bream

bream

bream

8'

most species pack into deeper water in front of dam during winter

10'

8'

4'

3'

lilies

tench

tench

lilies

tench

reed mace

reeds

Though of modest proportions this reed-lined, man-made estate lake is typical of these prolific fisheries in that it is stream fed from the northern end and dammed at the southern, through which excess winter water escapes via a boarded sluice. Mineral richness seeps in from the adjacent farmland creating a wealth of soft-rooted weeds and zooplanktons such as daphnia in abundance. Small wonder the rudd, perch and carp here reach specimen proportions.

ESTATE LAKES

We have the aristocracy of the 18th and 19th centuries to thank for the beautiful estate lakes that provide such prolific fishing for tench, bream, carp, rudd and pike.

Landscaping and estate-lake design took place on a grand scale, allowing landowners to look out across a carefully planned valley. It became fashionable to have a stream dammed at the bottom of a valley to create an ornamental lake, and most estate lakes follow a similar format. They are shallow at the narrow end, where the stream or surface water collects, gradually deepening and widening to the dam itself. Dams were usually constructed in brick, with a sluice so that surplus water could escape into a stream (fig. 35).

Organic particles from the feeder stream sink to the bottom of the lake long before the water spews over the sluice at the dam end, and in this build-up of rich silt over the bottom of all estate lakes, sometimes to a depth of 3-4ft, live massive concentrations of *bloodworms (Buzzers; Baits, freshwater - Naturals)*. This in turn is responsible for the large average size of bream, tench and carp living in these lakes. They have a wealth of natural food at their disposal: bloodworms (midge larvae), aquatic insect larvae of countless other species, freshwater shrimps, water-boatmen and molluscs from the tiniest peacockle up to the giant swan mussel, plus clouds of zooplankton.

Of the aquatic fleas, Daphnia is the largest. It reproduces so prolifically in warm weather, occurring in the water in dense red clouds, that it becomes impossible to see the bottom in marginal shallows, even through crystal-clear water (*Plankton*).

Roach, and especially rudd, fare well in the warm, shallow, fertile water of estate lakes. Those rich in soft, rooted weeds and beds of reeds and lilies may breed both species in profusion. They, in turn, provide an excellent food larder for predators such as perch and pike.

Not every estate lake can hold a stock of all species, let alone specimens of each one, but one fish guaranteed to be present in the silt is the freshwater eel. Most estate lakes are cropped of their eels every two or three years by professional eel catchers, who use a series of *fyke nets* staked out from the marginal growth.

Estate lakes invariably offer the best sport during the warmer months for traditional summer species such as tench and bream, whose feeding bubbles can easily be detected through binoculars in the shallower end of a lake. Once winter sets in, however, it is as well to remember that all species tend to pack into the deepest channel close to the dam itself, and on a mild day excellent sport can be enjoyed there.

EYED HOOKS

See *Hooks*.

Ff

FARM AND VILLAGE PONDS

Farm and village ponds may not always look particularly inviting, but acre for acre they are among the richest of British fresh-water fisheries.

Even tiny ponds of no more than ½ acre often contain large specimens, a much higher stock level, or even a greater variety of species than do more visually attractive lakes and meres. In addition to the more common species found in ponds, such as crucian carp, roach, rudd and perch, some may contain tench or wild carp, perhaps a large eel or two and even goldfish.

Many a fairground goldfish has ended up in the village pond on the way home, enjoying its new-found freedom and hybridizing with the crucian carp. There are all sorts of weird and wonderful coloured crosses to be found when crucians, goldfish, shubunkins and even koi carp are allowed to mix (see *Carp hybrids*). However,

the novelty of occasionally hooking into something pretty that you cannot positively identify is only a part of the mystique of pond-fishing.

Some ponds are obviously richer, shallower, deeper or better stocked than others. So first of all, do a bit of exploring. Look closely at any 6in-square on a local Ordnance Survey map (well worth the money spent) and count up those little blue dots. All denote tiny ponds by the side of a road, in farmyards, in the middle of fields and woodlands, or even in the middle of a village. Of these, roadside ponds usually receive little attention. Anglers assume that because they are within easy reach of everyone, sport on them will have deteriorated. And while everyone thinks likewise, the fish live an undisturbed life.

On some ponds the fishing is free, some are available on a day or season ticket, while many more will rarely have been fished because few anglers bother to seek permission to do so. However, don't go round and ask the farmer when he is having his dinner, or march across his cornfields to have

a look. Go along smartly dressed and at a civilized hour.

Many ponds, especially those in and around farmland, are particularly rich in nutrients that leak in from the land. Most - and these invariably turn out to be the best wild-carp fisheries - are pea-green in colour, so do not worry if aquatic plants are absent. Plants are not the hallmark of good fishing. Shallow ponds where cattle paddle, drink and foul the water are incredibly rich in phosphates, which in turn are converted into food by green plankton - hence the pea-green water. Zooplankton such as daphnia eat the green plankton (called phytoplankton), and then the fish eat the zooplankton.

On the bottom, among the detritus, all sorts of microscopic organisms make up another valuable food chain. The micro-organisms are eaten by shrimps, aquatic insect larvae such as the bloodworm, and asellus (a flat shrimp-like crustacean). These in turn are eaten by bottom-feeding fish such as carp and tench. As a result, at dawn (a natural feeding period) bubbles

Diminutive and hidden well away they may well be, but farm ponds are worth locating. Size for size, their rich water invariably contains prolific stocks of rudd, perch, roach or carp. Surprises in the form of a large eel or tench are not unlikely.

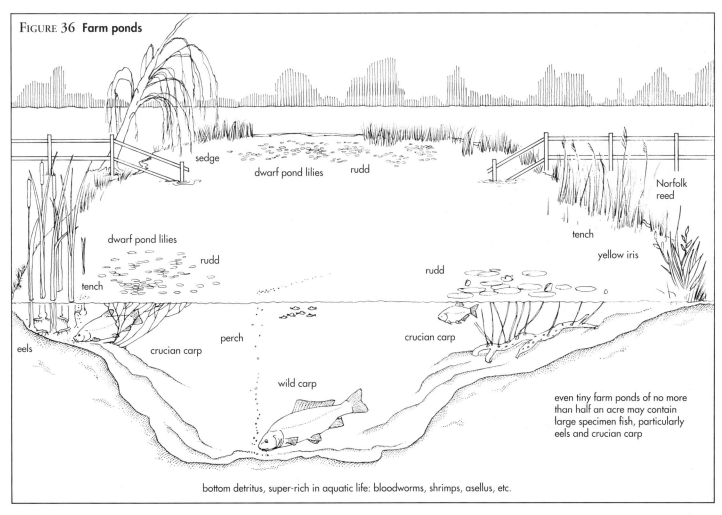

FIGURE 36 **Farm ponds**

sedge

dwarf pond lilies

rudd

Norfolk reed

dwarf pond lilies

rudd

tench

tench

yellow iris

rudd

eels

crucian carp

perch

crucian carp

wild carp

even tiny farm ponds of no more than half an acre may contain large specimen fish, particularly eels and crucian carp

bottom detritus, super-rich in aquatic life: bloodworms, shrimps, asellus, etc.

from carp that are rooting through the bottom detritus can be seen spewing up to the surface. The first rule of exploring a new pond, therefore, is to visit it during the early hours and see what's bubbling. This is an education in itself, so do not take a rod with you, just a pair of binoculars. Walk slowly and quietly along the bank, looking for clusters or streams of bubbles that move along the water surface, as these are caused by a fish rather than escaping gas.

Wild carp rooting quickly through the bottom sediment send up long streams of large bubbles or great swirling clusters. Crucian carp, however, are far more ponderous feeders, emitting groups or streams containing perhaps six to twelve bubbles at a time. The bubbles from tench are even smaller and are distinctly effervescent, not unlike the fizzing of health salts in a glass. Roach and rudd, owing to their small size, emit just the odd bubble or two when feeding on the bottom.

Fish also roll or jump when feeding in earnest, and it is thought that they come to the surface to shake irritating particles from their gills. Crucians, in particular, love to porpoise on the surface, which is handy for the angler as it pinpoints their preferred

area or swim.

In general terms, all the carp species prefer to feed close into the margins, where the water is warmer and the food larder better stocked. Ponds that vary between 18in and 5ft deep are the richest in both food and fish. Good areas for daytime fishing are beneath overhanging trees and alongside bushes that hang into the water, both of which provide shade. Thick reed beds or beds of reed-mace (often wrongly called bullrush) are also great hotspots. Fish go close to or even alongside them, for fish love to browse between the stems, gathering snails, aquatic nymphs including the caddis grub and damselfly larvae, and various beetles. Look especially for stems that twitch and knock when the rest remain still. In shallow, clear-water ponds with extensive beds of water lilies, expect most of the larger inhabitants to be beneath the pads, particularly during the heat of a summer's day. And if there are sizeable gaps between the pads within casting range, then consider these to be the choice areas.

At dusk, roach and rudd can be seen porpoising as they take the rising pupae of aquatic insects or the actual fly as it hatches. Where roach or rudd density is low, ex-

pect fish over the pound, but in ponds where roach, rudd or little crucian carp immediately grab the bait regardless of depth, they are liable to be stunted through overcrowding. That is not to say a good wild carp, which tends to dominate the lower food chain, or even a big perch, is not likely. Little ponds are renowned for producing small numbers of very large perch as they have an overstocked larder of stunted roach and rudd close at hand. As more lakes become stocked with king carp, either mirrors, leathers or commons, farm ponds also have them introduced. And provided that the carps' numbers are limited, they can create the chance of catching something really big. Even a weight over 20lb is not unlikely, and double-figure carp exist in countless ponds no larger than a couple of tennis courts.

A valuable gift provided by ponds is the yearly donation of millions of baby frogs, newts and toads. Most will have left the water by the end of August, and it is curious to note that while most fish consume frog tadpoles, they usually reject toad tadpoles. Perhaps they taste bitter, as the toad itself often does, causing many creatures that grab one to reject it quickly.

FEATHERING

The standard string of six brightly coloured mackerel feathers has long been the accepted way of acquiring a fresh supply of bait - usually mackerel - for a day's fishing. However, feathers are a very effective lure in their own right and catch a great deal more than just mackerel.

The traditional, dyed, hen hackle feather on its own is a good lure, but recent years have seen the arrival of several new styles. These vary from lures tied from long strips of coloured or silvery foil whipped to the hook, to various types and colours of tinsel. More recently, we have seen the arrival of a Far Eastern import known as the Hokkai lure, the original design of which has been much copied.

The Hokkai consists of a short, plastic body, roughly fish-shaped. The body is a pale, luminous green, with a silvery tint for added attraction, finished off with a tail tied out of natural feathers with silver tinsel mixed in. This style of lure has proved itself to be devastating, usually outfishing traditional feathers.

Apart from being invaluable for bait collection, feathers are excellent when fishing new ground for the first time. Fished on the drift, the feathers will help you to establish an accurate picture of the sea-bed topography. By jigging strings of lures, you will be able to pick out areas of clean ground, patches of heavy kelp and rock and other useful features.

Feathers are very effective at catching most common species of fish, such as pollack, bass, cod and coalfish, in addition to the various species of bait fish, such as mackerel, herring, scad and sand eels. You can greatly increase a feather's effectiveness by tipping it with a small strip of fish or worm (*Artificial lure fishing - Sea*).

The usual method of fishing feathers is to jig them down through the water, trying to establish at what depth the fish are stationed. Start at the surface, with the reel in free spool, and slowly drop the lures

During an exploratory trip in Danish waters, Dave Lewis and John used feathers to bag up with small codling just a few miles out from Ebeltoft.

down, stopping at intervals of about every 10ft or so and jigging them. Some anglers let the feathers plummet straight down to the sea bed, then work them back up towards the surface.

Many species inhabit the lower depths, around reefs, wrecks or beds of weed, so it is essential to work the lures as close to the fish-holding cover as possible. To minimize tackle losses, stay in close contact with your end rig and keep the lures working vertically. As soon as you feel the bottom, jig upwards and avoid dragging the lures across the sea bed behind the boat as this invariably results in a snag up.

FISHING TECHNIQUES

See *Artificial lure fishing - freshwater; Artificial lure fishing - sea; Babbing; Beachcasting; Drift fishing in freshwater; Drift fishing at sea; Downtide boat fishing; Feathering; Float fishing in harbours and off the rocks; Freshwater floatfishing techniques; Fly casting; Fly fishing; Freelining; Ledgering techniques; Trailing; Trolling; Uptide boat fishing; Wobbling deadbaits; Wreck fishing.*

FISH-FINDERS

The advances in marine electronics during the 1980s have been amazing. Not all that long ago, it was rare to see any form of fish-finder fitted to private angling boats, other than the very basic, flashing-dial sounders, which only indicated the depth. Today, however, it is unusual not to see an angling dinghy fitted with a state-of-the-art fish-finder.

There are several types of fish-finder/depthsounder available on the market. Paper graph sounders provide an incredible amount of detail, but modern sets tend to be limited to larger, commercial units, rather than the smaller versions suitable for installation aboard dinghies. The exception to this is the Eagle Mach 1, which has been very popular with anglers for many years. However, by far the most popular, not to mention the most practical, type of set for a small angling boat is the Liquid Crystal Display (LCD) type. Many of the latest sets incorporate a GPS navigator, plotter, and many more features.

Fish-finders work by transmitting a signal down to the sea bed and back again via a transducer, which can be fitted either in-

As artist Dave Batten illustrates, holding the transducer away from the boat in a horizontal plane 'side scanning' provides evidence of shoal fish (just look at the display screen) which are undetectable by any other means and obviously not directly beneath the boat.

board and shoot through a single skin of fibreglass, or outboard, usually on the transom below the water line. The information is displayed on an LCD screen. Objects such as wrecks reefs, shoals or even individual fish that interrupt the transmitted signal are then indicated on the screen.

The quality of the displayed information depends on several factors, and is dictated by the quality of the set. These factors include the output power of the set - the more power, the better; the amount of pixels (vertical and horizontal dots) that make up the LCD screen - again, the more the better; and the type of transducer fitted; and the ability of the set to compensate for the varying conditions encountered, particularly at sea.

Useful features to look out for include depth and fish alarms; automatic and manual control of display sensitivity; grey line, which gives an indication of bottom hardness; a zoom, to examine closely any portion of the depth covered; and a backlit screen for night-time use. Also ensure that

the set is waterproof, as indeed most LCD units are. Many sets can also display water temperature and speed if an additional sensor is fitted.

FISH LICENCES

See *National Rivers Authority.*

FLIES

See *Artificial flies.*

FLOATS

Made from various combinations of peacock quill, porcupine quill, bird feathers, balsa, cork, sarkansas reed (see Reed floats), dowel, polystyrene and plastic, floats - the most sensitive of bite indicators - are available in a galaxy of different patterns and sizes, and none more so than those designed and marketed for match fishing.

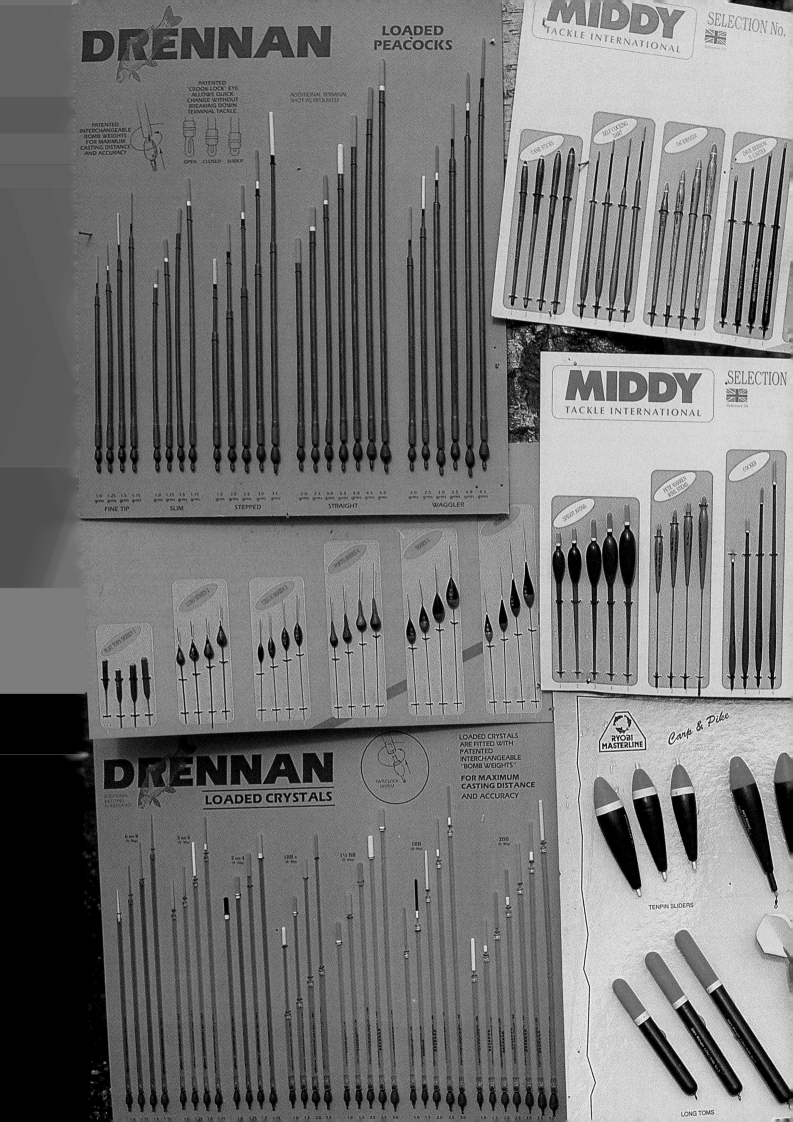

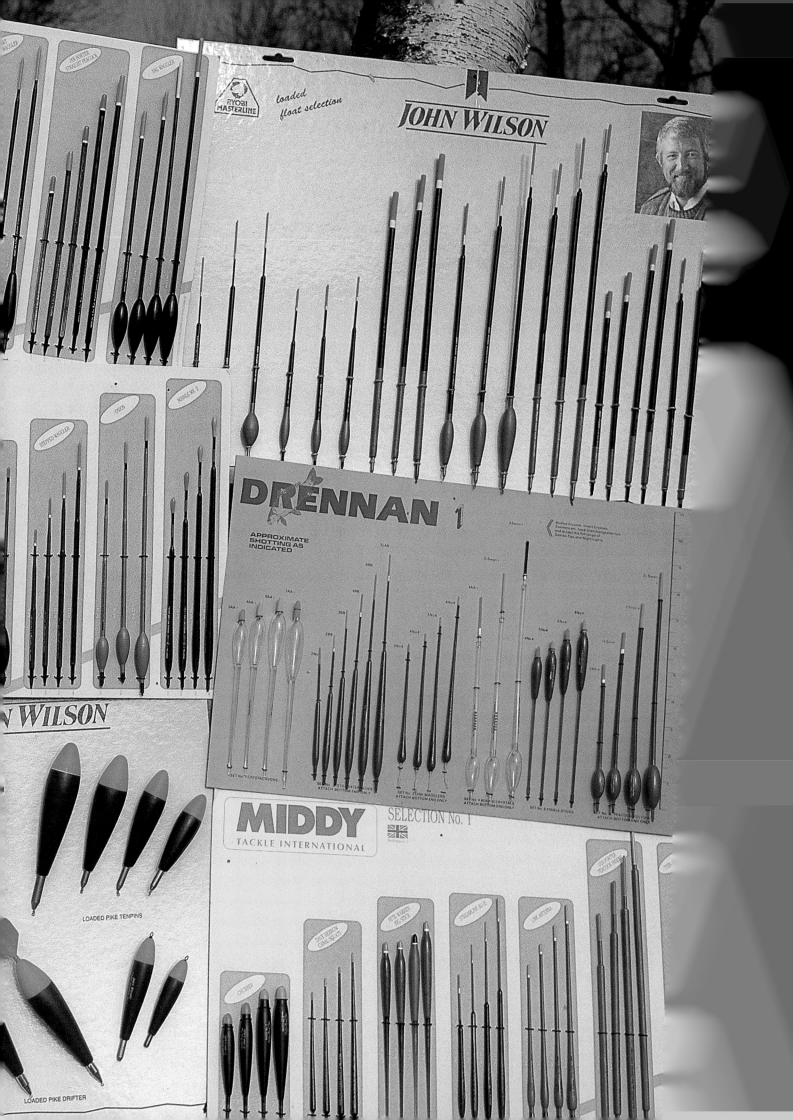

The novice can easily be excused for feeling confused, yet all floats, with a few exceptions, follow a basic principle that is worth remembering. Where maximum buoyancy is required for stillwater fishing, it is either evenly distributed throughout a straight peacock stem - the waggler; or concentrated in a bulb at the very bottom of the float - the bodied waggler. For running water the reverse is true. Any additional buoyancy (other than that of a straight peacock or balsa body, for instance) is concentrated in a bulb at the top of the float - the Avon or balsa trotter.

This makes it possible to distinguish immediately between different types of bodied floats, and to tell whether they are for still or running water. Obviously, straight or slim-bodied floats might suit both conditions. The waggler, for instance, usually made from peacock quill, is effective in both still and slow-moving water.

FRESHWATER FLOATS

Stillwater floats

The most sensitive float for fishing in canals, ponds, pits and even small lakes is the fine-tipped antenna in shotting capacities from two No. 1s up to 2-3AA. The loaded antenna or dart takes from two No. 4s to 2BB and is designed for fishing ultra light

on the drop.

To tackle larger waters, estate lakes, gravel pits and massive fisheries such as reservoirs and Irish loughs, waggler floats made from peacock quill are essential. You require a range of tipped (insert) wagglers (for sensitive registrations), plain straight wagglers, and bodied wagglers, in sizes from 2BB up to 3-4 swan shot capacity. In addition you need a range of loaded (almost self-cocking), straight and bodied wagglers (flyers) that require only a few small shots down the line, for both on-the-drop and on-the-bottom tactics (*Freshwater floatfishing techniques*).

Sliding floats

In years gone by, sliding floats were fitted with a tiny ring on the body, plus the end ring, through which the line could slide. Modern waggler-type floats, however, all come fitted with neat, small-diameter end rings against which a sliding stop knot will easily come to rest. Therefore they can all be used as sliders (*Freshwater floatfishing techniques - Sliding-float fishing for predators*) and there is no need for specialized patterns.

Stems of unpainted peacock quill of various diameters are useful when presenting the *lift method* and fishing the *flat float*, whether stillwater fishing or *stretpegging* in

rivers (*Freshwater floatfishing techniques*).

River floats

Both straight and bodied wagglers double up for use in slow-flowing water, but in moderate currents either plain or wire stem stick floats (fixed top and bottom as opposed to bottom end only) carrying from three No. 8s up to 4-5BB allow the bait to be eased gently along at close range. In stronger currents use either big sticks or balsa trotters that carry from 4BB up to 4AA, or Avon-style floats, which have even greater capacity due to their egg-shaped, cork or polystyrene body.

In exceptionally fast-flowing rivers, particularly those only 2-4ft deep, use a stumpy, wide-tipped chubber or loafer, which can easily be seen 30yd downstream and carries from two to five swan shots.

PIKE AND SEAFISHING FLOATS

Within this enormous range of large, specialist floats, selection largely depends on the size of the bait and whether it is to be supported off bottom or fished well over depth, in which case the float is used merely as a visual indicator. Most pike and sea floats have been designed to be used as sliders (in conjunction with a small bead and stop knot), with the line passing through either the middle or the bottom ring. Some

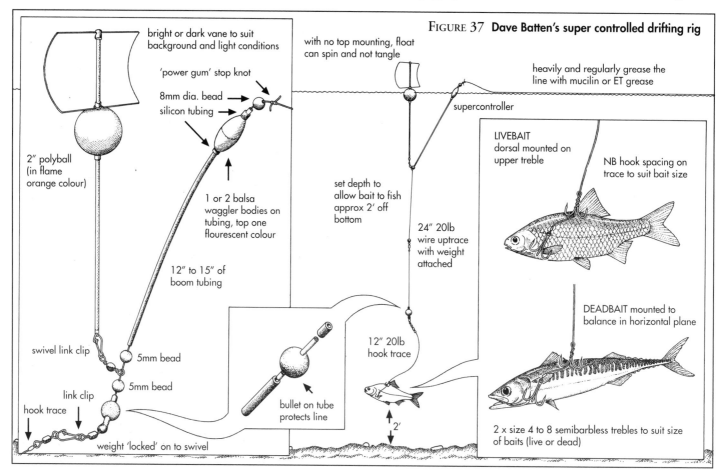

FIGURE 37 Dave Batten's super controlled drifting rig

bright or dark vane to suit background and light conditions

'power gum' stop knot

8mm dia. bead
silicon tubing

2" polyball
(in flame
orange colour)

1 or 2 balsa
waggler bodies on
tubing, top one
flourescent colour

12" to 15" of
boom tubing

swivel link clip

5mm bead

link clip

5mm bead

hook trace

weight 'locked' on to swivel

bullet on tube
protects line

with no top mounting, float
can spin and not tangle

heavily and regularly grease the
line with mucilin or ET grease

supercontroller

set depth to
allow bait to fish
approx 2' off
bottom

24" 20lb
wire uptrace
with weight
attached

12" 20lb
hook trace

2'

LIVEBAIT
dorsal mounted on
upper treble

NB hook spacing on
trace to suit bait size

DEADBAIT mounted to
balance in horizontal plane

2 x size 4 to 8 semibarbless trebles to suit size
of baits (live or dead)

patterns, such as Drennan's clear-plastic Zeppler range, have both a centre tube and a bottom ring, allowing either mode of presentation (see *Freshwater floatfishing techniques - Sliding-float fishing for predators*). Floats in the JW tenpin range from Ryobi-Masterline have wide bulbous tops for maximum visibility and come in both standard and loaded (weighted brass stem) patterns for presenting static deadbaits on the bottom when nothing needs supporting. There are also sight-vane versions, into which a fluorescent, dart-type vane is inserted for distance fishing.

For short- to medium-range fishing, long, slim, pencil-type sliders, such as the 'long tom' in both loaded and unloaded patterns, are excellent. The latter, which requires a heavy bullet to cock it, makes a fine float for sea fishing for pollack or wrasse off the rocks.

Through-the-middle sliders in plastic, polystyrene and balsa are also popular sea floats due to their extra shotting capacity. Simple through-the-middle floats can easily be made by threading a cork or polystyrene pilot float onto the reel line and plugging it at the desired depth with a short length of thin peacock quill. For perch, chub and zander, a ¾in-diameter pilot is ideal, while for pike use 1-1¼in-diameter pilot.

Drift floats

The tenpin, sight-vane drifter is designed for presenting small pike baits up to medium distances. For drifting both live baits and deadbaits to far off spots (70-150yd), however, there are several sail-like patterns available. The ET Drifter, for instance, has a long, counter-balancing, wire stem going through the centre of a polyball body. The plastic sail (available in yellow, black, red or orange) is then connected above the body and held in place with a rubber band.

The reel line first clips into a removable ring at the top of the float and then passes slider-fashion through the ring at the bottom. This ensures that the float folds on the strike, making it easy to retrieve. This does not always happen when fishing at extreme distances, however, and the 'Dave Batten', improved drifting rig incorporates a separate tube that keeps the line clear of the float, making drifting much more enjoyable (fig. 37).

Balloons

When sea fishing, drifting live or dead fish baits downtide for tope and all larger sharks, all you need is a selection of coloured balloons. For fishing close to the surface, partly inflate one and attach it to the trace swivel with a paperclip so that it releases on the strike. Alternatively, tie a tiny size 8 or 10 freshwater swivel onto the inflated balloon stem and use the balloon as a sliding float, with a bead and stop knot above it on the reel line, at any predetermined depth.

Sub-floats

For presenting a ledgered livebait well above bottom weed, use a sunken float such as the Drennan, clear-plastic sub-float, which has a centre tube through which the line passes, or a polyball painted dark green or black. Corks similarly painted and bored with a hot needle will do at a pinch.

FLOATING CONTROLLERS

For presenting both small and large floating baits, from casters to a huge chunk of breadcrust, in pursuit of species such as dace, rudd, orfe, chub, and especially carp, the floating controller is an indispensable item of tackle. Squat, dumpy controllers such as the tenpin (available in four sizes) can be cast long distances and are easy to see due to their wide, fluorescent-red top, which has a small, neat swivel glued into it through which the line passes. The distance between the hook and the controller is controlled by a sliding stop knot tied on the reel line below, with a small bead between the controller and the stop knot to act as a cushion. Controllers are self-cocking and thus sit vertically in the surface film with only the tip visible. You can watch the floating bait being sucked in or observe the line snake away and the controller bob gently as line passes through the swivel.

For close-range fishing, a mini surface controller is quickly made by fixing 2-5in of plain peacock quill to the line with a piece of silicone tubing at each end. To aid casting, shots can be placed at both ends. See *Surface-controller fishing*.

POLE FLOATS

Although there are hundreds of different pole floats, each available in a range of four to six models of varying shotting capacity, their design in principle follows that of all float patterns. For instance, those constructed with the traditional heart- or egg-shaped buoyant body are used for flowing water. Should the body be rather elongated, however, and positioned upside down with the narrow part at the top, the float is suitable for still or extremely slow-moving water because it creates less resistance to biting fish. As with all pole floats, these are attached by passing the line through a tiny ring on the top of the body and then through a fine sleeve of silicon tubing at the very bottom of the wire, carbon or cane stem.

Stillwater floats

For very fine-line, delicate, close-range presentation in calm conditions, a bristle-top, slim-bodied range taking from three to six no. 12 shots is ideal. When fishing over depth, the short-bodied, flat-topped dibber-type floats hold up well, even in a slow draw. Made from a short length of balsa or peacock quill with a wire stem beneath, they have a shotting capacity of between three and eight no. 10s. Peacock-quill patterns take a greater shotting load. When stability is essential in still water, choose a range of reversed, elongated heart- or oval-bodied, bristle-topped, wire-stem floats carrying between 0.2g up to 1.5g. When fishing at full pole length, say 8-12m out, a similar range with noticeably thicker tips will be useful.

River floats

These have heart- or egg-shaped bodies of balsa or dense polystyrene that do not lift easily from the surface when they are held back to slow down the bait's passage. These patterns may look bulbous and insensitive, but for easing the bait slowly along the river bed, especially in low water temperatures and in strong currents, a buoyant body above the wire stem is imperative.

To cover most situations, select a range taking from 0.2g up to 1.5g; another taking 1g up to 4g; and finally a range with a capacity from 5g up to 10g for combating excessive depth and currents. River patterns generally have thicker tips for greater visibility; bristle tips would be too sensitive.

FLOAT FISHING IN HARBOURS AND OFF THE ROCKS

The situations in which a float is an advantage are limited, but when the right conditions do occur float fishing can provide the angler with tremendous sport.

The usual species for the sea - in addition to sharks caught well offshore on balloon floats - are mullet, pollack, bass, garfish, wrasse and mackerel. Harbour walls, piers and rock marks that give access to deep

FIGURE 38 Float fishing in harbours

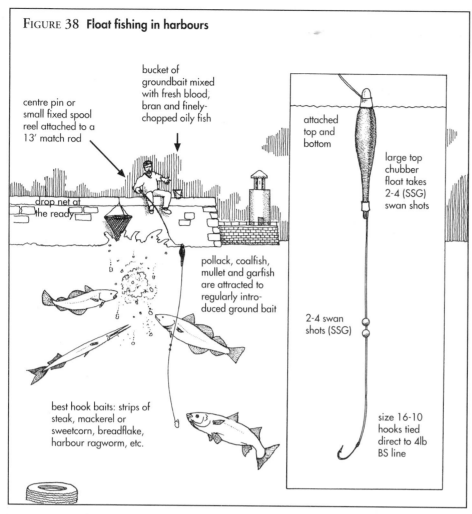

centre pin or small fixed spool reel attached to a 13' match rod

bucket of groundbait mixed with fresh blood, bran and finely-chopped oily fish

drop net at the ready

pollack, coalfish, mullet and garfish are attracted to regularly intro-duced ground bait

best hook baits: strips of steak, mackerel or sweetcorn, breadflake, harbour ragworm, etc.

attached top and bottom

large top chubber float takes 2-4 (SSG) swan shots

2-4 swan shots (SSG)

size 16-10 hooks tied direct to 4lb BS line

water are the type of places to consider when you are using a float - or anywhere else where the fish are likely to be within comfortable casting range.

Many of the traditional sea floats were huge polystyrene objects. Thankfully, most of these have now been replaced by more subtle freshwater designs, which are far more sensitive to bites and therefore allow the use of more sporting tackle. However, the larger, more buoyant designs should not be totally dismissed as they are useful for fishing in very turbulent water, around rocks for instance, or when extra casting

distance is necessary.

For fishing in the sea most anglers tend to use a sliding float with the line running through the middle of the float's body, as a waggler-style float (fixed to the line bottom end only) is constantly dragged under by the current or wave action, registering a lot of false bites. The sliding float is also the easiest type to rig for fishing at depths greater than can be comfortably cast with a float set at a fixed depth. In this situation, use a *sliding stop knot (Knots)*.

A sliding float is rigged as follows. A small bead is threaded on to the reel line,

followed by a float. A drilled bullet large enough to cock the float goes on next, followed by a second bead and a small swivel. The hooklength, generally 3-6ft, is tied to the other end of this swivel. A bunch of split shot instead of the bullet is preferable with smaller floats. A sliding stop knot is then tied at the required distance from the hook. On casting, the weight of the rig draws the line through the float until the top bead and the float come up against the stop knot, thus cocking the float (fig. 38).

To catch species such as mullet, garfish and small coalfish from clear, deep-water harbours that are protected from the sea proper, where sensitive presentation is imperative, scale down to freshwater tackle. Use a 12-14ft match rod, a centre-pin or small, fixed-spool reel loaded with 4lb-test line, and a chunky chubber float taking between two and five swan shot set 2-4ft above the hook. The hook itself should be between a 16 and an 8, tied direct to the line (fig. 38) and baited with slithers of raw steak or mackerel.

FLOAT LEDGERING

See *Freshwater floatfishing techniques.*

FLOUNDER

(Pleuronectes flesus)

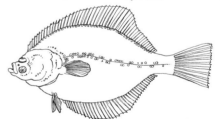

Average size: 8oz-1¼lb
Mega specimen: over 2½lb
British record: 5lb 11½oz (2kg 593g)

FLOUNDER

The flounder is a member of the pleuronectidae family of right-eyed flatfish, although reversed flounders, that is, flounders with both eyes on the left, are quite common. The flounder has the classic, compressed flatfish shape and a dorsal fin that almost fringes the entire body, while the anal fin is noticeably shorter, starting in a line directly opposite the pectoral. Overall colouration on top is warm grey, overlaid with dark brown blotches and small yellowy-brown spots. The distinct lateral line curves around the pectoral fin, where there are sharp denticles. Additional denticles exist at the base of both dorsal and anal fins. No other flatfish has these denticles. The belly is a dull off-white.

It feeds on worms, crustaceans and molluscs and reproduces in the spring. The fry change into flatfish within a few days of hatching, and sink to the bottom where they remain throughout their lives.

HABITAT AND DISTRIBUTION

Although the flounder is a shoaling sea fish, young flounders migrate high up into freshwater, returning to the ocean to reproduce 3 or 4 years later. It prefers a sandy or muddy bottom, and is widely distributed around the British Isles.

TECHNIQUES

Beachcasting; Downtide boat fishing; Floatfishing in harbours and off rocks. See also *Artificial lures - Spoons.*

FLY CASTING

In fly fishing more than in any other field of angling, it is vital to learn to cast properly if you are to maximize your chances of catching fish.

The simplest and most commonly used cast is the overhead. It is best described by employing the concept of a clock face (fig. 39). Imagine you are standing with a clock face sideways on beside you, 12 o'clock at your head, 6 o'clock at your feet, 9 o'clock in front of you and 3 o'clock behind. The cast should begin with about 5yd of fly line out beyond the rod tip. Place the foot on your rod side forward and put your weight on it. Then point the rod at the water at the 8 o'clock position and grip the fly line against the rod with your index finger.

Next bend your elbow and bring the rod back smoothly but progressively faster until you reach the 12 o'clock position. Stop here and allow the line to extend behind you in a straight line. Ensure that your wrist always remains straight so that the rod doesn't drop back towards the 2 or 3 o'clock position, from which it is impossible to execute a smooth forward cast. You will feel when the line has straightened out because the rod tip will be pulled back roughly to the 1 o'clock position.

Timing is most important here, and can only be perfected with practice. Wait too long and the line will begin to drop behind you, with the energy built up in it draining out. Begin the forward action too soon, and you will create a whiplash effect that can break the fly-line tip or crack off the fly.

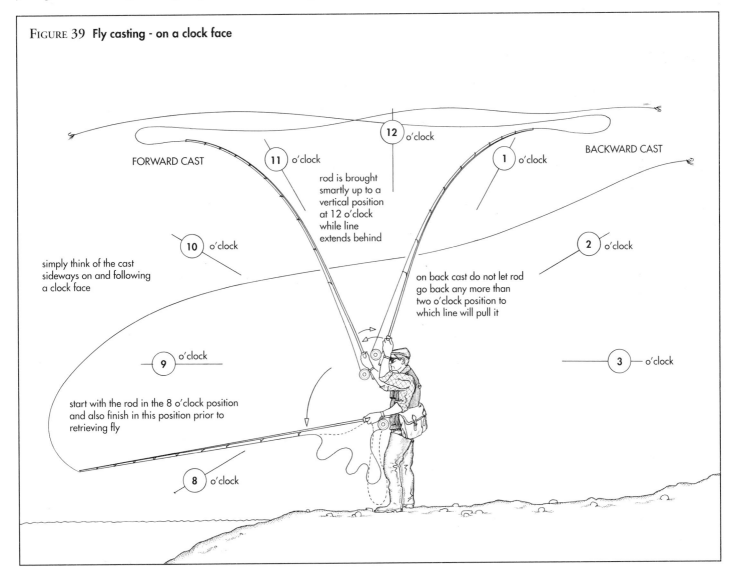

FIGURE 39 **Fly casting - on a clock face**

FORWARD CAST

BACKWARD CAST

12 o'clock

11 o'clock

1 o'clock

rod is brought smartly up to a vertical position at 12 o'clock while line extends behind

10 o'clock

2 o'clock

simply think of the cast sideways on and following a clock face

on back cast do not let rod go back any more than two o'clock position to which line will pull it

9 o'clock

3 o'clock

start with the rod in the 8 o'clock position and also finish in this position prior to retrieving fly

8 o'clock

When you can feel the rod tip pulling, push the rod smoothly forwards again, accelerating the movement as you do so. Stop smartly at the 10 o'clock position for an instant, and at the same time flick your wrist downwards in the same way that you would knock a nail in with a hammer. Then continue the downward movement of the rod towards the water, progressively slowing it as you do so, and finish with the tip pointing at the water surface. This will result in the line and leader lying out on the water in a nice straight line.

To cast a greater length of fly line using the simple overhead cast, pull line off the reel before commencing and let it lie on the ground beside you. Grip the line against the rod with your index finger as before. On the forward movement, as the rod reaches 10 o'clock, raise your index finger from the rod, so releasing the line. The momentum built up in the fly line by the casting action will result in the moving line pulling extra line up through the rod rings and out on to the water.

FALSE CASTING

Another way of casting a greater length of line is known as false casting. The rod is flicked continually backwards and forwards between the 10 o'clock and 1 o'clock positions. Extra line is pulled from the reel, left to lie to the side of you and gripped between finger and thumb around waist height by the non-casting hand. Each time the rod reaches the forward point, release a little of the extra line by relaxing your grip on it. The line will be pulled through between your finger and thumb.

Each rod can support a specific optimum length of line in the air. If you release too much line while casting, the rod will become overloaded and the line will fall to the ground. Again, practice will determine the correct amount of line to release.

DOUBLE HAULING

Double hauling is a technique employed in trout fishing to cast a much greater length of line than standard overhead casting can deliver, and is most popular with reservoir anglers casting from the shore. Greater casting distance is achieved by increasing the speed of the line through the air. The technique is a development of false casting, but differs from it in that the hand holding the line is pulled down sharply at the beginning of the backward movement of the rod, and is then allowed to be pulled up towards the butt ring by the weight of the fly line as it pulls out straight behind you. As the forward cast commences, the line is again pulled down sharply and is released completely as line shoots forward over the water. It is vital in double hauling to keep the line between the line-holding hand and the butt ring tight at all times or the velocity built up by the cast will be lost.

ROLL CASTING

Roll casting is useful for getting out a line on to the water where obstructions on the bank behind make back casting impossible. Start off by standing in the same position as you would for the overhead cast, and point the rod down towards the water. Smoothly bring up your casting hand to a little above your shoulder, to a point where the rod is angled back and pointing to the 1 o'clock position. This action causes an open loop of line to form between the rod tip and the water. Just as the casting hand reaches its backward point lift the rod slightly and then push it very quickly forward and down towards the water, stopping at the 9 o'clock position. As the loop of line turns over, straightens, and begins to fall towards the water, follow its progress on to the surface by lowering the rod tip still further.

SPEY CASTING

Spey casting is a development of the roll cast and is employed by salmon anglers using long, double-handed rods from banks that are steep or tree-lined and when wading. The big difference between roll and spey casts is that in the single spey cast the line is lifted clear of the water then dropped back on to it again in a new position ready for roll casting out. Timing is all important and needs to be perfected through a lot of practice.

The double spey cast is very much easier to accomplish than most anglers imagine. Following a roll cast with the rod still in the horizontal position at 9 o'clock, lift the rod up slowly until your hands are around head height. Then sweep the tip first to one side (the downstream side) then over to the other (the upstream side) in a long, flat, figure-of-eight movement with the rod tip. Finally, after a short delay, lay the line down smartly using a powerful roll-cast stroke. At this point, any loose line trapped beneath the fingers of your casting hand will shoot forward to achieve the desired distance.

FLY FISHING

DAPPING

Dapping is a technique used from boats on big stillwaters and one that is effective for salmon and sea trout as well as trout. A blow line made from several feet of featherweight floss replaces the fly line and is fished on a long rod up to 19ft in length in order that the fly can be fished some way out from the boat. Keep a spare fly reel well filled with 10lb monofilament and tie on (loop to loop) 10ft of floss, to which is added 6ft of 3-6lb monofilament and the fly or natural insect. To ensure that the floss is blown about in really light winds, it can be gently teased out in places to a fine web, which instantly becomes one again under the pressure of a fish. Flies are big and bushy and made to skip and skate backwards and forwards across the surface. In a strong wind some anglers like to use two flies, with the one on the point acting as an anchor. On some waters dapping is allowed with natural insects such as mayflies, daddy longlegs and grasshoppers.

DRY-FLY FISHING

Dry-fly fishing as its name suggests, involves using flies that sit on the water and is employed to catch fish feeding at the surface. On rivers, dry flies are normally fished upstream in order that rising fish can be approached from behind without being spooked. It is imperative to cast a snaky line, which is not immediately tightened by the current, so that the imitation is not dragged downstream in an unnatural manner. As the dry fly drifts towards the rod, the line should be carefully retrieved with the non-casting hand in order to be ready for a strike when a trout sucks down the imitation. When the trout gets its head down beneath the surface again, and only then, should the strike be made, simply by lifting the rod top and pulling the line simultaneously with the non-casting hand. Premature striking is the most common fault in dry-fly fishing. On stillwaters, the use of dry flies has become increasingly popular. So, too, have so-called emerger patterns, which are designed to sit in the surface film rather than directly on it, and represent insects in the process of hatching.

On rivers, dry flies are used singly and cast at rising fish, while on stillwaters one, two or even a team of three flies can be employed, and either cast at rising fish or simply fished blind.

FLY FISHING FOR COARSE SPECIES

As well as salmon, trout and sea trout, many coarse fish species will take a fly. The best known is the grayling, found in many clean rivers and streams. They are free risers and can often be taken on dry flies as well as nymphs and wet flies. Other species that can be caught on a fly include chub (particularly on leaded nymphs and bushy dry flies), perch and pike (lures), carp, roach and rudd (dry flies and nymphs) and dace (dry flies). Dace are the fastest risers of all freshwater fish, and to stand any chance of hooking them you need fast reflexes.

LOCH-STYLE FISHING

Also known as fishing on the drift, loch-style fishing involves casting a team of flies - usually wet flies, though it can be nymphs - over the front of a boat drifting side-on to the wind. It is effective for trout, salmon and sea trout, though for salmon fishing it is more common to use only two flies.

In windy conditions it can pay to fish a leaded fly on the point, not only to stabilize the team but also to improve line turnover during casting, thus reducing the risk of tangling. The fly on the top dropper is usually bushy and worked on the surface towards the end of the retrieve to create a disturbance that, hopefully, will attract a fish. Often on these occasions fish are attracted to this bob fly, but then turn away at the boat only to see the middle dropper or fly on the point, which they then grab. *Drogues* are often employed in windy weather to slow down the speed of the boat as it drifts along, thereby giving the anglers more control over the way the flies are fishing.

Loch-style fishing is normally conducted with a floating line, though in the early part of the season when the water is still cold and fish deep, it is practised by some anglers with a fast-sink line. With this tactic a long line is cast and the flies are steadily retrieved as they sink through the water. As the boat drifts down onto the team, the flies should be brought to the surface - but

Fishing guide, Jim Culp of Terrace in beautiful British Columbia, puts a wet fly downstream and across in the classical way, which is how the steelhead trout and char inhabiting the glacial-fed, boulder-strewn Copper River like it.

Everything you need for catching trout in waters large and small. The rods are 7½ft, 9ft and 10½ft long taking lines in sizes 4, 6 and 8 respectively loaded with plenty of backing on to lightweight magnesium reels. The folding net clips on to a D ring on the back of the waistcoat and most of the small items including scissors, leader material, leadersink, mucilin, aerosol floatant, priest and at least three small fly boxes containing an assortment of nymphs and dry flies, fit snugly into the pockets. A peaked hat and polaroid glasses are of course essential items, while large boxes of flies are accommodated in a tackle bag.

Following a lengthy acrobatic battle, Essex trout supremo Norman Bithell finally nets one of the superbly shaped, jumbo-sized rainbow trout for which Hanningfield Reservoir has become famous. It sucked in one of Norman's special super-buoyant booby nymphs on a short leader, retrieved slowly a few feet above the bottom using an extra fast sinking (Hi-D) line.

stopped when the top dropper appears. This is then held for as long as possible and watched very carefully for an unusual movement that might indicate that one of the flies below may have been taken.

NYMPH FISHING

Nymph fishing is widely used to catch trout from both rivers and stillwaters. Nymph patterns are tied to imitate the larval or pupal stage of many aquatic insects, such as *buzzers,* as well as adult invertebrates that spend their entire lives beneath the surface, such as corixae and shrimps. On big stillwaters such as *reservoirs* flies are most

often fished in teams of three and retrieved as slowly as possible. When a breeze is blowing across a fishing position, it may not be necessary to retrieve at all. Simply let the wind drift the flies round in a wide arc. On smaller lakes, particularly clearwater fisheries, trout are often stalked with weighted nymphs and cast to when spotted. In this induced-take style of fishing, only one fly is attached to the leader and it is observed through polarized glasses from the moment it slips through the surface film and starts to descend. Very often, a gentle twitch when the nymph is within the trout's vision brings a dramatic and immediate response.

On rivers, nymphs are most often fished upstream and singly. When the current is brisk, it may well be necessary to use weighted patterns in order to get down to where fish are feeding. In river fishing, nymphing trout are frequently looked for with polaroid glasses and cast to once spotted. In this situation, a trout can often be induced to take the fly. This is done by

raising the rod tip to lift the nymph just before it reaches the trout's nose. Watch the cast where it enters the surface and strike at the slightest indication. Sight of the trout's mouth (with its white insides) opening and closing is worth an instant response.

WET-FLY FISHING

On stillwaters and rivers normally wet-fly fishing involves the use of a team of two or three flies. On stillwaters they are given movement by being retrieved - either in short or long pulls or by a continuous figure-of-eight action. On rivers, wet-fly anglers usually cast across, or downstream and across, and allow the current to impart movement to the flies. Takes come as the team of flies swing round towards the bank.

Salmon and sea trout, as well as trout, are caught by fishing downstream and across, though for these two species either a single fly or a point fly with a single dropper above it are used. To cover a pool fully, it is customary to walk or wade a yard or

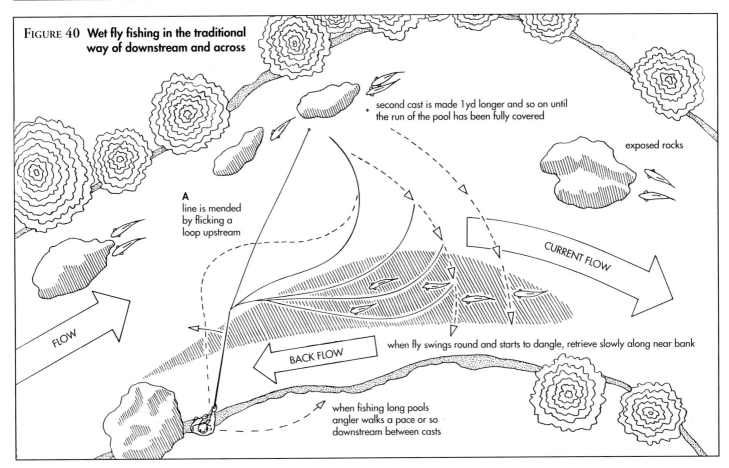

FIGURE 40 **Wet fly fishing in the traditional way of downstream and across**

second cast is made 1yd longer and so on until the run of the pool has been fully covered

exposed rocks

CURRENT FLOW

A
line is mended by flicking a loop upstream

FLOW

BACK FLOW

when fly swings round and starts to dangle, retrieve slowly along near bank

when fishing long pools angler walks a pace or so downstream between casts

so downstream after each cast until all the water has been worked. The artificial is liable to be grabbed virtually at any time as it swings across with the flow in front of fish as long as it isn't travelling too fast. To ensure that the fly comes around slowly, simply flick a loop of line between surface and rod tip upstream, immediately after casting downstream and across, in order to mend it (fig. 40A). At the end of the swing round, when the fly would otherwise sink to the bottom (a point in time known as the dangle), retrieve it slowly along the near bank before taking a pace down river and making a repeat cast (fig. 40).

FLY RODDING

A fly rod can be used to cast smaller spinners and even tiny plugs, plus American-style buoyant popping bugs with bulbous bodies made of deer hair to which wagtails and rubber frogs' legs have been added.

This opens up a whole new exciting field of fly rodding for coarse species, but these relatively heavy imitations can only be cast effectively by using a weight-forward floating line and short 4-5ft cast. The bass-bug taper line (*Lines - fly*) has been specifically

designed for popper casting and has a heavier section up front. Alternatively, chop a few feet from the front end of a standard weight-forward line, bringing the heaviest section of line and the imitation fairly close together. With other types of line, there is a delayed period during casting, which seriously affects casting accuracy.

Small, floating dog and cat biscuits can also be cast when fly rodding, and the largest of carp subdued. Simply exchange the tapered cast for 9-10ft of 8-10lb test, monofilament and hair-rig the biscuits on a size 8 hook as if floater fishing. The only prerequisite is to ensure that the reel has at least 75yd of backing beneath the floating line.

FLY TYING

Though seemingly highly skilled and intricate, the art of fly tying is easy to master and can be broken down into a series of mini exercises, as shown in fig. 41, tying a simple hackled dry fly.

The main benefit of home-tied flies is that they cost only a fraction of shop-bought patterns once the tools and an assortment of hooks and materials have been assembled. The basic tools include a fly-tying vice

complete with integral G-clamp for securing it on to a table-top, plus black fly-tying thread, hackle pliers, a bobbin-holder, sharp scissors, a whip-finish tool (optional), a dubbing needle, a piece of beeswax, and clear and black quick-drying head varnish. Red head varnish is also available for specialized patterns.

The most useful materials include coloured fly-tying threads, coloured floss, silver and gold oval wire and flat wire, peacock herl, black and coloured chenille, coloured wools, natural and coloured squirrel tail, turkey marabou in various colours, cock-pheasant tail feathers, duck and goose feathers, plus an assortment of cock and hen hackles, which come from the neck of a chicken. The entire cape from the neck of a cockerel is the cheapest way of obtaining hackles. The small feathers can be used for dry flies and the larger ones for winged lures or streamer patterns. Black and badger (black and white) capes are the most useful. Friends who shoot regularly can supply a host of free feathers, and a raid on someone's sewing or knitting box will provide more useful oddments of wool and thread. A walk beside rivers and lakes where geese and ducks abound will add to your stock of feathers, while roadside inspections of recently run-over pheasants and rabbits can provide additional materials.

TYING A SIMPLE DRY FLY

Select an up-eyed hook, size 14-10, and secure firmly by its point in the jaws of the vice (fig. 41A). The first operation is to lay down a bed of whipping thread along the entire length of the hook shank (41B), wound on with a bobbin-holder in tight, touching turns from just behind the eye to the bend. This non-slip foundation makes it much easier to tie in the tail, body and cock hackle that make up the dry fly. Use prewaxed fly-tying thread (black), or gently pull 2ft of thread through a piece of beeswax to make it waterproof.

First tie in a tail of several hackle fibres. Then, at the end nearest the bend, tie in any body or ribbing material (41C), which should then be wound back up to the head

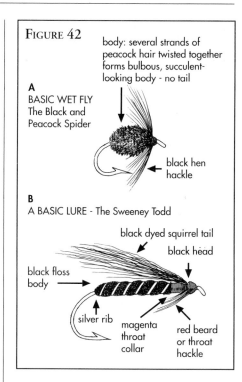

FIGURE 42

A
BASIC WET FLY
The Black and Peacock Spider

body: several strands of peacock hair twisted together forms bulbous, succulent-looking body - no tail

black hen hackle

B
A BASIC LURE - The Sweeney Todd

black dyed squirrel tail

black head

black floss body

silver rib

magenta throat collar

red beard or throat hackle

(41D) and the end trimmed off with scissors. If the fly has wings, these are normally tied in next and are selected from a pair of left and right feathers. For a simple hackled dry-fly pattern, however, next prepare a cock hackle (41E) and tie it on in front of the eye. Wind the hackle firmly and gently around the hook shank in the opposite direction to the whipping thread, using a forefinger and pliers (41F). Secure the end of the hackle with thread and trim close (41G).

The cock hackle not only aids buoyancy, but also represents the legs of the insect being imitated. Always use hackle feathers from cock birds as they are much stiffer and ensure that the fly will ride high when sitting on the water. Hen hackles are more fibrous and are perfect for tying wet flies, nymphs and lures.

Lastly, secure the head whipping by forming three or four simple slip knots over a forefinger, bedding each down and trimming them off. Alternatively, a whip-finish tool can be used. Then apply a coat of clear head varnish to the whipping using the point of a needle. Be miserly with the varnish or it will clog the eye of the hook and adhere to the hackles.

WET FLIES

The easiest wet fly pattern to tie, and one of the most effective, is the Black and Peacock Spider (fig. 42A). Put up a size 14-10, standard-shank, down-eyed hook in the vice and, as with the dry fly, wind black thread along the shank from the eye to the top of the bend. Then take four or five

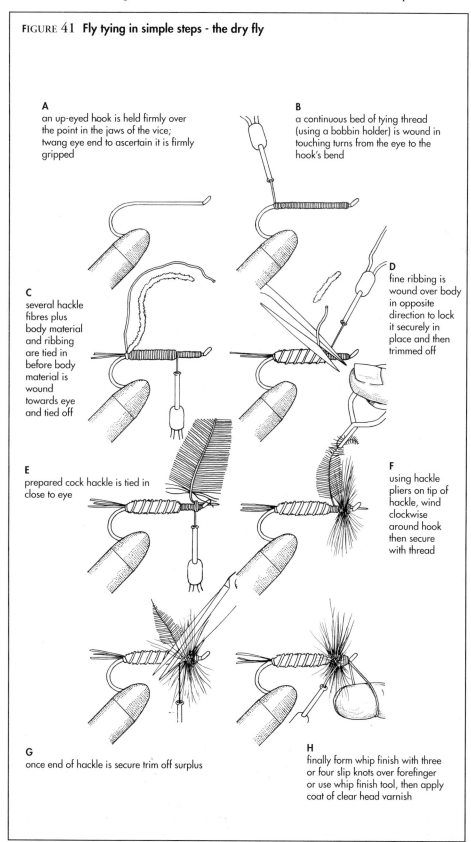

FIGURE 41 **Fly tying in simple steps - the dry fly**

A
an up-eyed hook is held firmly over the point in the jaws of the vice; twang eye end to ascertain it is firmly gripped

B
a continuous bed of tying thread (using a bobbin holder) is wound in touching turns from the eye to the hook's bend

C
several hackle fibres plus body material and ribbing are tied in before body material is wound towards eye and tied off

D
fine ribbing is wound over body in opposite direction to lock it securely in place and then trimmed off

E
prepared cock hackle is tied in close to eye

F
using hackle pliers on tip of hackle, wind clockwise around hook then secure with thread

G
once end of hackle is secure trim off surplus

H
finally form whip finish with three or four slip knots over forefinger or use whip finish tool, then apply coat of clear head varnish

strands of herl from a peacock quill and tie on by winding the thread back to the eye. There is no tail on this pattern.

Carefully twist the herl fibres together and wind them along the shank to create a bulbous body, finishing within ⅛in of the eye, and tie off. After trimming off the surplus herl, take a black hen hackle and prepare as for the dry fly, ensuring that the natural bend of the feather faces inwards, towards the bend of the hook. This ensures that it moves freely and attractively when retrieved.

Tie off the hackle and trim off the tip with scissors; make a neat head, bending the hackle forwards with the finger tips of your other hand. Finish with head varnish as for the dry fly.

LURES

Fix a long-shank, size 10-6, down-eyed hook firmly in the jaws of the vice, and form a base for the pattern by winding waxed tying thread around the shank from the eye to the bend. Tie in a tail of hackle fibres or wool at the bend, then use the thread to tie in both the rib and body material, also at the bend. Either silver or gold flat or oval wire can be used for the ribbing, and the body material can be floss, wool, herl or chenille, depending on the pattern. The body material should be wound up the hook shank first, in tight, touching turns. Then wind on the ribbing in evenly spaced turns and in the opposite direction to that used for the body to ensure that it doesn't pull into the body material.

If a beard hackle is required, it is tied in next (42B), followed by the wing. Lure wings can consist of two matching cock hackle feathers tied in together as one (for streamer flies), or hair from squirrel, goat, skunk or a calf's tail (for hair wings). Marabou is another excellent wing material, pulsating enticingly when the lure is retrieved in a series of pulls. With all feathers, strip the herls from the base and then tie in securely at that end. Never tie just one fly at a time. Only by tying up several of the same pattern will you arrive at the correct proportions for each material. Initially, the body will be either too big or too small, and so on, and it will seem impossible to fit everything into its correct place on the hook shank, especially when you are using standard-sized hooks. So start the easy way, by tying large flies such as a lure on a size 6 long-shank hook, and then tie progressively smaller patterns.

FORCEPS

See *Disgorgers - Freshwater, Sea.*

FORKBEARD, GREATER

(*Phycis blennoides*)

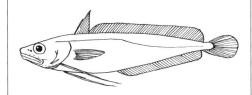

British record: 4lb 11¼oz (2kg 133g)

This member of the cod family is most common in the Mediterranean, but is also found around the British Isles, particularly in south-western waters. It has a greyish, thick-set, sharply tapering body and two dorsal fins, the first short and triangular, followed by a long, continuous fin reaching almost to the rounded tail. The anal fin is also long, about half the forkbeard's length, and its pelvic fins consist of an extremely long, single (fork-like) branched ray on each side - hence its name. Its mouth and eye are both large, and there is a single barbel under the chin. It feeds on small fish and crustaceans, and spawns during the early summer.

FREELINING

As the term implies, freelining involves presenting the bait without any shots, floats, tubing or bombs added to the line. The hook is tied on direct. It is the most sensitive technique of all as fish feel no resistance, but is restricted to close-range fishing because the only casting weight is that provided by the bait.

IN STILLWATERS

Species such as tench, catfish, eels and carp will confidently suck up the bait from the bottom, or sometimes even on the drop. You should strike as you see the line tighten. If you know these species are present, hold the rod all the time and keep your eyes glued to the bow in the line between rod tip and surface.

When you do not expect instant bites, for instance, when you are fishing for smaller species such as roach, orfe, rudd and bream, place the rod on two rests with the tip pointing directly at the bait to minimize resistance, and clip a simple coil indicator on a 2ft drop (*Bite indicators and accessories*) over the line between reel and butt ring (fig. 43).

If you are fishing in darkness, rig up an electric alarm in conjunction with the coil

The art of freelining a bait without any weight on the line is essentially a close range technique. It is therefore imperative also to practise the art of concealment as John illustrates here, by keeping low down and well back from the water whilst attempting to fool wary chub inhabiting an overgrown summer stream.

FIGURE 43 Freelining set-ups for fishing in stillwater

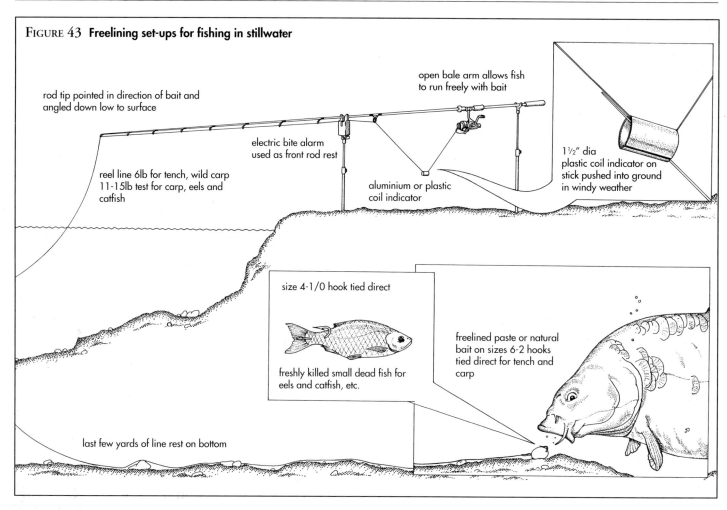

rod tip pointed in direction of bait and
angled down low to surface

open bale arm allows fish
to run freely with bait

electric bite alarm
used as front rod rest

reel line 6lb for tench, wild carp
11-15lb test for carp, eels and
catfish

aluminium or plastic
coil indicator

1½" dia
plastic coil indicator on
stick pushed into ground
in windy weather

size 4-1/0 hook tied direct

freshly killed small dead fish for
eels and catfish, etc.

freelined paste or natural
bait on sizes 6-2 hooks
tied direct for tench and
carp

last few yards of line rest on bottom

FIGURE 44 Wading whilst freelining

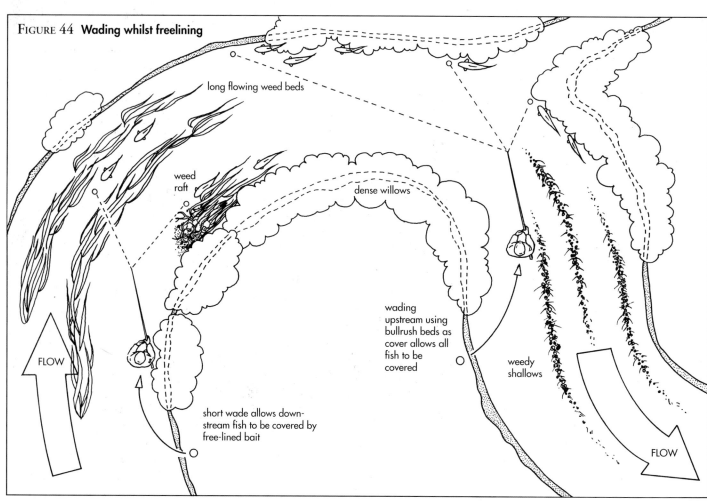

long flowing weed beds

weed
raft

dense willows

wading
upstream using
bullrush beds as
cover allows all
fish to be
covered

weedy
shallows

FLOW

short wade allows down-
stream fish to be covered by
free-lined bait

FLOW

indicator. When freelining for tench, eels, carp or catfish at night, leave the reel's bale arm open to allow several yards of line to peel off the reel and let a positive run develop before closing the bale arm and striking.

IN RIVERS

This is a roving, opportunist technique that depends on stealth and concealment. Species such as chub, bream and barbel, and even specimen roach, can often be seen, particularly in smaller, clear-flowing rivers and streams, and the idea is to locate and cast to individual fish. Don't forget to wear polarized glasses, which allow maximum visibility in clear water.

There is nothing to beat the versatility of an 11-12ft Avon-style, carbon rod of around 1¼lb test curve for freelining in running water (*Rods- freshwater*). Such a rod possesses the backbone to land big barbel, yet provides enjoyment from the smaller species. To achieve maximum casting distance, for instance to chub inhabiting an awkward lie on the opposite bank, use a heavy bait such as cheese paste, a big slug or two lobworms and punch it out using a gentle, double-handed lob. For all short- to medium-range casting, however, accuracy is more easily achieved by hooking the line over the ball of the forefinger (to feel the bait's weight) and flipping it out with an underhand, pendulum-type swing. Alternatively, if you find this one-handed method unsuitable, use the same underhand swing and flip, but hold a loop of line in your other hand with the rod tip pointing at the target, to build up momentum before letting go. The bait will then fly effortlessly through the air (provided the reel's spool is full to the rim) until you 'feather' it down with your forefinger to land exactly over the desired spot.

Allow the current to sweep the bait downstream while you keep a bow in the line from rod tip to the point where the line enters the water. And watch it like a hawk - it is a resistance-free bite indicator *par excellence*. Bites will consist of an initial twitch or two, followed by a positive tightening of the line (hence the importance of keeping a bow) or a sudden and exaggerated tightening, indicating that a fish has sucked in the bait and moved immediately downstream.

When a bait is freelined upstream, the line can momentarily fall slack. This is caused by a fish swimming a few feet downstream and towards the rod, and should be

The rewards of stretpegging. John hooked this 25lb river carp close into the margins of a deep, fast run beside a dense bed of yellow lilies, on a large lump of breadflake covering a size 4 hook, tied direct to just 8lb reel line.

met with an immediate sweeping strike to take up the loose line.

For species such as roach, perch and small to medium-sized chub, use a 3lb reel line. For quality chub, especially those inhabiting snaggy or weedy parts of the river, and barbel, a 5-6lb reel line is none too heavy. When double-figure barbel and sizeable carp are on the cards, step up to a 6-8lb reel line. In all cases, tie hooks direct to the reel line.

Very occasionally, a small shot needs to be pinched on to the line (12in above the hook) to anchor buoyant baits such as breadflake or a cube of luncheon meat, or an extremely light bait such as a bunch of maggots, in a particular spot. This is perfectly in order. Any more than a single swan shot, however, and you are then ledgering rather than freelining.

In order to present a freelined bait to chub or barbel in particularly weedy, overgrown stretches of rivers that are seldom fished, wade carefully into a casting position and swing the bait in. You'll have a good chance of a few easy bonus fish. Study fig. 44 for opportunist potential.

FRESHWATER FLOATFISHING TECHNIQUES

THE LIFT METHOD

This method is particularly well suited to catching species such as tench, bream, carp and crucian carp, which tilt downwards and stand on their heads to suck up a bait from the bottom, in still or exceptionally slow-flowing rivers. The secret of the 'lift' is to set the float (a length of peacock quill or waggler) a little overdepth, attached bottom end only with a sleeve of silicone tubing - not with locking shots (*Waggler fishing*). All the shot loading, whether a single BB or a swan shot or two, is pinched on 3-4in from the hook (fig. 45).

When the fish inhales the bait and rights itself, as in 45A and B, the float 'lifts' and may even keel over. Once the float is flat, however, the fish (not the float) is fully supporting the shots, at which point it may eject the bait. So strike while the float is lifting. Should the fish suck in the bait and

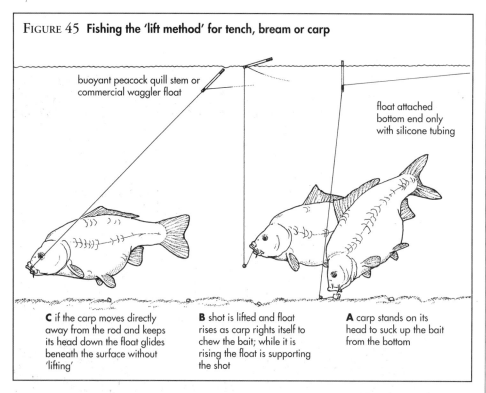

FIGURE 45 **Fishing the 'lift method' for tench, bream or carp**

buoyant peacock quill stem or commercial waggler float

float attached bottom end only with silicone tubing

C if the carp moves directly away from the rod and keeps its head down the float glides beneath the surface without 'lifting'

B shot is lifted and float rises as carp rights itself to chew the bait; while it is rising the float is supporting the shot

A carp stands on its head to suck up the bait from the bottom

move directly away, the float will immediately disappear in the conventional way (fig. 45C). To fish this rig after dark, add a luminous chemical light to the top of the float with the sleeve of clear tubing. This applies to fishing most float techniques at night, even *stretpegging* (below) in flowing water, where the float lies flat.

The lift 'bolt' rig

It is simple to convert the basic lift into a 'bolt' variation to catch carp, by adding more shots than are actually needed to cock the float. Four or five swan shots pinched on 4in from the hook will ensure that a carp really belts off with the bait - so hold the rod at all times. Baits can be side hooked or presented on a hair.

LAYING-ON WITH THE FLOAT FLAT

This method (fig. 46) permits presentation at close range to large species like tench and carp along reed lines or overgrown margins, where ledgering and most other float-fishing methods are impractical. The rig is simplicity itself. Attach 1-2in of plain peacock quill to the line with silicone bands at each end and pinch on a small shot below the float slightly deeper than the swim, leaving 2-3ft between the shot and hook so that it lies along the bottom. There are two main benefits from employing this rig: line bites from large fish moving close in along the margins are minimized, and bites are invariably glorious 'sail-aways'.

FLOAT LEDGERING

Whenever extra weight is required to reach

distant stillwater swims and present the bait hard on the bottom, float ledgering is the answer. As can be seen from fig. 47, the straight or bodied waggler can be attached to the line with silicone tubing through both tubing and bottom eye, or fished slider-style with a nylon *stop knot* tied on the reel line (*Knots*) slightly deeper than swim depth.

All the casting weight is pinched on to a separate mini-ledger link (two to four swan shots or a small bomb) stopped 10in above the hook by a single AA shot.

WAGGLER FISHING IN RIVERS

Wagglers are the most commonly used of all freshwater floats, in both still and moving water, and are made from peacock quill or, sometimes, sarkansas reed. Some have straight stems, while others have a polystyrene body at the base for extra stability and shotting capacity (*Floats*). As can be seen from fig. 48A, bulk shots are pinched on either side of the float (slightly deeper than the swim), with small shots at regular intervals between float and hook. As long as the line is freely given, the bait (maggots or casters) will trundle smoothly along the bottom behind the waggler. Do not attempt to hold back or straighten the line. For dace, roach, chub and bream this rig is unbeatable. Use a reel line of 2-2½lb-test and a 13-14ft match rod (*Rods - freshwater*). In fact, a 2½lb-test reel line harnessed

Carp readily fall to float rigs, this was taken on a mini surface controller rig

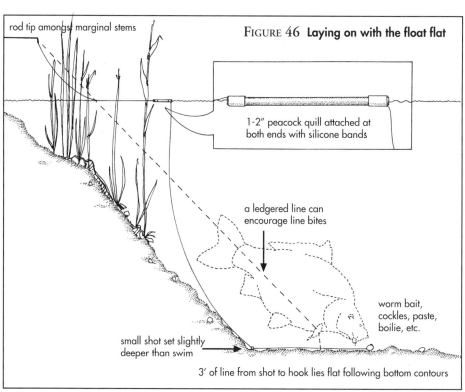

rod tip amongst marginal stems

FIGURE 46 **Laying on with the float flat**

1-2″ peacock quill attached at both ends with silicone bands

a ledgered line can encourage line bites

worm bait, cockles, paste, boilie, etc.

small shot set slightly deeper than swim

3′ of line from shot to hook lies flat following bottom contours

FIGURE 47 Float ledger rig

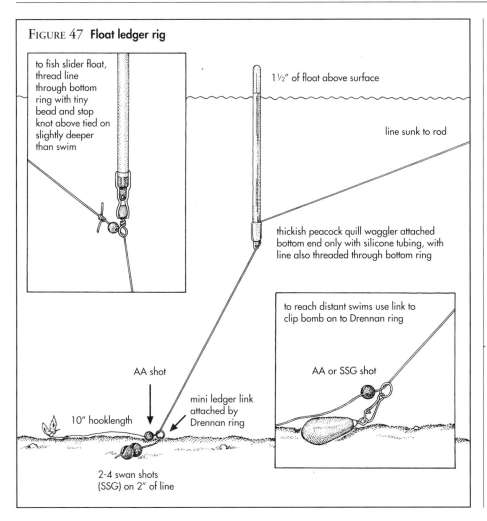

to fish slider float, thread line through bottom ring with tiny bead and stop knot above tied on slightly deeper than swim

1½" of float above surface

line sunk to rod

thickish peacock quill waggler attached bottom end only with silicone tubing, with line also threaded through bottom ring

AA shot

10" hooklength

mini ledger link attached by Drennan ring

2-4 swan shots (SSG) on 2" of line

to reach distant swims use link to clip bomb on to Drennan ring

AA or SSG shot

to a 13ft, waggler-style rod can be considered standard for most float-fishing techniques, carp excepted.

To lay the bait hard on the bottom, perhaps with bream in mind, fix the waggler well overdepth, 'lift' style, with a sleeve of silicone tubing and pinch on its entire shotting capacity grouped 5-6in from the hook (as fig. 48B). This is an excellent rig for presenting large baits such as breadflake or worms to large species.

For trotting in medium-paced to fast swims for species like chub and barbel, bulk most of the shots at two-thirds depth with just a couple of small shots between these and the hook (as in fig. 48C). Fix the float on to the line with silicone tubing or just a small shot either side of the eye.

Laying-on with the waggler in slow currents over weed is easily accomplished by joining a swan-shot link to the reel line using a four turn water knot (fig. 48D). This permits the shorter hooklink to lie on top of dense aquatic vegetation such as cabbages (sub-surface leaves of the yellow water lily); the swan shots hold the rig steady, with the tip of the float still visible above surface. To avoid the problems caused by water pressure from strong currents, which can force the float under, fish several feet

FIGURE 48 Waggler fishing in rivers

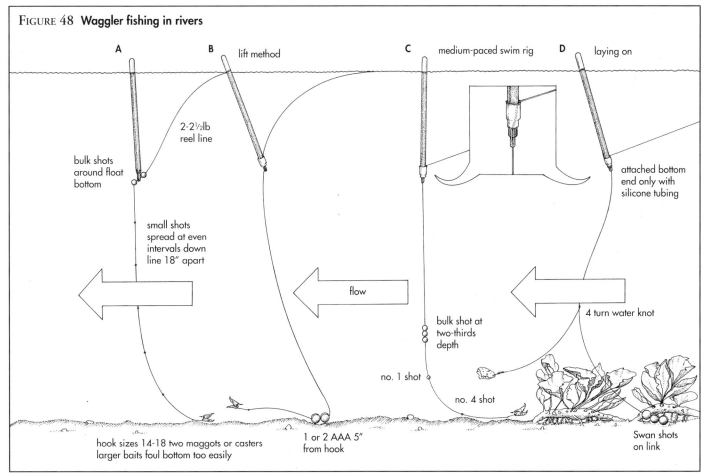

A

B   lift method

C   medium-paced swim rig

D   laying on

bulk shots around float bottom

2-2½lb reel line

small shots spread at even intervals down line 18" apart

flow

bulk shot at two-thirds depth

no. 1 shot

no. 4 shot

attached bottom end only with silicone tubing

4 turn water knot

Swan shots on link

hook sizes 14-18 two maggots or casters larger baits foul bottom too easily

1 or 2 AAA 5" from hook

FIGURE 49 Fishing the sliding float

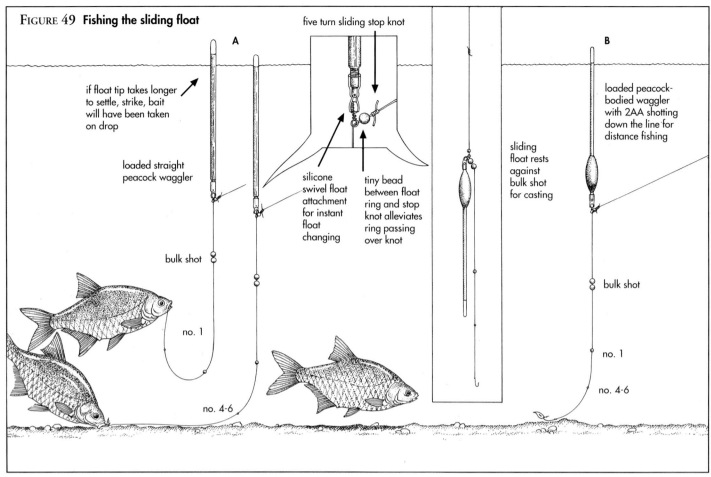

five turn sliding stop knot

A

B

if float tip takes longer to settle, strike, bait will have been taken on drop

loaded straight peacock waggler

silicone swivel float attachment for instant float changing

tiny bead between float ring and stop knot alleviates ring passing over knot

sliding float rests against bulk shot for casting

loaded peacock-bodied waggler with 2AA shotting down the line for distance fishing

bulk shot

no. 1

no. 4-6

bulk shot

no. 1

no. 4-6

FIGURE 50 Float-fishing from a boat in stillwater

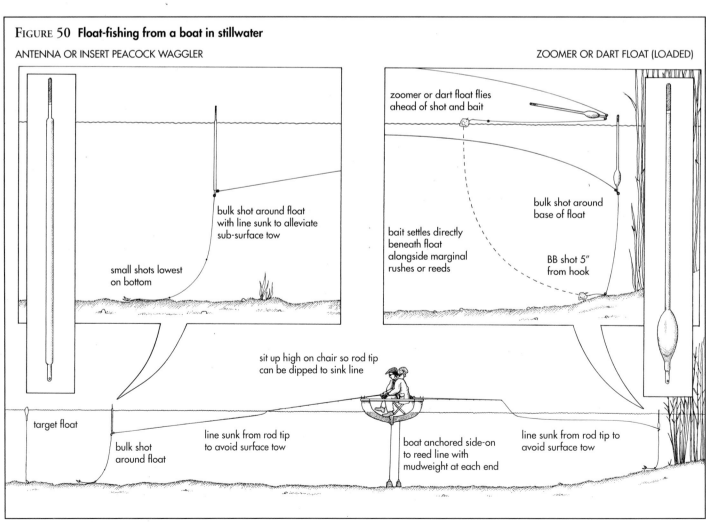

ANTENNA OR INSERT PEACOCK WAGGLER

ZOOMER OR DART FLOAT (LOADED)

zoomer or dart float flies ahead of shot and bait

bulk shot around float with line sunk to alleviate sub-surface tow

bulk shot around base of float

bait settles directly beneath float alongside marginal rushes or reeds

small shots lowest on bottom

BB shot 5" from hook

sit up high on chair so rod tip can be dipped to sink line

target float

bulk shot around float

line sunk from rod tip to avoid surface tow

boat anchored side-on to reed line with mudweight at each end

line sunk from rod tip to avoid surface tow

overdepth and keep the rod tip high above the water, positioned on two rod rests.

FISHING THE SLIDING FLOAT

To present the bait hard on (or close to) the bottom, even on the drop, in excessively deep stillwaters beyond the reach of a fixed float - depths of 10-12ft or more - you must fish 'slider fashion'.

This means tying a *sliding stop knot (Knots)* on the reel line above the float so that the float locks at the desired depth once the hook and shotting pattern have descended. Keep the reel's bale arm open while this is happening or the rig will eventually come to settle much closer in than you planned. Consider fig. 49, which illustrates that bites can be detected both on the drop (fig. 49A) and once the bait has settled on the bottom (fig. 49B). Strike immediately if the float takes any longer than it should do in reaching its final position once the lower shots have settled. Floats with colour-banded tips are useful here.

Use a silicone swivel float adaptor to facilitate quick changes from one float to another. The *sliding float* can also be used in slow-moving rivers (*Floats*).

FLOAT FISHING FROM A BOAT IN STILLWATER

Once the mudweights have been lowered and the boat has settled sideways on to the wind (*Dinghy fishing in freshwater*), casts should be made directly downwind. Aim to sit up high (using a comfortable folding chair) so that you can dip the rod tip and sink all the line to counteract surface tow.

The best floats to use are antennae or tipped (insert) wagglers (fig. 50) with most of the shotting capacity locked around the float's bottom ring and two small shots down the line. This simple rig will enable you to see bites on the drop (the tip taking longer to settle than it should) and once the bait comes to rest on the bottom. So plumb the depth carefully.

To fish up close against reed or sedge beds, loaded floats (darts or zoomers) are recommended with just a single small shot 5in from the hook.

FLOAT FISHING WAGGLER-STYLE IN STILLWATER

Whether you are using a tiny antenna float (fig. 51A) in a farm pond, or a long insert waggler (fig. 51B) or a bodied waggler (fig. 51C) in a huge estate lake, the technique is exactly the same. Group the bulk shots around the float's bottom ring (use a sili-

cone swivel float adaptor to facilitate quick changes from one float to another) leaving just two small shots to go down near the hook. The bait can then be presented either on the drop or on the bottom, catering for most species from rudd to bream.

Tie hooks in sizes 10-16 direct to a 2-2½lb reel line for baits like breadflake or sweetcorn. But to achieve the slowest possible descent with small baits like casters, maggots or punched bread, use fine-wire hooks in sizes 18-22 on a 1-1½lb hooklength.

To ensure that the line sinks between float and rod tip, dab a small amount of neat washing-up liquid over the spool. Surface drift pulls a floating line, and thus your float and bait, unnaturally along the bottom. Remember to cast several yards beyond the target area and instantly plunge the rod tip a foot beneath the surface before winding quickly for a few turns to sink all of the line.

Hooked on a bunch of maggots over 30 yards downstream using a wide-topped chubber float holding 3 swan shot, Bruce Vaughan nets a specimen grayling from a southern chalk-stream.

FIGURE 51 **Float-fishing waggler-style in stillwater**

tip always takes longer to settle when bait has been sucked in 'on the drop'

A antenna

bulk shot around float

C bodied waggler

B insert waggler

for the slowest possible descent to encourage bites 'on the drop' use casters, maggots or punched bread

use fine wire hooks sizes 18-22 on a 1-1½lb hooklength

no. 6 or dust shots 18" apart

two small shots down the line nos. 4-6

hook sizes 10-16 tied direct to reel line for bread baits or sweetcorn, etc.

FIGURE 52 **Long trotting**

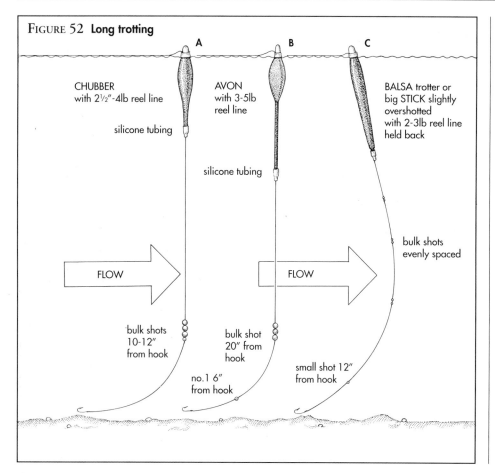

CHUBBER
with 2½″-4lb reel line

silicone tubing

AVON
with 3-5lb
reel line

silicone tubing

BALSA trotter or
big STICK slightly
overshotted
with 2-3lb reel line
held back

FLOW

FLOW

bulk shots
evenly spaced

bulk shots
10-12″
from hook

bulk shot
20″ from
hook

small shot 12″
from hook

no.1 6″
from hook

and push the float (a length of peacock quill, waggler or balsa trotter fixed at both ends) several feet overdepth, so that it lies completely flat once the bait and shots have settled, with an exaggerated bow in the line between (fig. 53). Set the rod in two rests (or hold it steady) and raise the tip until most of the line is clear of the water, otherwise the rig will be pushed into the margins by the current pressure.

STICK-FLOAT FISHING

This, the most sensitive of all running-water techniques, is only effective for swims up to 1½ rod lengths out, and is best executed using a 12-13ft, sharp-actioned match rod (preferably one with a spliced tip), a 2lb reel line, and with the float set slightly deeper than swim depth (fig. 54), using either maggots or casters. Because the line is not threaded through any part of the float (stick floats are always attached at the top and bottom with silicone tubing) changes from one to another are both quick and easy.

In order to ease the bait slowly through the swim just above bottom by holding the

LONG TROTTING

This probing, searching method of presenting the bait far downstream to species like dace, roach, chub, grayling and even barbel, demands a float that carries plenty of shot. In shallow streams and rivers use a squat, fat 'chubber', which has a wide tip visible at distances up to and over 40yd. Keep the shotting pattern simple (fig. 52A) with the entire load pinched on 12in above the hook.

For presenting maggots, breadcrust or flake in deep, fast water use an Avon or 'cork on crowquill special' with a line of AA bulk shots 2-3ft above the hook and a No. 1 halfway between (fig. 52B). Every so often hold back to make the bait swing forwards enticingly. For slower currents in medium to deep swims use a balsa trotter or big stick and slightly overshot it so that you can hold it back gently through much of the run (fig. 52C).

STRETPEGGING

As opposed to ledgering for roach, chub or barbel occupying swims along marginal fringes, even those with a fair current pushing through, you can present the bait static, hard on the bottom - the stretpegging style of float fishing.

The secret is to cast directly downstream

FIGURE 53 **Stret pegging**

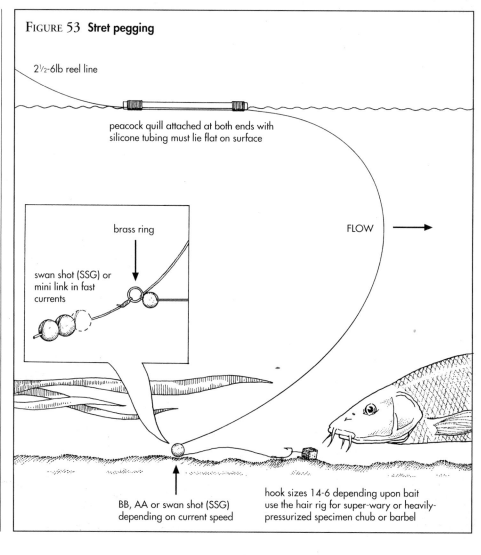

2½-6lb reel line

peacock quill attached at both ends with silicone tubing must lie flat on surface

brass ring

swan shot (SSG) or mini link in fast currents

FLOW

BB, AA or swan shot (SSG) depending on current speed

hook sizes 14-6 depending upon bait use the hair rig for super-wary or heavily-pressurized specimen chub or barbel

float back gently, distribute the shots evenly, 'shirt-button style', between the float and the hook.

Do not be afraid to overshot the float when holding back hard as this will make the bait swing enticingly upwards ahead of the float (fig. 54).

Both dace and roach respond well to this ruse, particularly when presenting a single *caster* in cold, clear water (*Baits, freshwater - Maggots*).

As illustrated perfectly in the photo below, to fish stretpegging style effectively the float should actually lie flat. Otherwise (with a half-cocked float) resistance is instantly felt by a fish sucking in the bait. In the confines of this narrow and shallow, clear-flowing stream which contains small numbers of specimen dace, continual trotting of the bait through each run could easiliy spook them. But with a static bait stretpegged on the bottom several yards downstream in the deepest part of the run, bites are usually confident, the float gliding purposefully beneath the surface following an initial twitch or two.

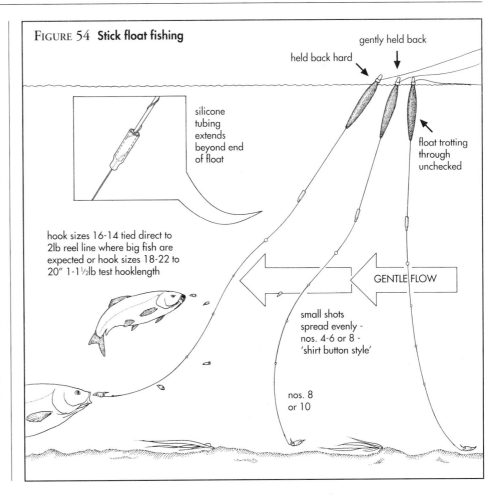

FIGURE 54 **Stick float fishing**

gently held back

held back hard

silicone tubing extends beyond end of float

float trotting through unchecked

hook sizes 16-14 tied direct to 2lb reel line where big fish are expected or hook sizes 18-22 to 20" 1-1½lb test hooklength

GENTLE FLOW

small shots spread evenly - nos. 4-6 or 8 - 'shirt button style'

nos. 8 or 10

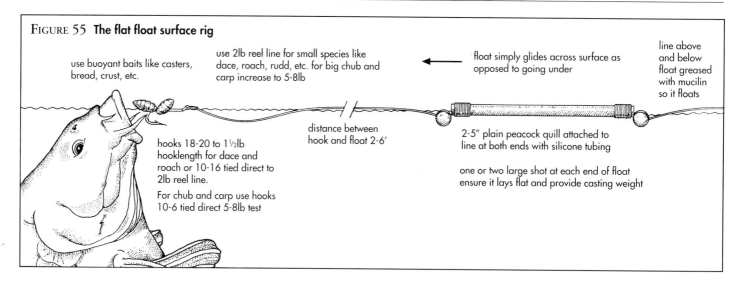

FIGURE 55 **The flat float surface rig**

use buoyant baits like casters, bread, crust, etc.

use 2lb reel line for small species like dace, roach, rudd, etc. for big chub and carp increase to 5-8lb

float simply glides across surface as opposed to going under

line above and below float greased with mucilin so it floats

hooks 18-20 to 1½lb hooklength for dace and roach or 10-16 tied direct to 2lb reel line.

For chub and carp use hooks 10-6 tied direct 5-8lb test

distance between hook and float 2-6'

2-5" plain peacock quill attached to line at both ends with silicone tubing

one or two large shot at each end of float ensure it lays flat and provide casting weight

SURFACE-CONTROLLER FISHING

The flat-float surface rig

To catch small species, such as dace, roach, chub and rudd when they are feeding from the surface, in both still and flowing water, use a small waggler or plain 2-5in section of unpainted peacock quill.

Instead of locking the bulk shot around its base, however, distribute the shot evenly (just one or two large shot) at each end so that the float lies flat and glides effortlessly across the surface when a fish bites instead of going under (fig. 55).

· The line should be greased with mucilin below and above the float for several yards so that any bow formed by wind drift can periodically be lifted up and mended.

All *floating baits (Baits - freshwater)* from casters to breadcrust can be loose-fed well 'upwind' or 'upstream' with the aid of a catapult.

PRESENTING FLOATING BAITS USING A LOADED SURFACE CONTROLLER

This is one of the most successful techniques for catching chub and carp in both still and flowing water, and relies on a self-cocking, 'loaded' surface controller such as the tenpin (*Floats*), which can place even tiny floaters accurately over 50yd out, or be trotted downstream to chub occupying awkward lies. In reverse to all other sliding floats, the ring of a controller is at the top, with a small bead and a sliding stop knot on the hook side of the float. This is to enable a chub or carp to suck down the floater and make off while feeling only minimal resistance, because it does not have to tow the float under. The line merely runs out through the float's tip ring while the float bobs gently.

As can be seen from fig. 56, baits can be side-hooked or threaded on to a hair rig, with a slither of black foam along the hook

shank to help it float horizontally, in order to fool super-wary fish. Hold the rod at all times, periodically lifting the line (treated with mucilin) to straighten any bow caused by wind drift, and watch the hook-bait like a hawk. Observation with binoculars of the way in which carp approach the floating bait often provides clues as to how to entice them to suck it down. Some can be seen to shy away from the hooklink long before they reach the bait, for instance, in which case replace the stop knot with a tiny swivel, to which a finer-diameter hooklink can be tied. A heavy hook can be replaced by a lighter model in a smaller size. The actual size of, for instance, dog-biscuit floaters can be reduced, or several tiny ones can be sleeved on to a long hair. Improvisation and an open mind allow you to obtain the best results from this fascinating technique.

The clear, silicone-rubber 'bait band' is a quick, easy and most effective device for

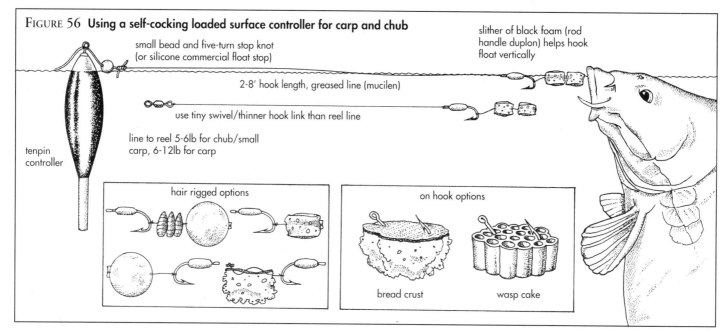

FIGURE 56 **Using a self-cocking loaded surface controller for carp and chub**

small bead and five-turn stop knot (or silicone commercial float stop)

slither of black foam (rod handle duplon) helps hook float vertically

2-8' hook length, greased line (mucilen)

use tiny swivel/thinner hook link than reel line

line to reel 5-6lb for chub/small carp, 6-12lb for carp

tenpin controller

hair rigged options

on hook options

bread crust

wasp cake

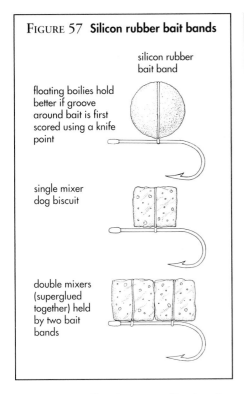

FIGURE 57 Silicon rubber bait bands

silicon rubber
bait band

floating boilies hold
better if groove
around bait is first
scored using a knife
point

single mixer
dog biscuit

double mixers
(superglued
together) held
by two bait
bands

mounting small, mixer-type, floating dog biscuits and for presenting peanuts, tiger nuts and boilies 'pop-up' style. Simply pierce the indent with the hook point on the flat side of the tab and sleeve it along the hook shank. Then ease a mixer into

the band, which ensures that the hook is presented directly below the floater (fig. 57). For a larger mouthful, rig two mixers, each held by a separate bait band, and join together with a squeeze of superglue.

ANCHORED FLOATER RIGS

There are situations, owing to the position of lily beds, weeds, snags or fallen trees, or because carp will only bite in a particular area, when a drifted floating bait does not work. The bait has to be anchored over a particular spot.

As can be seen from fig. 58, there are two ways of achieving this. With the sub-float, (58A), simply sleeve a clear (Drennan-type) plastic sub-float (or small, black, through-the-middle pike slider) on to the bomb link. This will then float up and present the hooklink (plus floater) in any fixed location, held steady by the 1½oz bomb. Sink all of the line between rig and rod tip and set the rod in two rests on a buzzer/indicator set-up, keeping your eyes glued to the floater for carp that may suck it in without moving off and registering a bite.

When properly executed (far easier from swims in high-banked gravel pits) the

'beachcaster rig' (47B) allows very natural presentation of the floater with little hooklength on the water surface to scare super-intelligent carp. The rig consists of a heavy, 2-3oz bomb and a large black, bulbous, through-the-middle sliding pike or sea float, set with a bead and stop knot to a couple of feet deeper than the swim. After casting, the hooklink should only just dangle the floater on to the surface film. Use a *four-turn water knot (Knots)* for the hooklink, which may be of a finer diameter than the 8-10lb reel line.

Support the rod up high on a beachcasting monopod or a pair of long telescopic rod rests and tighten up to the pike float. Then keep your eye on the floater and strike immediately it is sucked in, before the carp feels resistance and rejects it.

SLIDING-FLOAT FISHING FOR PREDATORS

For chub, perch, zander and pike.

The versatility of the *sliding float (Floats)* coupled with the right rig for the job, permits presentation of both livebaits and deadbaits at any depth band from 2ft below the surface down to 20-30ft and more.

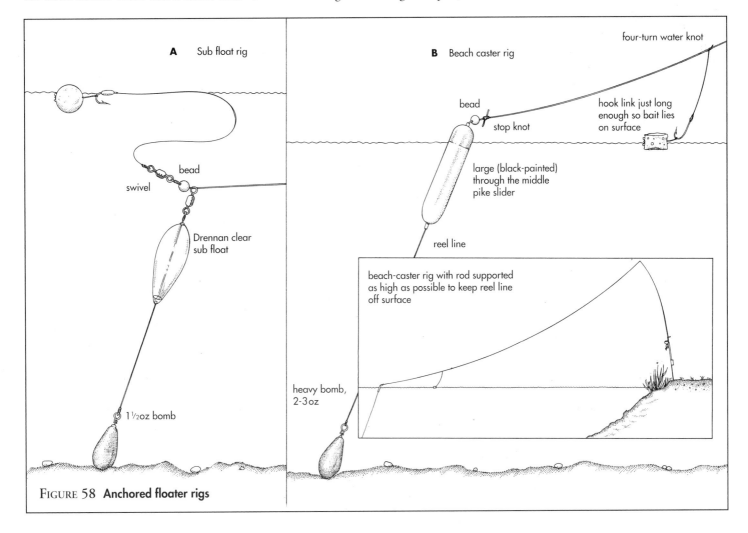

A Sub float rig

B Beach caster rig

four-turn water knot

bead

stop knot

hook link just long
enough so bait lies
on surface

large (black-painted)
through the middle
pike slider

reel line

bead

swivel

Drennan clear
sub float

beach-caster rig with rod supported
as high as possible to keep reel line
off surface

heavy bomb,
2-3oz

1½oz bomb

FIGURE 58 Anchored floater rigs

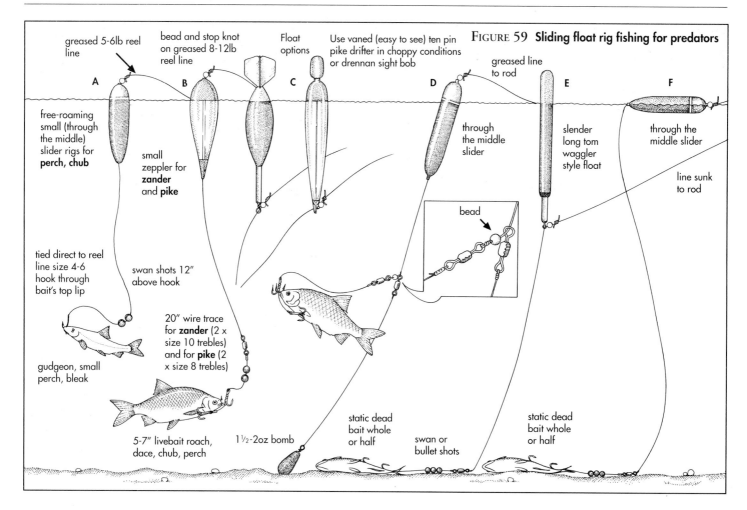

FIGURE 59 **Sliding float rig fishing for predators**

To accomplish this, tie a sliding *stop knot* (Knots) on to the reel line above the float, with a bead between knot and float, at the desired depth (fig. 59).

Figs. 59A and 59B both show small, through-the-middle sliders (for close-range work), used in 59A for chub and perch with a reel line of 5-6lb test with a single eyed hook tied direct, while 59B is intended for zander and pike, with a heavier reel line of 8-12lb and a 20in 15lb-test, alasticum wire trace holding a pair of semi-barbless trebles. In both rigs swan shots are pinched on 12in above the bait to keep it working down in the depth band at which the float has been set.

It is of paramount importance that the reel line above the stop knot is treated with mucilin so that it floats high on the surface. Even small baits can then cover and consequently search large areas of water. If the line between float and rod tip is sunk, the bait cannot go anywhere.

When fishing for either pike or zander at a distance, particularly if the surface is choppy, use one of the floats in fig. 59C: either a tenpin vaned drifter or a Drennan sight-bob waggler. Both are presented waggler style with the line passing through the bottom ring only, with a bead between

the float and a sliding stop knot.

To search a particular area thoroughly using a livebait, especially in deep or coloured water, use the running-paternoster float rig as shown in fig. 59D. Utilize a buoyant, through-the-middle slider stopped slightly deeper than the swim, with a 1½-2oz bomb on a separate swivel link. The bait then works only at the predetermined depth (equal to the length of the bomb link) above the bottom. Keep as much line off the surface as possible and keep the reel's bale arm open, with a loop of line retained beneath either a run-clip or an elastic band over the rod handle, in case a big fish happens along and screams off with the bait.

To present a static deadbait on the bottom, figs. 59E and 59F are both proven methods. For windy conditions and for distance fishing when wind drift and sub-surface tow in still waters can prove troublesome, the rig in 59E is best. The slender, loaded long tom, waggler-style sliding float is attached through the bottom ring with three swan shots or a small bullet on the line immediately above the trace swivel and set a little overdepth. As with all wagglers the line is sunk between float and rod tip (keep a small bottle of neat washing-up liq-

uid handy for dabbing on to the spool), thus overcoming the draw from sub-surface tow and wind drift. For close-range fishing and when presenting a deadbait in the lee of the boat or bank, use a through-the-middle slider as in 59F, with two or three swan shot pinched on to the wire trace just below the swivel.

DRIFT-FLOAT FISHING FOR PREDATORS

An exciting method for pike and zander is to use the force of the wind plus a vaned drifting float to work either a livebait or a deadbait well downwind from an anchored boat or from the bank. You can use a standard drift-float rig as in fig. 60 or go for the improved Dave Batten rig in fig. 37.

Either way, the reel line needs to be well greased so that it floats high on the surface film. As can be seen from fig. 59, a bullet or three or four swan shot keeps the bait at the desired depth, with the line attached at the very top of the stem via a pull-out eye. This means that when the bait is taken, a firm strike (made after winding until constant pressure is felt) converts the drifter into a waggler that 'folds' (because the eye pulls out) on impact for a resistance-free retrieve. Remember that deadbaits should

FIGURE 60 Drift float-fishing for predators

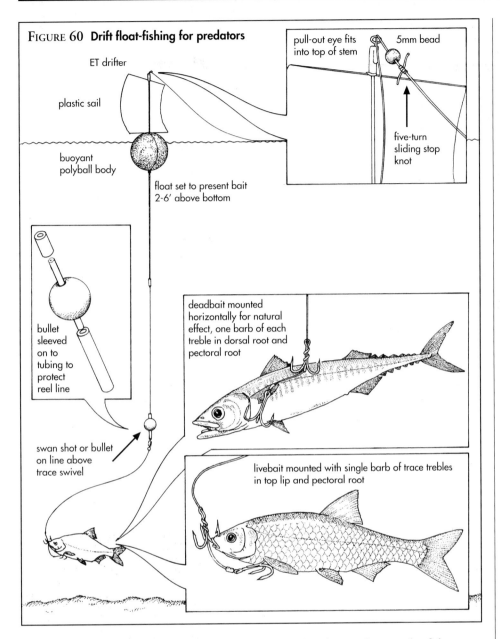

ET drifter

plastic sail

buoyant
polyball body

float set to present bait
2-6' above bottom

pull-out eye fits
into top of stem

5mm bead

five-turn
sliding stop
knot

bullet
sleeved
on to
tubing to
protect
reel line

swan shot or bullet
on line above
trace swivel

deadbait mounted
horizontally for natural
effect, one barb of each
treble in dorsal root and
pectoral root

livebait mounted with single barb of trace trebles
in top lip and pectoral root

be mounted horizontally for maximum authenticity, with the lower treble set into the pectoral root and the upper firmly embedded into the dorsal (fig. 60). Keep the reel's bale arm open and allow line to peel from the open spool as the wind 'sails' the rig downwind into virgin territory.

FYKE NET

Often called a Dutch fyke net, this extremely long net is not dissimilar to a keep net. It has inner steel hoops, and is purpose-built for catching eels and being staked out along the bottom of lakes and river beds.

To guide eels into the mouth of the net, a length of side-netting stretching out from the shallow margins connects with the main entrance. Once inside, the eels worm their way through an inner funnel into a chamber of no return (fig. 61). Other species, particularly tench, bream and even pike, are regularly trapped in fyke nets, and are released by the eel netsmen. A netting licence is required from the National Rivers Authority.

GAFF

Although gaffs are still used in freshwater by salmon fishermen, their days are over for landing pike now that large, strong-framed landing nets made from soft, knotless material are readily available. Even the majority of sea fishermen who once wielded gaffs now prefer to net their quarry when possible for catch-and-release.

However, there are certain species, such as big cod, ling, conger eels and big sharks, and tropical species with horrendous teeth such as barracuda, that are best gaffed to minimize the chance of injury to the angler. Some skippers prefer to lift even big congers up to the gunnel on a small, strong, narrow-gape gaff in order to unhook them carefully - or cut the trace - and release them quickly.

Salmon-type gaffs are available in both standard and telescopic models, and can be clipped on to a belt or shoulder strap. They consist of a chromium-plated, steel (barbless) hook, with a gape of 2-3in

FIGURE 61 Fyke net

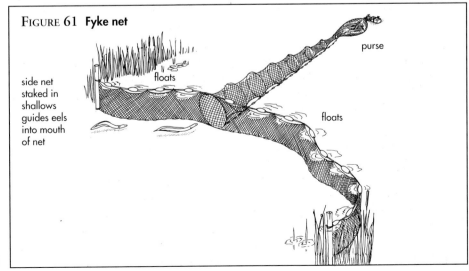

side net
staked in
shallows
guides eels
into mouth
of net

floats

purse

floats

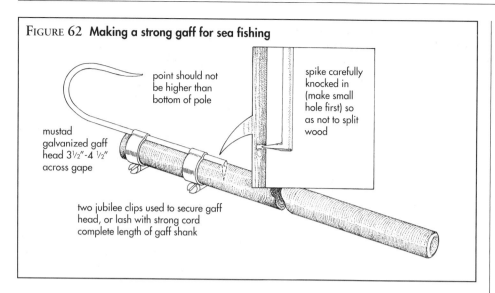

FIGURE 62 **Making a strong gaff for sea fishing**

point should not
be higher than
bottom of pole

mustad
galvanized gaff
head 3½"-4½"
across gape

spike carefully
knocked in
(make small
hole first) so
as not to split
wood

two jubilee clips used to secure gaff
head, or lash with strong cord
complete length of gaff shank

protected by a sleeve or cover. Chromium-plated, steel gaff-heads with a ³⁄₈th BSF standard thread are also available.

The best type of gaff for sea fishing is made by carefully knocking a galvanized, spiked gaff-head (the top ½in is bent at right angles as an alternative to a screw thread) into a strong, hardwood handle 6ft long and securing it along the shank with two jubilee clips. Alternatively, it can be lashed on with strong cord (fig. 62).

The flying gaff has been designed for the rigours of shark fishing when creatures up to 500lb may need to be landed. It consists of a strong, wide-gape gaff-head that slots on to the end of a stout pole. A long length of strong nylon rope is connected to the gaff head. When the gaff head is pulled into the shark with the pole it immediately flies clear and you are attached to the shark by the gaff head and rope only.

GARFISH
(*Belone belone*)

British record: 3lb (1kg 368g)

Coloured a metallic greeny-blue along the upper flanks and back, with shimmering silver sides and belly, plus a long, tooth-laden beak with a slightly protruding lower jaw, it is difficult to confuse the garfish with any other British sea species. It characteristically catapults its long, slender, elongated body high into the air when it is hooked, and it feeds on tiny fish and crustaceans in addition to thin slithers of raw steak and fish. Reproduction occurs in coastal waters during May and June. The

eggs have long filaments that adhere to floating algae at the surface.

HABITAT AND DISTRIBUTION
A migratory species that arrives inshore around the British Isles during the late spring, it regularly frequents harbour piers and rocky outcrops.

TECHNIQUES
Float fishing in harbours and off the rocks.

GARFISH, SHORT-BILLED
(*Belone svetovidovi*)

British record: 13¾oz (390g)

This species is similar in features and colouration, but with a slightly shorter beak and comparatively smaller teeth than *Belone belone*, the garfish regularly caught around the British Isles. It is occasionally caught from south-western waters.

GILTHEAD BREAM
(*Sparus aurata*)

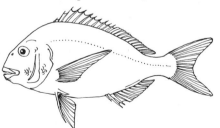

British record: 9lb 15¼oz (4kg 515g)

Although a Mediterranean sea bream, this deep-bodied, powerful shoal fish is very occasionally taken from British south-

western waters. Its name comes from a golden stripe running across the forehead between the eyes. It is blue-grey along the back, fusing into silver on the flanks and underbelly.

It has the classic bream arrangement of fins, with spined rays on the first half of the long, continuous dorsal fin and at the start of the anal fin. The pectoral fin is long and pointed and the tail forked.

It has strong, curved teeth at the front of its powerful jaws and flattened teeth, designed for crunching molluscs and crustaceans, at the sides. It breeds in deep water during the winter months.

GLOVE, UNHOOKING

Once a pike has been netted and deposited on the bank or on the bottom of the boat ready for unhooking, the greatest aid to the pike fisherman is an industrial-type rubber glove, worn on the left hand if the angler is right handed.

Keeping an eye on where the treble hooks are situated, slip all four fingers gently into the pike's left gill slit and clamp the thumb down hard against the forefinger. You can hold up the pike's head with this grip, whereupon its mouth will conveniently open for easy unhooking. It is then a simple case of removing the trebles using *artery*

See how John grips the pike (using a gloved left hand) using four fingers into its left gill opening, then clamping the thumb down on the outside.

forceps. Use the same grip for lifting modest-sized pike from the water if a landing net is not at hand, or if the loose trebles are liable to catch in the mesh and create tangles. Be careful of flying treble hooks at all times, easing them out with forceps while the pike is still in the water if in doubt.

The Normark Fillet Glove, made from fine, chain-mail-type stainless-steel, 'newtwist' yarn is absolutely perfect for gripping and unhooking pike, combining the safety of steel flex (you can run a sharp filleting knife across your hand without harm) with the comfort of man-made fibres. In addition, the glove is machine-washable and fits either hand, so you need only one. It is also an excellent general glove for the sea fisherman.

GOBY, BLACK
(*Gobius niger*)

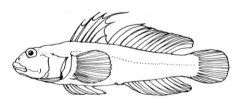

British record: 2¼oz (63g)

The black goby is common around all British and European shorelines and estuaries, although it is rarely taken on rod and line due to its tiny size. Like all gobies, it has fan-like membranes to each pelvic fin, which help it adhere to the bottom, and two dorsal fins, the first being high with stiff rays, and a rounded tail. It is dirty brown all over with dark brown markings along the back and sides. It lays a mat of eggs on the bottom during the summer, which the male guards until they hatch. It feeds upon tiny fish and crustaceans.

GOBY, GIANT
(*Gobius cobitis*)

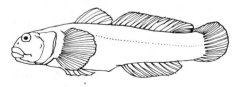

British record: 6¾oz (190g)

Thicker set than other species, and with a big head, the giant goby is by far the largest European goby, although it only ever reaches 10-12in long even when fully mature. The giant goby is marbled in shades of grey, brown and olive with darker markings along the flanks. It has the typical goby fin arrangement with a lighter rim around the dorsals and anal fin and a rounded tail. It breeds in the late spring, laying its eggs beneath stones. It feeds on crustaceans and algae off rocks, and loves rocky pools.

GOBY, ROCK
(*Gobius paganellus*)

British record: 1¼oz (35g)

Along with the marine stickleback, this is one of the smallest sea fish an angler is likely to catch on rod and line. It has the typical goby arrangement of fins, with membranes edging the pelvic fins, a thick tail root and a large, rounded tail. The short first dorsal has stiff rays. It prefers to live along rocky shorelines and is thus coloured in mottled, camouflaged shades of brown. It feeds on crustaceans and small fish, and reproduces in the late spring.

GOLDFISH
(*Carassius auratus*)

Average size: 2-6oz
Mega specimen: over 1lb
British record: none

Smooth, carp-like, fully-scaled body and a small, slightly upturned mouth. Its lips are level, without barbels. Owing to the breeding of fancy goldfish for the ornamental fish trade, colouration can vary enormously from the classic reddish-gold to yellow, white, and all kinds of combinations from the goggle-eyed blackmoor to Cambridge blue shubunkins. Shubunkins and other variants may be partly scaled or have scales of several different colours. Unlike the crucian carp, with which it can interbreed, the goldfish has a concave dorsal fin with a ser-

rated first spine, and often sports a fancy, fan-like tail. Some have triple tails.

In the wild its food consists of aquatic insect life, zooplankton and soft plant tissue, but it is easily weaned on to flaked or pelleted commercial fish foods. Reproduction occurs in the summer, the eggs being distributed over soft weeds or around marginal grasses. The fry are often drab, changing colour during their first two years.

HABITAT AND DISTRIBUTION
It prefers small, warm-water ponds, pits and lakes, particularly those containing lily beds and soft weeds. Common throughout the British Isles in garden ponds, it also thrives in the wild in isolated natural ponds, especially those with a dense weed growth that protects it from predatory birds such as the heron.

TECHNIQUES
It is rarely fished for, but accepts maggots and punched bread.
Freshwater floatfishing techniques - Lift method; Waggler fishing; Pole fishing.

GRAVEL PITS

Although gravel pits are excavated solely for the purpose of extracting gravel and sand for the building industry, mature pits with a variety of well-established flora and fauna hold the key to the future of freshwater fishing within the British Isles, especially in England.

As river systems slowly decline due to the demand for water from agriculture and commerce, fishermen will rely more and more on the wealth of sand and gravel workings, both old and new, for quality fishing. Indeed, angling clubs who once rented long stretches of river now use their membership fees to obtain long leases on gravel pits or to buy them freehold. It is the only way to ensure that the sport cannot be affected by the actions of other parties.

Of course, not all pits fill up with water once the minerals have been removed, and these are usually back-filled with household waste by the local council contractors (fig. 63A). An excavation needs to be within the local river's water table (63B) to ensure that it will always hold sufficient water and, once landscaped and stocked, become a worthwhile fishery.

Most pits are dug dry so that heavy machinery can remove the gravel-bearing

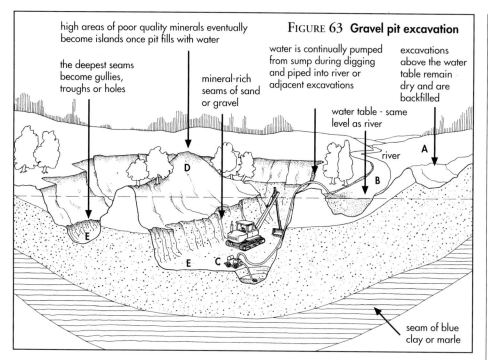

FIGURE 63 Gravel pit excavation

high areas of poor quality minerals eventually become islands once pit fills with water

the deepest seams become gullies, troughs or holes

mineral-rich seams of sand or gravel

water is continually pumped from sump during digging and piped into river or adjacent excavations

excavations above the water table remain dry and are backfilled

water table - same level as river

river

seam of blue clay or marle

seams with accuracy. The water that would otherwise seep in and fill the site (up to the water table level 63B) therefore needs to be pumped out, constantly, either into the adjacent river or another pit (63C). The places where the richest and deepest seams are removed become the deep troughs, gullies and holes (63E). Areas of poor-quality minerals and seams of clay or marle are not removed, and eventually become shallow bars, plateau, or even islands if they are above the level of the water table (63D) once excavation ceases and the pit is allowed to fill up from the water table. Some gravel pits are dug wet, which means that during excavation water is not continually being pumped out. The sand and gravel can then only be excavated with the shoe of a dragline crane, resulting in more even bottom contours.

An understanding of how gravel pits are excavated can really help your fishing, especially when you are investigating a new and previously unfished pit. Preferably, try to get out on the water in a dinghy and investigate the bottom with an echo-sounder (*Fish-finders*). If this is not permitted, spend some time viewing the visible features, such as islands and shallow

lily-clad plateau, through binoculars during the summer months for signs of fish activity, or spend time during the winter months accurately plummeting the bottom for a mental picture of the sub-surface layout. Chuck-it and chance-it tactics rarely produce results in gravel pits, and one of the most effective plummet-while-fishing techniques is to explore a new pit using a heavy spoon. It can be cast distances of 60-70yd and counted down to the bottom on each cast, allowing about one second per foot of descent. If there is any soft bottom weed the treble will certainly bring back the odd sprig. So in addition to a mental picture of bottom contours and features, an idea of actual bottom structure can be gained by casting repeatedly in a grid-searching fashion. A detailed drawn outline

of the pit with the depths written in as you fish will stand you in good stead for future occasions. And remember that no two gravel pits are ever dug exactly the same. Each has a special identity, character and eco-system.

During the summer months all species tend to spread out, often over the shallowest bars and plateau. In these areas the water is warmest and there is a rich larder of natural food with protection overhead from surface plants such as broad-leafed potomogeton, amphibious bistort, dwarf pond-lily, or the large-leafed lilies such as *nuphar lutea* (the common yellow variety) and cultivated lilies. Tench, rudd and carp are attracted to these areas like bees to a honeypot. But when temperatures start to drop rapidly in the autumn following a few hard frosts, and the protective canopy overhead rots away, most species retreat into deeper water. Find perch, pike or zander in a deep gulley and their food - small shoal species such as roach or rudd packed tightly together for protection - will not be far away. It is no coincidence, therefore, that the best areas for catching a bag of roach invariably also produce the most, and often the largest, pike. In pits that contain a maze of troughs or gullies shelving steeply away from shallow bars, concentrate on the points where one gully meets another. These crossroads are regularly used by bream, tench and carp, which have favourite feeding and patrol routes along certain troughs or gullies. Wind direction, barometric pressure, water temperature and especially water clarity, of course, also have a direct bearing on fish movements (*Water temperatures*).

Though created through excavation of stone and sand deposits and initially a scar on the landscape, once fully matured, gravel pits hold the key to controllable freshwater fishing within the British Isles, now that river systems are on the decline through water abstraction and pollutants from industry and farming.

GRAYLING

(Thymallus thymallus)

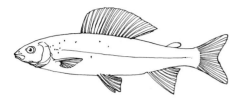

Average size: 6-14oz
Mega specimen: over 2lb
British record: 4lb 3oz (1kg 899g)

The grayling has a long, firm, wiry body with small flat scales and a distinct smell of thyme. The head is neat and conical with a protruding upper jaw and large jaw hinge. Colouration is dark grey-pewter along the back, fusing into lighter flanks tinged with mauve and dotted with a dozen or two small black spots, mostly towards the front half of the fish. There is a horizontal brownish line between the root of the pelvic fin and the pectoral fin and similar markings under the throat.

The grayling has a tiny, rayless adipose fin, a deeply forked tail and a sail-like dorsal fin with colourful lines of blue-black blotches between the rays and a fringe of scarlet on top. Males have huge dorsal fins, almost twice as long as the females', which is more squared when held open.

Its food consists of crustaceans such as shrimps and all forms of aquatic insect life, plus small molluscs, fish eggs and small fish. Reproduction occurs during the early spring over a gravelly bottom, and the eggs hatch some 20-25 days later. The grayling is disliked by many trout and salmon anglers because of its appetite for fish eggs and fry.

With its sail-like dorsal fin, the chance of confusing the grayling with other freshwater species is unlikely. It thrives in fast-flowing rivers and readily accepts long-trotted worms or maggots best presented beneath a squat, wide-tipped float.

HABITAT AND DISTRIBUTION

Though present in isolated stream-fed stillwaters, grayling are inhabitants of clear, pure, fast-flowing gravel and sandy bottomed streams and rivers. It exists in large numbers in Scotland and northern England, parts of Wales and in many of the southern chalk streams in the counties of Hampshire and Berkshire. It is absent from Ireland but common throughout Europe.

TECHNIQUES

Freshwater floatfishing techniques - Long trotting, Stretpegging; Fly fishing - Dry fly, Nymph, Wetfly.

Spawning

Larvae

Immature fish

GRAYLING

GROUNDBAITS - FRESHWATER

BREADCRUMBS

The universal bulk ingredient of most proprietary groundbaits, breadcrumbs can be purchased in bulk or in 2-3lb bags and in fine, medium or coarse form. Alternatively, you can make your own by crunching up dried or toasted bread scraps.

Various binders can be added to the dampened crumbs. If you want the bait to zoom straight down to the bottom, add maize meal, or even pearl barley and flaked maize, plus hook-bait samples. For species such as tench and bream, you can spice up plain breadcrumbs with dried or liquid molasses or very fine trout-fry crumb, a rearing food with a distinct, fishy aroma. A small quantity of brewers' yeast also adds aroma, particularly if the mix is left in a bucket to ferment for a few days. Fresh blood, obtainable from a butcher, is an effective additive for tench, in particular. Work on the basis of around 1pt of blood to a bucket (2-3 gal) of groundbait.

Open-ended plastic or cage swimfeeders should be filled with plain, medium to coarse crumbs, only slightly dampened so that they explode when the feeder touches bottom. To these, add a small quantity of hook-bait - maggots, casters, sweetcorn or stewed wheat and so on. To ensure that the mix breaks up quickly into a cloud, or goes straight down when squeezed lightly and thrown out by hand, match fishermen put their breadcrumb mix through an ⅛in riddle (as used for maggots and casters) to eradicate any hard, stodgy lumps, before adding a handful of hook-bait samples.

MASHED BREAD

For this you need bread that is at least five or six days old, preferably older. Put the bread in a large bucket and cover with water. After a couple of hours, strain off the excess water and mash the bread into a fine pulp by squeezing it firmly between your fingers. For roach and chub fishing in fast rivers, when you are using bread flake, crust, or even cheese paste on the hook, mould the mixture firmly into 'golf balls'. For bream, however, stiffen the mash with maize meal, coarse breadcrumbs or any proprietary groundbait, adding fragments of the intended hook-bait. For use in exceptionally deep, fast rivers, bind the mixture with flaked maize (plus hook-bait samples) and/or pearl barley and mould it into 'cricket balls'.

LIQUIDIZED BREAD

Remove the crust from fresh white bread, break it into chunks and pop them in a liquidizer. Switch on and you have a superb fine-particle groundbait for use with all forms of bread hook-baits, particularly *punched bread (Baits - freshwater)*.

CEREAL

In bulk groundbaits breadcrumbs can be replaced by various types of meal - bran, maize meal, layers' meal and so on. These are obtainable from the local corn store or pet shop and are well worth experimenting with.

GROUNDBAITS - SEA

RUBBY-DUBBY

This smelly concoction is used to attract sharks to a drifting boat and consists of oily-fleshed sea fish, such as herrings, mackerel, pilchards and so on, chopped up small (an old steel mincer is handy), plus extra bottled fish oil and a few handfuls of bran. Some fresh blood (obtainable from a butcher) is a most welcome ingredient. The ingredients are put in a large plastic tub and mashed mortar-and-pestle style with a length of wood until well mixed. Although an unpleasant job, it is well worth the effort of making up a large batch at the start of a day's shark fishing.

Once the boat is over the sharking grounds, with the engines cut to commence the drift, a generous helping of rubby-dubby is poured into an old onion or carrot sack and tied over the side of the boat so that the motion of the waves slaps it regularly against the water surface, creating a massive oil slick accompanied by a steady stream of groundbait particles, which drift down away from the boat through the deep blue void. Every hour or so a fresh batch of rubby-dubby is added to the bag. A rubby-dubby bag can also be tied to the anchor chain when boat fishing at anchor.

SHIRVY

This is a scaled-down rubby-dubby mix of finely chopped or minced meat and oily fish, to which bran, bottled fish oil and fresh blood is added. Once mashed up in a plastic bucket, the shirvy should have the consistency of chilli con carne. It is propelled out with a large dessertspoon (throwing it out by hand is not recommended) tied to a 24in length of stout garden cane. It is a fabulous groundbait for species such as mullet, garfish, small pollack and coalfish, when freshwater float tackle is being used to enjoy the delights of small sea species from harbour walls, rocks or jetties.

GUDGEON
(*Gobio gobio*)

Average size: 4-5in long, up to 1oz
Mega specimen: over 2½oz
British record: 5oz (141g)

GUDGEON

Hh

This small shoal fish has a barbel-like shape and snout, with an underslung mouth sprouting a single whisker or barbel from each corner. Barbel have four whiskers and loach six. Its blotchy, speckled body is dark pewter on top, bluish on the upper flanks, fusing into a silvery-white belly. The forked tail is heavily speckled with tiny dark markings, as is the dorsal fin. It has a distinct dotted lateral line.

It is an aggressive bottom-feeder, pursuing minute aquatic insect life, crustaceans, annelid worms and so on. It reproduces in the late spring, the eggs being distributed over gravel or willow moss, where they hatch 10-12 days later.

HABITAT AND DISTRIBUTION

Gudgeon are most prolific in, and colonize, sandy and gravel runs in rivers both big and small, although they also fare well in stillwaters - gravel pits in particular. They are common throughout the British Isles except for Scotland.

TECHNIQUES

Freshwater floatfishing techniques - Stickfloat fishing; Stretpegging; Ledgering techniques - Quivertipping; Pole fishing.

GURNARD, GREY
(*Eutrigla gurnardus*)

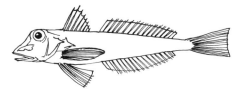

British record: 2lb 7oz (1kg 105g)

The grey gurnard has a large, angled head with a sharply tapering, slender body and short, fan-like pectoral fins, the first three rays of which are separate and used as food-locating probes while crawling along the sea bed. Two dorsal fins, the first of which has a distinctive, large, black spot, immediately distinguish the grey from other gurnards. The colouration is warm grey-brown along the back with a tinge of dull red to the sides and often covered in small white spots. It feeds on small fish and crustaceans, and prefers broken ground of rocks, sand and mud. It reproduces in deep water during the spring.

GURNARD, RED
(*Aspitrigla cuculus*)

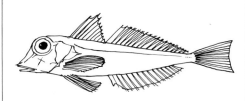

British record: 2lb 8½oz (1kg 148g)

This thick-set gurnard has a distinctive row of plate-like scales along its lateral line and a large, angled bony head. It has the usual gurnard fin formation, including two dorsals, short spines protrude from each side of the snout and it uses the first three rays of its pectoral fin as locating probes as it swims slowly along, almost crawling over the sea bed. Less colourful overall than the tub gurnard, it is bright red along the back, fusing into paler tones along the flanks.

It feeds on small fish and crustaceans over mixed ground of sand, mud and rocks, and reproduces during the summer.

GURNARD, STREAKED
(*Triglorporus lastoviza*)

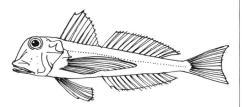

British record: 1lb 6½oz (637g)

Thicker set than the other gurnards, and with a large, blunt head, the streaked gurnard has the usual fin formation of two dorsal fins with separated lower rays in its pectoral fins for probing - or almost walking - along the sea bed. Its fan-like pectorals are warm grey with large blue spots. Its entire body is covered with ridges of skin originating at the lateral line, and it is dull red along the back with paler sides.

It feeds on crustaceans, frequenting areas of sand, mud and rough, rocky ground, and reproduces during the summer.

GURNARD, TUB OR YELLOW
(*Trigla lucerna*)

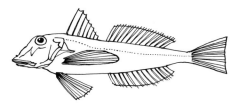

British record: 12lb 3oz (5kg 528g)

By far the largest of the gurnards to be caught from European waters, the tub, or yellow, gurnard, frequents sandy, muddy bottoms in small groups, feeding on small, bottom-living fish, molluscs and crustaceans. It is easily distinguished from other gurnards by its distinctive, bright, pinky-red back and upper flanks and golden-cream undersides, two dorsal fins and a squared tail. The top sides of its large, fan-like pectoral fins are bright blue, spotted in white or green, with a red band around the edge. It has the typical steeply angled, bony gurnard head, and the lower three rays of its pectoral fin are separate from main fin, and used as food-locating probes as it crawls slowly along the sea bed. It reproduces during the summer.

GWYNIAD

A whitefish that lives in Lake Bala, Wales. It is also called the *vendace*.

HACKLE

See *Artificial flies.*

HADDOCK
(*Melanogrammus aeglefinus*)

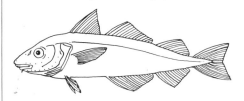

Average size: 2-3lb
Mega specimen: over 8lb
British record: 13lb 11¼oz (6kg 215g)

This member of the cod family, all of which are distinguishable by their soft-ray fins, has three dorsal fins, two anal fins, a forked tail and a distinctive dark spot immediately above its pectoral fin. The head is small with a large eye and a short barbel on the chin. The upper jaw noticeably overhangs the lower. Colouration varies between dark green and brown along the back, fusing into lighter flanks with a silvery tinge. It has an unmistakable, black lateral line and a white belly.

It lives close to the bottom, feeding upon crustaceans, molluscs, brittlestars, worms and small fish. It reproduces in the spring, the buoyant eggs drifting near the surface until they hatch.

HABITAT AND DISTRIBUTION

Localized in its distribution around the British Isles, it is most common around the west coast of Scotland and off Northern Ireland. It often lives in large shoals in deep water over areas of rough or broken ground.

TECHNIQUES

Drift fishing; Downtide boat fishing; Feathering.

HADDOCK, NORWAY

(*Sebastes viviparus*)

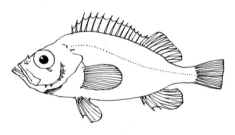

British record: 1lb 13½oz (836g)

Not a true haddock, nor a member of the cod family, this small, stocky, perch-like fish is distinctly rosy-red on the back, fusing into lighter sides. The inside of its large mouth is pink and the eye large. Its long, continuous dorsal fin consists of strong spines for the first half and soft rays for the remainder. There are three strong spines at the leading edge of the anal fin, followed by soft rays.

It prefers to live in the colder, more northerly seas around the British Isles, in deep water over rough ground. It feeds on small fish and crustaceans, and gives birth to live young.

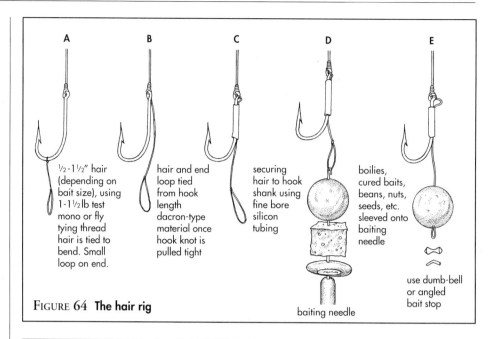

A B C D E

½-1½" hair (depending on bait size), using 1-1½lb test mono or fly tying thread hair is tied to bend. Small loop on end.

hair and end loop tied from hook length dacron-type material once hook knot is pulled tight

securing hair to hook shank using fine bore silicon tubing

boilies, cured baits, beans, nuts, seeds, etc. sleeved onto baiting needle

use dumb-bell or angled bait stop

baiting needle

FIGURE 64 **The hair rig**

HAIR RIG

Devised and used originally by carp fishermen in order to induce more confident takes from super-wary fish that have been caught before, the hair rig is a simple yet devastatingly effective trick for making fish believe that they are sucking in only the bait, because it appears unattached (fig. 64).

But because the bait is presented off the hook, on a fine hair (hence the terminology), it is confidently sucked in together with the hook. The hair rig can be used to catch other cyprinid species - tench, chub and barbel, in particular - as well as carp, and is most useful for clear-water, crafty-fish situations.

The hair itself can be made from fine monofilament, or fly-tying thread with a small loop at the end (64A), or as a combination of the hook knot, using any of the soft, dacron-type, hook-length materials now available from specialist tackle shops (64B) (*Lines*). The hair can hang from the eye of the hook, or, better still, be fixed firmly to the shank using fine-bore silicone tubing (64C).

The hair can vary between ½in to 1½in long, depending on the bait size, and virtually any bait can be presented singly or as a string - meat or cheese cubes, casters, boilies, cat and dog biscuits and all particle baits such as peanuts, stewed wheat or beans (*Baits, freshwater - Particles*, fig. 22) - and by fishing a floating controller (fig. 56).

The bait is sleeved on to a baiting needle, then carefully hooked around the loop (64D), and gently slipped on to the hair. A tiny dumb-bell or angled bait-stop prevents the bait slipping off (64E). To make

Eggs and fry

HADDOCK

Spawning and development

HALIBUT

a hole through really hard particles such as tiger nuts, or through floating dog biscuits, which easily crumble, use a specialized nut-drill.

Most anglers use the hair in conjunction with a bolt rig in order to make the carp panic away with the bait and thus hook itself (*Ledgering techniques - Bolt rig ledgering*). This ruse works equally well when freelining, quivertip ledgering and floating controller fishing, when float fishing all the pre-mentioned baits. The *lift method,* the *lift-bolt rig* combination, and *stretpegging* (*Freshwater floatfishing techniques*) are particularly well suited to hair-rig presentation.

HAKE
(*Merluccius merluccius*)

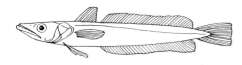

Average size: 5-8lb
Mega specimen: over 12-15lb
British record: 25lb 5½oz (11kg 494g)

The hake is similar in appearance to the ling, but has a much larger head and strong jaws holding large, curved teeth. The lower jaw protrudes. The body is slender and slate grey along the back, fusing into lighter sides and a white belly. The gill cavity and the inside of the cavernous mouth are distinctly black. Of two dorsal fins, the first is short and triangular and the second long. The tail is square, the anal fin is the same length as the second dorsal fin, and the lateral line is straight.

An aggressive nocturnal feeder on fish and squid at mid depth and on the bottom, the hake prefers deep water marks on the edge of the continental shelf. It reproduces

during late spring and summer.

It is not a common angler's fish around the British Isles, but is consistently caught in Irish waters. Anglers usually catch it while fishing for other species.

HALIBUT
(*Hippoglossus hippoglossus*)

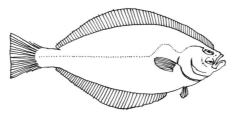

Average size: 25-75lb
Mega specimen: over 150lb
British record: 234lb (106kg 136g)

By far the largest flatfish caught around the British Isles, the halibut is right-eyed, with a long, thick-set body, neat head and large expandable mouth with a protruding lower jaw. Both jaws are well equipped with large teeth. The long, frill-like dorsal and anal fins widen to a peak halfway along the body, giving the halibut a diamond-shaped outline. The tail is large, powerful and squared. Colouration is dark greenish-brown on top and white underneath. The lateral line curves noticeably around the pectoral fin.

The halibut is an aggressive feeder on crustaceans, squid and other fish, particularly coalfish, hunting at all levels from the bottom up to mid water. It reproduces during the winter in deep water, and the eggs drift close to the bottom before they hatch up to 2 weeks later.

HABITAT AND DISTRIBUTION
Only very occasionally taken from shallow inshore waters, the halibut prefers deep, fast

water over rocky or broken ground. Distribution is limited to deep-water marks around the western, northern and north-eastern coastline of the British Isles, such as the Orkneys or Shetland.

TECHNIQUES
Artificial lure fishing - sea; Driftfishing at sea; Wreck fishing.

HANDICAPPED ANGLERS TRUST (HAT)
The HAT is a registered charity that, through a wide range of sponsors, promotes the use of special craft, called 'wheelyboats', that enable wheelchair-bound anglers to go afloat on stillwater fisheries. Contact the Trust's Director, John Barrow, Southleigh House, Ginger's Green, Herstmonceux, East Sussex, BN27 4PT. Tel: 01323 833139.

HEMPSEED
See *Baits, freshwater - Particle baits.*

HERRING
(*Clupea harengus*)

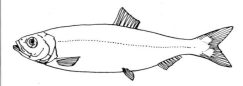

British record: 1lb 1oz (481g)

A member of the worldwide family of bony fish, to which the famous tarpon also belongs, the herring has the classic 'flat-sided' body covered in bright, silvery scales. The back is dark blue and the belly white. The head is plated and bony with a large eye and an upturned mouth. The lower jaw protrudes and has enormous expansion due to a long jaw hinge. The fins are small and the tail forked.

It feeds on plankton and lives in huge shoals, though these have now been greatly depleted in the North Sea due to commercial fishing. It reproduces between spring and autumn, the shoals shedding massive mats of eggs over a gravel or shell bottom.

It is only occasionally caught by anglers, but provides a first-class bait for both sea and pike fishermen (*Baits - sea; Baits - freshwater; Live and deadbaits - freshwater, sea*).

HOOKS

Being the vital link connecting a fisherman to his fish, this, the smallest and very often the cheapest item of tackle, becomes the most important of all.

Hook choice depends on both the type of bait being used and the size of fish expected. For instance, a single maggot will not look or behave naturally impaled on a size 4 hook, even if its inner juices remain intact. Conversely, a bunch of several maggots intended to catch heavyweight carp

or barbel will impair penetration if they are all crammed on to a tiny size 16 hook, which would quickly straighten or snap anyway should the point miraculously find purchase. So careful consideration should always be given to bait size and shape in relation to hook size and strength, remembering that hook strength is determined more by the gauge of the wire than by any other factor, be the pattern the very latest design in carp hook or a giant 10/0 shark or conger special.

Hooks derive their strength from being tempered by heat treatment, which obtains maximum benefit from the high-carbon, steel wire used in their manufacture. Points are usually needle ground (some have cutting edges) using a process similar to that used in the production of surgical needles, and popular models are then chemically etched to make them even sharper. Partridge of Redditch call their chemical etching process flashpointing, whereby only the thinnest parts of the wire are affected - namely the point, surplus metal being eaten away to refine it to an ultra-sharp degree.

Hooks are available in a variety of finishes and in a choice of carbon or stainless-steel wire. Carbon-steel wire can then be bronzed, blued, nickel-plated,

cadmium-plated or blackened and so on. Particular colours are also available, such as the bright red, extremely fine-wire, spade-end hooks produced especially for the delicate presentation of bloodworms.

Partridge of Redditch, Britain's largest hook manufacturer, offers a unique Niflor finish to some of their hook patterns, trout and treble hooks in particular. This is a special nickel/phosphorous, hard, protective process incorporating PTFE, making the surface extremely hard but at the same time very slippery. Being wear-resistant and corrosion-resistant, hooks treated with the dull grey Niflor finish last longer than other brands, and their durable, sharp points hold their sharpness for a long time.

Spade-end or flatted-shank hooks (hooks with no eye), being lighter than other types, provide the most natural presentation for small freshwater baits such as casters, maggots and bloodworms, and for feather or tinsel lures for sea species, mackerel in particular. Eyed hooks form the bulk of patterns used by pleasure anglers and include an unbelievable choice of sizes, shank lengths, bends, points and barbs.

As can be seen from fig. 66, which describes the various features of Mustad patterns, hooks are available in either

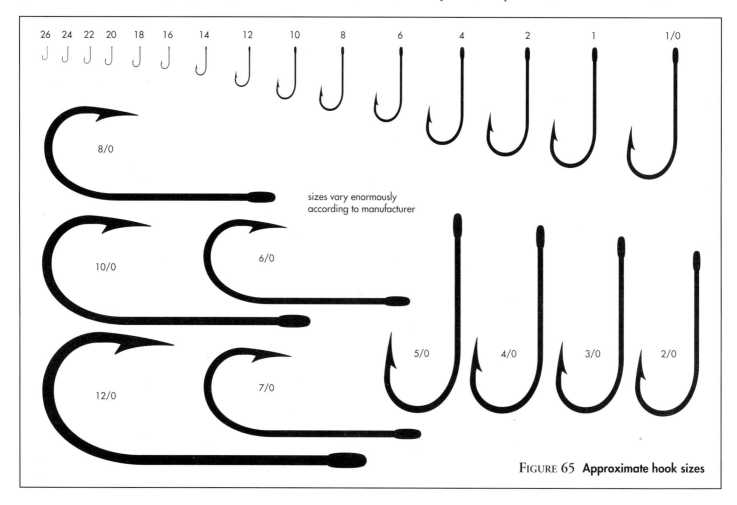

FIGURE 65 **Approximate hook sizes**

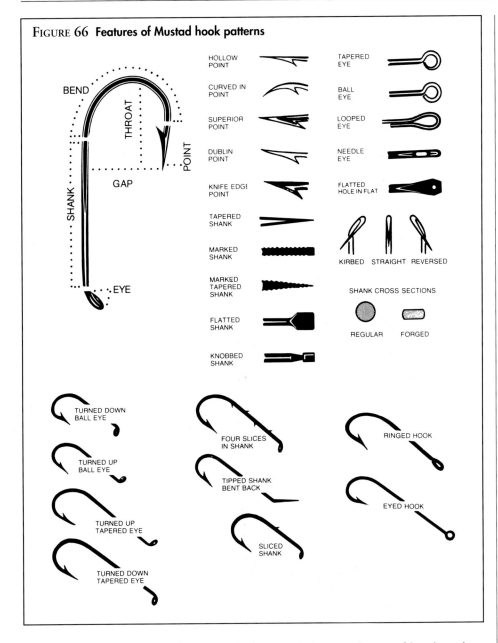

FIGURE 66 **Features of Mustad hook patterns**

regular (unforged) or forged (stronger) wire. They can be either straight, up, or down eyed, and ball or needle eyed as in treble hook patterns fitted into tube flies, or (for tying up salmon flies) simply a loop that becomes an eye once the head whipping is completed. Hooks that have neither eye nor spade end, simply a marked shank, are designed to be whipped on to a nylon trace. This ensures delicate freshwater baits like casters or small redworms etc and sea worms (lug and small ragworms) are not burst (by the eye and knot) when threaded on.

In addition to the point shape, length and cutting angle, barb size varies from quite large barbs to micro barbs, down to completely smooth, barbless points. When viewed head on, the bend of the hook can be straight, kirbed (twisted to the left) or reversed (twisted to the right), which on occasions aids penetration. There are also

several distinct shapes of bend, such as roundbend, crystal, O'Shaughnessey, with narrow, regular and wide gapes.

Barbless hooks are becoming increasingly popular, but rather than make do with the limited range of barbless patterns available, you can use the desired pattern of barbed hook and gently crunch down the barb using artery forceps. This applies to single hooks when carp or tench fishing and to treble hooks when seeking pike or zander. Crunch down two of the treble's barbs, leaving just one for holding the bait, thus converting it to a semi-barbless treble.

The following selection of popular coarse, game and sea patterns is only a tiny proportion of the thousands of models available, but illustrates the differences between various eyed and spade-end hooks, the sizes available, and the purpose for which each is best suited.

COARSE FISHING PATTERNS

MUSTAD 60175R
Bloodworm
Sizes 28-22

Spade end. Bright red, fine wire, long shank, crystal bend, chemically etched. Suitable for bloodworms.

MUSTAD 90340BR
Barbless maggot
Sizes 22-16

Spade end, barbless. Bronze, fine wire shank, crystal bend, chemically etched. Suitable for maggots, casters, etc.

KAMASAN B520
Sizes 24-12

Spade end, whisker barb. Bronze, fine wire, medium shank, crystal bend, chemically etched. Suitable for maggots, casters, seeds etc.

KAMASAN B511
Sizes 26-18

Spade end, micro barb. Nickel, fine wire, medium shank, wide gape, crystal bend, chemically etched. Suitable for punched bread, squatts etc.

DRENNAN
Carbon Chub
Sizes 24-10

Spade end, micro barb. Bronze, medium shank, crystal bend, chemically etched. Suitable for maggots, casters, seeds etc.

KAMASAN B640
Sizes 24-12

Spade end, forged. Bronze, short shank, round bend, reversed, chemically etched. Suitable for all small baits.

DRENNAN
Superspade
Sizes 22-8

Spade end, forged. Bronze, short shank, reversed, in-curving point, chemically etched. Suitable for all small baits.

KAMASAN B525
Sizes 22-14

Eyed, fine wire, whisker barb. Bronze, long shank, crystal bend, chemically etched. Suitable for maggots, casters, seed baits, punched bread etc.

DRENNAN
Carbon specimen
Sizes 20-2

Eyed, forged. Bronze, medium shank, reversed, round bend, chemically etched. Suitable for general use with all baits, large and small.

DRENNAN
Superspecialist
Sizes 20-2

Eyed, forged. Medium shank, bronze, reversed, special bend, heavy wire, chemically etched. Suitable for specimen-sized fish using all baits, large and small.

MUSTAD 34021
Carp
Sizes 12-2

Eyed, forged, Black, long shank, O'Shaughnessey bend. Suitable for specimen-sized fish using medium to large baits from particles to lobworms.

DRENNAN
Starpoint
Sizes 14-4

Eyed, forged, micro barb. Pearl black finish, anti-eject bend, swept reverse, chemically etched (also available barbless). Suitable for all particle baits and boilies. A designer carp hook.

DRENNAN
Boilie hook
Sizes 14-1

Eyed, forged. Blackened, medium shank, wide gape, reversed, incurving point, chemically etched. For presenting boilies, but can be used with most baits.

PARTRIDGE Z15
Boilie carp hook
Sizes 10-2

Eyed, forged. Blackened, short shank, wide gape, strong wire, incurving point. Designer carp hook for presenting boilies, but good for all-round carp fishing.

OWNER
Fly liner livebait
Sizes 8-2

Eyed, forged, strong wire. Black chrome, short shank, wide gape, special bend, slightly incurving cutting point, chemically etched. Suitable for specimen-sized fish with all medium to large baits.

PARTRIDGE X1BR
Out point treble hooks
Sizes 10-3/0

Straight eyed, forged. Bronze, out point, medium shank, treble hooks. Also available in black and silver finish. Ideal for livebait and deadbait fishing and for artificial lures. (Also available in semi-barbless 'Z3'.)

DRENNAN
Carbon trebles
Sizes 12-4

Straight eyed, forged. Bronze, long shank, crystal bend, chemically etched, treble hook. Ideal for all-round pike and zander fishing live or dead baiting.

PARTRIDGE CS9PK
Extra strong treble
Sizes 10-2

Straight eyed, forged. Heavy wire, medium shank, out point, treble, black finish. Super-strong pike and salmon treble hook for lures, live and dead baiting.

GAME FISHING PATTERNS

DRENNAN
Dry fly
Sizes 18-10

Up eyed. Bronze, medium shank, round bend, chemically etched. For tying dry flies.

PARTRIDGE
'Stronghold' long shank
Sizes 16-8

Down eyed. Grey Shadow (Niflor) finish, long shank. For tying streamers, long nymphs, mayflies, daddy longlegs etc.

DRENNAN
Wet fly supreme
Sizes 16-8

Down eyed. Lightly forged. Bronze, medium shank, round bend, medium wire, chemically etched. For tying standard wet-fly patterns and short-bodied nymphs.

DRENNAN
Wet fly sproat
Sizes 16-8

Down eyed. Forged. Bronze, medium shank, sproat bend, chemically etched. For tying traditional wet-fly patterns.

PARTRIDGE
Goldhead hooks
Sizes 14-8

Down eyed, forged. Bronze, medium shank, round bend, wide gape. Designed to take gold or silver beads for wet-fly patterns.

DRENNAN
Carbon lure hooks
Sizes 12-4

Down eyed, forged. Bronze, very long shank, round bend, chemically etched. For tying lures.

DRENNAN
Carbon nymph
Sizes 14-8

Down eyed, forged. Bronze, long shank, round bend, chemically etched. For tying long-bodied nymphs.

PARTRIDGE GRS 12ST
Emerger/nymph
Sizes 18-8

Straight eyed. Grey Shadow (Niflor) finish, curved shank, whisker barb, chemically etched. For tying emerging flies, nymphs and shrimps.

PARTRIDGE K4A
Grub/shrimp hook
Sizes 18-8

Down eyed. Bronze, curved short shank. For tying grub, shrimp and some emerger fly patterns.

PARTRIDGE H3ST
Draper flat-bodied nymph hooks
Sizes 16-6

Straight eyed. Bronze, broad bodied. For tying all types of flat, broad-bodied nymph patterns.

PARTRIDGE N
Low-water hooks
Sizes 10-8/0

Looped-up eye, forged. Black finish, very long shank, limerick bend. For tying salmon and sea trout flies.

PARTRIDGE CS42
Extra strong streamer hooks
Sizes 8-1

Looped-down eye, forged. Black finish, extra long shank, limerick bend. For tying streamer flies.

PARTRIDGE Q1
Double low-water hooks
Sizes 12-3/0

Up eyed, forged. Black finish, double hook, limerick bend, extra long shank. For tying low-water salmon flies.

PARTRIDGE CS18
Treble hook
Sizes 16-12

Straight eyed, forged. Black finish, extra long shank, treble hook with out-bend points. For tying sea trout and salmon flies. Often used in place of *Waddington* shanks.

PARTRIDGE X2B
Treble hook
Sizes 16-2

Up eyed, forged. Black finish, long shank, out point treble hook. For tying salmon flies.

PARTRIDGE X3BL
Tube-fly treble hook
Sizes 12-2

Straight needle eye, forged. Black finish, medium shank, treble hook. To fit snugly into *tube fly*.

PARTRIDGE X7
PM tube-fly hooks
Sizes 12-4

Straight eyed, forged. Black finish, medium shank, treble hook with spike to fit into plastic tubing of tube flies. Specifically for tube flies.

SEA FISHING PATTERNS

MUSTAD 3261 BLN
Aberdeen hook
Sizes 6-6/0

Straight eyed. Black nickel finish, long shank, round bend, Aberdeen medium-fine wire, chemically etched. Allows worm baits to be threaded on without bursting.

MUSTAD 4446B
Nordic bend
Sizes 3-6/0

Straight eyed. Blued, slightly kirbed, hollow point, small barb, fine wire (sizes 3/0-6/0 are in forged wire - 4447B). Good for live worms and presenting plastic worms.

MUSTAD 92608
Beak hook
Sizes 6-6/0

Straight eyed, forged. Stainless steel, long shank, reversed round bend, incurving hollow point. Good for worms, fish strip, etc.

PARTRIDGE
Uptide extra
Sizes 2-7/0

Straight eyed, blackened forged. Short shank, round bend. Good for crab, worms and fish baits.

MUSTAD 2363DT
Square haddock
Sizes 6-4/0

Spade end, forged. Medium shank, tinned. Bait, or for tying up snoods of mackerel or cod feathers.

MUSTAD 3134
Kirby
Sizes 8-6/0

Down eyed. Bronze, extra long shank. General-purpose hook for worms or fish strip.

MUSTAD 92647
Beak hook
Sizes 10-6/0

Straight eyed. Nickel plated, long shank, beak hook with splices on shank for holding bait. Good for crab, squid and fish strip etc.

OWNER
Gorilla livebait
Sizes 10-6/0

Straight eyed, forged. Black chrome finish, short shank, heavy-duty wire curved, cutting point. For crab or live baits when seeking large fish.

PARTRIDGE
Meat hooks
Sizes 6/0-10/0

Straight eyed, forged. Short shank, heavy-duty wire, blackened, round bend, reversed. For squid and cut or whole fish baits when seeking large fish, conger eels etc.

DRENNAN
O'Shaughnessey
Sizes 6-8/0

Straight eyed, forged stainless steel. Heavy duty wire, O'Shaughnessey bend, chemically etched. Squid baits, strip-cut or whole fish.

MUSTAD 7731D
Sea demon
Sizes 4/0-9/0

Straight eyed, brazed ring, forged. Short shank, wide gape, round bend, heavy-duty wire, knife-edge point. For cut and whole fish baits when after big fish, sharks etc.

MUSTAD 7699D
Sea master
Sizes 1/0-14/0

Straight eyed, brazed ring. Medium shank, kirbed, knife edge, long point slightly incurved. Heavy duty wire. Whole fish baits for big fish, sharks etc.

HOOK LENGTHS

See *Lines*.

Ii Jj Kk

HOUTING

See *Powan*.

HYBRIDS

See *Bream; carp; roach; rudd; trout.*

IDE

See *Orfe*.

INSURANCE

Insurance is something that every angler should consider. Modern fishing tackle is very expensive and even a modest outfit is likely to cost several hundred pounds. Should any of your equipment be stolen or damaged, replacement costs can be considerable.

Include items of fishing tackle on your home-contents insurance policy, or, if you have an extensive collection of tackle, take out an additional policy designed to give adequate cover. Make sure that your policy covers you for breakage during use, and check on any excess or liability-limiting factors written into the policy.

An increasing number of anglers own a boat, which usually represents a hefty financial investment. If you have a boat, you need to take out a separate small-craft insurance policy, the value and cost of which will be determined by the value of the complete outfit and, usually, its maximum speed or engine size.

Third-party liability is another area of insurance that anglers are advised to look into. Third-party insurance covers accidents to other persons or property. For example, the beach angler might accidentally snap off a 5oz lead, capable of inflicting horrific, even fatal injuries, in mid cast. Or that same lead might smash the hull of a boat offshore. Third-party insurance will cover such incidents as well as massive personal legal costs in the event of an accident.

Many clubs and federations provide group cover for their members, so club membership might be the cheapest way to acquire third-party insurance.

JIGGING

See *Artificial lures; Driftfishing at sea.*

JOHN DORY

(*Zeus faber*)

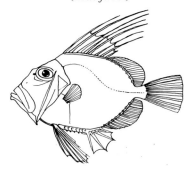

British record: 11lb 14oz (5kg 386g)

Also called St Peter's fish, this strange, almost ugly fish has a deep body and a huge bony head with vast jaws set in a fully protrusible mouth. It has two dorsal fins, the first of high spines and the second of soft rays. There is a similar set of strong spines in front of the anal fin. The pelvic fins are long and filamentous. It has horizontal yellowy lines across its brown back and silvery sides, with an unmistakable dark blotch ringed in yellow in the centre of each flank.

It feeds on small fish and crustaceans, which are sucked in at close range, and reproduces during the summer months. It prefers inshore habitats around harbours and breakwaters, and is most commonly caught from southern and south-western marks around the British Isles.

JOKERS

See *Baits - freshwater; Buzzers.*

KAPENTA

A freshwater sardine of African lakes and dams.

KEEPNETS

Used for retaining freshwater fish, during a match or for shorter periods while pleasure fishing, keepnets are available in a variety of diameters and mesh sizes and in lengths from 6ft to 14ft, with either round or rectangular rings spaced at regular intervals to support the net along the bottom. Soft, knotless micromesh, available in dark green, blue, grey or black, is by far the kindest material because it does not split the fins of small delicate species, but it is also the most expensive. Minnow, gudgeon and bream meshes are also available. The latter two, though cheap, are not recommended.

Quality nets are fitted with built-in, angle-lock top rings, enabling the top ring to be positioned horizontal to the water surface in any situation. The best have a 'protector net' facility. This allows large catches of bream, for instance, to be released with the minimum of fuss through the bottom of the net simply by unclipping a couple of plastic catches on each side of the bottom ring, without taking the net out of the water.

A good-sized net is 10-12ft long with a ring diameter of 20-21in. To ensure that the net does not swing about in high winds or strong currents, either stake it out with a bank stick or add a 3-4oz bomb to the bottom ring with a snap-swivel and large split ring.

KEEPSACKS

Ideal for retaining a large fish prior to weighing and photographing, keepsacks are rectangular, from 36x60in to 48x72in in size.

Keepsacks are made from black or dark brown, supersoft nylon material, well perforated to ensure that the captive fish receive sufficient dissolved oxygen. Some models have corners made from soft, large-mesh knitted nylon to ensure that the fish, which tend to nose into the corners, can breathe easily. Some sacks have drawstring tops while others come fitted with a long zip. All models should be thoroughly soaked before a fish is put inside, or its protective slime will be removed by the sack. It should then be staked horizontally in the marginal shallows, preferably in a shady spot (under a tree or overhanging bushes) so that the fish lies quietly. Never keep a fish sacked up for any longer than is necessary.

FIGURE 67 Knots for swivels and eyed hooks

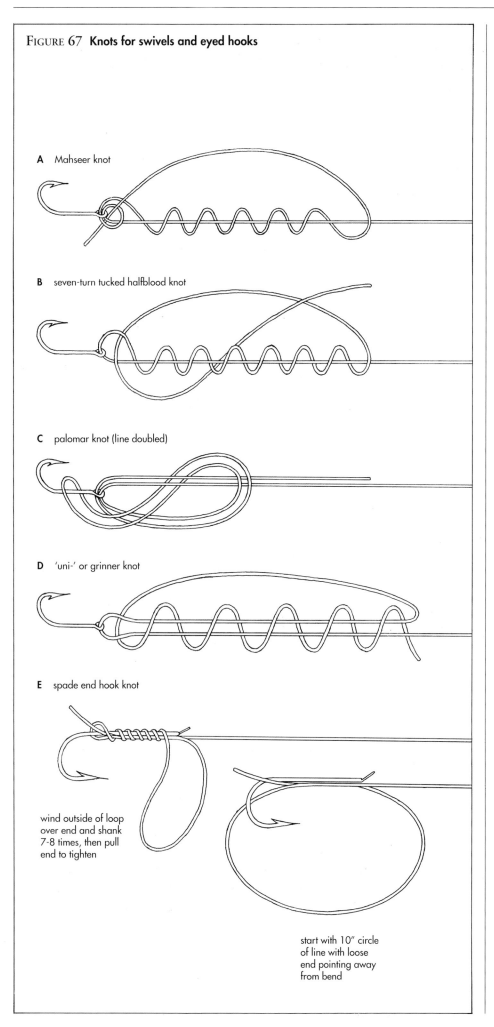

A Mahseer knot

B seven-turn tucked halfblood knot

C palomar knot (line doubled)

D 'uni-' or grinner knot

E spade end hook knot

wind outside of loop
over end and shank
7-8 times, then pull
end to tighten

start with 10" circle
of line with loose
end pointing away
from bend

KELT

A spawned out *salmon* or *sea trout*.

KNOTS

One of the most important skills in fishing, for obvious reasons, is the ability to tie a reliable knot, whether to join two lines together or to tie on a hook or swivel.

KNOTS FOR EYED HOOKS

Mahseer knot Devised to withstand the rigours of landing huge freshwater fish of up to 100lb from the fast rivers of India, this knot derives its strength from the fact that the end goes around the eye twice and is then trapped beneath two loops. The knot stretches under a full load, as opposed to constricting (fig. 67A), and is perfect for most freshwater situations and for saltwater hooks in sizes up to 6/0. Dampen the knot with saliva before pulling tight on both ends and trimming surplus.

The seven-turn, tucked, half blood knot (fig. 67B) is a quick, easy knot for all small-eyed, freshwater hooks used in coarse and game fishing. Dampen the knot with saliva and pull slowly to tighten it without crimping the line above.

The palomar knot For tying hooks to woven lines such as dacron and other braids, including specialized hooklength material, a knot is needed that causes minimal strangulation. The palomar knot can be used for freshwater and saltwater rigs. The line must be doubled into a loop and passed through the eye (fig. 67C). Pull steadily so that the knot does not bunch up, then trim off the end.

'Uni' or grinner knot (fig. 67D) The 'uni' or grinner knot is extremely versatile. It can be used for both braided and monofilament lines, and even for thick, sea-gauge monofilament over 100lb test. Wind the end of the line five times around the doubled-up length of line when tying on all freshwater hooks and small to medium-sized sea hooks. When using huge hooks and monofilament of 150lb plus, three times is sufficient, and tighten with pliers. Dab the knot with saliva and tighten it to ensure that the barrel beds down firmly; then pull the knot down to fit snugly against the eye or swivel and tighten again.

After pre-tightening, the knot can be left as a free-swinging loop about 1in long and the end trimmed, which gives large, artificial flies a more lifelike movement.

Spade-end knot For tying freshwater spade-end hooks to the finest monofilament, use the simple knot in 67F, which requires no threading or special tool. Alternatively, specialized spade-end hook tyers, such as the Matchman, are available for those whose eyes and fingers will not co-ordinate. Spade-end sea hooks are tied using the same knot.

SLIDING STOP KNOT

This useful knot (fig. 68A) is tied directly on to the reel line (using a 10in length of the same or power gum) above a sliding float so that the float rises and locks at knot depth. Wet the line with saliva while tightening the knot and when you move the knot in order to change depth. Trim the ends to 1in so that they fold flat when passing through the rod rings.

DOUBLE OR FULL BLOOD KNOT

This knot (fig. 68B) should be used for joining two lines together. Make four turns around the line with fine lines (3lb or less) and three times for thicker lines. Wet the line and tighten the knot slowly before trimming off the ends.

FOUR-TURN WATER KNOT

This reliable knot (fig. 68C) can be used for joining links or droppers of the same test strength to the reel line, and for joining lighter or heavier links to the main line for use as short droppers (fly fishing), hook-lengths or paternoster lead links. This knot is also useful for adding several feet of lighter line to the reel line or to a fly cast, and for making paternoster snoods for sea fishing with heavy-gauge monofilament. Always wet the knot before pulling it tight, and trim away the unwanted end. This knot is also effective for shark-fishing or blue-water game-fish rigs, when, to provide a safeguard, use the last 60ft of line to form a double length of line 30ft long.

DOUBLE OVERHAND LOOP

This is a strong loop that can be formed at the end of the reel line to join it to a 'hook to nylon', which comes with pre-tied loops, or at the thick end of a fly leader (fig. 69A).

BLOOD DROPPER

To make snoods for a feather, jig or bait to a sea trace (*Artificial lures*) follow fig. 69B.

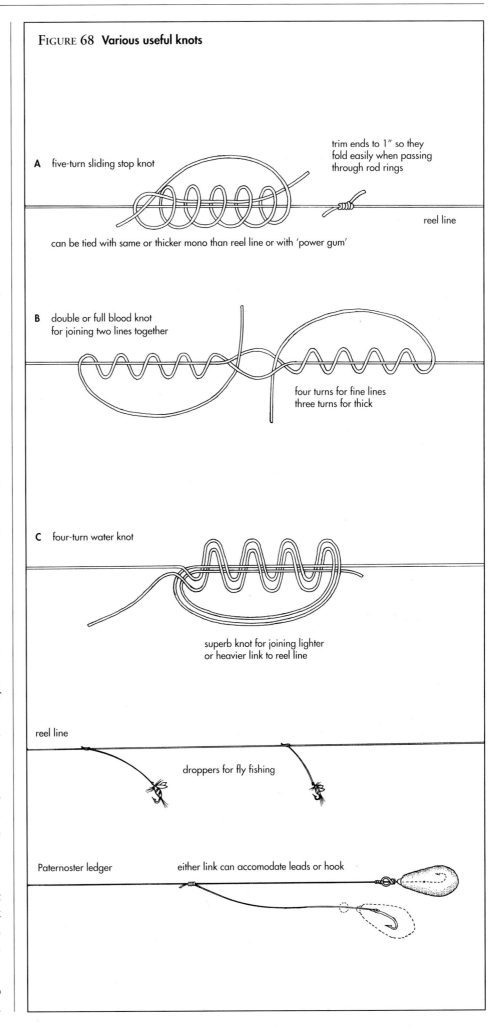

FIGURE 68 **Various useful knots**

A five-turn sliding stop knot

trim ends to 1″ so they fold easily when passing through rod rings

reel line

can be tied with same or thicker mono than reel line or with 'power gum'

B double or full blood knot for joining two lines together

four turns for fine lines three turns for thick

C four-turn water knot

superb knot for joining lighter or heavier link to reel line

reel line

droppers for fly fishing

Paternoster ledger   either link can accomodate leads or hook

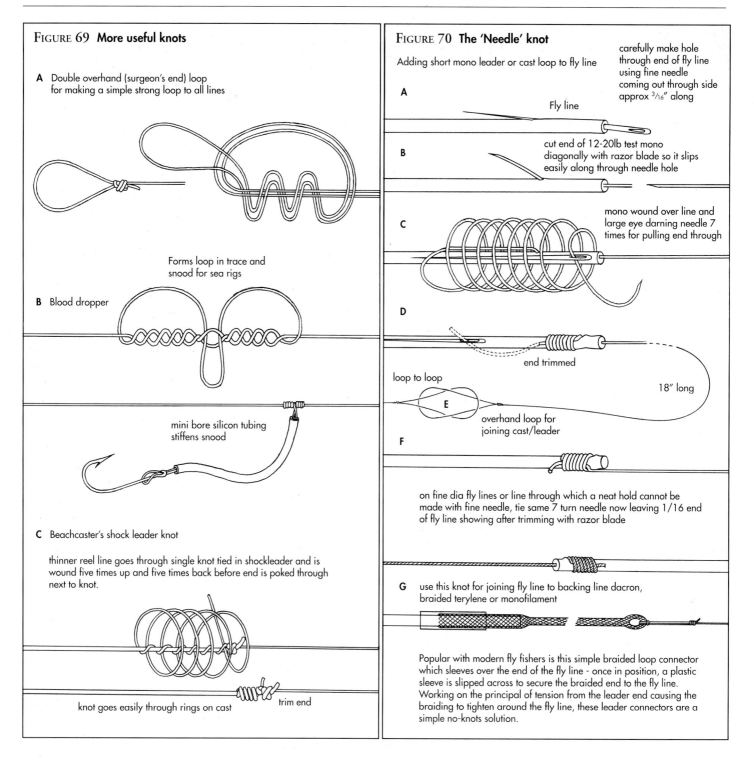

FIGURE 69 More useful knots

A Double overhand (surgeon's end) loop for making a simple strong loop to all lines

Forms loop in trace and snood for sea rigs

B Blood dropper

mini bore silicon tubing stiffens snood

C Beachcaster's shock leader knot

thinner reel line goes through single knot tied in shockleader and is wound five times up and five times back before end is poked through next to knot.

knot goes easily through rings on cast trim end

FIGURE 70 The 'Needle' knot

Adding short mono leader or cast loop to fly line

A Fly line

carefully make hole through end of fly line using fine needle coming out through side approx ³⁄₁₆″ along

B cut end of 12-20lb test mono diagonally with razor blade so it slips easily along through needle hole

C mono wound over line and large eye darning needle 7 times for pulling end through

D end trimmed

loop to loop

E overhand loop for joining cast/leader

18″ long

F on fine dia fly lines or line through which a neat hold cannot be made with fine needle, tie same 7 turn needle now leaving 1/16 end of fly line showing after trimming with razor blade

G use this knot for joining fly line to backing line dacron, braided terylene or monofilament

Popular with modern fly fishers is this simple braided loop connector which sleeves over the end of the fly line - once in position, a plastic sleeve is slipped across to secure the braided end to the fly line. Working on the principal of tension from the leader end causing the braiding to tighten around the fly line, these leader connectors are a simple no-knots solution.

After pulling the dropper tight, sleeve on a length of silicone tubing to stiffen the snood prior to adding the hook.

BEACHCASTER'S SHOCK LEADER KNOT

This is the knot to use for joining a shock leader to the main line for beachfishing, as it can take the strain of repeatedly punching out several ounces of lead. It is also good for uptide boatfishing over rough ground (fig. 69C). Simply tie a knot in the end of the shock leader and thread the reel line through it. Then wind it five times up the shock leader and five times back, before poking the end through the last turn next

to the knot. Now pull hard on the end of the shock-leader knot with a pair of pliers and bed down the barrel formed by the reel line. Wet the knot with saliva and pull steadily on the end of the reel line until the barrel knot tightens and butts up to the single shock-leader knot. Trim off both ends.

THE NEEDLE KNOT

To add a short leader loop to the end of a fly line, form a seven-turn, barrel-type knot using a large-eyed darning needle (fig. 70C). Once tightened (evenly), the knot cuts into the fly line's plastic coating to form a strong, neat junction (70D).

The leader loop will lie flatter if the monofilament is threaded through the middle of the line, through a hole made with a fine needle, before the knot is tied (fig. 70A and B). However, this can weaken the ends of exceptionally fine-diameter lines, so with these form the needle knot without piercing the line (70F). To finish, form a small overhand loop and join loop to loop with leader/cast (70E).

Both ways of joining the leader loop (70G) can be used for joining the other end of the fly line to the backing, whether dacron, braided monofilament or shooting-head monofilament (*Lines*).

LAMPREY, BROOK

(*Lampetra planeri*)

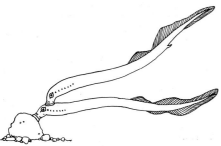

Smallest of the lampreys, rarely exceeding an adult length of 10in, the brook lamprey lives only in clear-flowing streams and rivers. It is slate grey along the back and sides with a dirty white belly, and has the customary seven gill holes and sucker-type mouth. Its teeth, however, are rather weak, and because it spends much of its life buried in thick silt, first in a blind, larval form and then during its short adult life, its sucker-type mouth is used only for adhering to the undersides of stones. It is non-parasitic, and is commonly found throughout European upper river systems.

LAMPREY, RIVER

(*Lampetra fluvatilis*)

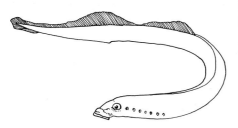

Also called the lampern, the river lamprey has a similar shape to, and the seven gill holes of the sea lamprey, but its sucker-type mouth contains beak-like inner jaws as opposed to rasp-like teeth. It has a grey, greeny-brown back, golden flanks and a white belly. The adult grows to a maximum length of 18-20in and lives in the sea prior to migrating into river systems to lay its eggs. Following egg laying, adult lampreys die. The resulting larvae remain blind for up to six years, living in silt or mud, before developing into adults and migrating to sea, where they feed on the flesh and body fluids of small fish.

LAMPREY, SEA

(*Petromyzon marinus*)

Though never likely to be caught by angling methods, except by foul-hooking, this primitive parasitic fish is, like all lampreys, scaleless and has no supportive rays in its fins. In place of the normal gill plates there are seven holes, and in place of a mouth and jaws is an awesome sucker-type mouth full of rasp-like teeth, with which the lamprey grinds away the flesh of its unfortunate victim.

Colouration along the back and sides is mottled shades of olive and dark brown, and the undersides are dirty white. The average adult length for this eel-like fish is 2-3ft. Although it spends much of its adult life at sea, the sea lamprey migrates into clear-flowing rivers to spawn, depositing its eggs in a redd cut by the male. The adult lamprey then dies. The blind larvae spend up to five years in freshwater before developing into adults and migrating back to sea.

LANDING NETS

Landing nets are indispensable for safely landing fish that are considerably heavier than the breaking strain of the line used to catch them, and comparatively small fish that the match fisherman cannot afford to risk swinging in.

Landing nets are available in a range of shapes, frame sizes and net meshes to suit the coarse, sea and game fisherman.

For small to medium-sized coarse species, a 15-20in frame size is ideal, either round, triangular or spoon shaped, with a net of soft, knotless micromesh or minnow-mesh sides and a micro-pan base, from which fish can easily be picked because they are not hidden in any folds and ultra-light terminal rigs and shots do not become snagged in the mesh. Monomesh nets are excellent on these smaller frames, which are available in plastic-covered alloy,

fibreglass or lightweight carbon. A round mini net of just 12in in diameter is used by canal fishermen in pursuit of tiny fish on ultra-light terminal tackle.

For general coarse fishing, a 24in round frame with a 24in deep net of minnow-mesh sides and a micro-pan base will easily land species such as tench and bream as well as roach, rudd and perch, plus even the occasional big carp or barbel if care is taken. For large fish - pike, carp, catfish and eels - the extra strength provided by triangular nets, which have lightweight carbon or fibreglass arms supported in a spreader block, allows the heaviest specimens to be landed. A nylon cord stretches between the tip of each arm, keeping the net slightly bowed, and you have a choice of knotless net meshes. Twin-meshes are extremely popular. The larger, side-wall mesh allows the net to be steered easily through the water (resistance from small meshes is considerable, especially against flowing water) while the soft micromesh or 'punched' material base ensures that the fish's body mucus is not removed nor its fins damaged. A triangular net with 42in arms will cover all situations, although 36in and 50in models are also available.

Landing-net poles are fitted with a standard BSF ³⁄₈in thread, into which all these nets will screw. Strong, 5½-7ft, one-piece fibreglass or carbon poles are available specifically for landing big fish, while telescopic models with two to four joints extend to lengths of 7½-11ft. Poles made from carbon are more expensive but much lighter to lift. Choose one that has the end thread accommodating the net braised into an overfit collar. Those with the end thread fitted inside the end of the hollow pole and held with a rivet weaken and eventually pull out.

Trout and salmon nets are available with short, telescopic handles or single stems, with strong clips for belt or waistcoat attachment. You have a choice between triangular nets (with a cord stretched between the tip of each arm to keep it rigid when open) and spoon-shaped nets, which have rigid alloy frames. Both have flick-up hinges at the junction of net and pole to facilitate immediate, single-handed use. By pulling on a sprung collar, you can instantly fold the net again.

Large, round or spoon-shaped salmon nets, the frames of which slide along a pole to be slung comfortably around the back on a belt, out of the way, are also available. As the fish are not returned, the nets are made from a large, knotted mesh of thick nylon cord, which is more easily guided through fast water than smaller meshes. Such nets double for boat fishing at sea, being large enough to accommodate most species from thornback rays to specimen cod and ling. To prolong the life of a net used in salt water, rinse both the mesh and the alloy frame well in fresh water.

LAUNCE (GREATER SAND EEL)

See *Sand eel.*

LEADERSINK

A preparation for degreasing monofilament line to ensure that it sinks quickly. This can easily be made by mixing Fuller's earth with liquid detergent (i.e. washing-up liquid). An essential piece of equipment for wet fly or nymph fly fishermen as a floating leader will prevent the fly sinking.

LEDGERING TECHNIQUES

BOBBIN LEDGERING IN STILLWATERS

When used for ledgering in stillwater at distances in excess of 50yd for tench, specimen roach, rudd, bream, perch and even medium-sized carp, with large baits and big hooks, standard ledger and quiver-tip rods are not capable of picking up sufficient line on the strike in order to set the hook, particularly a large hook.

An 11½-12ft Avon, or stepped up Avon, with a test curve of 1¼-1½lb is then the right tool for the job (*Rods - freshwater*), coupled to a 5lb or 6lb reel line and an electric bite alarm/bobbin set-up with the rod set on two rests and pointing directly at the bait (fig. 71A). Heavy bobbins (set on an 18in drop between reel and butt ring) (*Bite indicators*) are ideal for distance fishing because they hold the line down to counteract sub-surface tow. Alternatively, up to three or four swan shots can be pinched on to the retaining cord immediately below the bobbin, which should ideally have provision for a betalight luminous element for fishing during darkness (*Night fishing*).

Choice of end rig depends largely on the species sought. For instance, if large paste baits or worms are presented for carp or perch, a running paternoster rig (fig. 71B) permits the fish to run away with the bait, even with the bobbin set on a 2ft drop, without feeling resistance. For bream especially, plus tench and rudd, the fixed paternoster shown in fig. 71C is a proven distance rig, the short hooklength presenting buoyant baits such as breadflake attractively on top of dense bottom weed. When tiny lifts or drops of the indicator are continually experienced (tench are past masters at twitch bites), reduce both paternoster and hook links to 6in and 10in respectively (fig. 71D), which will provide an earlier indication of the moment to strike and give more exaggerated bites. Quite simply, the tench are no longer moving off with the bait to another pile of free food, they are consuming the hook-bait on the spot, as skinned or sucked maggots left on the hook (without a bite having registered on the indicator) will prove.

On really calm days, it pays to forget the indicator and watch the line where it enters the water close to the rod tip, instantly hitting any movement. In really shallow water, remember to strike sideways so that the line is pulled through and not

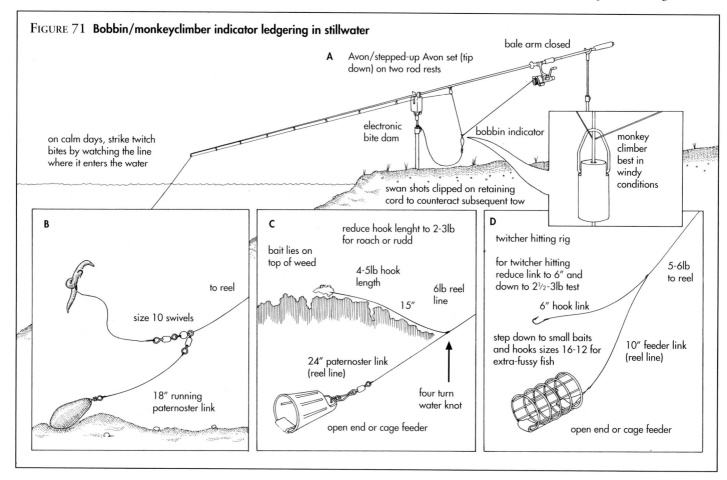

FIGURE 71 **Bobbin/monkeyclimber indicator ledgering in stillwater**

A　Avon/stepped-up Avon set (tip down) on two rod rests

bale arm closed

electronic bite dam

bobbin indicator

monkey climber best in windy conditions

on calm days, strike twitch bites by watching the line where it enters the water

swan shots clipped on retaining cord to counteract subsequent tow

B　to reel

size 10 swivels

18″ running paternoster link

C　reduce hook lenght to 2-3lb for roach or rudd

bait lies on top of weed

4-5lb hook length

6lb reel line

15″

24″ paternoster link (reel line)

four turn water knot

open end or cage feeder

D　twitcher hitting rig

for twitcher hitting reduce link to 6″ and down to 2½-3lb test

6″ hook link

step down to small baits and hooks sizes 16-12 for extra-fussy fish

5-6lb to reel

10″ feeder link (reel line)

open end or cage feeder

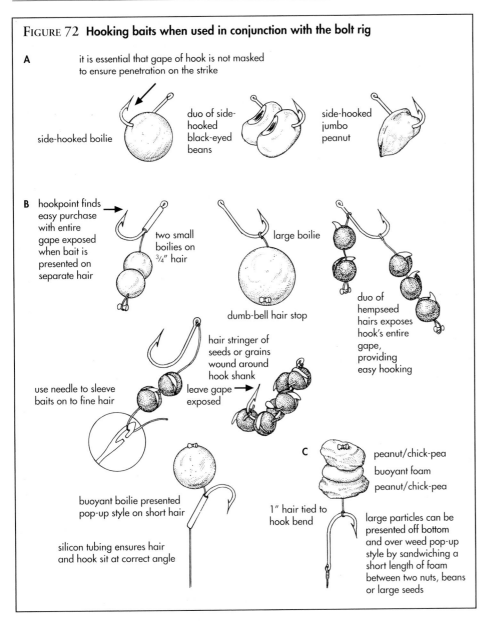

FIGURE 72 Hooking baits when used in conjunction with the bolt rig

A

it is essential that gape of hook is not masked
to ensure penetration on the strike

side-hooked boilie

duo of side-hooked black-eyed beans

side-hooked jumbo peanut

B hookpoint finds easy purchase with entire gape exposed when bait is presented on separate hair

two small boilies on ¾" hair

large boilie

dumb-bell hair stop

duo of hempseed hairs exposes hook's entire gape, providing easy hooking

use needle to sleeve baits on to fine hair

hair stringer of seeds or grains wound around hook shank

leave gape exposed

buoyant boilie presented pop-up style on short hair

silicon tubing ensures hair and hook sit at correct angle

C

peanut/chick-pea
buoyant foam
peanut/chick-pea

1" hair tied to hook bend

large particles can be presented off bottom and over weed pop-up style by sandwiching a short length of foam between two nuts, beans or large seeds

against the surface tension. Conversely, when ledgering into deep water, an upwards, sweeping strike straightens the line and bangs home the hook.

THE BOLT RIG

Sometimes referred to as the shock rig because it panics fish into bolting off with the bait, this rig was originally devised to make carp give strikable runs. It is, however, also extremely effective for tench. Because carp wise-up to the same old baits, they soon learn to suck them up and instantly reject them if they feel the hook, without giving much more than a twitch on the line. However, a heavy lead added to the terminal rig, which the fish senses as soon as its lips close over the bait, causes the fish to forget all about the bait and rush off, usually hooking itself in the process.

Generally speaking, only hard baits such as most particles (beans, nuts and seeds) and boilies, which the carp sucks back to

its pharyngeal teeth for chewing, work effectively with the bolt rig. And although baits can be side-hooked (fig. 72A) the hook point finds purchase more easily and the bait is picked up with more confidence, if the entire gape is exposed and the bait presented off the hook on a separate hair (fig. 72B) (hair rig fig. 64).

Alternatively, the bait can be presented as a pop-up (fig. 72C), either by using a floating *boilie* (*Baits - freshwater*) or by sandwiching a short length of buoyant foam between two large particles such as tiger nuts, chick-peas or peanuts.

The secret, when presenting the bait on the bottom in conjunction with a bolt rig, lies in having exactly the right distance between bait and lead. Carp vary enormously in size, and you need to experiment with this if you do not hook fish or they come off the hook repeatedly for no apparent reason. A distance of 6-10in is recommended. Fig. 73A shows a

simple bolt rig incorporating a short, anti-tangle boom that takes a semi-fixed, 2oz bomb.

This holds together for casting, but will slide up the line once a carp is on. The hooklength is 6-10in of reel line, dacron, or specialized super-soft hooklength material of a fine diameter. The bait can be side-hooked or presented on a hair to make the carp suck it up confidently.

After casting and catapulting loose feed around the hook-bait, fix a monkey-climber indicator on to the line halfway between the butt ring and the reel and switch on the electric bite alarm. If you are using a reel with a baitrunner facility, which disengages the spool, keep the bale arm closed and simply wait for the spool to revolve as a carp goes belting off with the bait, having hooked itself in the process - the reason for leaving the hook point exposed.

A hefty strike, therefore, is not required unless you are fishing at extreme range. Simply bend into the carp when all is nicely tight from reel to fish, having first closed the bale arm on non-baitrunner reels. When the sub-surface tow is strong, causing the monkey to rise continually and the buzzer to give false alarms, clip up the line beneath an elastic band or a run-clip positioned on the rod handle immediately above the reel and the bale arm (open if it is not a baitrunner reel).

For close-range bolt-rig situations, consider the rig in fig. 73B, which is simplicity itself and ditches the lead should a carp go belting off through dense weed. This rig is also excellent for presenting the bait popped-up above bottom weed (alter the length of the hooklink accordingly). Note how the two AA shots, pinched on at 12in intervals immediately above the swivel, iron the reel line to the bottom and hide it in the weed or soft silt so that an approaching carp is not alarmed (fig. 74).

If the rig is presented on a tight line between bait and rod tip, a proportion of would-be runs never happen, because carp sense the line and avoid the area. Where possible, do not fish clipped-up just because everyone else does. Dip the rod tip beneath the surface after casting, and with the left hand (assuming you are holding the rod in your right hand) gently pull the line until it is straight. Then allow a little slack from the reel to form a bow in the line and set the rod horizontally on two rests pointing at the bait.

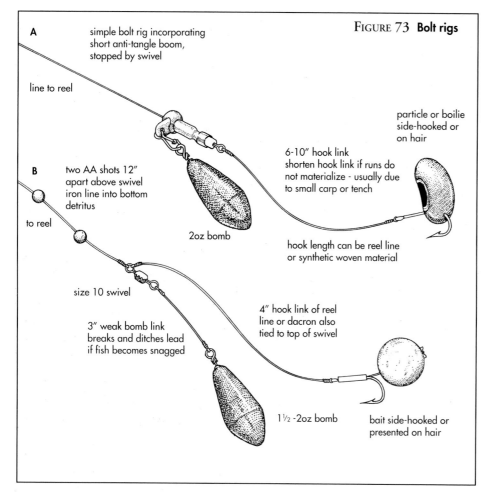

FIGURE 73 Bolt rigs

A   simple bolt rig incorporating short anti-tangle boom, stopped by swivel

line to reel

particle or boilie side-hooked or on hair

6-10″ hook link shorten hook link if runs do not materialize - usually due to small carp or tench

B   two AA shots 12″ apart above swivel iron line into bottom detritus

to reel

2oz bomb

hook length can be reel line or synthetic woven material

size 10 swivel

4″ hook link of reel line or dacron also tied to top of swivel

3″ weak bomb link breaks and ditches lead if fish becomes snagged

1½ -2oz bomb

bait side-hooked or presented on hair

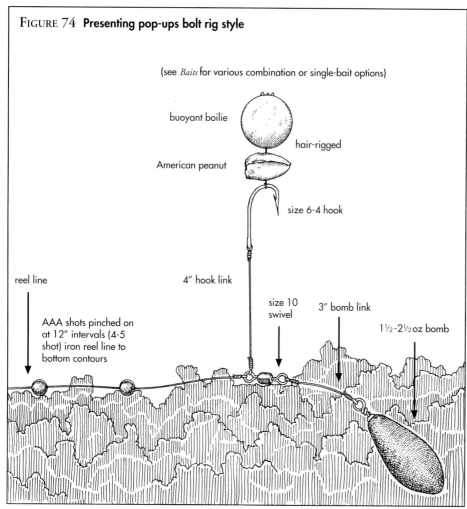

FIGURE 74 Presenting pop-ups bolt rig style

(see *Baits* for various combination or single-bait options)

buoyant boilie

hair-rigged

American peanut

size 6-4 hook

reel line

4″ hook link

size 10 swivel

3″ bomb link

1½-2½oz bomb

AAA shots pinched on at 12″ intervals (4-5 shot) iron reel line to bottom contours

LEDGERING LIVEBAITS AND DEADBAITS

A running ledger rig with a short, 5in, silicone covered, nylon bomb link sliding above a double-swivelled trace with a cushioning bead between them (fig. 75), allows predators like perch, zander, catfish, eels and pike to run off with the bait without feeling resistance. This is why the reel's bale arm is left open and the line clipped into a *drop-arm indicator (Bite indicators)* for zander and pike, and a monkey-climber indicator for eels, perch and catfish.

For pike use a 20in wire trace of 15lb test holding a duo of size 8 semi-barbless trebles, and for zander size 10 semi-barbless trebles on 10lb wire, whether presenting livebaits or deadbaits. For cats and perch, 15in monofilament traces made from the reel line are quite adequate. These species also generally prefer freshwater livebaits or deadbaits, although sprats can be used at a pinch. Make eel traces from supple 15lb-test wire holding a single, size 4, eyed hook baited with fresh sprats or small freshwater deadbaits.

When livebaits become over-active and when ledgering livebaits or deadbaits in running water, retain a loop of line (on the rod-tip side of all indicators) beneath a small run-clip or elastic band. This prevents false bites setting off the alarm, but allows a predator to run off with the bait and subsequently activate the indicators.

QUIVER-TIP LEDGERING
In flowing water

One step on from *freelining* is to add weight (usually on a separate link to the hooklength) for casting and for anchoring the bait in a particular spot in strong currents, and then to watch the rod tip for bites. Prior to the invention of the quiver tip (*Bite indicators*), river fishermen seeking roach, bream, chub and barbel watched the considerably thicker tip of standard Avon-type ledger rods. And in fierce currents demanding in excess of, say, a 1oz bomb, where a sensitive quiver tip would be pulled round, a standard rod tip is fine. But for most situations, particularly in hard-fished rivers where a large proportion of bites

The most effective method of detecting bites when ledgering for dace, roach, chub and barbel, etc. in fast flowing water is quivertipping. The finely tapered, super-sensitive solid glass or carbon tip, registers the tiniest of bites.

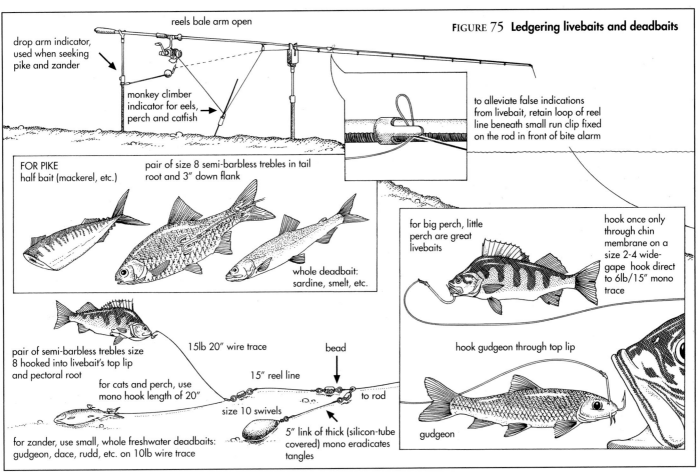

FIGURE 75 **Ledgering livebaits and deadbaits**

reels bale arm open

drop arm indicator, used when seeking pike and zander

monkey climber indicator for eels, perch and catfish

to alleviate false indications from livebait, retain loop of reel line beneath small run clip fixed on the rod in front of bite alarm

FOR PIKE
half bait (mackerel, etc.)

pair of size 8 semi-barbless trebles in tail root and 3" down flank

whole deadbait: sardine, smelt, etc.

for big perch, little perch are great livebaits

hook once only through chin membrane on a size 2-4 wide-gape hook direct to 6lb/15" mono trace

pair of semi-barbless trebles size 8 hooked into livebait's top lip and pectoral root

15lb 20" wire trace

bead

15" reel line

for cats and perch, use mono hook length of 20"

size 10 swivels

to rod

hook gudgeon through top lip

gudgeon

for zander, use small, whole freshwater deadbaits: gudgeon, dace, rudd, etc. on 10lb wire trace

5" link of thick (silicon-tube covered) mono eradicates tangles

FIGURE 76 **Basic quivertipping paternoster rig for river fishing**

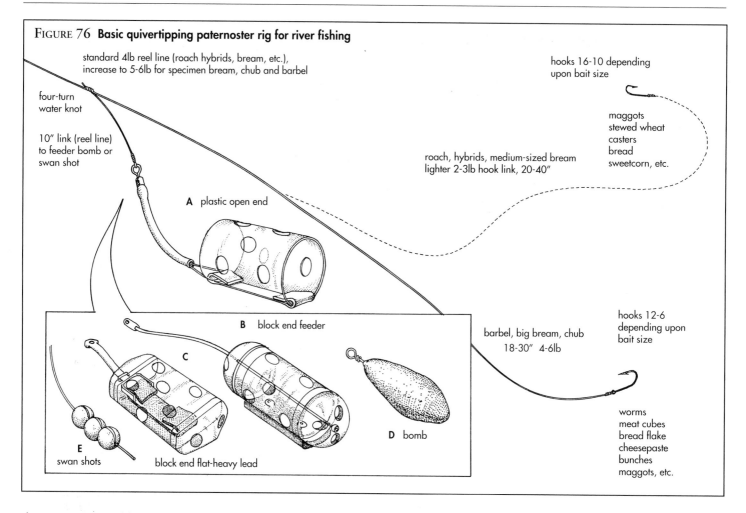

standard 4lb reel line (roach hybrids, bream, etc.),
increase to 5-6lb for specimen bream, chub and barbel

hooks 16-10 depending
upon bait size

four-turn
water knot

10" link (reel line)
to feeder bomb or
swan shot

maggots
stewed wheat
casters
bread
sweetcorn, etc.

A plastic open end

roach, hybrids, medium-sized bream
lighter 2-3lb hook link, 20-40"

B block end feeder

C

hooks 12-6
depending upon
bait size

barbel, big bream, chub
18-30" 4-6lb

D bomb

E
swan shots

block end flat-heavy lead

worms
meat cubes
bread flake
cheesepaste
bunches
maggots, etc.

show as mere trembles on a standard rod tip, quivertipping allows more time to strike before the bait is dropped (*Rods - freshwater*). Therefore choose the most sensitive quiver tip to match current strength, in order that even tentative pulls from dace, roach and bream will register. Avon-style ledger rods of 11-11½ft with built-in or screw-in quiver tips, coupled to a small fixed-spool reel with a sensitive clutch and loaded with 4-6lb mono, should handle most river fishing situations. Remember to use the minimum weight, whether rigged with feeder, swan shots or bomb ledger, so that drop-back bites are indicated instantly. Fish do not always swim downstream with the bait and pull the tip round. They move sideways with it across the current and even swim upstream. Both movements are indicated by a relaxing, or springing back, of the tip. Strikes at these drop-back bites will put many bonus fish in the net.

When quivertipping in large, wide rivers for roach, hybrids and bream, where shoals might contain hundreds of fish rather than dozens, deposit loose feed on the bottom, close to the hook-bait, using a *swimfeeder* as a built-in ledger weight (fig. 76). For deep, steady water, the plastic open-end feeder (76A) ensures that damp-

ened breadcrumbs plus fragments of hook-bait aren't released until it hits bottom. Don't cast straight out, because the bait will be scattered across the river bed as the flow drags the feeder round until it settles. Cast downstream and across, just slightly further out than where you intend to present the bait. To alleviate extra drag from the line, keep most of it above the surface by positioning the rod on two rests with the tip set high. The feeder will then settle quickly and not drag further. That way, even the slightest drop back will be a bite, and not the feeder resetting itself. Whenever possible, set the rod so you can strike with the current (fig. 77). The anglers fishing from positions A and B are both striking with the current and pulling the line through it, rather than against it. In C, the angler sits side-on to the river, having cast far out, and strikes not upstream as in B, but at a downstream angle, pulling the line through the water following the bow caused by the flow. C is not striking upstream and against the flow, which would create massive resistance and much reduced striking power.

In gentle currents, or where the slow dispersal of maggots or casters is imperative (during low water temperatures), use a

feeder-link block-end (fig. 76B). For holding and releasing maggots, hempseed or casters in extremely fast or steady, deep water, the best feeder is the flat block-end (76C). And when loose feed is not required, or can be introduced by hand or catapult, as when fishing for chub, barbel or big roach from small rivers while feeding in maggots or mashed bread, simply use a bomb (76D) or a string of swan shots (76E). The swan-shot link is the most versatile ledger of all because shots can be added or taken off as required so that the bait only just holds its position in the flow.

As can be seen from the basic quivertipping paternoster rig (fig. 76) various lengths and strengths of hooklength can be joined to the reel line using a four-turn water knot (fig. 68C). Running ledgers using swivels and beads are no more effective, and the basic paternoster rig keeps everything nice and easy. Simply increase or decrease the hooklength as required, changing hook sizes to match the bait.

To place the bait in tempting swims that cannot be reached by a cast made downstream or downstream and across - a situation that regularly occurs when quivertipping for roach, chub and barbel inhabiting the smaller rivers - simply ledger

FIGURE 77 Correct rod positioning when quivertipping in rivers

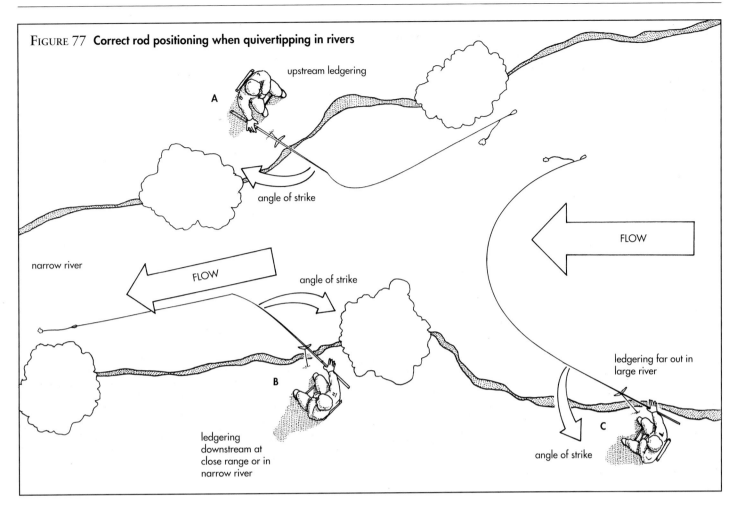

upstream ledgering

A

angle of strike

FLOW

narrow river

FLOW

angle of strike

B

ledgering far out in large river

C

angle of strike

ledgering downstream at close range or in narrow river

upstream. Sit facing upstream and across, with the rod tip high on two rests to minimize current pressure on the line. As most bites will be sudden drop-backs, strike in a long, sweeping movement to pick up all the slack and bang the hook home (fig. 77A).

In stillwater

Most of the basic principles of ledgering in rivers apply to quivertipping and swingtipping in stillwaters (*Bite indicators*). The swing tip is especially good when bream are biting shyly as it provides the absolute minimum of resistance to a biting fish. However, owing to the quiver-tip rod's superior casting performance (compared to swing tips, which dangle) and to the fact that tips of varying tapers can be employed to match the conditions, quiver tips are now widely used, even by match fishermen, on stillwaters. The main factor to consider, particularly when the surface is ruffled by strong cross winds, is sub-surface tow, which can greatly impair striking if the rod is angled downwind. While the surface layer of water is being blown by the wind against the shore (fig. 78A), most of the sunken line between bait and rod tip is bowed in completely the opposite direction by the lower water layers (78B).

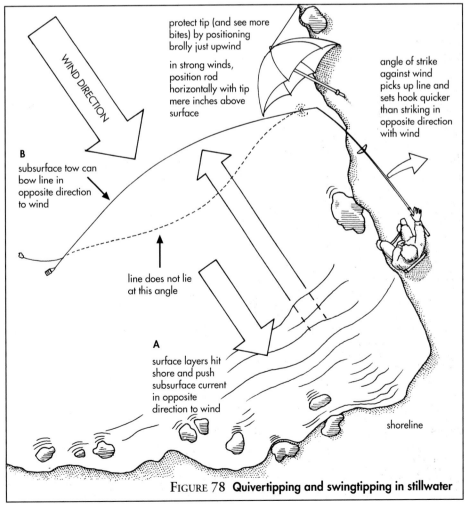

WIND DIRECTION

protect tip (and see more bites) by positioning brolly just upwind

in strong winds, position rod horizontally with tip mere inches above surface

angle of strike against wind picks up line and sets hook quicker than striking in opposite direction with wind

B
subsurface tow can bow line in opposite direction to wind

line does not lie at this angle

A
surface layers hit shore and push subsurface current in opposite direction to wind

shoreline

FIGURE 78 Quivertipping and swingtipping in stillwater

A basic fixed paternoster is used for the end rig in conjunction with an open-end/cage feeder (fig. 79A), a bomb (79B) or a block-end with small holes for a slow dispersal of baits such as maggots in cold water (79C). For feeding the swim with a breadcrumb/hook-bait-fragment mix (*Groundbaits - freshwater*) cage feeders (fig. 79A) are best. They release the load on impact with the bottom, and the feed spreads in a cloud around the hook-bait. If you are catapulting groundbait or loose feed, simply use a plain bomb (fig. 79B), and during cold, winter weather, when a slow dispersal of maggots is imperative, opt for a block-end feeder with small holes (fig. 79C).

During warm weather, when bream and rudd especially feed in the upper water layers, use a long hooklength and buoyant bait to encourage bites on the drop. Tighten up quickly after casting and watch the indicator like a hawk. The swing tip will refuse to ease back once the bomb or feeder has settled as it should, while the quiver tip will either rattle or refuse to tighten

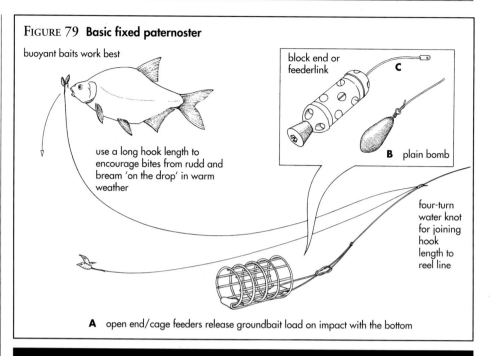

FIGURE 79 Basic fixed paternoster

buoyant baits work best

use a long hook length to encourage bites from rudd and bream 'on the drop' in warm weather

block end or feederlink **C**

B plain bomb

four-turn water knot for joining hook length to reel line

A open end/cage feeders release groundbait load on impact with the bottom

When ledgering for roach, bream and tench in large stillwaters, use a basic fixed paternoster ledger in conjunction with an open-end or wire cage feeder. Choice of bite indicator varies between swing or quivertip and a clip-on bobbin or monkey climber. When distance fishing for specimen tench and bites may be few and far between, most enthusiasts, like this angler, prefer a clip-on bobbin electronic bite alarm set up.

gently. A few sudden turns of the reel handle to move the feeder or bomb along the bottom and send up little clouds of silt, will give the bait life and often produces an immediate bite, particularly with animal baits such as maggots and worms. To see those really gentle flickers, position a target board immediately behind the tip. In severe winds, an umbrella set up-wind of both board and tip will drastically improve your concentration (fig. 78).

LEDGER WEIGHTS - FRESHWATER

While almost the entire world over ledger weights are made of lead, since 1987 it has been illegal to use lead weights of 1oz or smaller in the UK because of the number of swans that died from swallowing them. Small weights are now manufactured exclusively from non-toxic metals, while those of 1¼oz upwards are still made of lead.

The counter of any tackle shop has a huge variety of shapes and sizes, each designed to suit a particular purpose. Both barrel and bullet ledgers (with holes through the middle) can be used to cock large, sliding *pike and sea floats (Floats)* or used as a running ledger to make the bait roll across the gravel or sandy bottom of fast-flowing rivers. If a moving bait is not desired, it can be anchored with flat weights such as the coffin ledger.

For all general needs most anglers tend to use the pear-shaped Arlesey bomb ledger, which has a built-in swivel and casts accurately. Once any bomb over 2oz was considered a sea lead, but no such distinction is now made because carp anglers might use bombs of up to 3-4oz when bolt-rig fishing (*Ledgering techniques - Bolt Rig*). So that a carp does not have to drag the lead around if the terminal rig breaks, tadpole or helicopter leads come fitted with instant-release stems that automatically disconnect the weight from the hook trace.

Looking rather like an Arlesey bomb cut in half lengthways, the vaned, riser lead is useful for fishing over dense weed or snags because it angles straight up to the surface on the retrieve.

A useful ledger weight system with a unique design, called the Dexter Bomb, permits brass bottoms from ⅛oz to 1oz to be screwed into the same swivel-top male thread. This enables you to switch from a light to a heavy rig within seconds. This can also be done by making up various nylon link-ledgers (fig. 80) and pinching on sufficient swan shots to hold bottom. First brought on to the market in 1994, the heavier 2xSSG and 3xSSG shots add enormously to the versatility of the link-ledger.

Though not strictly a ledger weight, the Wye lead (also available in non-toxic metal) with trace attachments at both ends is used by salmon fishermen to work a buoyant lure (a wooden devon minnow) above the rocky bottom while the banana-shaped lead bumps over it (fig. 13). Another salmon/pike lead is the now rather outdated jardine weight, which has a wire spiral at each end enabling the line to be wound around the body and quickly replaced by one of a smaller or larger size.

LEDGER WEIGHTS - SEA

Most forms of sea angling are variations of ledgering, and a wide variety of ledger weights are available to suit different circumstances. Ledger weights can be split into two categories - those with grip wires and those without.

GRIP LEADS

The main purpose of the grip lead is to hold the baited rig in the required spot, usually hard on the sea bed, and prevent the tide or wave action from moving it, possibly into snags. Two types are available: those with wires that are fixed; and those with wires that break away when the angler retrieves or a fish takes the bait. The big advantage with the break-away type is that retrieving the lead is far easier than when using a fixed-wire lead. Another bonus with either type of grip lead is that fish will often hook themselves against the resistance of the wires. A variation on the grip lead is the Gemini System, which is essentially a break-out grip lead with a wide variety of different components designed to help the angler construct a lead that is just right for the various conditions encountered on the day. For example, different lengths of grip wire set at various angles can be adjusted to control the amount of grip exerted by the lead.

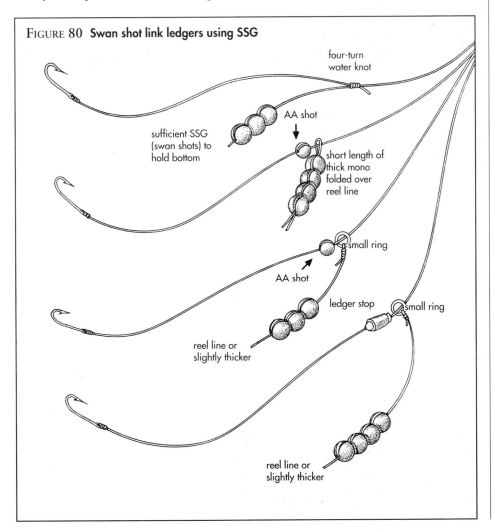

FIGURE 80 Swan shot link ledgers using SSG

four-turn water knot

AA shot

sufficient SSG (swan shots) to hold bottom

short length of thick mono folded over reel line

small ring

AA shot

ledger stop

small ring

reel line or slightly thicker

reel line or slightly thicker

Virtually any ledgering situation within the British Isles can be tackled with this collection which includes fixed and breakaway leads from 3-8oz, the 'Gemini System' and bell leads up to 1½lb. Amongst freshwater patterns are jardine and Wye leads, drilled bullets, Arlesey Bombs, pear leads, risers, tadpole leads and in-line designer carp bombs.

PLAIN LEADS

Plain leads are more universal in application and are widely used by both shore and boat anglers. One of the big advantages with a plain lead is that it can be used to allow the tide or waves to move the bait in a very attractive manner across the sea bed. By selecting just the right weight and shape of lead, this very effective method can be fully utilized. For example, a 4oz flat-sided or circular-studded watch lead will tend to hug the sea bed, whereas a 4oz bomb will roll across it a lot more easily.

Drilled bullets and barrel leads, which take the line threaded through their centres, are further variations on the plain lead. They are used primarily for spinning or float fishing, but they should not be dismissed for other applications. Massive, bell-shaped leads up to and in excess of 2lb are regularly used in deep water if there is a strong tide run.

LICENCES

See *National Rivers Authority.*

LINES

BRAIDED FLY CASTS AND LOOPS

Braided fly casts are made from monofilament and are available in floating (for dry-fly fishing), sinking, fast-sinking, neutral-density and heavyweight formats suitable for all game fish. These supple casts turn over superbly and are particularly hard wearing. Braided casts are tapered, and the end of the fly line is sleeved into the thicker end. A special 1in long silicone sleeve is then pulled over the junction for a firm connection.

At the fine end, some casts have a tiny pre-formed loop by which they can be joined to a monofilament tip of 4-6ft loop to loop. With those that do not have a pre-formed loop, simply tie a single knot and pass through the mono tippet. Then tie a beachcaster's knot around the braided end.

Braided-loop, fly-line connectors are also available and are easily joined to the line with a sleeve of silicone tubing (provided). The braided leader is then connected loop to loop.

BRAIDED HOOKLENGTHS

To minimize refusals from the most suspicious carp, braided hooklengths are used for their suppleness and abrasion-resistant properties. These are generally available in breaking strains of 5-25lb and have an incredibly fine diameter. The Octo Splice hooklink material comes with a needle, enabling knotless hooklengths to be constructed by passing the ends through the hollow centre, resulting in junctions 20 per cent stronger than any knot. The revolutionary Multistrand, made by Kryston, consists of numerous individual, limp, gossamer-like strands (similar to dental floss), which separate between the bait and hooklength swivel, appearing virtually invisible to fish. Hooklinks in these braided lines are usually made up in short lengths - 6-15in.

BRAIDED TROLLING LINE

Dacron is available with a lead core for trolling lures deep down behind the boat (*Trolling*). This heavy, specialized line changes colour every 10yd to indicate the length of line being trolled and comes in connected spools of 100yd each of 20lb-test. Lead-cored trolling line has now largely been made redundant by the technique of downrigger trolling.

DACRON

Due to its low stretch - only 15 per cent, compared to 25 per cent in standard and fine-diameter monofilament - woven lines such as dacron are popular with boat anglers at sea because they provide noticeably more contact with the end rig or pirk when fishing at depths in excess of 100ft than standard monofilament does. For the same reason, many shark fishermen use dacron, but charter-boat skippers dislike monofilament and dacron reel lines to be used at the same time because of the inevitable line

tangles that result when bottom fishing. Owing to its limpness, dacron is much used by carp fishermen for hooklengths and as backing line for fly fishing. However, because it is hollow, strangulation occurs if blood knots are used for tying on hooks or swivels. The *palomar* and *grinner* knots are ideal (*Knots*).

An entirely new type of line made in the USA from gel-spun, braided polyethelene, called Outcast, is considerably thinner than dacron, with just 5 per cent stretch. It is extremely limp and can be used on both multipliers and fixed-spool reels for freshwater and saltwater fishing. Its specific gravity is slightly less than water so it always floats, which makes it particularly useful for *drift-float fishing (Freshwater floatfishing techniques)* for pike at long range and for presenting floating surface baits for carp. Hooks and swivels should be tied on with the line doubled, using a seven-turn *tucked blood knot* or an eight-turn *grinner* (*Knots*). Outcast is available in either green or fluorescent yellow and, owing to its extremely narrow diameter, is a workable alternative to wire line for fishing offshore in deep water and fast tides with light leads.

FLY LINES

Modern fly lines are made in one of two ways. Those of American origin are based on a vertical PVC plastisol technique, while those manufactured in the UK tend to be made from extruded PVC and production is computer controlled.

American dry lines, for instance, incor-

porate microscopic glass beads as their floating agent, while British manufacturers use blowing agents, resulting in tiny bubbles of gas within the line's outer coating. Nearly all lines vary in length between 27yd and 35yd, and have a core of nylon braid over which the plastic coating is fused. Floating sink tip (a floating line whose first 10ft is fast sinking), intermediate (a neutral-density line that sinks exceptionally slowly), slow sinkers, medium sinkers, fast sinkers and extra-fast sinkers (hi D) lines are all available.

Floating lines are generally available in light colours so that they can easily be seen by the angler, while sinking lines, because they are retrieved through the water close to the fish, are made in darker colours. Several tapers are available (fig. 81).

Level fly lines (81A) are used as backing in conjunction with a shooting head to obtain maximum casting distances. The shooting head consists of just 10yd of rapid-taper line (81E).

Double taper lines (81B) are at their thickest in the middle, and taper gradually towards each end. They are most frequently used for presenting the dry fly, rollcasting and spey casting. The double-taper line is reversible, and so after a year or two's use it should be turned around and a new backing knot tied.

Weight-forward lines (rocket taper) (81C) have the bulk of the casting weight locked up in the first 10yd of the line, which makes casting into the wind and long-distance casting much easier.

Bass-bug/saltwater taper (81D) is an

FIGURE 81 **Fly line tapers**

A level fly line

B double taper fly line

C weight-forward fly line

D bass-bug/saltwater taper fly line

E 30' shooting head to which specialized mono or braided mono is joined for distance casting

90'   60'   30'   0'

extreme forward-taper line with a shorter, heavier section at the front end, enabling long casts to be made using large or heavy flies, popping bugs and small spinners.

A shooting head (81E) is a 30ft rapid-taper line (joined to level line or specialized monofilament or braided monofilament backing) for extra-long casting.

MONOFILAMENT

Despite enormous improvements in woven lines, monofilament continues to be the automatic choice of British anglers. Some brands are more abrasion resistant than others and therefore more suitable to the rigours of lure fishing, beach fishing, or presenting the bait over the pinnacles, plateaux and bars of gravel pits. Others are extremely soft and supple, and ideal for freelining over soft bottoms in stillwaters.

Line colour is important. Freshwater anglers demand muted shades in sorrel, mist green, grey and so on, while many sea anglers prefer a yellow line, which is highly visible - an important factor for trolling or fishing at anchor, when several outfits could easily become tangled if the lines are difficult to see.

When two or more reels need to be filled, it makes economic sense to buy monofilament in 500yd or 1000yd spools rather than 100yd spools. The vast majority of monofilament sold in the UK is manufactured in Germany or Japan, although US brands such as Berkeley Trilene, which holds over 2000 IGFA world records, are becoming more popular.

Standard monofilament (as opposed to the pre-stretched, low-diameter type) is a suitable reel line for most situations in coarse, sea and game fishing. For specialized techniques, however, such as long-range carp fishing or drift-float fishing for pike, a low-diameter, pre- or low-stretch monofilament reel line increases casting potential and hook setting when fishing in excess of 100yd.

Low-diameter monofilament, such as Double Strength or Ashima, is also excellent for hooklengths, especially when floater fishing for carp, and for fly casts for fishing in crystal-clear water, when presentation of the artificial is open to the closest scrutiny. Fine-diameter lines are also used extensively by match anglers for hooklengths. However, on no account should pre-stretched or low-diameter monofilaments be employed as a reel line for close-range fishing, where the inherent stretch of regular monofilament is required to cushion sudden runs or acrobatic leaps, thus preventing almost certain snap-offs (*Knots*).

Fly casts/leaders

Monofilament fly casts are available in knotless, tapered form for precise presentation of a single fly; and in level monofilament to which one or two short droppers have been added. The latter (called wet casts) are easy to make from spools of monofilament in varying strengths simply by learning to tie the *four-turn water knot* (*Knots*).

WIRE LINE

Only when boat fishing at sea, fishing on the bottom in extremely deep and fast water, is there a need for wire reel line. Specialized, stainless-steel, braided wires in 20lb, 30lb, 40lb and 50lb test, such as Tide-cheater marketed by Ryobi Masterline, permit the use of considerably lighter leads (due to its narrow diameter) than would be needed to keep a bait on the bottom with a monofilament or dacron reel line of the same breaking strain. Penn Reels of the USA make a narrow-drum multiplier, called the Super Mariner, specifically designed for use with wire.

Owing to its minimal stretch, wire line registers the tiniest of bites and is joined at the trace swivel with a slim-line gauge crimp. Use a monofilament hooklength of at least one third less than the test of the wire reel line so that minimal torque is exerted in the event that you snag up on the bottom and have to pull for a break.

LINE SIZE

All fly lines are rated in specific sizes. The lightest line is size 3 and the heaviest (salmon) line a size 12. All fly rods are marked (just above the handle) with the line weight recommended for best performance by the manufacturer, and it is imperative to use a line of the right size. If too light a line is used, far more effort than is necessary will be needed to cast the fly. If too heavy a line is used, the rod will have insufficient backbone to achieve any useful distance. Most rods are rated for a choice of two line sizes, say a 4/5 or a 8/9, in which case either can be used.

LING

(*Molva molva*)

Average size: 5-15lb
Mega specimen: over 40lb
British record: 59lb 8oz (26kg 987g)

The ling has a long, slender, rounded body with a flattish head, large jaws with sharp teeth, and a single barbel under the chin. Colouration is brown, grey-green along the back, fusing into lighter sides and an off-white belly. It has two dorsal fins, the first short, the second almost half the fish's length, a long anal fin and a small, slightly rounded tail. Most of its fins have a noticeable white fringe.

It preys upon crustaceans and smaller shoal fish. It reproduces during the spring, laying huge numbers of eggs, which float until they hatch.

Breeding

LING

at the base of a champagne bottle and fix a piece of cloth over the neck with an elastic band. Then tie cord around each end and join to a long pole or extending landing net handle. Pop a few bread scraps into the bottle, lower it with the neck pointing upstream on to the gravelly shallows where minnows congregate, and leave for half an hour.

ELVERS AND BROOK LAMPREYS

Baby eels are thin and transparent but, provided they are cast gently, will catch perch, chub and trout. Hook them gently through the head or middle with a size 8 hook.

BROOK LAMPREYS

Average 2-5in long and are found beneath stones in small streams and rivers. Hooked once only through the mouth with a size 4 hook tied direct, they are an electric bait for chub, trout and barbel, whether trotted or bumped across the bottom with a light ledger.

BLEAK, GUDGEON AND DACE

Whether float-fished, paternostered or ledgered live or dead, these species make great baits for perch, chub, eels, catfish and zander.

RUDD, ROACH, BREAM, CHUB, PERCH, TROUT, CRUCIAN AND COMMON CARP

All are taken readily by zander, pike and, to a much lesser extent, catfish, which also have a liking for small, live tench.

Large livebaits do attract pike, in particular, but problems arise when you try to set the hook. It is therefore more productive (in terms of pike in the net) to use livebaits in the 5-7in range. It can also be argued that to use large roach or rudd as bait for a pike that will be returned to the water, reduces the quality of another angler's sport. So take only enough small baits for your own requirements. River authority by-laws that permit the use of small rainbow trout as bait for pike and zander help not only to minimize pressure on shoal species, but also allows the predator-hunter to purchase his baits for immediate use, rather than having to buy maggots in order to try to catch shoal fish, for bait, that many fisheries cannot really afford to lose. An increasing number of trout farmers are now, as a winter sideline, only too pleased to sell small trout at a sensible price. This facility has an additional benefit, in that it reduces the pressure put on small shoal species that would otherwise be used for live baits.

With this near 50lb monster which took a pirk, angling journalist Dave Lewis actually broke the Danish ling record whilst fishing with the author aboard *Thailand* over the famous Yellow Reef, 40 miles off Hansholm in north-east Jutland.

HABITAT AND DISTRIBUTION

The ling prefers deep-water marks where the bottom is rocky, submerged reefs and sunken wrecks, where it lives in large colonies. It is found all around the British Isles wherever the habitat is suitable.

TECHNIQUES

Artificial lure fishing - sea; Downtide boat fishing; Drift fishing at sea; Wreck fishing.

LIVE AND DEAD BAITS - FRESHWATER

MINNOW, STONE LOACH, BULLHEADS AND STICKLEBACKS

These small, freshwater naturals are easily gathered in the shallows with a fine-mesh aquarium net for presenting, either float-fished or ledgered, to chub, trout, perch and zander. Stone loach and bullheads are found by turning over large pieces of flint on the bottom, while minnows can be caught in a home-made wine-bottle minnow trap. Knock out the inverted funnel

The choice of deadbaits that pike will accept is considerably more varied than the eels, mackerel, smelt, herrings and scad shown here. Whilst fresh naturals invariably prove most effective, in certain circumstances there is a call for colouring deadbaits which is a simple matter that takes just a few minutes. After blotting off excess water, either brush on liquid food colouring straight from the bottle or immerse in a concentrated solution made by mixing powder colouring with a little water in a plastic bait tin. The baits can then be used immediately or packed into poly bags and frozen.

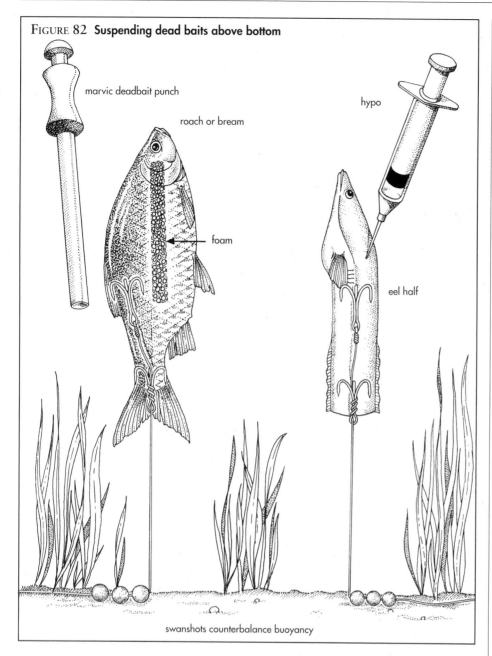

FIGURE 82 **Suspending dead baits above bottom**

marvic deadbait punch

roach or bream

hypo

foam

eel half

swanshots counterbalance buoyancy

DEADBAITS

All of the previously mentioned species work well as deadbaits as well as livebaits. The fresher they are, the better, although it makes sense to freeze batches for future use when available. One of the most effective natural freshwater baits is the common eel, which can be caught during the summer, or purchased directly from eel nets-men, and popped into the freezer for winter use. Eels in the 8-14in range can be wobbled whole or cut in half and used as static deadbaits. To suspend the head end above bottom weed or debris, inject a little air with a hypodermic syringe or use a length of pop-up foam inserted with a Marvic deadbait punch (fig. 82), which will suspend any small species above bottom.

SEA DEADBAITS

There is a noticeable difference between the smell of a freshly killed fish and one

that has been stored in a freezer, particularly when it has been there for some time. And if we can differentiate between the two, to predatory fish the difference must be enormous. So either purchase your deadbaits straight from the fishmonger and freeze them immediately, wrapping each in clingfilm if you have the time, or buy them in ready-wrapped, blast-frozen packs from specialist tackle shops. All silvery saltwater species of 5-12in long, such as mackerel, sandeels, sardines, mullet, herrings, smelt and sprats make fine deadbaits for pike, and can also be used as half baits. Strangely, zander are only occasionally caught on sea baits. Oddball fish from the Mediterranean, such as gurnard and various sea breams, which are now regularly on show at wet-fish shops, are well worth a try. Squid and even baby octopus are also effective for pike.

COLOURING DEADBAITS

Any deadbait can easily be coloured for use in both clear and green water (yellow is then effective) should pike not respond to naturals. You can use liquid food colouring applied to both sides of the bait with a brush, or mix up some powdered carp-bait dye with a little water in a plastic bowl and gently swish each bait slowly around, gripping it by the tail with artery forceps until it is evenly coloured. The most effective colours are orange, red and golden yellow.

INJECTING DEADBAITS

Deadbaits can also be spiced up by injecting them, using a large-bore hypodermic needle, with various fish oils, such as pilchard oil, herring oil, squid extract and so on. In heavily coloured water especially, the scent permeates a long way and draws predators towards the hook-bait.

LOACH, SPINED
(*Cobitis taenia*)

A smaller and much slimmer fish in cross-section than the stone loach, the spined loach also has six small barbels and a double-pointed spine (hence its name) beneath each eye. The smooth body is light brown on top, fusing into lighter sides that have horizontal lines of minnow-like blotches. It prefers slower-moving ditches, streams and canals, where it lives hidden on the bottom, feeding on minute crustaceans. It reproduces in the late spring.

It is localized within the British Isles to certain parts of England only.

LOACH, STONE
(*Noemacheilus barbatulus*)

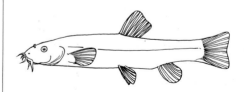

Rarely exceeding 6in in length, this barbel-like bottom-dweller has a smooth, wiry, olive-brown body and an underslung mouth sporting six whiskers (barbel have four and gudgeon two), which it uses to

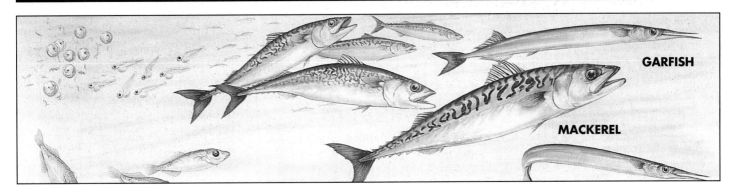

GARFISH

MACKEREL

locate aquatic insect larvae and crustaceans. It lives beneath large stones in the brooks, streams and tributaries of most river systems within the British Isles, and reproduces during the late spring. It makes a fine livebait for perch, trout and chub.

LONG TROTTING

See *Freshwater floatfishing techniques.*

LOOSEFEEDING

See *Baits - freshwater.*

LUMPSUCKER

(Cyclopterus lumpus)

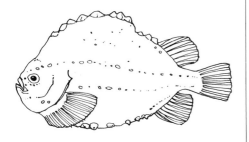

British record: 20lb 9¾oz (9kg 347g)

Only occasionally caught by anglers on worm, crab or fish-strip bait intended for other bottom-feeding species, the strange, armour-plated lumpsucker is generally found over rough and rocky ground. Fitted with rather weak fins and an almost round body, it has a large sucker disc on its belly for anchoring itself to the bottom in fast tides. The body is greeny-brown with rows of spined plates running horizontally along the back, flanks and belly.

It reproduces during the spring, the male guarding the clump of eggs until they hatch. It feeds on crustaceans, worms and small, bottom-dwelling fish.

MACKEREL

(Scomber scombrus)

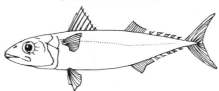

Average size: 6-14oz
Mega specimen: over 2½lb
British record: 6lb 2½oz (2kg 790g)

Caught in larger numbers than almost any other shoaling sea species around the British Isles, the mackerel is one of the smallest members of the migratory mackerel and tuna family. It has a streamlined body, round in cross-section, with two dorsal fins and a single anal fin followed by a series of five finlets. The forked tail has two small keels on the base of the fin lobes and is translucent grey like all the fins. The back is bright blue-green overlaid with irregular wavy lines, fusing into lower flanks and belly of metallic silvery white. It has strong jaws fitted with fine teeth and feeds on small crustaceans, young shoal fish and baby squid. It reproduces during the summer months, laying eggs that float on the surface.

HABITAT AND DISTRIBUTION

Common around the British Isles, often in huge shoals, it generally occupies mid water up to the surface layers. It is a migratory species, some fish travelling north during the summer months and returning to the south as winter sets in. Stocks in the English Channel are quite distinct from mackerel off the Scottish coast and upper North Sea, which have an oilier flesh due to richer feeding grounds.

TECHNIQUES

Artificial lure fishing - Sea; Drift fishing at sea; Feathering.
See also *Artificial lures; Baits - Sea.*

MACKEREL, SPANISH

(Scomber japonicus)

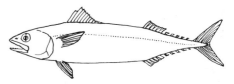

British record: 1lb ½oz (464g)

The Spanish mackerel is similar to the mackerel, but is distinctly oval in cross-section with flattish sides and more diffused, greeny, silvery-blue colouration along the back, with faint wavy dark markings and a larger, more pointed head. Its silvery flanks sport numerous dark round blotches and the belly is silvery white. It inhabits the warm upper water layers, feeding on pelagic crustaceans and small shoal fish.

The Spanish mackerel grows much larger than the mackerel and, being a pelagic species of tropical and warm, temperate seas, is extremely rare around the British Isles.

MAGGOTS

See *Baits - freshwater.*

MARGINAL PLANTS

See *Waterside flora - Rivers; Waterside flora - Stillwaters.*

MARROW SPOON

An elongated, narrow, spoon that is put down a trout's throat and into its stomach to ascertain what it has been feeding on (*Priest*).

MAYFLY

See *Artificial flies.*

MEGRIM

(Lepidorhombus whiffiagonis)

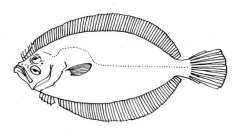

British record: 3lb 12½oz (1kg 715g)

This left-sided, rather slim-bodied, deep-water flatfish, is not commonly caught by anglers around the British Isles. It has a large head and eyes, a slightly protruding bottom jaw, and long dorsal and anal fin frills stretching almost to the small, rounded tail. It is light brown on top, overlaid with darker blotches and white on its blind side. It feeds on crustaceans and squid but mainly on small fish. It reproduces in deep water during the spring.

MIDGE

See *Buzzers.*

MINNOW

(Phoxinus Phoxinus)

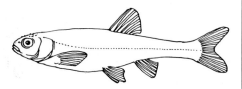

British record: 13 drams (23g)

Found throughout the British Isles in clean, clear-flowing brooks, streams and river systems, the minnow is an excellent barometer of water quality. It has the distinction of being the smallest British cyprinid shoal species.

The minnow is slim, rounded and quite smooth to the touch with tiny scales, large eyes and a small mouth. It is grey-brown along the back, with silvery-yellow flanks overlaid with a dotted line of olive-brown markings stretching from gill plate to tail root. The tail is forked and has a dark blotch at the base. The belly is silvery white, and the fins are translucent grey.

The minnow feeds on tiny forms of aquatic insect life, crustaceans and worms. It reproduces in the late spring, when eggs are deposited over a gravel bottom.

MOLLUSCS

In freshwater, the mollusc family is represented by a range of bottom-living bivalves, from the tiny peashell cockle, to numerous types of snails and the huge swan mussel. In saltwater there is a far greater range, including squid, cuttlefish and octopus (all technically molluscs), plus razor fish, limpets, mussels, cockles, scallops and oysters.

MONKFISH

(Squatina squatina)

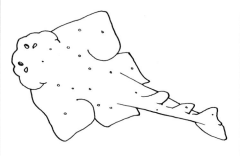

Average size: 25-30lb
Mega specimen: over 45lb
British record: 66lb (29kg 936g)

The monkfish is more closely related to the shark family having lateral gill slits and a shark-like lower body. But it appears half way between shark and a ray with a distinctly flattened front end which incorporates its wide pectoral fins. The mouth is wide and cavernous with sharp teeth, and it has large appendage-type nostrils, each covered with a broad flap of skin. Its skin is rough, like that of a tope, and is coloured sandy brown on top, overlaid with small dark dots and white underneath. It feeds on molluscs, crustaceans and other bottom-living fish. Reproduction takes place in the summer. The eggs are fertilized inside the female by the male, and after a 6-mouth period litters of live young, between 10-12 pups, are born.

HABITAT AND DISTRIBUTION

The monkfish prefers a muddy or sandy bottom (often in shallow water) where it can lie in wait half buried for its prey to pass by. It is found all around the British Isles, although it is more common in southern and south-western waters. Owing to its importance as a commerical species, the monkfish is not now regularly or specifically sought by anglers, although one turns up occasionally to the boat angler who presents a large fillet of fresh fish or squid on the bottom.

TECHNIQUES

Downtide boat fishing.

MONKEY CLIMBER

See *Bite indicators and accessories.*

MUDWEIGHTS

See *Anchors & Mudweights.*

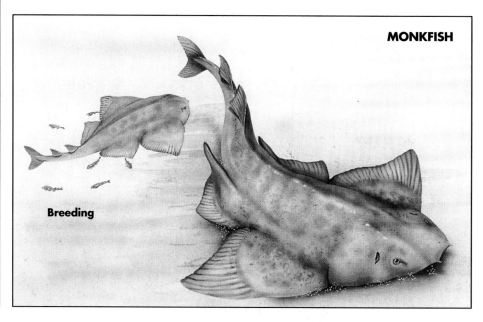

Breeding

MONKFISH

Young mullet

Red Mullet

MULLET

MULLET, GOLDEN-GREY
(Liza aurata)

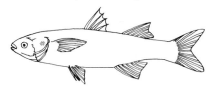

Average size: 10oz -1¼lb
Mega specimen: over 2lb
British record: 3lb ¼oz (1kg 368g)

The golden-grey mullet is not dissimilar in overall colouration and physical appearance to the thin- and thick-lipped varieties, but it is noticeably slimmer in cross-section and has a distinct golden spot on the gill plate. In addition, the pectoral fin of this mullet, if folded forward, overlaps the edge of the eye, whereas the pectoral of both the thin- and thick-lipped mullets does not. It has a narrow upper lip with noticeable (though weak) teeth, and feeds on bottom algae and organic muds.

HABITAT AND DISTRIBUTION
It is most commonly found in harbours and estuaries around the British Isles, but rarely in completely fresh water.

TECHNIQUES
Float fishing in harbours and off the rocks.

MULLET, RED
(Mullus surmuletus)

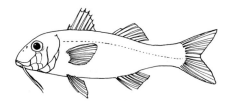

British record: 3lb 10oz (1kg 644g)

This small shoal fish is nothing like the grey mullet (below), in either looks or colouration. The only similarity is its two dorsal fins. The red mullet has a gudgeon-like body, with a steeply angled forehead and a small mouth with two long barbels beneath the lower jaw. Colouration is either warm brown or red overlaid along the flanks with yellow stripes. It feeds by grubbing along the bottom for crustaceans, and reproduces during the summer. It is only occasionally caught around the British Isles, and rarely by design.

MULLET, THICK-LIPPED GREY
(Chelon labrosus)

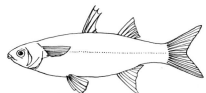

Average size: 2-3lb
Mega specimen: over 6lb
British record: 14lb 2¾oz (6kg 427g)

The thick-lipped mullet is similar in overall appearance and colouration to the thin-lipped; differing in its noticeably thicker upper lip and lacking the dark blotch at the base of the pectoral fin. It feeds on the top layer of the sea bed and filamentous plant tissue, and on small molluscs and crustaceans. It reproduces in the sea and in estuaries in the spring, laying eggs that float.

HABITAT AND DISTRIBUTION
It is common around the British Isles in harbours, marinas, breakwaters, piers, lagoons, estuaries and so on.

TECHNIQUES
Float fishing in harbours and off the rocks.

MULLET, THIN-LIPPED GREY
(Liza ramada)

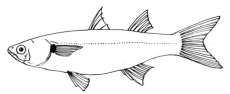

Average size: 1-2lb
Mega specimen: over 4lb
British record: 7lb (3kg 175g)

A shoaling sea fish, the thin-lipped mullet nevertheless spends much of its life in rivers, travelling far up into freshwater. It has the classic, mullet, torpedo shape with a bullet-like head (wide in cross-section) and low-set eye. It has a narrow upper lip (hence its name), extremely fine teeth, and a distinct, dark blotch around the pectoral fin root that distinguishes it from other mullets. It has a grey back and silvery sides that have faint horizontal stripes.

Feeds heavily on algae and nutrient muds found in an estuary or river bed, and on filamentous algae growing from the sides of harbour walls and so on. It reproduces in the sea and in estuary mouths in the spring, laying eggs that float.

HABITAT AND DISTRIBUTION
The most common of all the European grey mullet, the thin-lipped is found all around the British Isles except for the colder Scottish seas. It is attracted to sewage discharge pipes and is a common fish in marinas.

TECHNIQUES
Float fishing in harbours and off the rocks.

MULTIPLIERS

See *Reels - multipliers.*

Nn

MUPPET

See *Artificial lures*.

NATIONAL FEDERATION OF ANGLERS (NFA)

The NFA is one of the UK's largest sporting bodies, looking after the interests of over 500 affiliated organizations and, through them, nearly 500,000 coarse fishermen.

Since its formation in 1903 by a group of pioneer anglers, the Federation has striven to tackle the ever-present problems of pollution, water abstraction and land drainage. Today, the pressures and demands made on the Federation's full and part-time staff are staggering in their complexity.

The NFA has eight Regional Councils comprised of club representatives, and these councils concern themselves with matters of local and regional significance. The Regional Councils also give early warning of any problems that may assume national significance.

Complementing the work of the regions are the four key policy-making committees: Finance, Administration and Planning/Legal, Educational and Constitutional/Fisheries and Environment Protection, and Promotion Events. All four committees are represented on the National Executive.

The NFA sees itself shouldering two main areas of responsibility:
1. Protection of the aquatic environment.
2. Representation of the interests of angling to Government bodies, water authorities and conservation groups.

For further information contact: The National Federation of Anglers, Halliday House, 2 Wilson Street, Derby DE1 1PG. Tel: 01332 362000.

NATIONAL FEDERATION OF SEA ANGLERS (NFSA)

The NFSA is the governing body of sea angling in the UK, recognized by both the Government and the Sports Council, who provide it with funds. The Federation is administered by a National Executive, with regional seats of administration, known as divisions, and is backed by a full-time development officer.

There are currently over 550 affiliated clubs and nearly 2,000 personal members, which probably makes the NFSA the largest sea-angling administration body in the world. Today the NFSA is represented on most Sea Fisheries Committees, and this representation has been very successful in securing recognition for sea anglers on what were purely commercial regulatory bodies.

The NFSA is also responsible for the processing of claims for British Records for sea fish, which it prepares for ratification by the British Record Fish Committee. All affiliated clubs can take advantage of the Federation's block, third-party public liability scheme for a small annual cost per club. Fees for club affiliation are based on a sliding scale related to that club's membership figures. Personal membership is also available at a most modest cost.

Highly sought-after specimen certificates are awarded to members at the end of each year, based on a percentage of the amount by which a fish exceeds the target weight in force at the time of its capture.

For further information contact: D. Rowe, NFSA Development Officer, NFSA Office, 14 Bank Street, Newton Abbott, Devon TQ12 2JW. Tel: 01626 331330.

NATIONAL RIVERS AUTHORITY (NRA)

The NRA is an independent, impartial body set up by the Government under the 1989 Water Act to control, regulate and protect the water environment.

Its main functions are flood defence, conservation, navigation, recreation, fisheries, pollution control and water resources.

The National Headquarters are at Eastbury House, 30-34 Albert Embankment, London SE1 7TL, Tel: 0171 820 0101 - Fax: 0171 820 1603 and at Rivers House, Waterside Drive, Aztec West, Almondsbury, Bristol BS12 4UD, Tel: 01454 624400 - Fax: 01454 624409.

The NRA is split up into eight regions, each with its own administration, pollution and fisheries department. They are the Anglian Region, Southern Region, Yorkshire/Northumbrian Region, Thames Region, Severn-Trent Region, South West/Wessex Region, Welsh/Cymru Region and the North-West Region.

The NRA does not cover Scottish waters. These are governed by separate purification boards to each catchment area.

October 1993 saw the NRA free, 0800 'Hotline' launch, where by simply ringing 0800 80 70 60 members of the public can immediately report incidents of pollution, poaching, flooding or fish deaths via its National Emergency number. Calls are automatically connected to the nearest NRA control centre wherever the caller is telephoning from in England or Wales. Public vigilance in reporting incidents relating to water problems plays a key role in the NRA's administration, and the fisherman on the riverbank is extremely well placed to notice anything unusual. Make a note of what you have seen and where, and immediately ring 0800 80 70 60 to report what you saw, giving as much information as possible and leaving your name and telephone number if possible.

FISHING LICENCES

Anyone aged 12 or over who goes freshwater fishing in England and Wales must have a current NRA rod licence. Concessionary licences are available to juveniles (12-15 years) and to retired or disabled persons. Short-term licences are also available. NRA licences are sold at all post offices throughout England and Wales and run from 1 April to 31 March.

NAVIGATION AT SEA

Navigation is the term used to describe the method by which seafarers plot their present position and find their way to another position, both within sight of land and beyond the horizon.

In its simplest form, the route, known as a course, is followed with the assistance of a magnetic steering compass. More complex courses require an accurate understanding of several variables, which include the tide, the weather, running times and the boat's speed.

The technique for establishing the boat's position at sea is known as taking a fix. Within sight of land, a decent magnetic compass will provide a reasonable fix on the boat's position, the accuracy of which will diminish as the boat's distance from the shore increases. Out of sight of land or fixed marker buoys, it will only be possible to establish the boat's estimated position. The accuracy of this position will be determined by the accuracy of the last fix established when within the sight of land.

In order to establish as accurate a fix as possible, it will be necessary to acquire at least three bearings from prominent landmarks illustrated on an Admiralty sea chart for that area. These could include any prominent land-based features, such as lighthouses, church spires, factory chimneys, the peak of a prominent hill or the left or right edge of a distant island. Floating buoys and channel markers should be treated with a degree of caution as their position can vary depending on the state of the tide, and they can move during gales.

One of the most accurate bearings that the navigator can take is known as a transit bearing. Two prominent features are observed directly in line with each other, such as a lighthouse in line, or in transit, with a church spire on a distant headland, and that line is then projected out to sea. The navigator can then be sure that his boat is somewhere along that line, known as a position line. Plotting another two bearings should determine just where on the line.

It is far more practical to take bearings with a hand-held compass rather than trying to read them off the steering compass. For the greatest degree of accuracy, bearings should, where practical, be taken from objects approximately 90 degrees apart. A good depth-sounder or fish-finder can also be useful when trying to establish the boat's position, especially where there is a considerable difference in water depth in any one area, such as in the vicinity of sandbanks and deep channels.

There is a difference between the reading taken from a magnetic compass, which will be a magnetic bearing relative to magnetic north, and the bearing taken off the chart, which will be a true bearing, relative to true north. The difference lies in local variation, caused by differences in the earth's magnetic field at different locations, and deviation, which is an error caused by

magnetic influences aboard the boat. There will probably be a degree of error on the compass itself, known as an index error. Reference to any basic navigation handbook will show how to determine and allow for these errors.

At sea today many small boats are fitted with some form of electronic navigational aid, such as Decca or, increasingly, GPS. The accuracy obtained from these sets is usually far greater than could possibly be achieved using the tried-and-tested traditional methods, especially when out of sight of land, and as such they are a great aid to angling, not to mention safety. Using such devices, it is possible for small boats to locate and fish isolated wrecks many miles offshore, and then return again even in fog.

Decca sets receive signals from land-based transmission stations, sited in various parts of the country. The set accepts the transmitted data and displays the boat's position in latitude and longitude: Latitutde and longitude are the imaginary horizontal and vertical lines that are drawn on the earth's surface and used to establish the boat's position. The position will be given as being in degrees either north or south of 0 degrees latitude (the Equator) or east or west of 0 degrees longitude (the Greenwich Meridian).

The GPS (Global Positioning System) establishes the boat's position via signals transmitted from satellites in space. The accuracy available with GPS is nothing short of phenomenal, as was seen during the Gulf War when the GPS system was used by the American military forces to target bombs and missiles with outstanding accuracy.

It should be noted that the accuracy of the data is strictly controlled by the US and can be upgraded or downgraded according to their needs. However, it is still a very accurate system for establishing a boat's position. An even higher degree of accuracy can be acquired by using DGPS (Differential Global Positioning System). This system utilizes land-based stations to intercept the GPS signals. These are processed by the differential station, which then retransmits upgraded data to the GPS receiver fitted aboard the boat.

NIGHT FISHING

Not only are wary, freshwater species such as tench, bream, carp, catfish and eels sometimes easier to catch during the hours of darkness, because they feed with more confidence (this can also apply to sea species, bass and conger eels in particular), there is also a special magic about night fishing.

At no other time, for instance, are the angler's natural senses of smell, touch, hearing and sight used to their full potential than when fishing at night. Unfortunately, few anglers use their natural sight at night; the beach fisherman, for instance, must rely on a bright pressure lamp in order to see his rod tip at night (which reflects more light if painted matt white or if fitted with reflective tape). Bright lights shining directly on the water in rivers and lakes, however, can not only deter wary species from biting but also ruin the natural vision of everyone around the fishery.

Once your eyes have adjusted to the ambient light (and it is never as dark as you think), you can bait up, net fish and unhook them without the use of a torch. However, have a small pocket-sized torch at the ready for undoing tangles, tying on another hook and so on. In so far as freshwater species are concerned, the most fascinating method of fishing at night is float fishing. Chemical lights that sleeve on to the tip of most floats via a length of silicone tubing are easily seen and give a bright, luminous green light for up to eight hours. These are available in three sizes, minis, small and large, and are activated simply by bending the plastic element and shaking it. They fit most waggler-style floats and work effectively with the *lift method* and for *stretpegging (Freshwater floatfishing techniques)* in flowing water. Alternatively, a betalight element of 600 microlamberts (the most powerful available) can be glued into a length of peacock quill or temporarily fixed on to almost any float tip via ¾in-long sleeve of silicone rubber. A betalight element (sometimes called isotopes) consists of a phospher-lined glass tube into which tritium gas is forced. This creates luminosity that reduces by approximately 10 per cent yearly. Betalight elements (available in other colours as well as green) are now mainly used in ledger bobbins or monkey-climber indicators when ledgering in stillwater. For long sessions in stillwater, an *electric bite alarm (Bite indicators and accessories)* together with an indicator allows you to relax and enjoy the tranquillity of night fishing, while simultaneously being prepared for action.

The exception is ledgering in a strong

Oo

current on a river, when a finely tapered quiver tip is necessary for bite indication from species like roach, bream and chub. This is the only occasion when you might choose to break the 'no lights at night' rule and use a narrow-beamed torch to illuminate the quiver tip, which shows up well if painted matt white. Angle the torch from a downstream position so it shines upstream and slightly out across the rod tip, affecting neither the fish nor your night vision.

This method allows you to concentrate for hours on end, because you will see the slightest bite on the quiver tip, perhaps even more easily than during daylight hours. Alternatively, a 600 microlambert element or chemical element can be connected to the quiver tip (or swing tip) by whipping on a short length of silicone tubing $\frac{1}{2}$in from the tip ring and leaving $\frac{3}{8}$in clear, into which the element can be pushed.

The secret to successful night fishing lies in being well prepared. Most problems can be solved with common sense, but the presence of a friend to natter to can make the occasion that much more enjoyable. Remember that even the warmest of summer evenings can turn cold or wet during the early hours, so put up the brolly before you start and take along extra clothing such as waterproof over-trousers and a warm, three-quarter-length coat. One-piece thermal suits are extremely popular with night hawks.

In addition to warm clothing, take along plenty of hot drinks and food. Instant noodle meals, which require the simple addition of boiling water, are ideal; they take up minimum space in the tackle bag and a flask of boiling water can also be used to make coffee or tea. Whenever possible, plan a night-fishing session around fine weather. Don't set off in the middle of a downpour when the forecast suggests continual rain or strong winds, simply because promises have been made to friends. Think about reorganizing the trip for a time when conditions will be more favourable. Fish do not suddenly go on a feeding spree as soon as darkness falls if temperatures are falling drastically or heavy rain is imminent. It is well worth waiting for favourable conditions to coincide with darkness, because then optimum results can be enjoyed.

OPAH
(Lampris guttatus)

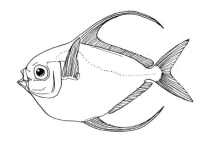

British record: 128lb (58kg 57g)

This colourful pelagic sea fish is found world wide in both tropical and temperate oceans, but is rarely caught on rod and line. It has a deep, broad body with a small, protrusible mouth and feeds on a diet of fish and squid in mid water in the deep open sea. Hence, it is rarely offered a meal by fishermen. Colouration sets the opah apart from most other sea fish in that all its fins are bright orangey-red. The back changes from deep blue to green across the flanks and silver along the undersides, overlaid with distinctive large cream spots.

OPTONIC

See *Bite indicators and accessories.*

ORFE, GOLDEN
(Leuciscus Indus Var Auratus)

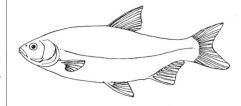

Average size: $\frac{3}{4}$-$1\frac{1}{2}$lb
Mega specimen: over 4lb
British record: 6lb 2oz (2kg 778g)

The golden orfe is unlikely to be confused with any other species due to its unique peachy-orange colouration, sometimes flecked with dark blotches, which blends into silvery undersides. All fins are also orange with a reddish tint, and the tail is deeply forked. It has smooth lines, rather like a giant dace, and can be sexed in the same way as dace during the early spring,

GOLDEN ORFE

GRASS CARP

when the males grow tiny spawning tubercles over their body and feel extremely rough. Spawning takes place during April or May. The eggs are deposited over stones or fibrous marginal vegetation and hatch after 16-20 days.

It feeds on all stages of aquatic insect life and hatching flies on the surface, where it darts around sucking them down, plus other small natural food items.

HABITAT AND DISTRIBUTION

The golden orfe prefers a clear water environment, either still or running, with plenty of aquatic plants. Although originally imported by the ornamental pond-fish trade, the species is now becoming a popular angler's fish due to being stocked in modern, man-made fisheries throughout the British Isles. It has isolated distribution in a handful of rivers in southern England.

TECHNIQUES

Fly fishing - for coarse fish; Freshwater floatfishing techniques - Surface controller fishing.

ORFE, WILD
(Leuciscus idus)

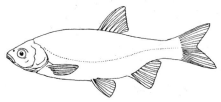

Although the occasional, neutral-coloured wild orfe (called *ide* throughout Europe) finds its way into British freshwaters via the ornamental pond-fish trade, it is rarely caught.

Pp

The wild orfe has the same lines and smooth, rounded body of the golden variety, with a greeny-brown back fusing into brassy-buttery flanks. The fins are tinged with red, almost rudd-like. In fact, large, wild orfe look very much like a cross between a rudd and a chub, and reach weights in excess of 8lb throughout Europe, where they are most commonly found in large river systems. They are highly prized by British coarse fishermen, who travel to Sweden, in particular, to catch them.

OSMOSIS

Osmosis is the term used to describe the delamination of fibreglass due to the ingress of moisture. It is generally used in reference to glass-reinforced plastic (GRP) boat hulls.

The fibreglass matting is protected by a high-gloss resin finish, known as the gell coat. This, when intact, prevents water from reaching the glass matting beneath, which gives the material its strength. Should the gell coat become damaged, water can percolate into the matting, and in severe cases cause delaminate of the fibres. This obviously reduces the strength and overall integrity of the boat's hull.

It is therefore essential that all damage to the protective gell coat is repaired as soon as it is noticed, particularly where the damage has occurred below the waterline. Even in the short term, water that has soaked into the fibreglass matting can cause severe damage during cold conditions, as the water expands when it freezes, thus forcing the fibres apart and allowing more water to enter.

If there is a universal bait for the perch, an offering that attracts specimens both large and small, it is a big, fat, juicy lobworm.

PEACOCK QUILL

See *Floats*.

PERCH
(Perca fluviatilis)

Average size: 4-12oz
Mega specimen: over 3lb
British record: 5lb 9oz (2kg 523g)

The perch is the most distinctive of all British freshwater fish, with its hump-backed, thick-set body and double dorsal fin, the first heavily spiked with a dark blotch at the base of the last two spines, the second soft-rayed. The dark green back fuses into golden olive flanks that are overlaid by between six and nine dark, vertical stripes. The belly is white. The pelvic and anal fins and the lower half of the tail are bright scarlet-orange, while the pectoral fin is colourless. The perch has a large eye and a large, expanding mouth that incorporates a bony jaw hinge in the top lip. Teeth are absent, but there are bristle-like gripping pads on the tongue and in the throat. The scales are rough to the touch.

Reproduction occurs during the early spring, when strings of large, sticky, white

Spawn

PERCH

Spawning

Larvae

PIKE

eggs are laid across sunken branches or through reed beds. The goggle-eyed fry hatch 8-9 days later. The perch's food consists of crustaceans and small fish of any species, including its own.

HABITAT AND DISTRIBUTION

The perch makes use of its camouflage to ambush small shoal fish passing through reed stems and old boathouses, lock cuttings, in weir-pools and against wooden pilings. It is found throughout the British Isles in most lowland river systems, ponds, pits, lakes and reservoirs, although it has been less common in some areas since the 1970s, when 'perch disease' wiped out huge numbers, particularly in England.

TECHNIQUES

Artificial lure fishing - freshwater; Freelining; Freshwater floatfishing techniques - Waggler fishing, Long trotting, Sliding-floatfishing for predators; Ledgering techniques - Bobbin ledgering in stillwaters, Ledgering livebaits and deadbaits.

PERCH, DUSKY
(*Epinelphelus marginatus*)

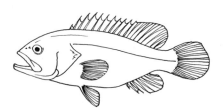

British record: 28lb (12kg 700g)

This common Mediterranean perch (also called dusky grouper) is a rare visitor to the British Isles and is only occasionally caught from south-western waters. It has the typical perch-like fin arrangement, the first half of the long dorsal fin being heavily spiked, as is the start of the anal fin.

The pectoral and pelvic fins and the tail are rounded. It has a large head and cavernous mouth. The strong jaws are set with strong teeth at the front, and a large, bony jaw hinge. Overall colouration is reddish brown overlaid with light mottling. It feeds on crustaceans and other fish, and prefers a rocky bottom.

PHARYNGEAL TEETH

All cyprinid species, from the tiniest gudgeon to 50lb-plus carp, are equipped with powerful pharyngeal teeth positioned in the rear of the throat for the purpose of chewing food by grinding it against a hard pad in the roof of the pharynx.

These strong teeth are an extension of the pharyngeal bones situated behind the gill chamber.

Hybrids resulting from the cross-breeding of compatible cyprinids such as roach, rudd and bream can be positively identified by the number and formation of these teeth.

The huge set of pharyngeal teeth on the right come from a golden mahseer of 40lb. Those on the left are from carp (top), chub (middle) and bream at the bottom.

PIKE
(*Esox lucius*)

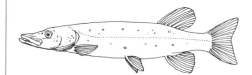

Average size: 5-12lb
Mega specimen: over 30lb
British record: 46lb (20kg 884g)

The most notorious and easily recognized of all freshwater fish the entire world over, the pike has a long, sleek, athletic body and a dorsal fin set right back near the tail for sudden bursts of speed in pursuit of prey. The head is large and flattened, with eyes set into the very tip of the skull. The snout is pointed and the jaws immensely strong, with large canine teeth set into the lower jaw, while the roof of the upper jaw contains hundreds of tiny backward-slanting teeth, ensuring that what goes in rarely comes out. The lower jaw protrudes slightly.

Colouration along the back is brownish to dark olive (with lighter vertical bars) fusing into flanks of olive green overlaid with creamy white spots. The belly is matt white. The fins often show a tinge of pale orange-yellow and are noticeably barred.

Pike prey upon amphibians, large crustaceans such as crayfish, all species of fish including their own kind, and occasionally on swimming rodents and waterbirds such as young cootes, moorhens and mallard duckling.

Reproduction occurs in the early spring, when the fat-bellied females, each accompanied by up to three or four males (often called jacks), shed their eggs on reed stems and soft, rooted plants. These hatch after 2 weeks, and the young pike commence a diet of small fish when only a few inches in length.

HABITAT AND DISTRIBUTION

Pike are common in all river systems and most stillwaters throughout the British Isles, relying on their wonderful camouflage to stalk and ambush prey among natural features such as reed beds, sub-surface branches of fallen trees, side-stream entrances, river confluences and so on. They also hunt shoal fish in open water lacking ambush features, and scavenge from the bottom.

TECHNIQUES

Artificial lure fishing - freshwater; Fly fishing for coarse species; Drift fishing in freshwater; Freshwater floatfishing techniques - Sliding-float fishing for predators, Drift-float fishing for predators; Wobbling deadbaits. See also Artificial lures.

PILCHARD
(*Sardina pilchardus*)

British record: 8oz (226g)

The pilchard is similar to the herring but has a more rounded body and larger, easily detached scales. Its blueish back fuses into brassy flanks and a white belly. It has a longer anal fin than the herring, and the last few rays are noticeably longer. It is pelagic shoaling fish of great commercial importance, but is only occasionally caught on rod and line, usually from southern and south-western waters around the British Isles.

PIPEFISH, GREATER
(*Syngathus acus*)

British record: 4oz (113g)

This long, thin (pipe-like), rather strange fish is rarely taken on rod and line because it feeds on tiny crustaceans and fish fry, sucking them into its tubular snout via a small mouth. The body has armour-like skin divided into segments, similar to the sea horse (which belongs to the same family), and is greeny-brown along the back and sides. It has a weak arrangement of fins except for the long dorsal fin.

It is found all around the British Isles in shallow coastal waters and estuary mouths. It reproduces during the summer, and the males incubate the fertilized eggs in a special brood pouch, from which the young eventually emerge.

PIPEFISH, SNAKE
(*Entelurus aequoreus*)

British record: 1oz (28g)

One of the tiniest sea fish to be recorded taken on rod and line, the snake pipefish is a similar shape to the greater pipefish with a tubular snout through which it sucks in plankton. Its yellow-brown body, however, is smooth, round in cross-section, and it lacks both pectoral and anal fins. The males brood fertilized eggs during the summer months. It is an offshore species pre-

ferring deep waters, where it congregates in the surface layers.

PIRKING

See *Drift fishing at sea; Wreck fishing.*

PLAICE
(*Pleuronectes platessa*)

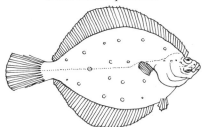

Average size: 1-2½lb
Mega specimen: over 6lb
British record: 10lb 3½oz (4kg 635g)

The plaice is a member of the Pleuronectidae family of flatfish, the adults of which have both eyes on the right side of the head. Left-sided plaice do occasionally occur, however. The plaice has a small, neat head with upturned jaws and a flat, rounded body that is brown on top overlaid with distinctive orange spots. The underside, or blind side, is white. It feeds on worms, crustaceans, molluscs and brittlestars, and reproduces during the latter part of the winter, its eggs floating on the surface until they hatch.

HABITAT AND DISTRIBUTION

Common all around the British Isles, plaice prefer a bottom of sand or mud (sometimes gravel) in relatively shallow waters, both offshore and inshore.

TECHNIQUES

Beachcasting; Downtide boat fishing; Drift fishing at sea; Uptide boat fishing.

PLAICE

Development

Spawning

DABS

Note how this carp fisherman crouches on one knee whilst playing a good fish and has sunk the other rod tip beneath the surface so the two lines do not tangle.

PLANKTON

Plankton consists of the swimming and floating microscopic vegetable and animal organisms that drift with the wind and currents.

It is found in great masses in both fresh and salt water, and many life forms ultimately depend on it. The green-pea colouration in freshwater, for instance, is caused by an over-abundance of single-celled vegetable plankton, or phytoplankton, which reproduce prolifically in sunlight. Animal plankton are called zooplankton - for instance, freshwater fleas, of which Daphnia is the largest, are examples - and these feed upon phytoplankton. This accounts for the fact that stillwaters can change from green to clear water within a few days - the zooplankton have simply eaten the phytoplankton.

PLAYING AND LANDING

Whether saltwater or freshwater fishing, the prerequisite for maximum enjoyment from playing fish and for making sure that a fish is safely landed is balanced tackle. The line should match the rod so that they stretch simultaneously, giving that wonderful elastic feeling throughout the fight. For instance, when freshwater fishing for big pike at close range, a powerful, stepped-up rod is only asking for trouble regardless of line stretch or strength. For close-in work it is much better to use an all-through-actioned rod, which bends immediately, absorbing any sudden lunges or fast runs.

Enormous fish can be landed on the softest rods. Take the fly rod, for instance, which must bend readily or the line could not be cast. As there is little stretch in the fly line, the rod also absorbs all the sudden lunges and acrobatic antics of a trout or salmon.

For the majority of sea anglers, particularly those who need to fight big fish such as conger, cod and rays almost vertically up to the boat, often from great depths, the only reel for the job is the *multiplier (Reels)*. Adjustment of the lever or stardrag, which either increases or lessens drag upon the fish, is absolutely crucial. If the reel locks up the line could easily snap with a big fish on its very first dive. Conversely, use insufficient drag and a big fish will either swim around happily for hours close to the bottom or take the line quickly into the rusting ironwork of a wreck. So from the very start, adjust the clutch to the breaking strain used, allowing firm pressure from the fish to pull line from the spool, but able to stop the spool from slipping when you are pumping the fish upwards. To gain line, simply wind down while lowering the rod tip, but stop winding while you bring the rod back up to the vertical again. Smooth, unhurried repetition of this pumping action is the only way to beat big sea fish, whether they are hooked from a boat or from the beach. Gentle thumb pressure applied to the spool while pumping the rod upwards can help enormously.

Playing fish on a centre-pin reel comes naturally because thumb pressure on the rim dictates how little or how much line is given. And this feeling is transmitted directly from drum rim to thumb.

To play a fish with a fixed-spool reel, you must first adjust the clutch tension carefully to match the breaking strain of the line. With the anti-reverse on, turn the drag knob until line can be firmly and quickly pulled from the spool but still be wound in under normal fishing situations. The spool will then rotate or slip (hence the name slipping clutch) only when a good fish starts to pull hard or runs, stopping the line from snapping. Gentle pressure from a forefinger on the rim of the spool can eventually slow down the biggest fish and at the same time provide an idea of its power and size. When the fish is about to stop or change direction, clamp the forefinger tightly down on the spool rim and pump the rod up and backwards before winding down to regain line. This pumping action is the only way to regain line safely and land monster fish when you are fishing a reel line or hooklength considerably lighter than the fish's weight. Always keep the rod tip up so that it can act as a shock absorber, and use side-strain to turn big fish should they be moving towards snags. This is done by lowering the rod tip towards the direction the fish is taking and then applying pressure at the lowest possible angle. Sink the rod tip beneath the surface if this helps to reduce the angle. Few fish will fail to yield to these tactics, but be quick to recover line before the fish changes direction again. Some anglers prefer not to use the clutch system, and back-wind with the anti-reverse off to give line. There are times when this method is unsatisfactory, however, such as when a carp or salmon is running so fast that you cannot keep hold of the reel handle. So learn to use the slipping clutch properly, remembering to stop winding when a fish is taking line from the spool, or the line will twist.

Check the tension of the drag knob regularly throughout the day as atmospheric changes may affect the setting, and be prepared to alter the setting at various stages throughout a fight with a very large fish. When the fish is all but beaten and ready for the net, under the rod tip on a short line, loosen the clutch before slipping the net beneath it. The hook will then not pull out should the fish decide to make one last run for freedom or perform a roll and dive down deep.

During these final stages of the fight, be careful not to crunch about or wade into the water. The angler's shadow could easily frighten the fish as it fights in clear-water shallows. When it is about ready, sink the rim of the net a few inches under the surface and slowly draw the beaten fish over it, keeping the net perfectly still. Avoid taking the net to the fish or stabbing at it. When the fish is inside, drop the rod tip, lift the net rim above the surface a few inches and slowly draw it towards the bank. Never lift the net upwards; too much strain will be put on the screw head, or spreader block (*Landing nets*). Finally, lift the fish well away from the water's edge on to a grassy spot. If the bank is hard gravel, use an *unhooking mat* so its body mucus and scales are not disturbed while you remove the hook.

Wherever the water is extremely shallow, and only inches deep immediately beyond the marginal plants, an effective way of landing a big fish is to beach it. Wait until it is on its side and completely exhausted. Then simply draw it towards the shore in one long, smooth, fluent movement until it becomes grounded. This is a most effective way of landing pike or zander that have flying treble hooks or an artificial lure outside their mouth, which would otherwise become tangled in the mesh of a landing net. For pike, wear a glove on the left hand (*Glove, unhooking*) and insert the fingertips into the pike's left gill opening and squeeze hard with the thumb, which will enable you to lift the pike well away from the water on to an unhooking mat.

To stop a big fish from flapping about and hurting itself, pull part of the landing-net mesh over its head so that its eyes are covered.

The shore fisherman has no alternative but to beach his catch, and the only way to do this without the line or trace snapping is to use the force of a wave (once the fish is completely exhausted) to glide the fish up on to the sand or shingle. Allow the wave to recede before trying to lift the fish.

Lastly - and this really only applies to freshwater species - as an alternative to transferring specimen fish into a *weigh-bag* or *sling,* you can simply unscrew the landing net from the pole immediately after landing the fish and hoist the net on to the scales. Then deduct the weight of the wet net. This is far kinder and far less stressful for the fish than transferring it to a second receptacle.

A comprehensive selection of clip-on and cork-bottomed plummets. You cannot ascertain swim depth without one.

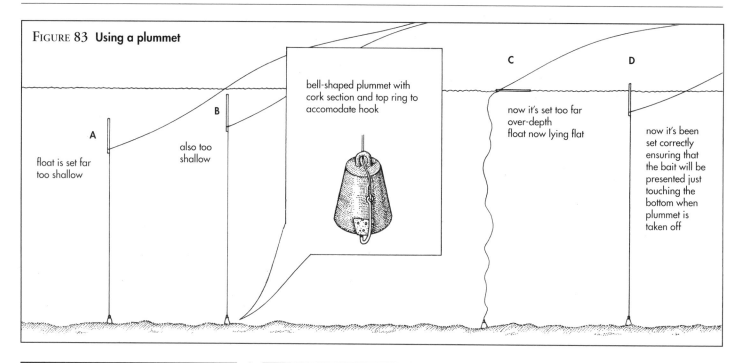

FIGURE 83 Using a plummet

A — float is set far too shallow

B — also too shallow

bell-shaped plummet with cork section and top ring to accomodate hook

C — now it's set too far over-depth float now lying flat

D — now it's been set correctly ensuring that the bait will be presented just touching the bottom when plummet is taken off

PLUMMET

The plummet is used for determining water depth for float fishing (fig. 83) and for ascertaining depths in a previously unfished water. Plummets are made from brass or non-toxic metal and come in two shapes. The classic bell-shaped plummet has a flat bottom into which a small cube of cork is glued. To attach the plummet, thread the hook through a ring in the top and push the hook point gently into the cork. The Little Nipper plummet comes in two halves, held together with a strong spring. It can either be nipped around the hook, or around the lowest shot for laying on or presenting the lift method. The inside of the rounded end is hollowed out to take shot up to SSG in size.

Brass plummets are available for pole fishing. One is shaped like a coin, the other like a 1gal-sized demi-John. Both have tiny, stainless-steel loops through which the hook is passed and are held in place by a length of silicone tubing.

In fig. 83A and B, the float has been set too shallow. In 83C it has been moved too far up the line and lies flat on the surface. In 83D the depth has been plummeted perfectly so that when the plummet is removed the bait will just touch bottom.

For plummeting distant or large, unknown and previously unfished areas, tie a 2oz bomb on the end of the line to act as a plummet, and use a sliding pike float above it with a bead and stop knot (see fig. 59 and *Freshwater floatfishing techniques - Sliding-float fishing for predators*).

POGGE

(Agonus cataphractus)

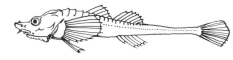

British record: 1¾oz (46g)

Also called 'hook nose' due to the pair of robust hooks on the top of its snout, this 5-6in long fish has a large head, and a sharply tapering body constructed of bony plates. Numerous whisker-like sensory barbels sprout from beneath the head, and each gill cover sports a strong spine. It has large pectoral fins and two dorsals, the first being spined. The pogge is brown on the back, overlaid with darker bars, and cream underneath. It feeds on worms, brittlestars, tiny molluscs and crustaceans and reproduces during the spring. It is common around the British Isles, usually in shallow waters, but is rarely caught on rod and line due to its small size.

POLARIZED GLASSES

These invaluable glasses not only reduce glare from direct sunlight, they eliminate reflected glare from the water's surface, enabling the angler to spot a fish through clear water before it becomes alarmed.

They do not turn muddy water into clear; they simply remove unwanted glare and reflections. In strong sunlight amber or grey lenses are recommended, while in the low light conditions of dawn, dusk or an overcast day, yellow lenses allow more to be seen by providing a brighter image below the surface in addition to cutting out unwanted reflections.

POLE FISHING

There is no finer or more exact method of presenting baits such as bloodworms, maggots, casters and punched bread than with a pole.

Because the pole tip can be positioned upwind or even directly above the float, the bait can be eased through the swim at current speed or held back and swung enticingly up from the bottom at any time during the trot-through. And on stillwaters it takes but a second to lift the rig a couple of feet to make the bait flutter enticingly or allow it to freefall down through the swim again as though it had just arrived. Consider fig. 84A, a stillwater situation where a slim-bodied, bristle-top pole float (*Floats*) has been shotted with evenly spaced No. 12 shots specifically to catch clear-water roach and rudd 'on the drop' at fairly close range. If the float takes longer to settle than it should, an immediate strike should be made. Otherwise, wait until the bait dangles at the end of the drop, just off bottom, before lifting again.

Cradle the pole in your left hand (if you are right-handed), with the butt across your right knee. To strike, grip the very end of the pole tightly with your right hand and twist it smartly, which will cause the entire pole to lift and set the hook. The type of strike that you make with a waggler rod is totally impossible with a pole.

Alternatively, with 1ft of the pole protruding behind your right elbow, lay your forearm along the top of the pole and grip tightly with the right hand. Then cup and steady the pole in your left hand, which should rest across your right knee.

A good, though tiring, technique for landing sizable fish from deep, fast-flowing rivers when you are not using elastic in the rig is to pivot the end of the butt under your crotch against the seat-box top and, using your arm at full stretch, hold the pole in your right hand. As long as the float rig is slightly shorter than the pole, you can then swing both bait and hooked fish easily to hand.

Fishing to hand is best reserved for deepish swims. When you are tackling canals, shallow ponds or slow-moving rivers, where only 3-4ft of line should be used between pole tip and float, you will need to unship the pole, or take it apart, in order to unhook a fish. Match fishermen have a

ruse for expediting this unshipping procedure (taking apart all the lower joints is just not on). They simply unship the pole at the fourth or fifth joint (whichever is level with the hook) and slide the rest behind them over a pole roller. The rig then comes easily to hand for unhooking and rebaiting. They then reconnect the pole and push the rig back out to the desired spot.

During times when bites are slow, and while you are feeding in either loose feed or groundbait, a custom pole rest to suit your particular tackle and seat-box or stand is extremely useful.

A reversed, heart-shaped float rig (84B) is ideal for use with a long whip or when fishing to hand in deep water using a 10-12 metre pole especially for bream. With most of the shotting capacity concentrated in a single 0.30-1g olivette fixed 30in above the hook, and a couple of dust shots between them, this rig indicates bites occurring during that last 30in of the bait's descent through the water and as it settles just on the bottom.

A similar rig, illustrated in 84C, is good

for easing the bait along close to the bottom in slow-moving water in pursuit of dace, roach and chub. The bulk shot, a 1-2.5g olivette, is set at roughly two-thirds depth, followed by a string of evenly spaced styl leads. These ensure a slow passage of the bait and will also indicate bites on the drop.

A heart-shaped, wire-stem float with a 3-5g capacity (84D) is the float to use for easing the bait along just above bottom in a steady flow. The single olivette is fixed low down, just 20in above the hook, with a pair of No. 4-6 shot between them. To keep the bait down in deep, fast rivers, where the force of the current creates an accentuated bow in the line between the float and the hook, use 4-5lb rig line and a single 6-10g olivette fixed just 12-20in from the hook (84E). A No. 1 or 3 shot, 4-8in from the hook, ensures that the bait drags along the bottom. The large, bulbous float must be held back hard throughout the swim in order to present the bait correctly.

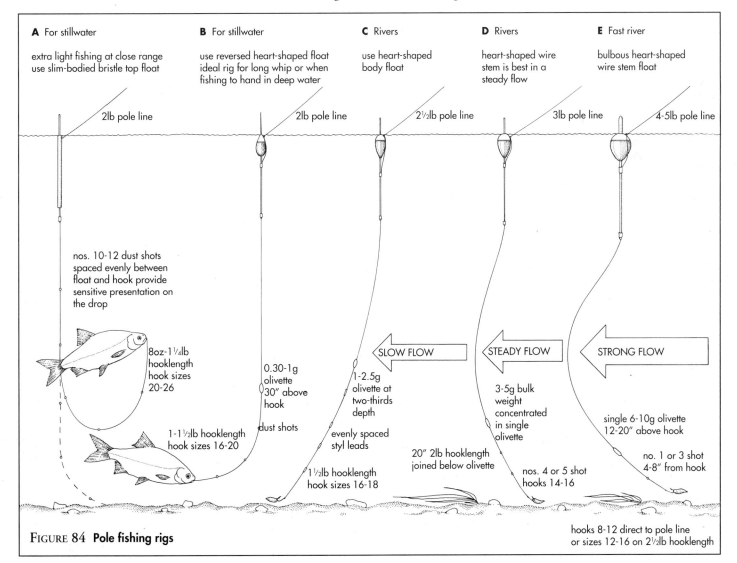

A For stillwater

extra light fishing at close range use slim-bodied bristle top float

2lb pole line

nos. 10-12 dust shots spaced evenly between float and hook provide sensitive presentation on the drop

8oz-1¼lb hooklength hook sizes 20-26

1-1½lb hooklength hook sizes 16-20

B For stillwater

use reversed heart-shaped float ideal rig for long whip or when fishing to hand in deep water

2lb pole line

0.30-1g olivette 30" above hook

dust shots

1½lb hooklength hook sizes 16-18

C Rivers

use heart-shaped body float

2½lb pole line

SLOW FLOW

1-2.5g olivette at two-thirds depth

evenly spaced styl leads

20" 2lb hooklength joined below olivette

D Rivers

heart-shaped wire stem is best in a steady flow

3lb pole line

STEADY FLOW

3-5g bulk weight concentrated in single olivette

nos. 4 or 5 shot hooks 14-16

E Fast river

bulbous heart-shaped wire stem float

4-5lb pole line

STRONG FLOW

single 6-10g olivette 12-20" above hook

no. 1 or 3 shot 4-8" from hook

hooks 8-12 direct to pole line or sizes 12-16 on 2½lb hooklength

FIGURE 84 **Pole fishing rigs**

Steadying the pole comfortably across the right knee with the left hand cupped around it in front and the right gripping the butt end, makes for relaxed fishing.

POLLACK

(Pollachius pollachius)

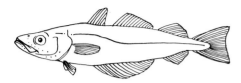

Average size: 2-8lb
Mega specimen: over 18lb
British record: 29lb 4oz (13kg 267g)

Pollack are members of the cod family and sport three dorsal fins and two anal fins, the first of which is noticeably long. The lateral line curves above the pectoral fin, while that of the coalfish, with which pollack are sometimes confused, is perfectly straight.

The lower jaw protrudes way beyond the upper and there is no chin barbel. Colouration is brownish green along the back, fusing into brassy flanks that have a metallic sheen. The belly is silvery white. All the fins including the forked tail are grey.

Pollack feed on crustaceans and small shoal fish. They reproduce in deep water between January and April. The resulting eggs and fry drift towards inshore waters, where young pollack spend the first year of their life.

HABITAT AND DISTRIBUTION

Pollack love feature marks close inshore around rocks and the deep water of sunken reefs and wrecks. They are found all around the British Isles, but they are most common in southern, south-western and western waters.

The shoals of pollack living around previously unfished wartime wrecks are often enormous.

TECHNIQUES

Artificial lure fishing - sea; Drift fishing at sea; Feathering; Float fishing in harbours and off rocks; Wreck fishing.
See also *Artificial lures.*

POLLAN

Another name for *powan.*

PONDS

See *Farm and village ponds.*

POLLACK

Sea Angler magazine editor Mel Russ practises what he preaches and fought this magnificent 16lb pollack up from over 100ft down where it grabbed a rubber-tailed, lead-headed jig, bounced around the rusting ironwork of a wartime wreck resting on the bottom of the English Channel.

POOR COD
(*Trisopterus minutus*)

British record: 11oz (311g)

Though a member of the cod family and cod-like in shape, with the characteristic three dorsal fins and two anal fins, the poor cod appears more like an underweight pouting. It has similar colouring too, with coppery-yellow back and flanks and a dirty white belly. There is even a long barbel beneath the chin and a black spot at the base of the pectoral root. But this tiny fish seldom exceeds 10in long, and because it masses in huge shoals in deep water around the British Isles it is rarely caught by anglers. It reproduces in the early spring, and it feeds on tiny fish and crustaceans.

POUTING
(*Trisopterus luscus*)

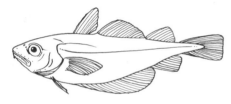

Average size: 6oz-1½lb
Mega specimen: over 2½lb
British record: 5lb 8oz (2kg 494g)

Also called a bib or pout, this member of the cod family is sometimes confused with the haddock. It has three dorsal fins and two anal fins, the bases of which almost touch each other, and a distinct black spot at the base of the pectoral fin. The had-

POUTING

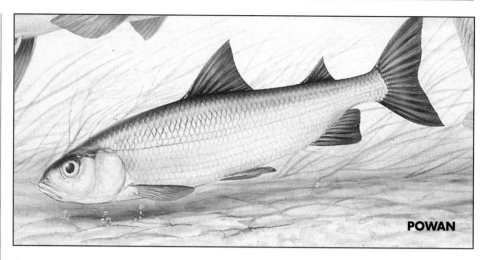

POWAN

dock also has a black spot, but it is above the pectoral fin.

The pouting has a particularly deep, thick-set body (deeper than all other members of the cod family) with a neat head and large eye. Its snout overhangs the lower jaw, beneath which there is a long chin barbel. Its pelvic fins (unusually short on most members of the cod family) are long, reaching past the start of the first anal fin.

Colouration is coppery brown along the back, fusing into lighter sides (often with a metallic yellow sheen) and a white belly. Adult pouting caught from deep water well offshore over rocks and rough ground sport four or five vertical, dusky (perch-like) bars down their flanks. It feeds on crustaceans, molluscs, worms, brittlestars and small fish, and reproduces in the early spring.

HABITAT AND DISTRIBUTION

A common shoal fish, pouting frequents inshore waters around the British Isles, particularly along the south coast. Young pouting congregate in huge numbers around piers and jetties. Adult pouting prefer deeper water around rocks, sunken reefs, over rough ground and especially around wrecks, where shoals can be dense.

TECHNIQUES

Beachcasting; Downtide boat fishing; Drift fishing at sea; Feathering; Float fishing in harbours and off rocks; Uptide boat fishing.

POWAN
(*Coregonus lavaretus*)

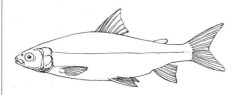

British record: 2lb 1½oz (950g)

Also called schelly, gwyniad and houting, the powan is a shoal-fish member of the whitefish family. It is similar to a grayling in shape, complete with a tiny adipose fin, but lacks the sail-like dorsal. It has a slim, silvery-white body of small, flat scales, translucent grey fins, including a forked tail, and a noticeably protruding upper jaw. These rare fish have been caught in a time warp since the last ice age, so their features vary according to the particular environment in which they live. They inhabit deep, cold, clear-water lakes and lochs, and feed on aquatic insect larvae, plankton, molluscs and crustaceans, plus the eggs and fry of other fish.

Reproduction takes place during the winter months, and distribution is restricted to Lake Bala in Wales, the Lake District and Irish and Scottish lochs.

Now included on the endangered species list, it is illegal to catch powan intentionally.

PRESSURE LAMPS

The paraffin pressure lamp, or storm lantern, has been the traditional angler's lamp for many years. Many original brass-bodied Tilley lanterns are still in use, along with modern, imported designs, but many anglers are switching away from lamps that run on paraffin, preferring those that run on either unleaded petrol or a specially formulated fuel.

Paraffin lamps provide an excellent light and they are not affected by strong winds, but lighting them can be a bit of a performance. Before the actual mantle can be lit the paraffin reservoir needs to be pressurized, and the vapourizing tube and mantle pre-heated, usually with a small clip-on bowl containing a wick and methylated spirits. Some of the more modern paraffin lamps have the facility for self-contained rapid pre-heating using paraffin, which dispenses with the meths. But by and large, paraffin lamps can take some lighting.

On the other hand, the American-made Coleman range of lamps run off either standard unleaded petrol or Coleman fuel and require no pre-heating. They provide instant light at the application of a match or a lighter. One litre of fuel provides up to 12 hours of light, and as it becomes increasingly difficult to find a supply of paraffin more anglers are using lamps that run on petrol.

PRIEST

This weighted device is used to despatch game fish - salmon and trout - quickly. It is available in brass, stainless steel, aluminium, staghorn and various other materials.

Some models have a screwed end that converts into a *marrow spoon* for examining the contents of a trout's stomach.

PUFFERFISH
(Lagocephalus lagocephalus)

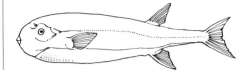

British record: 6lb 9¼oz (2kg 983g)

This pelagic species, which is also found in the Indian Ocean, is common in warmer parts of the Atlantic and only rarely caught along the south coast of Britain. In outline its bluish body is roughly cod-shaped with numerous small spines embedded in the belly skin. These become erect only when its unusual defensive mechanism is displayed.

Pufferfish are so called because they can blow their body cavity out to three times normal size in order to scare off predators. At this point, its already weak arrangement of fins are virtually incapable of propulsion, but as few predatory fish attempt to eat it the puffer simply deflates when they swim off in disgust.

It has a parrot-like mouth with strong teeth bones, which it uses to crunch crus-

taceans and molluscs living on sunken reefs and rough ground.

PUMPKINSEED
(Leponis gibbosus)

British record: 4½oz (129g)

Originally imported from the USA by the ornamental pond-fish and aquarist trade, this colourful and smallest member of the American freshwater sun bass family has been stocked into isolated ponds, pits and canals throughout England. The chances of catching one are rare, although they bite readily on maggots and worms presented on light float tackle.

It has a deep, laterally compressed, perch-like body mottled in turquoise-blue and brown along the back, fusing into a golden-orange belly and throat. Males have a colourful red spot at the corner of the gill plate. The lower jaw protrudes and both

Aptly named for dispatching trout and salmon, priests come in a variety of types and weights. Those on the left have double-threaded ends which unscrew and convert into marrow spoons for ascertaining what creatures trout have been feeding upon.

Qq, Rr

the first dorsal fin and the leading edge of the anal fin are spined. It feeds upon aquatic insect larvae, crustaceans, plus fish fry, and reproduces during the summer, the male guarding the eggs in a depression on the bottom until they hatch and vacate the nest.

QUIVER TIP

See *Bite indicators and accessories.*

QUIVERTIP LEDGERING

See *Ledgering techniques.*

RAY'S BREAM
(Brama brama)

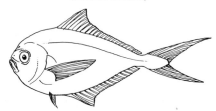

British record:　　6lb 3¾oz (2kg 829g)

This oceanic, mid-water species occurs in small schools and is an irregular visitor to the seas around the British Isles. It has a deep, laterally compressed body with long continuous dorsal and anal fins reaching almost to the large, deeply forked, swallow-like tail. Its eye is large and the bony mouth decidedly upturned. It has a metallic, greeny-brown sheen along the back, which lightens across the flanks, large, yellow pectoral fins and tiny pelvic fins with prominent ancillary scales just above. It feeds on fish and crustaceans and reproduces in late summer.

RAY, BLONDE
(Raja brachyura)

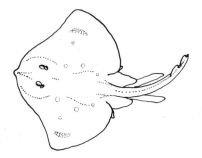

Average size:	10-18lb
Mega specimen:	over 25lb
British record:	37lb 12oz (17kg 122g)

This thick-set ray has large eyes, a short snout, and spines across its entire back, which is a light, warm brown overlaid with much paler patches and completely covered in small, dark brown spots the size of AA and SSG split shot. The underside is white, and there is a prominent line of spines along the top of the tail. Its food consists of bottom- dwelling crustaceans, worms and fish. Reproduction occurs during late spring and summer. The eggs, fertilized inside the female, are released in oblong, leathery cases which adhere to bottom structures, and from which the young blonde rays finally emerge.

HABITAT AND DISTRIBUTION

Very much an offshore species preferring fast tide runs over banks of shingle and sand, the blonde ray is seldom caught from inshore waters. It is reasonably common around the British Isles, particularly off the south and western coasts.

TECHNIQUES

Downtide boat fishing; Uptide boat fishing.

RAY, BOTTLE-NOSED
(Raja alba)

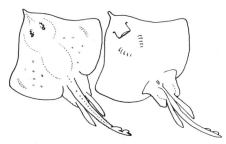

British record:　　76lb (34kg 471g)

Also known as white skate, the bottle-nosed ray is only very occasionally caught from southern and south-western offshore waters around the British Isles. It has a reasonably long snout and wide wings that curve inwards between snout and tips, a brown-grey back sporting spines, with rows of more spines along the tail, and white undersides.

It feeds on crustaceans and fish, and reproduces during the late spring. The eggs, fertilized inside the female, are deposited

in horned cases, from which the young skate emerge over a year later. It is caught by accident when downtide boat fishing for other bottom-feeding species.

RAY, CUCKOO
(Raja naerus)

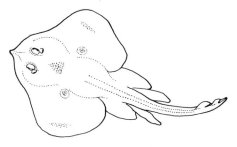

British record:　　5lb 11oz (2kg 579g)

This small species is immediately recognizable by a black and yellow, large round mark in the middle of each wing. The back and tail are greyish brown and covered with rows of tiny spines, the undersides are dirty white.

It feeds on fish, worms and crustaceans, and reproduces during the winter and spring. The eggs are fertilized inside the female, and are laid in small egg cases, from which the young rays emerge some 9-10 months later.

The cuckoo ray is found all around the British Isles, but is most commonly caught from southern and south-western seas in fairly shallow water over sand.

RAY, EAGLE
(Myliobatis aquila)

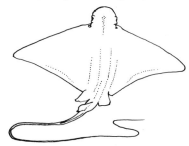

British record:　　61lb 8oz (27kg 894g)

The eagle ray has a wide, triangular, brownish-grey, thick-set body and a noticeably raised and prominent head. It has a long, thin, whip-like tail with a small dorsal fin at the tail root. Immediately behind this is a serrated bone projection - also called its sting. Its large mouth is filled with flattened, mosaic-like teeth, which it uses to crush molluscs and crustaceans. It prefers a sandy or muddy bottom and is only very occasionally caught from British water, usually off the south and south-west coasts by boat anglers seeking other bottom-feeding species. It gives birth to live young.

RAY, ELECTRIC
(Torpedo nobiliano)

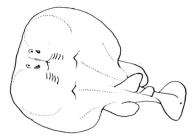

British record: 96lb 1oz (43kg 571g)

With a body shaped rather like a flattened pumpkin and enough clout in its pectoral fins to give a nasty jolt of electricity, British sea anglers are fortunate that the electric ray is a fish of warmer seas and only very rarely caught off the south and southwestern coasts.

The colour over its top side, which is smooth and lacking any kind of spines, is dark grey-brown; the undersides are white. It has a thickish tail with two dorsal fins (the first considerably larger than the second) and a proper tail, which is squared. No other skate or ray (except the marbled electric ray - a smaller species) has a classic tail, so the electric ray can be recognized instantly. It feeds on crustaceans and bottom-feeding fish. It gives birth to live young following a long gestation period.

RAY, MARBLED ELECTRIC
(Torpedo marmorata)

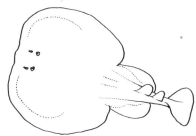

British record: 13lb 15¾oz (6kg 341g)

Similar to the larger, electric ray, with a rounded but longer body, the marbled elec-

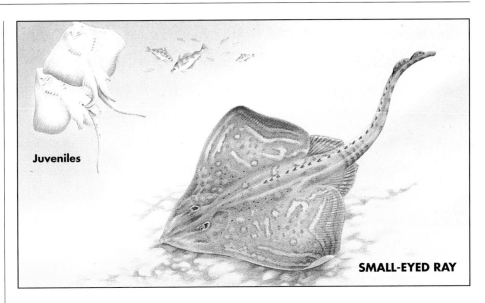

Juveniles

SMALL-EYED RAY

tric ray can also produce a jolt of electricity. The skin is smooth, without spines or protrusions, being dark brown on top and creamy white underneath. The thick tail root has two dorsal fins of similar size (whereas the first dorsal of the electric ray is considerably larger than the second) and a proper tail, which is squared. It feeds on bottom-living fish and gives birth to live young. It is only rarely caught around the British Isles, both shore and boat records for the species being caught in the Channel Islands.

RAY, SMALL-EYED
(Raja microcellata)

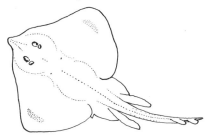

Average size: 3-6lb
Mega specimen: over 10lb
British record: 17lb 8oz (7kg 938g)

As its name implies, this ray has extremely small eyes. It is grey to yellow-brown on top, strongly overlaid with large cream patches and streaks running in line with the wing edges. It has a short snout and a row of spines (all bent at right angles) down the back and along the top of its tail. Underneath it is white. It feeds on crustaceans and fish, and reproduces during the summer months. The eggs are fertilized inside the female and then laid in egg capsules, and the young, fully formed rays emerge 4

to 5 months later.

HABITAT AND DISTRIBUTION
The small-eyed ray prefers sandy ground and moves into shallow water to feed, especially at night. Distribution limited to southern and south-western seas only, around the British Isles.

TECHNIQUES
Beachcasting; Downtide boat fishing; Uptide boat fishing.

RAY, SPOTTED
(Raja montagui)

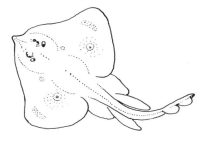

British record: 8lb 5oz (3kg 770g)

One of the smallest rays to be caught around the British Isles, the spotted ray has a short snout and is a light, warm brown on top, overlaid with large, dark brown spots. The underneath is white. A line of spines start midway down the back and reach to the dorsal fin, and there are a few scattered spines over the head. It feeds on crustaceans and small fish, and reproduces during the summer. Following fertilization inside the female, the eggs are laid in capsules in shallow water, and the fully formed, young ray emerge some 6 months later.

It is common around much of the British Isles, but because it prefers to live in deep water is not often caught by anglers.

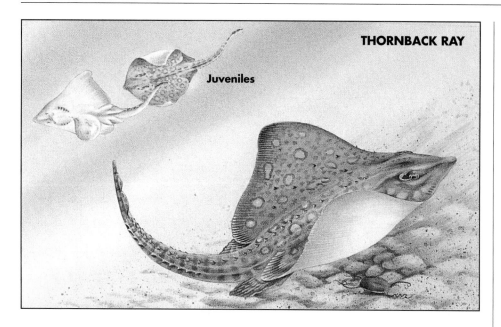

THORNBACK RAY

Juveniles

RAY, THORNBACK
(Raja clavata)

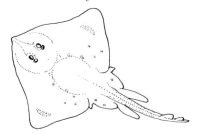

Average size: 4-10lb
Mega specimen: over 20lb
British record: 31lb 7oz (14kg 260g)

Also called roker, the thornback is by far the most commonly caught ray around the British Isles. It has more spines on its body than all other rays, with dense prickles over the entire back and larger thorns, or spines, down the back and over the tail. Colouration on top is grey-brown with irregular brown and yellow mottling; the underside is creamy. The short snout is noticeably translucent.

The thornback feeds on worms, molluscs, crustaceans and fish. Reproduction takes place during the spring and summer when, following internal fertilization by the males, females deposit their eggs in leathery pouches, often called mermaids' purses. The fully formed young ray emerge from these 5 months later.

HABITAT AND DISTRIBUTION
It is common all around the British Isles in shallow waters over sand, mud and gravel.

TECHNIQUES
Beachcasting; Downtide boat fishing; Uptide boat fishing.

RAY, STING
(Dasyatis pastinaca)

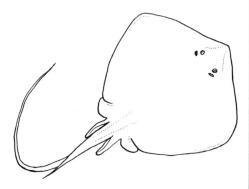

Average size: 10-12lb
Mega specimen: over 40lb
British record: 68lb 4oz (30kg 958g)

This sting ray has a typical thick-set ray body with a short snout and rapidly tapering tail that sports one or two serrated spines half-way along it. These spines measure 3-5in long and are covered in a gelatinous, poisonous substance that enters the wound inflicted by the serrated spine, causing extreme pain, and even hallucinations.

The body is smooth and dark olive-grey above. The underneath is cream with grey-blue tips to the undersides of the wings. Sting rays feed on worms, molluscs and crustaceans, but will not refuse the angler's fresh fish fillet. They give birth to live young in litters of several at a time.

HABITAT AND DISTRIBUTION
It is found all around the British Isles, more commonly in the south, and even in shallow waters, such as river estuaries, where it feeds over soft bottoms of mud and sand.

TECHNIQUES
Beachcasting; Downtide boat fishing; Uptide boat fishing.

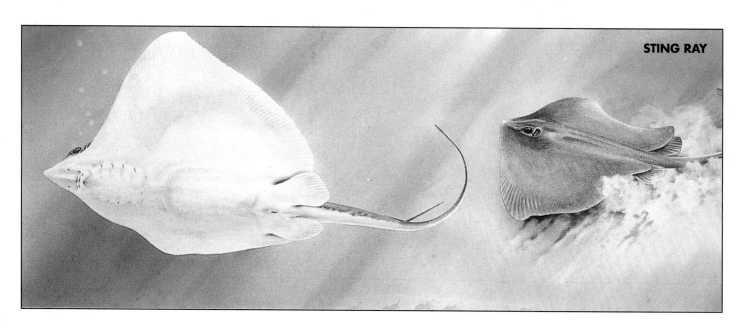

STING RAY

Ray, Undulate

(Raja undulata)

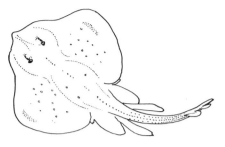

British record: 21lb 4½oz (9kg 652g)

The undulate ray has the classic ray shape, with a short snout covered in coarse prickles and more spines in a line down the back and on the tail, including between the two dorsals. Its distinct colouring consists of brown, sometimes yellowy-brown, on the back overlaid with irregular, wavy, dark markings edged in white or yellow, and white underneath. It feeds on molluscs, crustaceans and fish, and reproduces in late summer. Following internal fertilization by the males, the females lay egg capsules from which the fully formed young rays emerge within several months.

It is generally found only in southern and south-western waters around the British Isles, and prefers a sandy bottom.

Record Fish - Claiming a British (Rod-caught) Record

All claims for a British record are judged by the British Record Fish Committee (BRFC), an independent committee whose membership consists of representatives of the three disciplines of angling - game, coarse and sea - along with a scientific adviser. The Committee adjudicates claims for British fish caught by fair angling means. If an angler catches a potential British record, he/she should make their claim to one of the three disciplines:

GAME fish record claims should be made to the Salmon & Trout Association, Fishmongers' Hall, London Bridge, London EC4R 9EL. Tel. 0171 283 5838.

COARSE fish record claims should be made to the National Federation of Anglers, Halliday House, Egginton Junction, Derbyshire DE65 6GU. Tel. 01283 734735. All coarse fish claims are scruti-

nized by a committee comprised of NASA and NFA members.

SEA fish record claims should be made to the National Federation of Sea Anglers, 51A Queen Street, Newton Abbot, Devon TQ12 2QJ. Tel. 01626 331330.

All three disciplines have a 24-hour answerphone facility and require that the following procedures are complied with:

Identification

Claims for a record fish are scrutinized for identification of the species. Clear photographs of the fish (with some kind of scale) are required, and for some small sea fish the body may have to be produced.

Capture

The catch must have been made by fair angling with rod and line. A reliable witness to capture must be prepared to support the claim (if there is no witness to capture, the claimant must formally verify his statement by affidavit).

Weighing

The fish must be weighed accurately on appropriate scales, which will need to have a current Weights & Measures Certificate, and there must be two independent witnesses who will vouch for the weight.

Claims

All the details of the claim must be registered on the BRFC claim forms, which are available from the appropriate discipline. These will be checked and presented by the discipline to the BRFC for consideration for a record.

Only the BRFC can award the record and, far from being a rubber-stamping operation, each claim is critically examined and if it falls short on verification it can be rejected. The Secretary of the BRFC is David Rowe, 51A Queen Street, Newton Abbot, Devon TQ12 2QJ. Tel. 01626 331330, and the committee is sponsored by Messrs Barbour, who present a Barbour jacket to each successful claimant.

Red Band Fish

(*Cepola rubescens*)

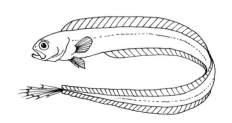

British record: 6½oz (180g)

This long, slender fish has long dorsal and anal frills that taper to a point where the tail should be. It has a large mouth for such a thin fish, filled with curved teeth, and a very large eye. It is bright pinky, orangey-red and quite unmistakable. It is only occasionally caught off the south and western coasts of the British Isles. It lives in a vertical burrow, which it leaves to feed on planktonic crustaceans.

Reed Floats

Reed floats are easily made from the tall, common reed, which not only abounds in thick marginal beds along the banks of many river systems and stillwaters, but is the very same 'phragmites' reed used for thatching the roofs of houses (Waterside flora).

For both thatching and float-making, the reeds must be free of moisture and harvested by being cut off neatly above the waterline with a rape hook, some time between January and April when they are parchment brown. Bundles of cut reed can often be seen stacked beside a river, drying out in readiness for thatching, and a polite word with the reed-cutter will usually result in a small bundle for float-making.

Before cutting into sections, using a sharp modelling knife, bend each stem gently. Those that flex and quickly straighten are perfect. Discard any that feel spongy or crack. Reed is formed like bamboo, and has a hollow (buoyant) centre between each knot. To make a simple, straight waggler float (*Floats*) cut gently through a stem on the other side of two knots, beside a knot. Then cut through the far side of the next knot along (fig. 85A). This will give a buoyant tube of 6-12in long, depending on the reed selected. As reed stems vary in diameter, wagglers of varying shotting capacities are easily made.

The next step is to smooth each end with a piece of medium sandpaper. And there it is: a natural tube that takes about two-thirds of the shotting capacity of an identical length of peacock quill. The stem can be stained (green or brown wood preservatives are ideal), coloured with matt black or grey paint, or simply left in its natural state, which is enhanced by two coats of clear varnish. To the tip apply one coat of matt white, followed by the desired fluorescent shade to a depth of ½in. The reed waggler can now be attached to the line

With just a sharp modelling tool or razor blade, plus glass paper, waterproof glue, woodstain, varnish and some coloured paints, anyone can transform a bundle of dried reed stems into beautiful floats. Straight or tipped wagglers, stick floats, trotters, the permutations are endless and the raw materials are absolutely free.

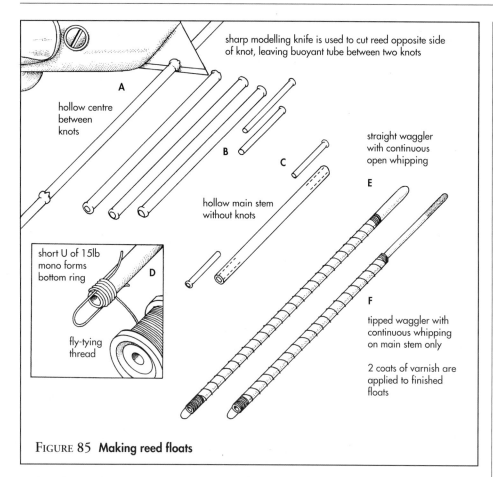

sharp modelling knife is used to cut reed opposite side of knot, leaving buoyant tube between two knots

A

hollow centre between knots

B

C

straight waggler with continuous open whipping

E

hollow main stem without knots

short U of 15lb mono forms bottom ring

D

fly-tying thread

F

tipped waggler with continuous whipping on main stem only

2 coats of varnish are applied to finished floats

FIGURE 85 Making reed floats

with a sleeve of silicone tubing; or a bottom ring made from 15lb monofilament whipped on to the reed, through which the line can be threaded (85D). Use fly-tying thread for the whipping. For a fancy effect that also helps to protect and strengthen the stem, continue an open whipping (with a ^{1}/16th gap) all the way along to the coloured tip (85E). Give the whippings two coats of varnish to finish, and leave at least for a couple of days to fully harden before using.

To make the main stem of tipped or insert wagglers, cut through the stem just below one of the knots, revealing the hollow tube, and gently sandpaper the rim smooth. Prepare several in this way, all of varying diameters, and then prepare the shorter inserts from reed of finer diameters, making sure that the knots of each stem are smoothed over with sandpaper. It is then a simple case of inserting various tips into a stem (85B) until one fits tightly to a depth of at least 3/4in. Add a little clear waterproof glue. The float can be left plain or strengthened on the main stem only using an open whipping (85F).

Fig. 85C shows a stick-type trotting float using a completely hollow main stem (no knots), into which both a tip and a stem are glued once their knot-ends have been smoothed over with sandpaper.

There are numerous permutations worth considering once you have made a few basic reed floats and mastered the craft. Old-time float-makers, for instance, painstakingly decorated their stems with various drawings and motifs in Indian ink prior to winding on an open whipping and applying a matt varnish. And when fishing close beside reed beds in gin-clear water for wary rudd or tench, there is nothing more natural than a reed-stem float.

REELS - CENTRE-PIN

TROTTING REELS

The very earliest reel designs were based on a line-holding drum spinning freely on a centre pin or spindle. And for numerous float-fishing techniques, particularly *long trotting,* there is still nothing to beat a free-running centre-pin reel. No other type of reel gives line so freely and provides such immediate, sensitive tackle control.

The best modern centre-pin reels are 4½in in diameter, with a body and drum (the spool) machined from the highest-quality aluminium bar stock. Some have solid-face drums, others have a series of holes drilled in the face to reduce the reel's weight. Some have ventilated drums constructed around a centre hub (into which

the pin or spindle fits), accurately aligned by means of several spokes (known as the aerial design), and some even house a stainless-steel main bearing. The end float is adjusted by a grub screw located in the centre of the hub.

Top-quality, centre-pin reels are fitted with a micro-adjustable drag system which can be fine-tuned with a knurled knot and a spring unit fitted over one of the spokes, which imparts gentle pressure against the centre-pin itself - a design used with the famous aerial centre-pins first made by Allcocks of Redditch. Most centre-pins are fitted with an on/off ratchet lever on the backplate, which operates a simple pawl against a cog on the inside of the drum.

Large centre-pin reels, known as the 'Leeds' design, have drums up to 6in in diameter, and some specialized models lack handles. To play fish, a finger is inserted into one of the many large holes drilled into the outside of the drum to reduce its weight.

FLY REELS

All fly reels are centre-pins, but as they are not required to spin freely, but merely hold the line, engineering tolerances are nowhere near so exact as in trotting reels. Diameters vary from 2½in for a tiny brook reel, up to 4½in or more for the largest salmon fly reel. The material used can be reinforced hi-density plastic, carbon, aluminium or magnesium. To reduce the reel's weight, a series of holes are drilled in the outside (and inside) of the removable spool.

Some manufacturers offer reels of the same diameter with both narrow and wide spools to hold extra backing. At the very least, a fly reel needs to hold a full 30yd of line plus at least 50yd of backing beneath it. Large-diameter and wide salmon reels may have the capacity to hold up to 200yd of backing. Most fly reels are fitted with permanent ratchets, consisting of pawls and a cog, that are reversible for either left-handed or right-handed anglers. Winding-in should be accompanied by a light ratchet (some reels are silent), while pulling line out, or a fish running off, should be against a firm ratchet or an overrun could result.

Extra pressure can be exerted by gently pressing the palm of the non-casting hand up against the reel's rim. Some reels are also fitted with fully adjustable disc-type drags. For playing salmon in heavy water, or for tropical saltwater sportsfish, disc drags are excellent, but for the vast majority of fly-fishing situations in British freshwaters, a simple rim, fly reel is the most effective and practical type. Geared fly reels, which have a removable, locking centre stem to secure the spool (useful for speedily retrieving excess line from the ground or bottom of the boat), are the only exception to all those already mentioned, which are called single-action fly reels.

SEA CENTRE-PINS

Large centre-pins, such as the old wooden star back, were once commonly used for both beach and boat fishing, but only a handful of manufacturers now bother to produce centre-pins large enough for saltwater work, because multipliers and fixed-spool reels do everything a centre-pin can and more efficiently. The Australian company, Alvey, however, produce a comprehensive range of saltwater centre-pins with bodies made of high-density plastic and fibreglass with and without drag systems.

REELS - CLOSED FACE

These small format, specialized reels have been designed for match fishermen. The spool is totally enclosed to alleviate problems with the wind. They are therefore particularly well suited to all float fishing and light ledgering using lines up to 4lb test.

Replacing the fixed or open-face reel's bale arm is a ⅛in diameter stainless-steel pin, around which the line is gathered. Gentle pressure with a forefinger on the reel's centre button ensures that the pin clicks in, thus releasing the line, for single-handed casting. Turns of the reel make the pin click out again to gather the line and wind it around the spool. An outer housing of stainless steel or aluminium ensures that the line remains totally enclosed.

Some models are fitted with an anti-reverse, whereby line can be given via an adjustable clutch knob on the handle, while others only have a back-winding facility. Most closed-face reels are made for left-hand wind only, although a few manufacturers produce ambidextrous models.

REELS - FIXED-SPOOL

The vast majority of fixed-spool reels (sometimes referred to as spinning reels) are fitted with push-button, skirted spools to prevent line dropping off and fouling underneath the rotor.

Unlike the spool of both centre-pin and multiplier reels, which turn in order to recover line, that of the fixed-spool reel remains fixed after casting, while the line is gathered by the bale arm and transported around it. To make the line lie evenly, the spool moves slowly up and down throughout the retrieve.

The spool itself rotates, or slips, only under the pressure of a sizeable fish, when the line would otherwise break. And by using the reel's slipping clutch, even the largest fish can eventually be beaten on relatively light lines (*Playing fish*). To stop the reel handle from going backwards when the spool is turning, the anti-reverse lever should be used.

Despite a host of modern, largely cosmetic features, all fixed-spool reels fit into one of two categories: front drag, and stern or rear drag. On front drag models, the slipping clutch is built into the spool, which rotates on the main shaft and is fully adjustable by turning the drag knob anti-clockwise to reduce, or clockwise to increase, drag. On a rear-drag fixed-spool reel, the spool remains fixed while the main shaft rotates, and adjustments are made to the drag through a series of washers and discs via the large rear knob.

As line comes off the reel at right angles over the bale arm, most models incorporate a roller at this point to minimize friction and line wear. Some are fitted with ball-bearing line-rollers. A useful modern addition for pike and zander fishing, and especially for bolt/rig tactics (*Ledgering techniques*) in pursuit of carp and tench is the 'bait-runner' facility (also called bait-feeder and spool-free clutch). This allows the spool to be disengaged by pushing forward a lever at the rear of the reel behind the handle stem. The spool can then rotate freely, giving line as a fish runs off with the bait. Turning the reel handle clicks the reel back into gear to the clutch setting preset via the drag knob. While the reel is in the bait-runner mode, spool tension can be adjusted to suit fishing conditions by a separate collar or lever, depending upon the make of reel.

Standard gear ratios are around 5:1 - the bale arm turns five times around the spool for every single turn of the handle. Extra high speed reels are excellent for some forms of lure fishing and for match fishing, for which specialized, automatic, finger-dab, bale-arm models are available. Reels with a low ratio, however, are more

useful for playing large fish or winding in against pressure. This is why the large-format fixed-spool reels used for sea fishing are fitted with gear ratios of 3.5-4:1.

Many reels now come fitted with long-nosed, tapered spools (first designed for distance shore casting), which greatly improve casting potential. Whatever the spool size, it needs to be filled almost to the rim with line that is wound on firmly.

Medium-sized reels in the 2000 to 3000 format with a selection of spare spools holding 2½lb, 4lb, 6lb and 10lb test will cover most eventualities in British freshwaters, from roach and dace to specimen pike and carp. Really heavy freshwater work, such as salmon spinning, estuary fishing and long-range carp or pike techniques, demand reels in the 3500-4000 size with a spool capacity of 200yd of 14-16lb test. Fixed spool reels for surfcasting should have still greater capacity - at least 250yd of 15-20lb test - and should be corrosion resistant (many now have graphite bodies) and exceptionally smooth in operation. Models with a bale arm that stays rigid, and does *not* click over during the force of a powerful cast, are particularly recommended, as are those with short, manual pick-ups.

REELS - MULTIPLIER

The multiplier reel is accepted by many sea anglers as the standard reel for use in saltwater, especially when fishing afloat.

As the name suggests, gearing within the reel multiplies spool revolutions with each turn of the handle. For each turn the gearing increases the rate at which the spool turns. For example, 3½ times gives a retrieve of 3.5:1. Some models have a much higher gear ratio.

As with the fixed-spool reel, most multipliers are fitted with a clutch to allow fish to take line at a controlled rate under pressure, and there are two types of drag system, the star drag and the lever drag. The star drag is by far the most common, and works by varying the amount of pressure at which the spool slips, via a set of internal, fibre drag-washers. Turning the star drag anti-clockwise reduces pressure whilst turning it clockwise increases pressure.

Many of the better-quality multiplier reels are fitted with a lever drag. Again, this type of drag system allows the spool to give line under pressure, but the lever-drag

FRESHWATER REELS

Top row: **A selection of small multipliers in both left and right hand wind, plus three closed face reels.**

Second row: **Small to medium format fixed spool reels.**

Third row: **Medium to large fixed spool reels. The largest models are fitted with the free spool (baitrunner) facility.**

Bottom row: **Three free-running centre pins used for long trotting and four single action fly reels, with permanent ratchet.**

SEA REELS

Top row, L to R: **Fixed spool reels with both full auto bale arms and manual.**

Second row, L to R: **Medium large to large format multiplier boat reels with both star and lever drag systems.**

Third row, L to R: **A centre pin, plus small format uptide and standard multiplier boat reels.**

Bottom row, L to R: **Small format multiplier reels used for uptide boat fishing, beach casting and salmon spinning.**

system is far more efficient, allowing a much finer degree of control. In addition, the lever drag tends to be far smoother than the star drag, which has a tendency to stick before it gives line, which may result in line breakages. It is this high degree of control that has made the lever-drag reel popular with big-game anglers and light-tackle enthusiasts.

In order to minimize tangles, known as over runs, caused by casting, multiplier reels are fitted with braking systems to control the spool speed. In its most basic form, the braking system consists of spool-end float control knobs, which exert pressure directly on the spool spindle. For many years, only the spool-end float adjustment and careful application of varying grades of oils provided cast control. However, most modern multipliers are fitted with additional braking systems - usually either centrifugal brakes or a magnetic braking system.

The centrifugal system utilizes small brake blocks fitted to spokes attached to the spool spindle. The centrifugal force created when the spool revolves at speed during casting throws these brake blocks outwards, where they make contact with a friction plate, thus slowing the spool down.

By varying the size and quantity of blocks used, along with end float control and the use of oil, the angler has a degree of braking to suit his casting ability.

The magnetic braking system utilizes the magnetic field created by sets of very small magnets fitted inside the reel's end plate to control the speed of the spool. The degree of braking with a magnetic system is generally easier to vary on the beach without having to strip the reel down and change the size or number of brake blocks.

Multiplier reel spools are made from chromed brass, duralium, plastic or various types of graphite. Heavy metal and graphite spools are by far the strongest, and are generally favoured for boat reels, which are not used for casting. A metal spool, in particular, is much harder to control during casting because of the flywheel effect that occurs when it is forced to spin quickly. Reels intended for casting usually have spools made out of light alloys or in some cases plastic or graphite. However, reels with plastic spools should be used with great caution because plastic spools can distort under pressure.

Most multipliers have a cog at the gearing end of the spool, against which a pawl clicks to provide an audible ratchet. The

reel can then safely be left out of gear with the ratchet on and line can instantly be taken by a big fish running off. In strong tides it is better to keep the reel in gear on a drag setting just sufficient to stop line being pulled off.

Many of the smaller multipliers (6000-6500 size), which were originally designed for salmon spinning but are now commonly used by shore fishermen seeking maximum casting distances, are fitted with a level-wind mechanism. This winds the line evenly on to the spool, ensuring smooth, trouble-free casting. These reels, and narrow-spooled baby versions that hold just 150yd of 10lb-test line are much used for *trolling* and *trailing* for pike and when lure fishing in conjunction with a short, American bait-casting rod (*Artificial lure fishing*).

Top-flight models are fitted with a touch-'n'-trip casting thumb bar that disengages the spool immediately prior to casting on thumb pressure alone. Turns of the handle instantly put the reel back into gear. On reels that also have a 'flipping' feature, the thumb bar becomes a direct drive control to the spool once the flipping lever is switched on. This allows a lure or bait to be dropped back instantly and the hook

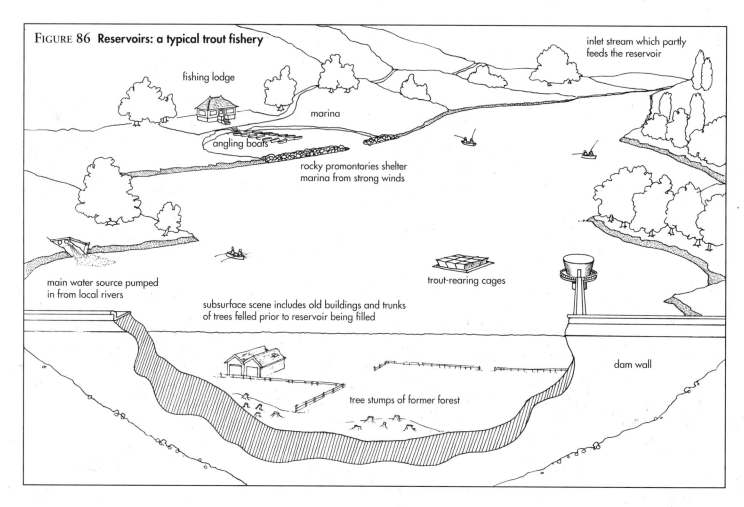

FIGURE 86 **Reservoirs: a typical trout fishery**

inlet stream which partly feeds the reservoir

fishing lodge

marina

angling boats

rocky promontories shelter marina from strong winds

main water source pumped in from local rivers

subsurface scene includes old buildings and trunks of trees felled prior to reservoir being filled

trout-rearing cages

dam wall

tree stumps of former forest

set without you touching the handle.

Some baby multipliers are convertible for both left- and right-handed wind, which allows you to enjoy single-handed casting and retrieving without having to change hands to perform the simple task of winding in.

RESERVOIRS

Reservoirs fall into several categories. Some are entirely brick built and raised completely above the local water table, so all the water has to be pumped in. Many of the London reservoirs and those in the home counties fall into this category. Others are flooded river valleys with completely natural banks that slope gently into the water and contain lush marginal growth exactly like a natural lake, the only man-made structure being the heavily reinforced, concrete or brick dam wall, which holds back and stores the water in readiness for processing by the respective water company. Some reservoirs are constructed with banks that are part natural and partly reinforced concrete or brick.

Reservoirs created by flooding massive areas of farmland, such as Rutland Water in Leicestershire (the biggest man-made lake in Europe) may even have old farm buildings, fences, walls and roads - present prior to flooding - on the reservoir floor. Even tall trees may still exist, although these are invariably felled before the reservoir fills up once the dam wall is completed.

Some reservoirs are fed entirely by surface run off from farmland and the original stream or river feeding the valley prior to flooding. Some are fed in part by a river or stream, with the bulk of the water piped in from adjacent rivers and even from river systems hundreds of miles away. Some are water storage reservoirs filled totally from piped river water.

Depths in reservoirs that are flooded river valleys vary according to the original contours, and could be 50-100ft deep, especially near the dam wall. Those constructed entirely of brick or concrete are more evenly contoured, with the greatest depths, 20-40ft, through the centre channel, shelving down to the vicinity of the valve tower. Many large reservoirs, both part-natural and man-made, are managed as trout fisheries (*Fly fishing - Loch-style*) and stocked on a regular basis, usually with

There is no better way of stocking the freezer than each taking a limit bag of rainbows. John teamed up with old pal Bob Church, whilst filming one of his television programmes on Rutland Water. And every fish came off the top, loch-style fishing with floating lines, G and H sedges and hoppers being favoured patterns on the day.

brown and rainbow trout reared-on with pelleted food in special floating cages. The cages consist of deep, nylon-meshed net enclosures, held in position within a wooden framework with anchor chains over the deepest areas. The most up-to-date fisheries use a grading machine for stocking. This sucks up trout from a holding pen and sends them through a special tank divided with baffles. Those too small for stocking are fed back into another holding pen to be reared-on, while those of a catchable size go straight down a chute into the reservoir. This puts minimum stress on the trout as they are not actually handled until caught. Most reservoir trout fisheries offer excellent facilities with a choice of

bank or boat fishing, and a lodge, often with tackle shop and restaurant, adjacent to the marina.

Water quality in reservoirs is excellent, being generally exceptionally clear yet holding an enormously rich larder of planktonic life, such as daphnia (*Crustaceans*) and aquatic insect larvae (*Buzzers*), which help to keep both trout and coarse species well fed. Coarse species, particularly roach, tench, bream and pike, grow to huge proportions in reservoirs. And reservoirs that are open only for coarse fishing offer the best prospects for breaking a British record. Having said that, however, the British pike record of 46lb came from Llandegfedd Reservoir in South Wales,

It's all systems go as over 100 anglers sharing two to a boat prepare for the start of a fly fishing tournament at the marina of famous Rutland Water, Europe's largest man-made lake, and one of the most prolific trout fishing reservoirs within the British Isles. Covering 27 miles around its perimeter, Rutland has depths to over 100ft and a capacity for holding 27,000 million gallons of water.

ROACH
(*Rutilis rutilis*)

Average size: 4-10oz
Mega specimen: over 2½lb
British record: 4lb 3oz (1kg 899g)

Roach is the most commonly caught, British freshwater shoal fish. It has the classic cyprinid shape with a neat head, small mouth, uniformly scaled body and distinct lateral line. Colouring along the back fuses from grey-brown to a blueish tint along the upper sides, which blends into scales of silver-pewter. During the summer months adult roach, especially, tend to be more brassy along the flanks.

which has been managed purely as a trout fishery. There is no way of preventing coarse species in a trout fishery from proliferating, and it is an open secret that more pike in the 35-45lb bracket are caught in trout-fishery reservoirs than in any other kind of habitat within the British Isles.

Many owners of trout fishery reservoirs (and large clear-water, trout-fishery gravel pits) now rent out their boats to pike fishermen throughout the winter months, once the trout season ends in October, and even provide, for a modest cost, fresh bait in the shape of small, live trout - a revenue-raising policy that all trout fisheries could easily adopt. It has been found beneficial to return all large pike caught (although they do grow fat on the trout diet), removing only the small ones. If large pike are removed, as was once the case, there is nothing to crop small pike, and within two or three seasons there is an explosion of small pike, capable of swallowing newly stocked trout.

Triple world match fishing champion Bob Nudd took this nice net of jumbo-sized Irish lakeland roach on quivertipped maggots, using a fixed paternoster open-end feeder rig 40yd out in 18ft of water. Note the blueish cast to their upper flanks. Rudd have deeper, more golden bodies with scarlet-orange fins.

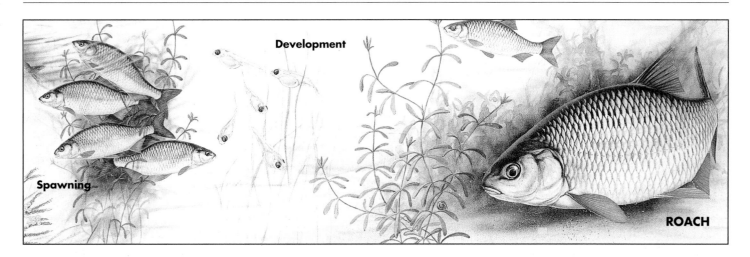

Development

Spawning

ROACH

The belly is matt white. The pectoral fin has a warm tinge, while the anal and pelvics are orangey-red. The forked tail is also warm, showing a touch of crimson in adult fish. The lips of a true roach are almost level when open, whereas in a *bream/roach hybrid* the top lip protrudes. With *roach/ rudd hybrids* the bottom lip protrudes slightly. In true *rudd* the bottom lip noticeably protrudes.

Roach feed on all stages of aquatic insect life, molluscs, crustaceans and occasionally plant tissue. Reproduction takes place during the late spring, when roach mass in shallow water, shedding sticky yellow eggs over sub-surface tree roots, soft weeds and marginal grasses. The fry hatch within 10-12 days. Should bream, silver bream or rudd be using the spawning area at the same time and milt from the male fish fertilizes the eggs of another species (a common occurrence), then hybrids will result.

HABITAT AND DISTRIBUTION

Roach thrive in most freshwater environments from tiny pits, ponds and streams, to wide river systems and huge sheets of stillwater. In reservoirs, for instance, they grow particularly large and form vast shoals. Roach are perhaps most common in well established, large gravel-pit complexes, where they can reach specimen proportions. Wide, slow-moving rivers also contain roach in huge shoals of up to 1,000 or more. Roach are common throughout the British Isles except for Scottish waters north of Perthshire, and have been introduced into Irish waters.

TECHNIQUES

Fly fishing - for coarse species; Freelining; Freshwater Floatfishing techniques; Ledgering techniques - Bobbin ledgering in stillwaters, Quivertipping/swing-tipping; Pole fishing.

ROACH HYBRIDS

When either bream, rudd or silver bream gather in the areas of shallow, weedy water that roach use for spawning, hybridization will occur.

ROACH/RUDD HYBRID

To the untrained eye, this is one of the most difficult of all hybrids to identify, and it is more common in stillwater fisheries than anglers imagine. It usually (though not always) has a slightly protruding bottom lip and a slight keel to the anal fin. In addition, the dorsal fin may be set slightly further back than on a true roach. Overall colouration is brassier than a true roach, but nowhere near the buttery-gold of the true rudd. Colouration of the pelvic and anal fins is generally more intense than in a true roach, with a decided orange-scarlet tint.

ROACH/SILVER BREAM HYBRID

As silver bream are now an extremely rare species throughout the British Isles, their distribution being limited to isolated fisheries in East Anglia and the Midlands, roach/silver bream hybrids are a most unlikely catch. However, recognition is helped by concentrating on the hybrid's colouration, which is extremely pale except for warmth in the pectoral, pelvic and anal fins. The top lip may protrude slightly (though not to the extent of a roach/common bream hybrid), and the scales will be noticeably larger than those of a bream of the same size. There will also be minimal body mucus.

ROACH/CHUB HYBRIDS

These hybrids are exceedingly rare, but do occur. Lack of warmth in the tail and a noticeably broader head and larger mouth are the pointers to look for.

ROCK FISHING TECHNIQUES

Many shore anglers avoid fishing rock marks because they are scared of losing tackle. However, very few marks are totally unfishable, and often the most effective rigs for fishing rough ground marks are also the most basic.

Before fishing any shore mark, rough ground marks in particular, it is a good idea to visit the area at low water. The best time to go is at low water on a spring tide, when much of the ground that you will later be fishing over will be uncovered. Look for features like gullies, weed beds, or patches of sand sandwiched between kelp beds. These are the places where items of food collect, and the places where the fish will feed once the tide has flooded. If you are unfamiliar with the mark, it is also very important to try to pick out any area where the flooding tide could cut off your retreat.

The first stumbling block for many anglers preparing to tackle a rough-ground mark is the choice of end rig. End rigs should be tied as simply as possible. Rock marks are certainly not the places to use complex rigs with lots of swivels, bait-clips and beads, all of which will increase the rig's snagging potential. Rigs should usually incorporate some sort of rotten bottom to attach the lead (try using an old spark plug) as this will break free if it becomes snagged. A simple running paternoster is an ideal rig. You seldom need to fish at any distance and at some marks species like wrasse can be more or less under your feet.

If long-range fishing is necessary, it is important to ensure that the lead will not break away from the rotten bottom during

Rugged shorelines often provide deep water close in and a variety of species from wrasse to small sharks. Inspect the sea bed at the very bottom of a low spring tide which will reveal features to which fish are attracted, such as sandy gullies between kelp beds, distinct clearings amongst dense rock, etc. In calm seas try float fishing, stepping down to freshwater tackle whenever bites are not forthcoming in clear water.

casting. One of the easiest ways to do this is to use a pulley rig tied from a minimum 50lb bs line with a loop at the bottom. The rotten bottom attaches the lead to the loop, and the loop is then pushed through the eye of the lead. A small nail pushed through a ¼in diameter polyball is then inserted through the loop of nylon, to hold it secure during casting. On contact with the water, the nail floats free, aided by the buoyant polyball, leaving the rig anchored by the rotten bottom. The addition of a lead lift can further assist end-rig recovery over rough ground.

Many anglers make the mistake of using too light a main line when fishing rough ground. You should expect to get snagged on the bottom from time to time, and you will need a fairly substantial main line to break even an 8lb rotten bottom. It is also inevitable that your line will get chaffed from constant contact with rocks, and chaffed 25lb line will give you a far better chance of landing a big fish than damaged 15lb line.

Too light a lead is another common mis-take. A light lead will get washed around by the tide or swell until it snags. It is far better to use a heavier lead, which will hit the bottom and stay put. If there is any lateral tide or swell consider using a grip lead, which will anchor your end rig firmly, preventing it from dragging into snags. The grip wires can even prevent the lead falling into tight crevices.

Another very common mistake is moving the lead after it has touched bottom, just to see if it has snagged. If the lead was not snagged, there is a good chance that you'll drag it into a snag when moving it. The first time that you attempt to move the end rig should be either when you strike or when you reel in to check your bait. In the latter case, lift the rig as high in the water as you can with one firm upward swoop of the rod. Then, keeping your rod tip high, wind furiously to get the rig up to the surface and clear of the worst of the snags.

The new generation of high-speed-retrieve reels are better suited for this sort of work than small, baitcasting multipliers.

ROCKLING, SHORE
(*Gaidropsarus mediterraneus*)

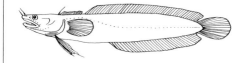

British record: 1lb 9¾oz (730g)

The rocklings are members of the cod family. The shore rockling has the classic rockling shape with a long dorsal fin, the first part of which is a low-set frill with a single, long ray at the front. This feature separates all rocklings from other species. It has a single barbel beneath the chin and one sprouting from each nostril. Colouration is a warm brown on the back and sides of the smooth body, blending into lighter undersides. A common inhabitant of rocky shorelines, it is found in rock pools around much of the British Isles. It feeds on crustaceans, worms and small fish, and reproduces in summer.

ROCKLING, THREE-BEARDED

(Gaidropsarus Vulgaris)

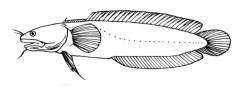

British record: 3lb 4¼oz (1kg 481g)

This is by far the largest of the rocklings; it has similar characteristics to the shore rockling, but with a larger mouth and head. It has a single barbel under the chin and one on each nostril; and large pectoral fins, a long dorsal fin preceded by a short frill of low-set rays and with a long leading ray. Its smooth, pinky-brown body is marked along the back and upper sides with darker bars and blotches. The undersides are pinkish. It is found all around the British Isles, preferring deeper, offshore marks over rocks and rough ground, where it preys upon small fish and crustaceans. It reproduces during the winter.

ROCKLING, FOUR-BEARDED

(Enchelyopus cimbraus)

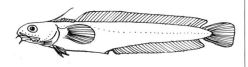

British record: 1½oz (40g)

Due to its minute size and preference for deep water over sand or mud, the four-bearded rockling is rarely caught on rod and line, although it is found all around the British Isles. It has a slim, smooth, warm-brown body and a distinct, overhanging snout, from which four barbels protrude: one under the chin, one directly above, sprouting from just above the upper lip, and one on each nostril. Its extremely long dorsal fin with a low-set fringe in front is preceded by a noticeably long first ray. It feeds on small worms, crustaceans and molluscs, and reproduces in summer.

ROCKLING, FIVE-BEARDED

(Ciliata mustela)

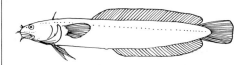

British record: 12oz (340g)

This has a similar fin arrangement to other rocklings, with a long dorsal preceded by a fringe of short rays with a single, long ray in front. It has a slim, smooth, reddish-brown body with a small head sporting five barbels: one on each nostril, one beneath the chin and a pair on the front of its top lip. It is common in rock pools all around the British Isles, feeding on small fish and crustaceans. It reproduces in early spring.

RODS - FLYFISHING

Fly rods are available in many designs, lengths and strengths to perform a wide range of tasks in a variety of conditions. Always choose a rod with care, basing your decision precisely on what is expected of it. And for optimum performance it is vital to ensure that the line matches the rating indicated on the rod.

Most fly rods these days are made of carbon fibre, which is light, extremely strong, and needs the minimum of maintenance, though there are still some game anglers who would rather use cane, preferring its feel and slower action despite its much greater weight.

The overall length of trout rods rarely exceeds 11ft, so the vast majority tend to comprise two sections, butt and tip, with an overfit or spigot connection. Salmon fly rods, on the other hand, can measure up to 15ft or 16ft, and as a consequence are built in three sections for ease of transportation. In recent years, multi-section rods have become increasingly popular with the travelling angler. Consisting of up to eight sections for a 9½ft model, they fit easily inside a suitcase. Telescopic fly rods are also available.

Trout rods are equipped with single grip handles, the longer models frequently being supplied with an extension butt that pushes or screws in below the reel seat and

produces greater leverage when playing big trout, salmon or sea trout. Rods designed specifically for salmon fishing tend to start at 12ft, and all are double-handled because of the different casting techniques employed with them.

The smallest fly rods are aimed at the trout angler who fishes streams and small rivers with a floating line in conjunction with a dry fly or nymph. Such rods tend to be 6-7ft long and are rated to take a number 3 or 4 line. At the other end of the scale are loch-style rods, which are available up to 12ft in length, but are more commonly around the 11ft mark and usually three-piece. They are normally used in conjunction with a 5-7 line, and the extra length is necessary to enable the top, or bob, fly in a team of three to be lifted high on the surface at the end of the retrieve and held there well away from the boat. Fish are wary of boats and will often follow flies a long way, only to be put off at the end of the retrieve by the sight of the boat.

Between the small stream and loch models are many fly rods in the 8-10ft range. Produced in a variety of actions, they are designed for many tasks on rivers, ponds, lakes and reservoirs, from fishing dry flies to throwing big lures long distances on sinking lines. The more powerful 10ft and 11ft single-handed trout rods are quite suitable for much salmon and sea trout fishing, but for salmon fishing in the early spring and autumn on powerful rivers where big, heavy tube flies need to be used, the longer, more powerful, custom-designed salmon fly rods become the order of the day.

RODS - FRESHWATER

The vast majority of freshwater rods are now made from carbon fibre. Short, inexpensive models in solid glass are still sold as youngsters' rods, and at the beginner and budget-price end of the market hollow, fibreglass rods are extremely popular. There is also a small market for built-cane (fly rods in particular), once the most popular rod-building material. However, owing to its narrow tube diameter, strength and rigidity, quick return and extreme lightness, nothing can compare with the qualities of carbon fibre.

The tubes or blanks of many top-of-the-range models are wrapped in a material

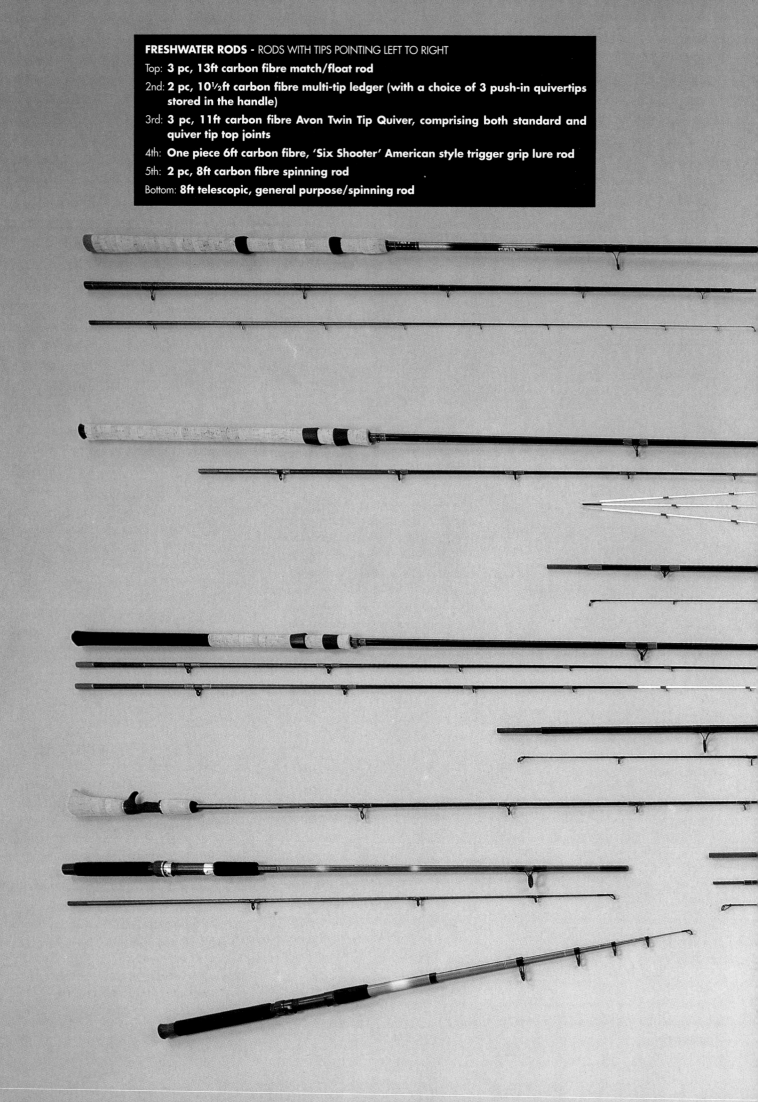

FRESHWATER RODS - RODS WITH TIPS POINTING LEFT TO RIGHT

Top: **3 pc, 13ft carbon fibre match/float rod**

2nd: **2 pc, 10½ft carbon fibre multi-tip ledger (with a choice of 3 push-in quivertips stored in the handle)**

3rd: **3 pc, 11ft carbon fibre Avon Twin Tip Quiver, comprising both standard and quiver tip top joints**

4th: **One piece 6ft carbon fibre, 'Six Shooter' American style trigger grip lure rod**

5th: **2 pc, 8ft carbon fibre spinning rod**

Bottom: **8ft telescopic, general purpose/spinning rod**

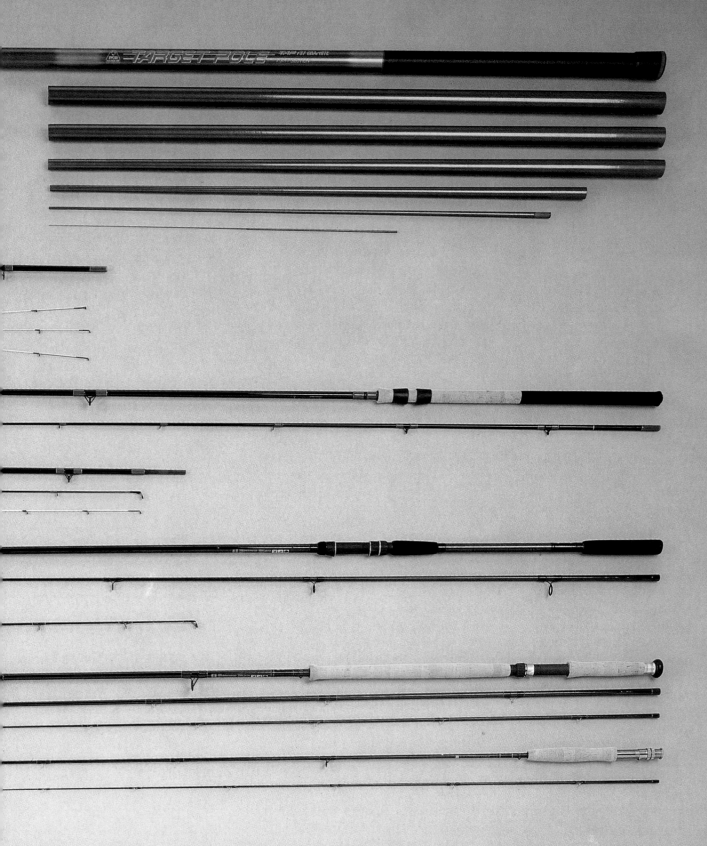

FRESHWATER RODS - RODS WITH TIPS POINTING RIGHT TO LEFT

Top: **8 section, 7m carbon fibre pole.**

2nd: **2 pc, 11ft carbon fibre Avon Specialist rod.**

3rd: **2 pc, 11ft carbon fibre carp/pike rod.**

4th: **3 pc, 14ft carbon fibre salmon fly rod.**

Bottom: **2 pc, 8ft carbon fibre trout fly rod.**

called Kevlar, which has good shock-absorbing qualities, or in carbon braid, which produces very light yet strong rods. Rod rings are important. If the centres of the rings are not lined, they will eventually be worn away by the line. Aluminium oxide centres are excellent, and the best rings have silicone-carbide centres.

FLOAT RODS

Also referred to as match or bottom rods, float rods are available from 11ft to 15ft long. Most come in three sections of equal length, and are capable of dealing with lines ranging from 1½lb to 4lb test. The most useful rod is a 13-footer with a waggler-style snappy yet forgiving action, unless you fish regularly in depths of 12ft plus, when a 14ft or even 15ft rod is advisable.

Super-fast-action rods have a 24-30in fine-diameter tip spliced into the top joint. These are often called stick-float rods because the finer, super-fast tip is designed to connect with fast bites when *stick-float fishing* in running water for small species like roach and dace (*Freshwater floatfishing techniques - Stick-float fishing*). Waggler-action rods (*Freshwater floatfishing techniques - Waggler fishing*) are more versatile and are capable of handling larger species, such as chub, barbel and tench, and even modest-sized carp, in addition to the smaller species.

Most float rods have overfit integral ferrules, which help to maintain the rod's rigidity and eradicate the problems caused by spigot joints, which wear away to the point when surgery to the female joint becomes necessary.

While inexpensive, three-piece, carbon float rods are fitted with a duplon (black foam) handle, a slimline, 22-24in cork handle of around 1in diameter, with sliding reel fittings, is the hallmark of quality rods.

Multi-joint, telescopic float rods are useful for the travelling fisherman lacking space, but their action is impaired by the number of joints and they cannot compete with three-piece rods. The only exceptions are the 20ft, telescopic Bolognese match rods. These have become popular for extreme deep-water trotting since the 1992 World Championships in Ireland, when most of the top catches were made by competitors using them. Rods of this length do not have conventional handles, but have a fuji-style, flat, snap-lock reel fitting whipped on. In any other format a rod of this length would be too heavy.

POLES

Also called roach poles because the original heavy brass-jointed bamboo poles were first designed for use on the Rivers Lea and Thames to catch roach, top-quality poles are now made from reinforced carbon fibre tubes. Short, inexpensive, telescopic poles are still available in fibreglass. Short, extremely slim poles (up to 6m) are also available in carbon. Called whips, these are designed for single-handed speed fishing and tiny fish. Long poles from 8-14 metres generally have put-over joints for easy assembly and breakdown (*Pole fishing*). Top-flight models come with an extra top three sections, enabling an alternative, elasticated rig to be made up at the ready.

Most manufacturers also supply spare top-three or top-four section kits for their poles of 9m and above, plus butt extension sections to increase the pole's overall length.

LEDGER AND SPECIALIST RODS

Basic ledger rods are usually of two-piece construction with either overfit or spigot ferrules, and are capable of dealing with lines of 3-6lb. Length varies between 9ft and 11ft and most are fitted with a threaded tip ring to accept either a *swing tip* or *quiver tip* for more sensitive bite detection (*Ledgering techniques*). As with float rods, the handle is either cork or duplon, or a combination of the two, with sliding reel fittings. Specialist quiver-tip rods vary from 10½ft to 12ft and have either a built-in, tapered quiver tip of 16-24in or tips that are interchangeable and fit into the top joint. Some models contain two or three spare tips of varying sensitivity in the rod handle. Avon-style, twin-tip rods comprising a butt and two top joints - one standard with a threaded end ring, the second with built-in quiver tip - are the most versatile. Quiver tips of different sensitivity, or a swing tip, can be used in the standard top, which also doubles as a powerful float rod for tench, bream, barbel and even carp.

Specialist carp and pike rods, most of which have abbreviated handles of the fuji type, with a screw reel fitting sandwiched between two short, hand-grip sized lengths of duplon, can be used for both float fishing and ledgering, and vary in test curves (*Test curves*) from 1¼lb to 3lb in ¼lb increments. Rods with a test curve above 3lb are not required for British freshwater fishing. The specialist range consists of two-piece rods (three-piece travelling and telescopic

models are available) with either overfit or spigot joints in lengths from 10ft to 13ft.

An ideal, all-round choice capable of most carp and pike fishing requirements from close-in to medium-range fishing is a 12ft, 1¾-2lb test curve rod possessing a medium-tip action. For close-range work only, choose an 11ft all-through-action, and for long range a powerful 12-13ft fast-tip-action rod.

SPINNING RODS

Rod choice in this department depends upon the kind of reel being used. Short, American-style, trigger-grip handle baitcasters, for instance, just 5½-7ft long, can only be used with baby *multipliers* (*Reels*), as can the longer 9-11ft salmon spinning rods, which incorporate a trigger grip immediately below the reel seat for the forefinger to go around.

All other spinning rods are fitted with a regular screw reel fitting, with a short grip of duplon or cork above the reel, plus a forearm grip of the same material below. Beware of spinning rods with overlong handles. Apart from being uncomfortable to cast and to play fish with, any more than a few inches sticking out beyond the elbow is a waste of the rod's effective blank length.

RODS - SALTWATER

SHORE FISHING RODS

For most general beach-fishing applications, the shore angler will need two rods. The first is a standard beachcaster, between approximately 11½ft and 13ft in length, balanced to cast approximately 5oz. This sort of rod is the workhorse of beach angling, where it is usually important to cast large baits a fair way out in order to catch fish.

There has been a tendency in recent years for anglers to buy extremely powerful, tip-action beachcasters in the belief that

the rod will automatically give them extra distance. This is far from true, and the result will rarely be an increase in distance. Indeed often the angler will not be able to cast as far as if he were using a medium-tip-action rod. In order for a rod to be used at anywhere near its maximum potential, it must first be made to bend and an efficient casting style is a must (fig. 23).

It takes time to develop the required technique (*Beachcasting*), and a medium-tip-action rod will greatly assist the novice. Any good tackle shop should be able to recommend a rod to suit your requirements and capabilities.

The second rod should be a lighter bass rod, between 10ft and 12ft in length and designed to cast up to about 4oz. This is a useful tool for fishing clean ground such as surf beaches and estuaries and for short-range work over rougher ground.

BOAT RODS

Boat rods also fall into two categories, one for use when fishing uptide, the other for more traditional downtiding.

Uptide rods are between 9ft and 10½ft in length and are rated by the size of lead that they are designed to cast, such as 2oz to 6oz, or 4oz to 8oz. An uptider should

have a sensitive tip for bite detection, a softer middle third to prevent the grip leads continually breaking out due to the rolling of the boat, and a stiff butt section to give the required strength to land big fish in a strong tide.

Downtide rods are rated in line classes that give an indication of the size of line to which they are most suited. A 12lb-class rod, for example, would be ideal for use with lines between 10lb and 15lb bs: perfect for plaice fishing, or drifting with redgills or other lures for bass and pollack. A 30lb-class rod is a good all-round rod, while a decent 50lb-class rod will be

SALTWATER RODS

RODS WITH TIPS POINTING RIGHT TO LEFT

Top: **5½ft 30-50lb line class, solid glass boat rod (roller tip ring), detachable handle.**

2nd: **6ft, 50lb line class, hollow glass boat rod, roller rings throughout, detachable handle.**

3rd: **6½ft, 30lb line class, carbon fibre, boat (pirking) rod, roller tip ring, detachable handle.**

4th: **5½ft, 20lb line class hollow glass boat rod.**

5th: **6½ft, 20lb class carbon fibre boat rod. Detachable handle.**

6th: **9½ft carbon uptide boat rod, separate handle.**

7th: **5ft, one piece heavy duty boat rod, roller tip ring.**

8th: **8ft telescopic, general purpose/spinning rod.**

RODS WITH TIPS POINTING LEFT TO RIGHT

Top: **12ft, 2 pc carbon fibre Beachcaster - rung for fixed spool reel.**

2nd: **As above with more rings and coaster reel fittings for use with multiplier reels.**

3rd: **9ft, 2 pc carbon fibre spinning rod.**

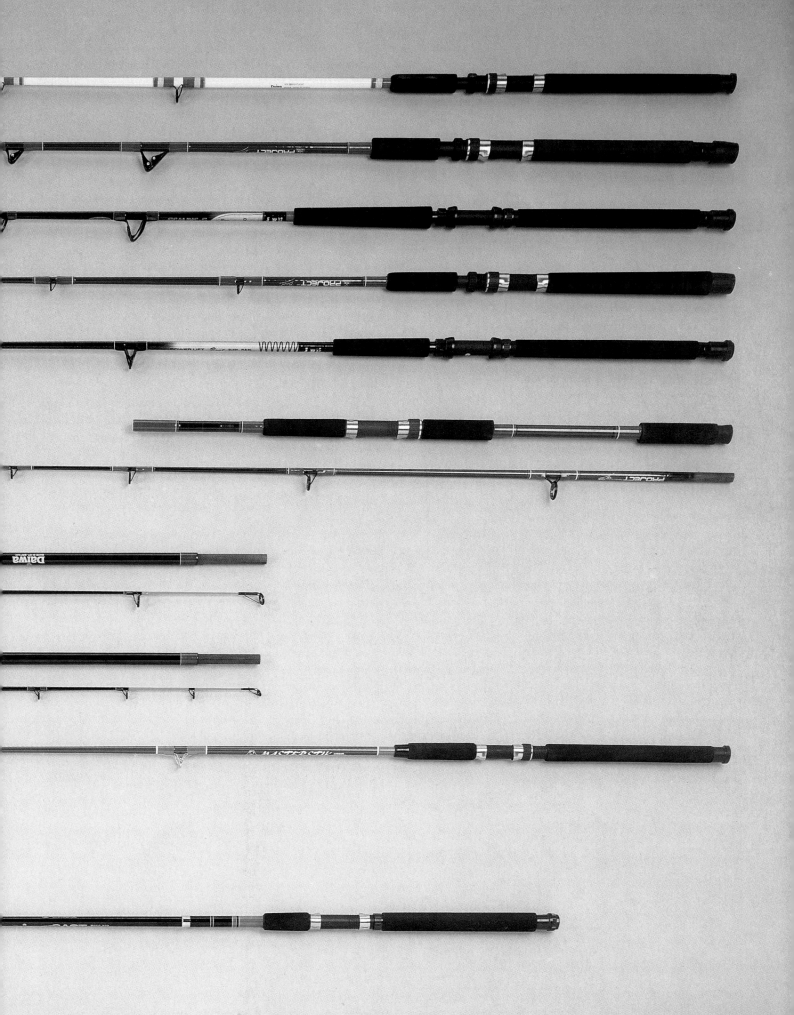

capable of landing any fish that swims in British waters.

Most downtide rods are between 6ft and 7ft in length and fitted with or without roller eyes. Roller eyes are recommended for the bigger fish, such as conger or shark, and they are a must when using wire line. A gimbled butt cap designed to lock snugly into a fighting harness is another must on rods intended for the larger species.

ROD RESTS - FRESHWATER

The choice of rod rests in various shapes and sizes is considerable, from matching buzzer bars beloved by carp anglers down to the easily bent, mild-steel shafts sold for youngsters. Each has a special purpose, however, and it is important to choose the correct rod rest for the method at hand.

The cheapest rests are those with shafts made from alloy, solid glass or mild steel, into which is fixed a permanent head of plastic or plastic-covered wire. Front rests have a keyhole, or carp-type, head so that the line is not trapped by the rod when you are ledgering with an indicator between rest and reel. Back rods rests have a simple V or U head to support the butt end. The fault with these cheap, basic rod rests is that they cannot be extended, so to get full use from rod rests in all situations it is wise to buy a pair of bank sticks that extend from 20-24in to 40-48in and into which any chosen head or bite alarm can be screwed. The thread of all rod-rest tops, banksticks and so on is the same - ⅜th BSF. The rod height can then be lowered or raised at either end to suit conditions or the tech-niques being used. Telescopic bank sticks come in tubular alloy, plastic-covered alloy, or stainless steel. Though expensive initially, the latter are stronger and last a lot longer. They have solid points that will not bend and go easily into a hard gravel bottom.

Popular with all float anglers, especially match fishermen because of the speed at which the rod can be put down, are the wide D-type heads. These have front supports of plastic tubing sleeved on to a light-weight, solid alloy frame, and are available in widths from 8in to 18in. On some, the angle of the head can be altered by an adjustable tilt. D-head rests also come fitted with a groove in the centre so that the rod does not slide about in the wind when ledger fishing. The Drennan quiver-tip rod-rest top, which has a series of mini grooves, goes one step further by allowing the ledger rod to be firmly rested in seven different positions.

For ledgering where two or even three rods are to be used, such as carp or pike fishing, the best set-up is provided by buzzer bars, horizontal bars that screw into the thread of any bankstick and are available with either two or three internal threads to accommodate rod-rest heads or electric bite alarms. The beauty of buzzer bars is that you only need one bankstick for each. They are available in coated mild steel or stainless steel, and some extend horizontally (*Bite indicators and accessories).*

Auto-locking plastic rests fitted to a ground spear, and which lock around the butt of a rod or lightweight pole when its weight is transferred to the front, are ideal for poles up to 16ft long. For longer, heavier poles, however, it's hard to beat the old-fashioned shepherd's crook and U-type heads, which come with standard bank-stick threads. Shepherd's crook and U sets are also available for screwing permanently on to the side of any large plastic, glassfibre or wooden, Continental-style tackle box/seat. For sliding a cumbersome pole up the bank behind you, specialized pole rests that incorporate two duplon rollers on a Vee frame above a bankstick thread are ideal.

For supporting a rod when trolling or trailing livebaits, deadbaits, lures and so on from a moving boat for pike, salmon, perch or trout (*Trolling; Trailing),* various quick-release rests incorporating a small G-clamp for fixing on to the side of the boat are available. These simple rod rests comprise a fully adjustable crook and U-type frame that can be rotated by loosening and tightening a large wing nut.

ROD RESTS - SEA

The most popular rod rest is the simple sand spike, made from 48in of 1¼in angle iron. This has a plastic-covered U welded on at the top to stop the rod bouncing sideways, and a cup to hold the butt welded on 18in up from the bottom, which is cut to a point.

Using a foot on the cup, you can easily tread it firmly into any sand, mud and even some shingle beaches. Home-made, lightweight versions of the above, using angled aluminium with shaped plastic tubing screwed on for the U and a round section screwed on for the butt rest can easily be put together. But as aluminium and saltwater do not mix, the aluminium angle will inevitably oxidize.

When fishing with two rods, the double sand spike with a bar at the top holding two U rests and a bar 18in from the

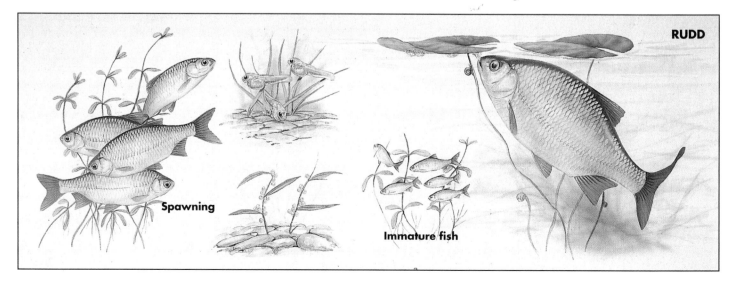

Spawning

Immature fish

RUDD

spike with a butt cap at each end, also made from angle iron, is hard to beat. This type of rest has a short bar welded on a few inches up from the spike, stopping it from twisting round in the sand or mud.

When fishing from heavy shingle or rocky beaches where sand spikes are impractical, tripod rod rests made from aluminium tubing are excellent, despite having a limited life due to saltwater corrosion. The plastic U-type rest is available with either single or double heads, into which all three poles screw via brass threads. On some models the poles are fixed together with a strong plastic housing that allows them to pack neatly together for carrying. Tripods provide a stable platform against which to rest the rod, but because the butt rests on the beach, the tip will be considerably lower than it would be if the rod was set in an angle-iron beach spike, thus creating more pressure on the line. For this reason, many beach fishermen still prefer spikes.

ROKER

See *Ray, thornback.*

RUBBY-DUBBY

See *Groundbaits - sea.*

RUDD

(Scardinius erythrophthalmus)

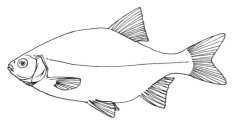

Average size: 4-8oz
Mega specimen: over 2¾lb
British record: 4lb 8oz (2kg 41g)

This beautiful shoal fish is much deeper in the body, size for size, than roach, with flatter sides burnished buttery gold, the scales being slightly larger than those of the roach. The rudd is also identified by its upturned mouth and considerably longer bottom jaw, designed for sucking in food from

above. The fins are orange-scarlet, the pelvics and anal being particularly bright. The anal fin is set on a sharp keel and overlapped in a vertical line by the end of the dorsal, which is set much further back than that of the roach.

Rudd consume all stages of aquatic insect life (much of which they suck in from the surface in warm weather), plus plant tissue and crustaceans. Reproduction occurs in the late spring, when translucent, pinkish eggs are deposited by the females over soft, rooted weeds and fertilized with milt from the males. The fry hatch 2 weeks later. During the act of spawning, cross-breeding sometimes occurs when roach or bream shed eggs and milt over the same weed beds as rudd (*Roach/rudd hybrids; Bream/rudd hybrids*)

HABITAT AND DISTRIBUTION

Rudd are nowhere near as common throughout the British Isles as the roach, except in southern Ireland where they are more prolific by far. Rudd prefer shallow, warm and weedy environments rich in aquatic insect life. It can always be found close to reed lines and lily beds, sucking down nymphs and hatching flies from the surface in warm weather.

TECHNIQUES

Fly fishing - for coarse species; Freelining; Freshwater float fishing techniques; Pole fishing.

RUDD HYBRIDS

See *Bream/rudd hybrids; Roach/rudd hybrids.*

RUFFE

(Gymnocephalus cernus)

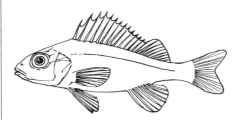

British record: 5¼oz (148g)

This aggressive, perch-like, shoaling freshwater fish has a thick-set body averaging

just 3-5in long, with two dorsal fins (joined together), the first being spiked and the second soft rayed. There are more spines on the gill plates. All the fins are transparent grey and heavily flecked with brown. The back is grey-brown and speckled in dark blotches that continue along the pewter flanks, which often show a tinge of silvery-olive. The belly is dirty white. The ruffe feeds on all stages of aquatic insect life, worms, crustaceans, plus the eggs and fry of other fish. It reproduces in the spring, and the fry hatch within 2 weeks. It can be a nuisance, greedily swallowing casters, maggots or redworms intended for larger species.

Distribution is limited to certain river systems in England where currents are gentle. It loves lock cuttings, deep pools, side drains and any slow areas of deepish water.

SAFETY AFLOAT

Safety should be paramount in the mind of every angler every time that he or she goes afloat. Many fatal accidents have occurred within close proximity to the shore and many of those when the sea conditions were perfect. The freshwater angler should also consider safety every time that he goes afloat. Conditions afloat on even a modest lake or reservoir can very quickly become rough, and in the past too many anglers have taken unnecessary risks and paid with their lives. The following is a list of safety precautions to be observed every time you fish in a boat.

LIFEJACKETS

At least one lifejacket should be provided for every angler, and ideally it should be worn at all times. Modern flotation suits designed for anglers are ideal, but it is still advisable to carry standard lifejackets as well. Do not be tempted to buy cheaper buoyancy aids, because unlike a lifejacket a buoyancy aid will not keep an unconscious person face up in the water.

Many companies now manufacture very neat, compact lifejackets that automatically inflate when wet. These are ideal as they can be worn in complete comfort at all times, while providing a high degree of personal protection should you end up in the water.

AUDIBLE WARNING DEVICE

Every boat should be equipped with an audible warning device. A whistle should be regarded as the bare minimum - most life-jackets are supplied with a whistle. Aerosol foghorns are excellent, and so too are electronically operated foghorns fitted to larger boats. Sound travels well over water, and the repeated blasts of even a small whistle could attract vital attention when needed.

COMPASS

No boat should ever go to sea without a good-quality compass. Visibility even on fine days can quickly deteriorate to nil, and even the most experienced sailors quickly become disorientated. A good compass will guide you home.

FLARES

No boat should ever venture offshore without a full set of fresh, in date, distress flares consisting of at least four hand-held flares and two parachute rockets. A pack of flares is a good precaution for the freshwater angler, too, especially if he fishes some of the larger lakes, reservoirs or lochs.

RADIO

It is strongly advised that any boat fishing at sea should be provided with an approved marine-band VHF, fitted with Channel 16, the international distress channel. Small, hand-held sets are all right but they are restricted to a maximum of 5 watts of transmission power, unlike a fixed installation, which can have up to 25 watts and a correspondingly longer transmission distance. CB radios and portable phones are useful as a backup, but they are not acceptable substitutes for a marine radio with a direct line to the nearest coastguard station and other shipping in the area.

FIRST-AID KIT

All boats should carry a first-aid kit. These are widely available in prepacked kits, but an excellent first-aid kit can be assembled by purchasing individual items from a chemist and storing them in an air-tight box. It is worth adding a small booklet on basic first-aid procedures.

FIRE EXTINGUISHER

A fire extinguisher is a must, especially on boats fitted with outboard engines. These are widely available through car mainte-

Captured on a tube fly in the failing light, a fresh run salmon rests cradled safely in the net of well-known tackle dealer Jack Simpson of Turnford in Hertfordshire. The river is Scotland's famous Tweed, just a few hundred yards downstream from the road bridge at Kelso, and this large grilse was the third fish taken by Jack within two hours, while the author fishing close by had not a nibble.

nance shops and garages. A stored-pressure, dry-powder type is the most suitable for use aboard small boats, or a stored-pressure foam type.

SPARE CLOTHING

It is always worth carrying a complete set of warm, dry clothing when fishing afloat, even when setting off on a warm, dry summer day. Conditions can deteriorate with alarming speed offshore, and you might end up spending longer afloat than you anticipated.

BAILER/BILGE PUMP

Some means of getting rid of either rain water or spray taken aboard is another essential requirement. A bilge pump is useful for shifting modest quantities of water

where there is a suitable collecting point from which to pump the water. However, large quantities of water can only be removed quickly using either a bailer or a bucket.

SPARE-PARTS KIT

A simple spare-parts kit consisting of a few spanners (including plug spanner), screwdrivers, pliers, tape, cable ties, WD40 or similar lube/water repellent spray, a length of starter cord, and so on can save a lot of trouble afloat.

REMEMBER Always make sure that a responsible person ashore knows where you are, what time you intend returning, and has full details of your boat *every time that you venture afloat.*

SALMON
(Salmo salar)

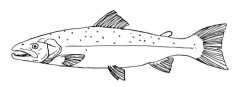

Average size: 6-12lb
Mega specimen: over 35lb
British record: 64lb (29kg 29g)

Though trout-like, the salmon's body is firm, more streamlined and powerfully built. When entering rivers fresh from the sea, it is a steely blue-grey along the back, blending into flanks of burnished silver liberally flecked with small asterisk-like spots, the majority of which are above the lateral line. Overall colouring darkens noticeably, however, the longer a fish remains in fresh water before spawning, at which time it becomes a dirty grey-bronze, often sporting large brown and red spots on the flanks. Males develop a hooked bottom jaw, called a kype.

The one distinguishing factor that easily separates the salmon from sea trout is its concave tail and narrow tail root, called the wrist, the outer edges of which are rigid allowing only the salmon to be gripped and lifted with one hand.

Salmon stop feeding when they enter freshwater, programmed thus to prevent them eating their own eggs and the eggs of others. Consequently, they fast until their reproduction cycle is over. However, they instinctively snap at and grab flies, worms, spinners and particularly shrimps (one of their staple foods at sea), motivated by aggression and territorial declaration. In saltwater, they consume shrimps and prawns, and small shoal fish. Reproduction occurs between October and January, when salmon mass on the gravel shallows, often high up in tiny rivers and streams, where they themselves were born. Females cut a depression, called a redd, in the gravel bottom and deposit large orange-coloured eggs, which are immediately fertilized by milt from the cock fish. The female then covers the eggs with stones by flapping her tail just above the redd. After a long, 3 to 4 month, incubation period the salmon fry, called alevins, emerge complete with their own yolk sac, on which they feed beneath the stones before massing in shoals. At 3-5in long the fry are called parr, and are recognizable by up to a dozen oval, blueish spots along the flanks with a red dot between each. When double this size they silver up and move down river towards the sea in readiness for a year (sometimes two or three) of rich feeding in saltwater. At this stage they are called smolts. When the smolts, now known as grilse, return to the river to spawn themselves one year later, they generally vary in weight from 3lb to 8lb. Those that remain at sea for more than a year return as fully mature salmon of large proportions. Though a percentage of adult fish die from exhaustion following spawning, many recover and, extremely thin, slowly make their way back to the sea. At this stage they are known as kelts. At sea they replace their body fats, before returning to spawn again the following year.

HABITAT AND DISTRIBUTION

At sea salmon follow shoals of herring and sprats in the North Atlantic, and will only tolerate pollution-free river systems when returning to spawn. The most prolific runs of salmon occur in Irish and Scottish rivers, with good runs in many Welsh river systems. English salmon runs are poor by comparison, with rivers entering via south and south-western coastlines enjoying the better runs.

TECHNIQUES

Artificial lure fishing - freshwater; Fly fishing; Spin fly fishing.
See also *Artificial flies; Artificial lures.*

SAND EEL, CORBINS'
(Hyperoplus immaculatas)

British record: 4½oz (128g)

This sand eel has a long, thin, smooth body, greeny-blue along the back blending into silvery-white lower flanks and belly. It has a long dorsal fin, forked tail and protruding lower jaw with large teeth in the upper jaw, which is not protrusible like those of smaller species. It feeds on planktonic life, including crustaceans and the eggs and fry of other fish, and it reproduces in the winter. An oceanic species, it is found around much of the British Isles, preferring deep water. It is caught for bait using tiny sets of feathers.

SAND EEL, GREATER
(Hyperoplus lanceolatus)

British record: 8½oz (239g)

Called launce by most sea fishermen, and the largest of the sand eels, this species has a distinctive black mark on each side of the

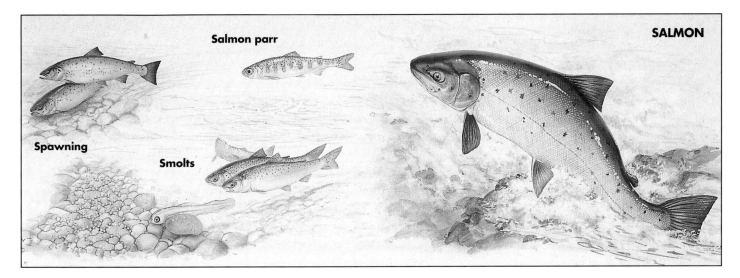

SALMON

Salmon parr

Spawning

Smolts

head. Its lower jaw protrudes and there are teeth in the upper jaw, which is not protrusible. The body is long, thin and smooth with a greeny-blueish back, blending down the sides into lower flanks and belly of silvery white. It is common around the British Isles in water over a sandy bottom, where it can easily be caught for bait using sets of very small feathers (*Feathering*). It feeds on small fish, crustaceans, fish eggs and planktonic life, and reproduces during the summer.

SCAD, OR HORSE MACKEREL

(*Trachurus trachurus*)

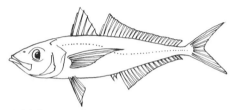

British record: 3lb 5¼oz (1kg 507g)

Though labelled horse mackerel, the scad is really a member of the jack family and sports the characteristic line of wide, bony scales along the tail root. In the scad, these cover the entire lateral line and are its instantly recognizable feature. The body is laterally compressed and rather slender, but the head is large and bony, with bony jaws (the lower protrudes) and a huge eye. There is also a dark mark on the edge of the gill plate. It has two dorsal fins, the first of spines, with a further two spines in front of the long anal fin. The tail is forked. Colouration is green-blue along the back with sides of metallic silver. The belly is white.

It feeds on squid, small fish and crustaceans, and reproduces in the summer. It is regularly caught on feathers (*Feathering*), and is common offshore all around the British Isles.

SCALES

Scales are available in three formats: tubular spring balances, clock-face scales and electronic scales with a digital read-out.

There is still a lot to be said for the simple spring balance available in brass, steel or in reinforced, glass-filled nylon, which is lightweight and easily slips into a jacket pocket. The Super Samson range, made by Salter, for instance, comes in models weighing up to 4lb in 1oz divisions, 11lb x 2oz, 22lb x 4oz, 33lb x 8oz and 44lb x 8oz. Calibrations are also marked in kg, and there is a useful rotating collar that allows for zero adjustment when using a weigh sling or bag. With tubular balances it is important to keep the spring itself in good order and free of rust (imperative for sea anglers), so the occasional spray from a moisture repellent aerosol such as WD40 is recommended. Salter also manufacture heavy-duty, steel-bodied spring balances (also calibrated in both imperial and metric divisions) up to 112lb x 1lb suitable for the sea fisherman. These have strong weighing hooks and adjustable zero knob.

Dial, or clock-face, scales are available in both large and popular, pocket-sized models, such as the Avon and Waymaster, which have clearly marked calibrations. Avon scales weigh to 40lb x 1oz, and the lightweight Waymaster is available in 12lb x ½oz and 30lb x 1oz models. Large clock-face units are most suitable for the big-fish freshwater specialist, the match fisherman and the sea angler. Reuben Heaton make several models, including a specimen hunter unit weighing up to 60lb x 1oz, while the Salter 235 6s model weighs to 110lb x ½lb divisions. Both are also fitted with zero knobs and are calibrated in kg. The Salter match clock-face scales are available in 8lb x 2dr, 20lb x 4dr, 50lb x 1oz and 100lb x 2oz, with zero adjustment. This unit comes with a weigh-bag and waterproof case.

Normark's electronic weigh-in scales are pocket-sized, battery-operated and provide an accurate digital read-out of a big fish via a liquid-crystal display on a 1¾in x ¾in screen. There are two models, weighing up to 10lb and up to 50lb, both in 1oz divisions.

SCHELLY

Another name for *powan.*

SEA SCORPION, LONG-SPINED

(*Taurulus bubalis*)

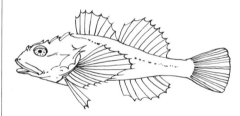

British record: 10oz (283g)

This species of sea scorpion is much smaller and squatter than the bull-rout, or short spined, scorpion, but it has a similar

Enthusiastic members of a small syndicate carp fishery bent on removing unwanted species, gently ease the diminishing circle of net held vertically by cork floats, towards the bank. The large buoy marks where the net's cod-end is situated.

appearance: two dorsal fins, the first spined, and huge pectorals; a bony head and jaws with a long spine on top of the gill plate; a membrane running from the bottom of the gill cover to the throat; and a spiny lateral line. Each pelvic fin has three distinct rays while the bull-rout's have more.

Colouration is greeny-brown along the back and sides, overlaid with darker mottling, and yellowy-orange underneath. It is common all around the British Isles over rocky ground, where it feeds on small, bottom-living fish and crustaceans. It reproduces in the spring.

SEA SCORPION, SHORT-SPINED
(*Myoxocephalus scorpius*)

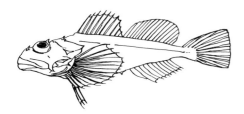

British record: 2lb 7½oz (1kg 119g)

Also called the bull-rout, this broad-headed sculpin has a quickly tapering body and lies half curled on the bottom just like the freshwater bullhead, which it closely resembles. It has two dorsal fins (the first spiked) and large pectorals; and a bony mouth with nasty spines on the top of its gill plates. The bottom of the gill plates extend to form a membrane under the throat. There are numerous small spines along both sides of the lateral line.

Colouration is a good camouflage of greeny-brown mottling on the back, slightly lighter along the flanks, and a colourful orange-red underneath. It feeds on crustaceans and small, bottom-living fish, and spawns during the winter. It is found all around the British Isles, preferring rough ground or rocks.

SEA TROUT

See *Trout, sea.*

SEINE NETTING

Seine nets are used by fish farmers, clubs and river authorities to net fish from still-

waters. Net depth can vary from just 8ft (for netting really shallow ponds) up to 25-30ft for deep gravel pits and reservoirs, while the length can vary from just fifty to several hundred yards long.

The knotless nylon mesh is generally quite small - minnow or gudgeon sized - and the top of the net is fitted with cork floats set at regular intervals to ensure that it stays on the surface, while the bottom (called the lead line) contains lead weights to ensure that the net lies on the bottom so that fish do not pass underneath it while it is pulled in.

The net is generally laid out in a circle by boat with one end remaining on the bank. When the other end has been taken back to shore, both ends are slowly pulled in until the lead line can be eased up on to the bank or into the shallows - with all the fish that were within the circle inside it. Some seine nets are fitted with a 'cod end' into which most of the fish swim.

SEWIN

Another name for *Sea trout.*

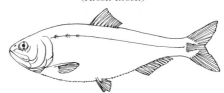

Only during the latter part of May or in early June do vast shoals of twaite shad enter the River Wye in order to spawn. And when he is not out in his boat sea fishing Dave Lewis loves to catch them on light spinning tackle.

SHAD, ALLIS
(*Alosa alosa*)

British record: 4lb 12½oz (2kg 166g)

This herring-like fish has a compressed side and deep body with a distinct keel along the belly. Its upturned mouth (the lower jaw protrudes) with bony hinges and a strange notch cut into the middle of the top lip denote that the shad is a plankton-feeder, although it also eats small shoal fish. It is blue-green along the back, fusing into flanks of burnished golden-silver. At the top of the gill cover there is usually a dark blotch, though not always. Though a sea fish, allis shad migrate far into freshwater to spawn during the late spring, but are not tolerant of pollution or man-made weirs that block their path. They are therefore now a rarity, though occasionally caught at sea on feathers.

SHAD, TWAITE
(*Alosa fallax*)

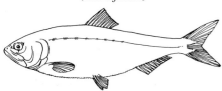

British record: 2lb 4¼oz (1kg 141g)

A smaller species, and less deep in the body than the allis shad, the twaite shad has similar characteristics and body shape, with silvery scales that, like those of its cousin, the herring, easily become dislodged. It has compressed flanks and a defined keel along the belly, the scales in ridge-like formation. It has a strange notch cut into the centre of the upper jaw, and the lower jaw protrudes and fits tightly against the upper. It feeds on crustaceans and small shoal fish.

Colouration blends from pewter or grey, with a touch of blue along the back, into silvery sides and belly and a line of several dark, round blotches along the shoulder, which are often just visible when the shad is in the water but seem to disappear when it is out of the water. Or they are not present at all.

This sea species is found all around the British Isles, though it is more common in warmer seas. In spring, it migrates up rivers into fresh water to spawn. More common than the allis shad, it is nevertheless becoming a rarity. It can be caught in fresh water on tiny spinners and on fry-imitating flies.

SHANNY
(*Lipophrys pholis*)

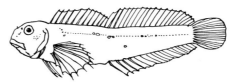

British record: 3oz (85g)

Easily distinguished from other blennies, which have a tentacle sprouting from the top of the head, the shanny has a smooth, rounded head. It has a long, double dorsal fin with a step down in the middle and a rounded tail. Its greeny-brown back and sides are overlaid with darker mottling.

It is a common in-shore fish around the British Isles, in rocky pools, where it feeds largely on crustaceans. It reproduces during the summer, when the male guards the eggs until they hatch.

SHARK, BLUE
(*Prionace glauca*)

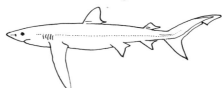

Average size: 40-60lb
Mega specimen: over 125lb
British record: 218lb (98kg 878g)

The blue shark is a shoaling or pack fish with a long, slender body and a long, sharply pointed snout, beneath which are strong jaws lined with pointed, serrated teeth. There are five gill slits and immediately beneath these, huge, curved pectoral fins. The upper tail lobe is elongated. Colouration fuses from bright indigo blue (which fades quickly to grey with death) along the back and upper sides into pale blue flanks and a white belly. It feeds on surface-shoaling species of oily fish, such as mackerel, pilchards and herrings, and squid. Following internal fertilization by the male, a female blue shark gives birth to live young, usually more than 40 to a litter.

HABITAT AND DISTRIBUTION
An open-ocean shark, the blue prefers deep, clear, warm waters, where it feeds actively in the upper layers close to the surface, well away from the coastline. It is most commonly caught from south-western and western seas off the British Isles, from Cornwall round to the Dingle peninsular in south-western Ireland.

TECHNIQUES
Drift fishing at sea.

SHARK, MAKO
(*Isurus oxyrinchus*)

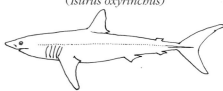

British record: 500lb (226kg 786g)

Members of this oceanic species, belonging to the mackerel shark family, usually travel alone and are caught to over 1000lb from tropical seas. It has a long, athletic body with a noticeably pointed snout and a rounded dorsal fin, which starts in a vertical line just back from the rear edge of the long pectorals. The tiny secondary dorsal is close to the narrow tail root, which

MAKO SHARK

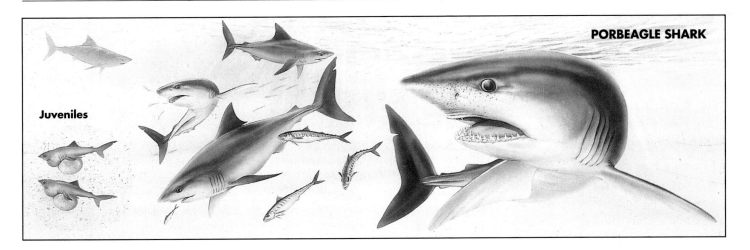

Juveniles

PORBEAGLE SHARK

has a strong keel on each side. There is a similar-sized fin directly below the second dorsal, set back from the anus. There are five gill slits and strong jaws lined with long, narrow-gape, triangular teeth, free of cusps. Those sprouting outwards from the lower jaw hang clear of the gums. Colouration is dark blue-grey along the back and half-way down the flanks, instantly changing to off-white along the lower flanks and belly.

The mako shark preys on oily-fleshed shoal species such as pilchards, herring, mackerel, sardines, squid and even turtles. It comes inshore to attack man in tropical oceans, and is fast and aggressive. It readily chases Kona-head artificial lures intended for marlin in tropical seas. It characteristically jumps completely clear of the water during a fight. The female gives birth to live young, usually single pups, following internal fertilization by the male and a long gestation period.

HABITAT AND DISTRIBUTION

This open-ocean species rarely comes inshore around the British Isles, although isolated captures have occurred well offshore along the south-western coastline between Plymouth and Falmouth. It likes any surge of water around wrecks and sunken reefs that is well-populated with food shoal fish such as pollack and various warm-water breams.

TECHNIQUES

Drift fishing at sea.

SHARK, PORBEAGLE

(Lamna nasus)

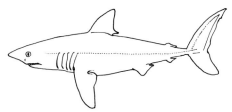

British record: 507lb (230kg)

The porbeagle is a member of the mackerel family of sharks, to which the similar-looking mako belongs. It has five gill slits and a large, round, thick-set body that is dark blue-grey along the back and upper sides, fusing into creamy white on the undersides. The large, rounded dorsal fin starts in a vertical line above the base of the wide pectorals, and there is a tiny secondary dorsal in front of the tail, with an identical-sized fin directly below, just back from the anus. The large, powerful tail has a noticeable V cut into the upper lobe, and keels on each side of the narrow tail root. The main feature, in addition to its body shape and fins, that sets the porbeagle apart from the mako is its teeth. These are triangular with a tiny cusp on each side of their base, whereas those of the mako are long, narrow and triangular, without cusps.

Porbeagles hunt mackerel, herrings, sardines, pollack and squid. The female gives birth to live young, up to four pups at a time, following internal fertilization by the male, which like all sharks is fitted with two large claspers for the purpose of reproduction.

HABITAT AND DISTRIBUTION

This open-ocean shark hunts in the upper water layers around the British Isles, and comes extremely close inshore should conditions suit. It is regularly caught from southern marks, such as around the Isle of Wight, off Devon and Cornwall, the southern, western and northern Irish coasts, and all around Scotland - the record porbeagle came off Dunnet Head, Scotland.

TECHNIQUES

Drift fishing at sea.

THRESHER SHARK

BLUE SHARK

SHARK, SIX-GILLED
(Hexanchus griseus)

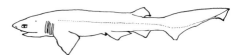

British record: 9lb 8oz (4kg 309g)

As its name implies, this primitive species has no less than six gill slits, while all other members of the shark family taken on rod and line from British seas have five. Its slender, classic, shark-shaped body has only one dorsal fin, set far back. The upper tail lobe is elongated, and the broad head has a relatively blunt snout. The back and sides are dark grey-brown, and the belly is a much lighter grey. An open-sea species generally found at great depths, it feeds on crustaceans, squid and bottom-living shoal species. The female gives birth to incredible numbers of live young (between 50 and 100) following internal fertilization by the male. It is rarely taken on rod and line.

SHARK, THRESHER
(Alopias vulpinus)

British record: 323lb (146kg 504g)

There can be absolutely no confusion between the thresher shark and other sharks, its identifying feature being the scythe-like upper tail lobe, which is as long as the shark's body and used for herding up food fish and then disorientating them by threshing the surface prior to attack. Colouration of its long, slim body is dark grey-blue to purple, slate-grey along the back, fins and flanks, with a white belly and grey beneath pectoral fins and snout. There are five gill slits, and the snout is very short and rounded. The jaws contain small, triangular teeth. It feeds on squid and shoaling species like mackerel, herring and other oily-fleshed species. The female gives birth to two to four pups at a time following internal fertilization by the male and a long gestation period. It characteristically jumps clear of the water. A lone species, thresher sharks occasionally hunt in pairs.

HABITAT AND DISTRIBUTION
Although never common around the British Isles, a large thresher shark (and they grow to over 700lb) can turn up almost anywhere. The most likely areas, however, are off the south coast of England, particularly around the Isle of Wight in the vicinity of the Needles.

TECHNIQUES
Drift fishing at sea.

SKATE, COMMON
(Raja batis)

Average size: 30-75lb
Mega specimen: over 100lb
British record: 227lb (102kg 961g)

Of all the flatfish inhabiting British waters, the common skate is second only to the halibut in potential size. It has a wide, diamond-shaped body with a long, thickish tail, and a pointed snout. It is brown to slate-grey on the top side with patches of prickles, and grey underneath with noticeable lines of pores. There are larger spines along the tail and between the dorsal fins.

It feeds mainly on fish, both on and off the bottom, plus molluscs, crustaceans and worms. It reproduces during late autumn and winter when, the eggs having been fertilized internally by the males, females lay large, purse-like capsules with horns at each end for attachment to weeds. The fully-formed young skate emerge after 4-5 months.

HABITAT AND DISTRIBUTION
More commonly found in seas around the north of the British Isles in deep, strong, flowing water over sand, mud or rough ground. Following heavy commercial fishing common skate are no longer plentiful, but anglers still have a fair chance of catching them from the seas off western Ireland, Northern Ireland and around the western Scottish Islands such as the Orkneys and Isle of Mull etc.

TECHNIQUES
Downtide boat fishing.

SKATE, LONG-NOSED
(Raja oxyrinchus)

British record: none

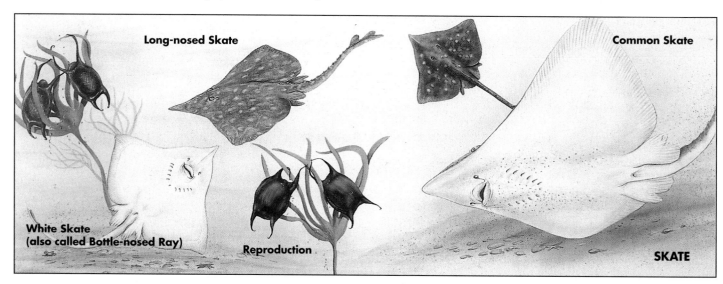

Long-nosed Skate

White Skate (also called Bottle-nosed Ray)

Reproduction

Common Skate

SKATE

The long-nosed skate has a much longer snout than the common skate, with a grey-brown top side overlaid with lighter spots. Underneath it is grey and scattered with small black dots. It has large spines along the tail and fine prickles on the snout.

Feeding on crustaceans and fish over soft bottoms in deep water, this skate is very rarely caught on rod and line, although it is not uncommon in seas bordering the western coastline of the British Isles. It reproduces in the spring. Once the eggs have been internally fertilized by the male, the female lays leathery egg capsules, from which the fully-formed young skate emerge several months later. It grows to over 100lb.

SKIPPER
(*Scomberesox saurus*)

British record: 5oz (141g)

Similar in appearance to a garfish, but smaller, and with thinner jaws and tiny teeth, this open-sea species is found all around the British Isles. Its long, slim body is rather deep, with compressed sides, and it is green along the back, fusing into metallic silver along the flanks and belly. It feeds on small, surface shoal fish and crustaceans and reproduces during the summer.

SMELT
(*Osmerus eperlanus*)

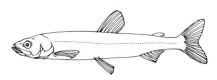

British record: 6¾oz (191g)

Averaging between just 4-8in in length, this tiny, fully-scaled shoal fish spends the greater part of its life in the sea and is common around the British Isles, only entering freshwater to spawn. It is often called cucumber smelt due to its distinct smell of cucumbers. It has a slim body, large eye and upturned mouth line, with large teeth, and a tiny adipose fin between dorsal fin and tail. All fins are translucent grey in colour, and the tail is deeply forked. The dorsal and anal fins are squared. Colouration is pale grey-green along the back, fusing into flanks of metallic silver.

It feeds on worms, crustaceans and the fry of other fish. It reproduces during the spring in the tidal reaches of large rivers, the eggs adhering to rocks and weeds. The resulting fry are taken out to sea by the tide. Smelt are only rarely caught on maggots by coarse fishermen, but make a fine *deadbait* for pike (*Baits - freshwater*).

SMELT, SAND
(*Atherina prespyter*)

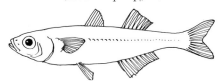

British record: 2½oz (72g)

Commonly found in huge schools around the British Isles, in estuaries and shallow inshore waters, the sand smelt has a fully-scaled, slim, silvery body with two dorsal fins, the first of delicate spines, the second of soft rays. It has a forked tail, big eye and upturned mouth with protrusible jaws. It feeds on minute crustaceans and planktonic organisms, and reproduces during the summer in the mouths of estuaries or in the sea proper.

SMELT, SAND - BIG-SCALE
(*Atherina boyeri*)

British record: 5dr (8g)

Second only to the stickleback as the smallest British record fish ever claimed, this slim shoaling species is quite localized around the British Isles, preferring estuaries of low salinity. It has a distinct silver streak along the flanks, a silvery-white belly and a greenish back with clearly defined scales. It has two dorsal fins, the first of fine spines, a huge eye and an upturned mouth. It feeds on tiny worms, molluscs and crustaceans.

SMOOTH HOUND
(*Mustelus mustelus*)

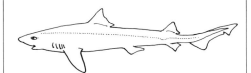

Average size: 3-7lb
Mega specimen: over 15lb
British record: 28lb (12kg 700g)

This small, athletic shark species has very similar physical characteristics to the starry smooth hound, but is not so common and is generally smaller. It has five gill slits and relatively large fins for its size. Colouration is light grey on the back and sides, with a creamy white belly. It has no white spots, which immediately distinguishes this species from the starry smooth hound. It is a bottom-feeder, consuming only molluscs and crustaceans, which it chews with flattish grinding teeth. Following internal fertilization by the male and a year-long gestation period, the female gives birth to live young in litters of up to a dozen or more pups.

HABITAT AND DISTRIBUTION
Found all around the British Isles, often in large packs, the smooth hound prefers inshore waters, where it hunts along the bottom over beds of gravel and sand.

TECHNIQUES
Beachcasting; Downtide boat fishing; Uptide boat fishing.

SMOOTH HOUND, STARRY
(*Mustelus asterias*)

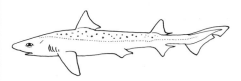

Average size: 3-8lb
Mega specimen: over 15lb
British record: 28lb (12kg 700g)

Athletic, small species of shark with five gill slits and relatively large, broad fins for its slender body. It is light grey along the back and sides fusing into a creamy belly and overlaid with a sprinkling of small, star-like white spots. It is equipped with flattened, grinding teeth for crunching up molluscs and crustaceans, including hermit crabs complete with whelk shells. Following internal fertilization by the male and a year-long gestation period, the female gives birth in summer to live young in litters of up to a dozen or more pups.

HABITAT AND DISTRIBUTION
This common, bottom-feeding shark is

found around the British Isles often in sizeable packs. It prefers inshore waters over beds of sand and gravel.

TECHNIQUES

Beachcasting; Downtide boat fishing; Uptide boat fishing.

SOLE

(*Solea solea*)

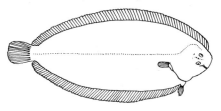

Average size: 12oz-1½lb
Mega specimen: over 2½lb
British record: 6lb 8½oz (2kg 966g)

The sole is a right-sided (i.e. both eyes are on the fish's right side), extremely slippery, long and smooth-bodied flatfish. Rather slim in cross-section, it has continuous, low-set dorsal and anal fin frills that almost taper into a tiny, rounded tail.. The head is small and so is the strangely curved, off-centre mouth. Colouration on the top side is mid brown overlaid with darker blotches and the underneath is creamy white. There is a small black spot on the pectoral fin. It feeds on worms, molluscs and crustaceans and is particularly active at night or in low light conditions. It reproduces in the summer, laying eggs that float until they hatch.

HABITAT AND DISTRIBUTION

Commonly-caught flatfish around the British Isles, the sole prefers a sandy or muddy bottom in fairly shallow water.

TECHNIQUES

Beachcasting; Downtide boat fishing; Uptide boat fishing.

SOLE, LEMON

(*Microstomus kitt*)

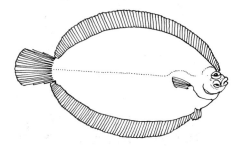

British record: 2lb 7¾oz (1kg 124g)

LEMON SOLE

SOLE

Dab-like in appearance, the lemon sole is a right-sided flatfish, with a thick-set body, small head and mouth, and a perfectly smooth body. Brown with darker patches on top and white undersides. The lateral line curves slightly around the pectoral fin and the long dorsal and anal fin frills almost join the rounded tail. The tail root is wide. The lemon sole feeds on worms, molluscs and crustaceans, and reproduces during the summer at great depths. It is widespread around the British Isles over bottoms of gravel, sand and mud, but is not commonly caught by anglers.

SPADE-END HOOK

See *Hooks.*

SPIN-FLY FISHING

This extremely effective method for presenting a fly deep down in cold water close to the bottom, even around boulders, for game species such as trout, sea trout and salmon, originates from Scandinavia.

A spinning outfit comprising a 9-10ft rod and a fixed-spool reel is used in conjunction with a special weighted end rig (fig. 87) plus the fly (or lure) of your choice.

The rig is easy to make and requires three items of tackle. Tie a tube fly (or large wet fly) to a 4-5ft long trace and on to a three-way swivel. To the top of the swivel tie the 6-12lb-test reel line (depending on the size of game species expected), and to the bottom tie a plastic-covered tubular weight or plain bomb on a 20-40in monofilament link. The lead-link length depends on the river-bed structure. For instance, if the bottom is smooth shingle, gravel or sand, 20in is ideal, whereas for boulder-strewn bottoms, 40-60in ensures that the lure or fly will be presented at the level where the fish lie. Make the cast down-

stream and across in the traditional manner, as though placing a wet fly, and after closing the bale arm once the lead has touched bottom, keep the rod tip high as the rig swings around in the current.

Once the rig has swung into the near bank and the tube fly starts to dangle, a slow retrieve brings the rig back upstream again. Takes can occur at any point from the moment when the fly starts swinging across the current (while the lead bumps over the boulders or gravel) to when it is lifted out for another cast. At this point, you wade or walk a yard or so downstream and repeat the procedure.

In exceptionally deep, fast rivers the tube fly can be exchanged for a small, light-weight, artificial lure such as a *Toby-type spoon, spinner* or a wooden *Devon Minnow,* or even a natural dead fish bait, such as a mounted minnow, or a *plastic worm/spinning jig* (*Artificial Lures*).

Remember to work the near (close range) lies first, then make progressively longer casts in order to cover the entire pool in a methodical fashion. Gently ease the bomb or tubed weight over rocks by lifting the rod tip whenever the rig feels heavy and catches up. Do not, however, be tempted to wind as the fly is swung around by the current, or it will travel too fast and be presented too high in the water for a fish to grab hold.

SPINNING

See *Artificial lure fishing.*

SPLIT SHOT

Prior to the British Government's ban on the sale and use of lead split shot larger than size 8 and lead ledger weights up to 1oz, which came into force in January 1987 following an escalating number of swan deaths caused by lead poisoning, all shots

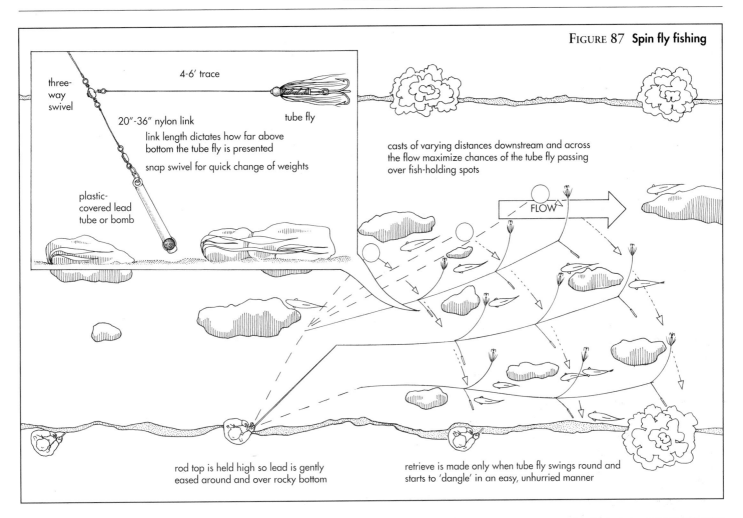

FIGURE 87 **Spin fly fishing**

three-way swivel

4-6' trace

tube fly

20"-36" nylon link

link length dictates how far above bottom the tube fly is presented

snap swivel for quick change of weights

plastic-covered lead tube or bomb

casts of varying distances downstream and across the flow maximize chances of the tube fly passing over fish-holding spots

FLOW

rod top is held high so lead is gently eased around and over rocky bottom

retrieve is made only when tube fly swings round and starts to 'dangle' in an easy, unhurried manner

Along with the groups of non-toxic split shot shown here in 13 different sizes are dispensers of the popular olivette and style weights much used by pole fishermen. Olivette-type weights thread on to the line, whilst style types are pressed on.

and ledgers were made from lead. Tiny dust shot from size 8 to micro size 13 are still made from lead, as are bombs of 11/4oz upwards (*Ledger weights*). All split shot in sizes 6, 5, 4, 3, 1, BB, AB, AAA, SA, SSG (swan shots) 2SSG and 3SSG are now made from non-toxic, lead-free metals. The easiest to use are those with a double cut - a deep slit takes the line and a smaller cut on the opposite side allows the non-toxic split shot to be opened and closed with ease. Open the slit with a thumbnail to remove the shot or reposition it on the line, and gently press tight again. Do not try to reposition the shot without opening it or the line will fracture. To make quick and inexpensive ledgers using split shot see fig. 80. Size for weight, non-toxic split shot is only slightly larger than the equivalent in lead shot.

As makes vary, equivalent shot sizes given in the following table may also need to be varied.

3SSG = 3SSG (swan shots)
2SSG = 2SSG (swan shots)
1SSG = 2AAA or 4BB or 8 No. 4s
1SA = 3BBS
1AAA = 2BBS
1AB = 2 No. 1s
1BB = 2 No. 4s, or 4 No. 6s or 8 No. 8s
1 No. 1 = 3 No. 6s or 6 No. 8s
1 No. 3 = 2 No. 6s
1 No. 4 = 3 No. 9s
1 No. 5 = 2 No. 8s
1 No. 6 = 2 No. 10s
1 No. 8 = 2 No. 12s

SPRAT
(*Sprattus sprattus*)

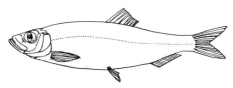

British record: none

This tiny, oily-fleshed sea fish averages 4-6in long, and masses in huge shoals, feeding on crustaceans and planktonic organisms. It is almost identical in shape to a herring, with an upturned mouth and flattened, silvery sides. It can easily be distinguished, however, by its dorsal fin, which starts on a vertical line with the pelvic fin root, whereas the herring's dorsal is set much further forward. Also, the sprat's back is more green than blue. Adolescent sprats (in their first year) are sold as whitebait.

The sprat reproduces in the summer. It is heavily preyed upon by other species, particularly cod, and makes an effective bait. (*Baits - sea*).

STICKLEBACK, NINE-
OR TEN-SPINED
(*Pungitius pungitius*)

British record: none

Similar in shape to the three-spined variety, but slimmer in the body, this stickleback averages around 2in long and has nine or ten short spines in place of a first dorsal fin. The second dorsal, anal and pectoral fins and the tail are rayed. Along the middle belly are two single spines, widely separated. It has a generally darker colouration than the three-spined, with an olive brown back fusing into dull, silvery flanks. Males develop a black throat during the spring, when the reproduction cycle and courtship ritual begins.

It feeds on minute crustaceans, aquatic insect life, and the young fry of other fish. A freshwater species of ditches, dykes, canals and small ponds, it is occasionally found in brackish marshland dykes. It is rarely taken by anglers, but like the three-spined stickleback, it can be lifted out when it gorges on the end of a maggot or worm.

STICKLEBACK, SEA
(*Spinachia spinachia*)

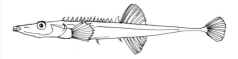

British record: ¼oz (7g)

Also called the fifteen-spined stickleback, this species is vastly different in shape to the freshwater sticklebacks and averages 3-4in long, with a long, slim body, a long, extremely thin tail root and a tiny mouth. It has between 14 and 17 short spines along its middle (where the first dorsal should be), preceding a second dorsal of soft rays. Its anal fin is also of soft rays with a tiny pelvic spine in front, and is situated immediately below the second dorsal. It is coloured a greeny-brown along the back and sides, overlaid with dusky bars, and is yellowy underneath.

It feeds mainly on crustaceans, and reproduces during the late spring, when males build nests well above the bottom in which several females lay their eggs. It is non-shoaling and lives entirely in shallow salt water all around the British Isles. It is rarely deliberately caught by anglers.

STICKLEBACK, THREE-
SPINED
(*Gasterosteus aculeatus*)

British record: none

This aggressive shoaling species, averaging just 2in long, is found throughout the British Isles in small ponds, pits, dykes, ditches, streams and sluggish rivers. It is also found in estuaries and in tidal pools with a high salinity content, where it appears to grow slightly larger. Its ungainly, bony, deep body rapidly tapers to a weak tail, and it is completely lacking in scales. It has three strong spines on the back (in place of the first dorsal fin) and a pair of spines in place of pelvic fins. The second dorsal fin is of soft rays, as are the anal fin, tail and pectoral fins, which are constantly working in a fanning movement.

It has a bony-plated head with large eye and upturned mouth with protruding lower jaw and thick-rimmed lips. Colouration along the back is dark pewter fusing down the flanks to yellowy-silver. Males have a distinct reddish tinge beneath the chin that intensifies during late spring when spawning occurs to bright red, with metallic green flanks and a turquoise blue outer circle to the eye. Males entice several females to lay their eggs in a nest made from weeds and fertilizes them immediately, standing guard until the young hatch. The stickleback feeds on worms, molluscs, aquatic insect larvae and even tiny fish fry. It will hang on to a maggot or worm without the hook penetrating its lips, and can often be lifted out.

STRETPEGGING

See *Freshwater floatfishing techniques*.

SUNFISH

(Mula mota)

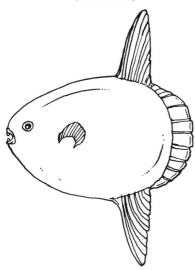

British record: 108lb (48kg 986g)

This huge, blueish-grey, round-bodied fish appears to have been cut in half through the dorsal and pelvic fins, but close inspection reveals that the wavy edging at the rear of its body is in fact a round-lobed tail. It has a light belly and decidedly rounded pectoral fins with a keel-like anal fin and a similar-shaped, erect dorsal directly above it. The eye is small, and the mouth tiny for such a huge creature (sunfish are known to reach weights in excess of 1½ tonnes), and it merely sucks in planktonic animals and jellyfish. This fish is widespread around the British Isles, but is rarely caught on rod and line although it prefers the warmer surface layers.

SWIMFEEDERS

Swimfeeders do exactly what their name implies: they feed either particle baits such as maggots and hempseed, or bread-crumbs, or a mixture of both, into the swim next to the hookbait.

Because feeders have built-in weights, a separate ledger weight is not needed. You simply add the desired feeder to a running ledger or paternoster rig (fig. 88), making sure that there is sufficient lead to hold bottom and to keep the feeder static in fast-flowing water.

Most feeders are cylindrical, flat or oval in cross-section, made from tough, clear or coloured plastic and drilled with holes through which the bait is distributed. Cage feeders are made from either wire or plastic

Note the swim feeder hanging just to the left of John's right shoulder. It is a plastic cage feeder into which dampened breadcrumbs are pressed that release on impact with the bottom. Used in conjunction with a simple fixed paternoster and baiting with breadflake, lobtail or a worm/maggot cocktail, there is no better combination for keeping slab-sided Irish bream coming to the net. John took this seven-pounder and another 30 of similar size in a morning session from Hodson's Bay Caravan Park at the south-western end of mighty Lough Ree, through which the River Shannon passes.

mesh, and dampened breadcrumbs are pressed into them for instant dispersal in still or very slow moving water. Open-end plastic feeders are also used for groundbait but do not release it until the feeder hits bottom, which is desirable when ledgering in deep, flowing water where premature release of the groundbait would result in it being dispersed too widely. Block-end feeders are fitted with a removable end cap (for baiting up) and distribute maggots, casters and particles, but not groundbait.

Some manufacturers offer weights of alternative sizes for their feeders. The Drennan Feederlink, for example, has a plastic spigot at the bottom to which weights varying between ⅛oz and 1oz can

be clipped. It makes sense to carry a supply of fold-over or strap leads in varying sizes from ½oz to 2oz so that any make of cage, open-end feeder or block-end can be doctored to remain static on the bottom regardless of current strength.

The holes of block-end feeders can be enlarged with a pair of small scissors to cater for large particles or to release small ones instantly. Don't be afraid to experiment. For instance, by removing the end of a large Drennan flat block-end, which come fitted with heavy weights, you can turn it into a superb open-end feeder, ideal for bream fishing in the deep, fast rivers of southern Ireland where continually depositing breadcrumbs is essential for success.

FIGURE 88 **Swimfeeders and rigs**

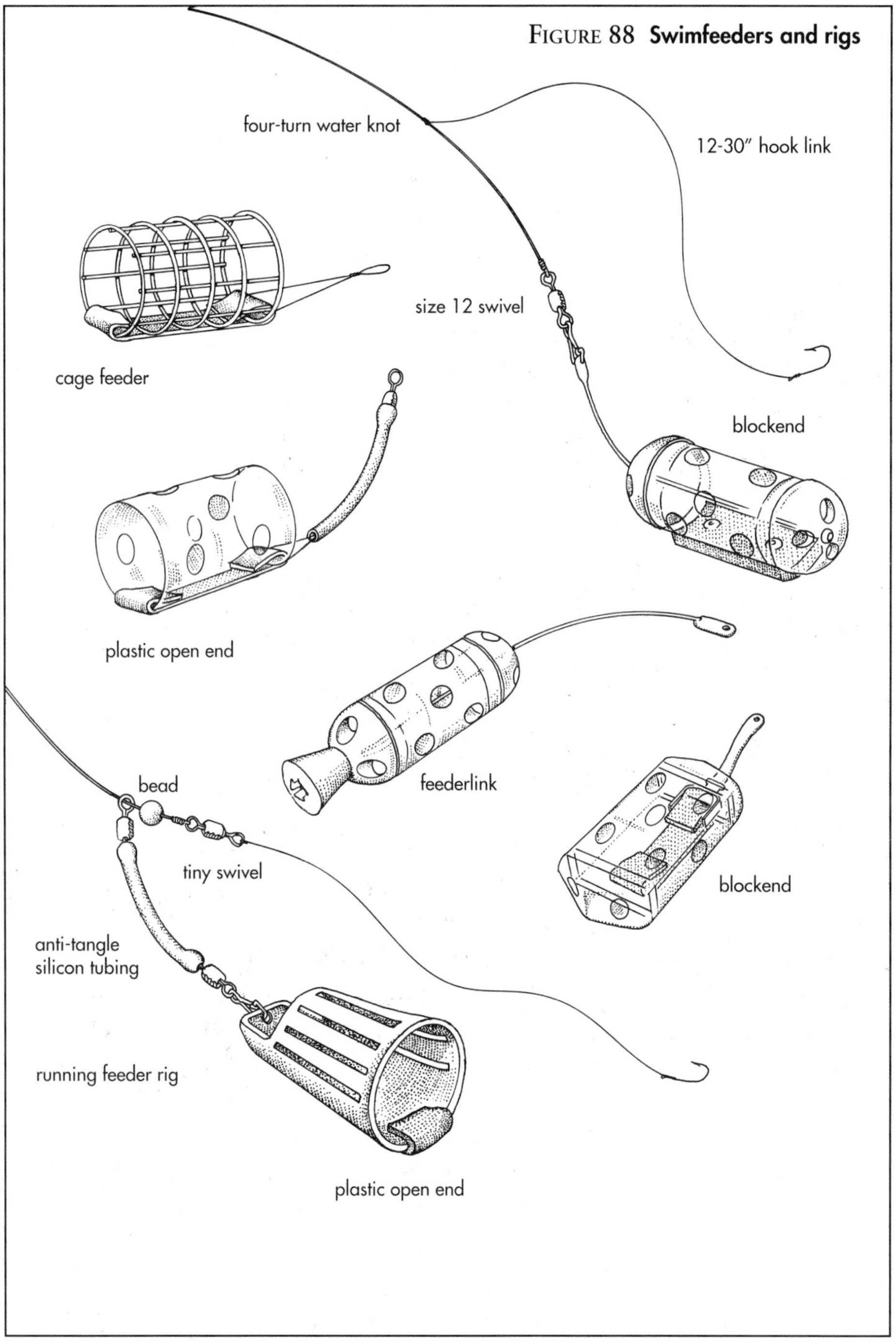

four-turn water knot

12-30″ hook link

size 12 swivel

cage feeder

blockend

plastic open end

bead

feederlink

tiny swivel

blockend

anti-tangle silicon tubing

running feeder rig

plastic open end

SWING TIP

See *Bite indicators and accessories.*

SWIVELS

Swivels are small but very strong junctions made from brass or stainless steel wire. Barrel swivels are generally used as a junction between hook trace and reel line. They revolve and thus eliminate line twist, and are available in about fourteen different sizes, from a tiny size 16, up to giant 6/0 models used for big game fishing.

Basic swivels are available in several shapes, with either round or diamond-shaped eyes, and in bronze, nickel, stainless steel or a blackened finish. Game-fishing swivels, such as the famous Berkeley range from the USA, are strength rated. Non-rusting, ball-bearing swivels are available (though expensive), and incorporate ten stainless-steel balls that absorb the torsion. Many salmon anglers prefer ball-bearing swivels when using artificial lures.

Various connectors can be added to a basic swivel to facilitate quick changing of numerous accessories, from swimfeeders and ledger links to artificial lures. Well proven types are the interlocking snap-swivels, American snaps, link-spring swivels and the cross-lok snaps. Snaps or snap-links are also available on their own. When joined to a plastic lead-slider, these snaps facilitate easy changing of leads when sea fishing. Some swivelled snaps are mounted on to wire or plastic, triangular or L-shaped booms, such as the Kilmore, Clements, Ashpoles or Eddystone booms, in order to minimize tangles and keep the lead away from the hook trace.

A buckle swivel is used to accommodate the monofilament trace loop when sea fishing, and the lead is attached via a corkscrew swivel.

For paternostering livebaits and for working lures on a paternoster link, three-

T t

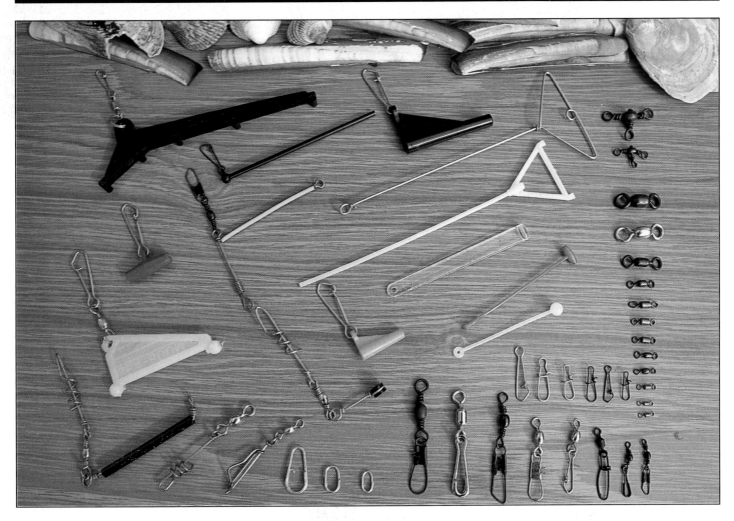

way swivels are often used. These consist of a barrel swivel to which a third eye has been joined, thus providing three junctions.

TADPOLE FISH
(*Raniceps vaninus*)

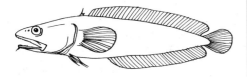

British record: 1lb 5¾oz (616g)

This rarely-caught member of the cod family is a solitary bottom-dweller. It is common among rocks, where it feeds on worms, crustaceans and small fish. It has a large head and mouth, with a single, small barb under the chin. The dorsal fin is a long, low-set frill preceded by a tiny first dorsal fin comprising just three rays. The anal fin is also long and the tail small and rounded. All the fins have a light edging. Colouration is dark along the back, fusing into warm-grey flanks and a grey belly. It reproduces in the late summer.

TAILER

A tailer, as the name suggests, is used to snare a fish by the tail when it is ready for landing. They are used mainly for salmon, but also for some saltwater species.

The tailer's great advantage over the gaff is that fish can be returned unharmed. Some charter-boat skippers along the east coast of England even use a tailor to bring Thames-estuary tope aboard by snaring the fish around its middle.

A tailer consists of a running loop of braided wire attached to a handle. The wire loop is slipped over the salmon's tail and pulled tight around the wrist just above it. Some tailers are equipped with wrist straps that prevent the tailer from being ripped out of the hand by the last lunge of a hooked fish. Some also incorporate an anti-swivel pin to stop the loop swinging away from the fish at the vital moment.

TARGET BOARD

See *Ledgering techniques - Quivertipping*.

TENCH
(*Tinca tinca*)

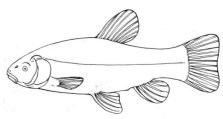

Average size: 2-3lb
Mega specimen: over 7lb
British record: 14lb 7oz (6kg 548g)

With its thick-set olive green body and nicely rounded, large and powerful, dark grey-brown fins, there is no chance of confusing the tench with another freshwater

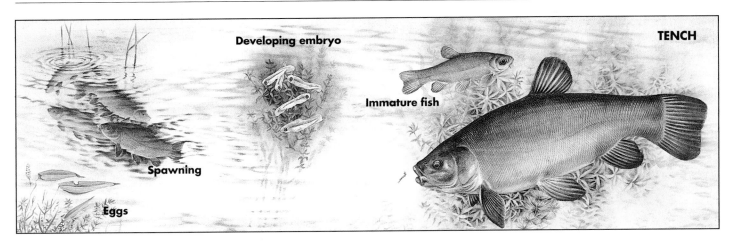

Developing embryo

TENCH

Immature fish

Spawning

Eggs

species. The small eye is red and the mouth semi-protrusible with thick-rimmed lips. At each corner of the mouth there is a tiny barbel. The scales are tiny, deeply embedded and covered in a thick, protective mucus. Males are easily distinguishable from females (which grow much larger) by their huge and crinkly, spoon-shaped pelvic fins, which overlap the vent when held against the belly. The female's pelvic fins do not overlap the vent and are slightly pointed.

Tench are slow, ponderous feeders, purpose-built for grubbing about on the bottom. They stand on their heads to suck in crustaceans, aquatic insect larvae such as bloodworms, and small molluscs. Spawning takes place during the summer in warm shallows, and the eggs are deposited among marginal grasses or soft weeds. These hatch within 10 days, and the young tench rarely leave the cover of weed until they are at least several inches long.

HABITAT AND DISTRIBUTION

The tench is widely distributed throughout the British Isles, but not common in Scotland. It prefers habitats lush in aquatic flora and grows to its optimum weight in clear, rich stillwaters. It proliferates in all ponds, pits, lakes and reservoirs, and also in canals and sluggish rivers.

TECHNIQUES

Freelining; Freshwater floatfishing techniques - Laying on, Lift method, Float ledgering, Waggler fishing, From a boat in stillwaters; Freelining; Ledgering techniques - Bobbin indicator ledgering in stillwaters, The bolt rig.

A nicely shaped early morning gravel pit tench for the author's brother, David Wilson, who ledgered lobworms together with breadcrumb packed into a wire cage feeder, 40yd out over a shallow plateau.

TENCH, GOLDEN
(*Tinca tinca*, var. *Auratus*)

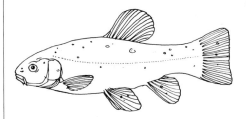

British record: none

Identical in physical characteristics, feeding, reproduction and body shape to the common (green) tench, golden tench are noticeably slimmer and do not grow to the same optimum size, specimens in excess of 3-4lb being quite unusual. Colouration is a distinct and striking, bright orangey-banana yellow, often irregularly flecked with dark spots and blotches. Banana fish is, in fact, a nickname given to this species. The eye is jet black and the fins are translucent, often with a pinkish tinge.

The golden tench is commonly available through the ornamental pond-fish trade, for which it is specifically bred. It is stocked as an angler's fish into a few stillwaters in England.

TEST CURVES

Devised by the late Richard Walker as a guide to suitable line strengths for use with two-piece rods, test curves simply refer to the pull on a spring balance required to bend the rod's tip round into a quarter circle.

That pull in lb and oz is then multiplied by 5 to give the ideal line strength. Multiplying by 4 gives its lowest suggested line strength and by 6 gives the upper limit. For instance, a carp rod with a 2lb test curve

will have an ideal strength of 10lb with the option of stepping down to 8lb test and going up to 12lb.

As test curves were originally devised for two-piece, through-action built-cane rods, they should be regarded only as an approximate guide with modern fast-taper carbon-fibre rods.

THERMOCLINE

See *Water temperature*.

THROWING STICK

The throwing stick is an alternative implement to the catapult for accurately propelling freshwater baits and groundbaits into a chosen area.

Designer throwing sticks, such as the aluminium Cobra range, have curled, open ends and can throw boilies accurately to over 100yd. The groundbaiter, spoon-type stick throws small deadbaits, groundbait, particle baits or even multiple boilies.

Throwing sticks for maggots, casters or boilies, and for groundbait, can easily be made from hollow-glass off-cuts obtainable from a tackle shop. To make a simple loose feed or boilie throwing stick (fig. 89A), take a tapered off-cut of around 24in long and 1-1¼in in diameter, and plug it 6-8in from the narrow end with a wine-maker's cork bung, reducing the bung to size with a rasp-type file. To finish, glue a moulded plastic hand-grip over the thick end.

To construct a groundbait stick (fig. 89B) use a 30in long off-cut blank, also of around 1-1¼in in diameter, and plug the narrow end with a cork. Then build up the top for a length of around 3-4in with three separate layers of masking or electrical tape so that it will take a 10in length of 2½-

FIGURE 89 Making throwing sticks

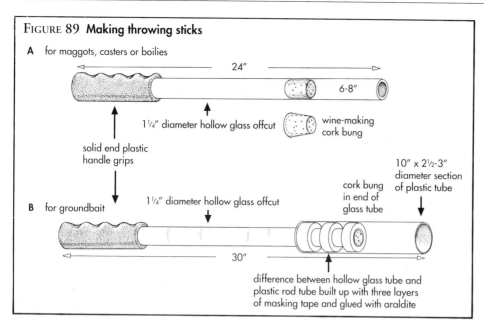

A for maggots, casters or boilies

24″

6-8″

1¼″ diameter hollow glass offcut

wine-making
cork bung

solid end plastic
handle grips

10″ x 2½-3″
diameter section
of plastic tube

cork bung
in end of
glass tube

B for groundbait

1¼″ diameter hollow glass offcut

30″

difference between hollow glass tube and
plastic rod tube built up with three layers
of masking tape and glued with araldite

3in diameter plastic rod tube. When the fit is tight, glue on permanently with a strong adhesive, and if you wish paint the entire unit either black or dark green. To finish, glue a moulded plastic hand-grip over the thick end.

To use either stick accurately, hold it upright and punch it out smoothly, as though laying the line down when casting a fly.

TIDES

There is no question that the tides affect the way sea fish move and feed, and the sea angler should always be aware of how the tides affect the fishing in his local area. The problem is that there are no hard and fast rules as to when fish do or do not feed, certainly not on a national scale. And even in the case of local feeding patterns there will always be exceptions to the rules.

Many species favour a strong tide run, others become more active at slack water or during more gentle tidal flows. Any change of tide is a good time for a bite, the altering conditions tending to stir fish into life. The first run of the tide, either the ebb or the flood, following a period of slack water can often be productive.

The size and consequently the flow of the tide is constantly changing between neaps (small tides) and springs (big tides). The height and times of tides are mainly governed by the moon and its gravitational pull on the earth, and this varies with the moon's orbit. The full cycle takes approximately one month. Spring tides coincide with either a new moon or a full moon,

when the gravitational pull on the earth is at its strongest.

However, friction against the coastline retards the tidal action, so that a place connected with the main ocean by long channels, such as the east coast of Britain, will not experience the highest tides on the actual day of the new or full moon, but perhaps two days later. This delay is called the 'age of the tide' for a particular place.

Neap tides fall midway between each sequence of springs. One week after a new moon, we will see approximately one-quarter of the moon in the sky. This is the first quarter. Two weeks later we will see the opposite quarter of the moon, and the tides are now said to be in the last quarter. Both times coincide with the smallest of neap tides, with little run of water.

Another factor that undoubtedly affects fishing is whether or not the tidal sequence is falling or rising; that is, whether the tides are getting bigger each day, building towards the next set of springs, or dropping back to neaps.

All sea anglers should purchase a set of local tide tables, which are available through most tackle shops. Consult them each time you go fishing, and if you keep accurate records you will start to see a pattern that shows which tides tend to be the most productive in your area.

TOPE
(Galeorhinus galeus)

Average size: 20-35lb
Mega specimen: over 60lb
British record: 82lb 8oz (37kg 422g)

A member of the requiem shark family, to which the blue shark also belongs, tope have a slender, athletic body with five gill slits and a pointed snout. The jaws are lined with sharply pointed, triangular teeth, and colouration is greyish-brown on top and midway down the flanks, changing to a white belly. Fins are large and powerful with an unmistakable deep notch in the upper tail lobe. The small second dorsal fin, set back close to the tail, is the same size as the anal fin positioned directly below.

Tope feed on shoal fish such as mackerel and herring, but also eat bottom-living species and crustaceans. They reproduce during the summer. After internal fertilization by the male and a gestation period of up to 10 months, the female gives birth to up to 30 pups.

HABITAT AND DISTRIBUTION
The tope is widely distributed around the British Isles and elsewhere in warm, temperate seas. It hunts over sand, shingle or a gravel bottom from midwater down to the ocean floor; young tope often coming close inshore to feed.

TECHNIQUES
Beachcasting; Downtide boat fishing; Drift fishing at sea; Uptide boat fishing.

TOP KNOT, COMMON
(Zeugopterus punctatus)

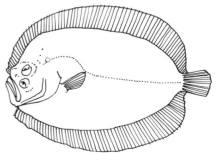

British record: 12½oz (352g)

A small, left-sided flatfish with rather localized distribution around the British Isles,

Breeding

TOPE

the top knot is generally found among rocks and over rough ground in shallow water. It has a wide brown body overlaid with dark brown blotches, a distinct round mark in the middle of its top side, and dark lines immediately above and below each eye. Both dorsal and anal fin frills fringe almost its entire body from forehead and chin, merging into the tiny, rounded tail. Its scales feel rough to the touch, and the upturned mouth is cavernous. It feeds on crustaceans, worms and tiny fish, and reproduces in the spring.

TORSK
(Brosme brosme)

British record: 15lb 7¼oz (7kg 5g)

Yet another member of the cod family, and looking very much like a giant rockling with a thick-set body, the torsk is grey-brown on the back fusing into lighter sides and belly. The long dorsal and anal fins merge into the tail, the edges fringed with white, similar to the ling. The mouth is large, with a long, single barbel under the chin. The distinct lateral line curves noticeably above the vent.

The torsk prefers a rocky bottom in deep cold water, feeding on crustaceans, molluscs and small, bottom-dwelling fish. It reproduces during the summer in deep water. It is occasionally caught off Northern Ireland and Scotland, and is common throughout Scandinavian seas.

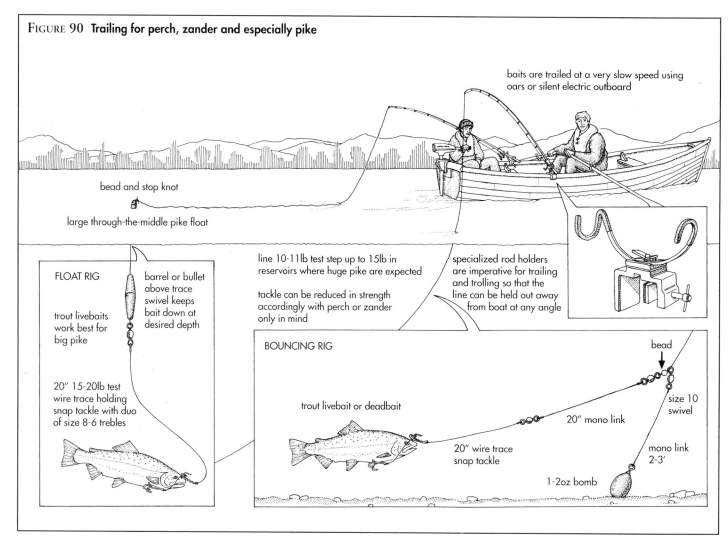

FIGURE 90 **Trailing for perch, zander and especially pike**

baits are trailed at a very slow speed using oars or silent electric outboard

bead and stop knot

large through-the-middle pike float

FLOAT RIG

trout livebaits work best for big pike

barrel or bullet above trace swivel keeps bait down at desired depth

20″ 15-20lb test wire trace holding snap tackle with duo of size 8-6 trebles

line 10-11lb test step up to 15lb in reservoirs where huge pike are expected

tackle can be reduced in strength accordingly with perch or zander only in mind

specialized rod holders are imperative for trailing and trolling so that the line can be held out away from boat at any angle

BOUNCING RIG

bead

size 10 swivel

trout livebait or deadbait

20″ mono link

20″ wire trace snap tackle

mono link 2-3′

1-2oz bomb

TRAILING

This fascinating method of catching predatory species such as perch, zander and pike revolves around slowly pulling, or trailing, either livebaits or deadbaits behind a moving boat propelled by oars. In some instances a silent, battery-operated outboard engine in its slowest mode is used.

An echo-sounder/*fish-finder* unit with a sizeable display screen showing bottom contours, depths, and even fish lying beneath the boat, is an invaluable aid when exploring large, deep, featureless stillwaters such as loughs, lochs and reservoirs and wide river systems. Although trailing is an effective technique, and probably best practised alone, it is quite possible for two anglers to work a pair of rods apiece from the stern and sides of a sizeable dinghy (with one angler working the oars). The dinghy should be equipped with specialized rod rests that support the rods on both sides of the reel (in either a shepherd's crook U or an adjustable, tubed holder) so the line can be angled out from the boat, enabling a wide search to be made.

When working feature venues such as small to medium-sized rivers, the baits should be trailed close beside all the obvious predator-holding lies, such as overhanging trees, confluences and dense reed lines, while the boat's speed and direction are controlled with the oars. If you slow up on the bends, where the depth is invariably greater, the baits can work deeper. If you speed up over the shallows or known snags, the lines will be pulled at a 45-degree angle from float to bait, enabling you to search the ever-changing bottom contours without snagging on the river bed too often. The same principles apply to trailing in large stillwaters. In heavily coloured water, the boat's speed must be reduced to a crawl, whereas in crystal-clear water pike, in particular, often respond to a fast trailing speed, especially if an occasional spurt from the oars suggests that the bait just might be getting away.

Two basic set ups work effectively when trailing (fig. 90), whether using oars or an electric motor: a livebait or deadbait fished on a sliding float, and bouncing ledger rig. The latter is especially effective in really cold or coloured water where pike and zander are hugging the bottom and will not

rise to attack float-trailed baits. If you use 12ft rods, you can use four different rigs in any combination to cover as large an arc as possible behind the boat without the lines tangling. If you stagger the baits at varying distances this will also help to prevent snarl ups.

The choice of reels lies between a smallish multiplier and a bait-runner type of fixed-spool reel. The former can either be left in gear with the ratchet on and with a light drag setting, allowing line to be taken without undue resistance or, when conditions permit, be left out of gear with the ratchet on.

A *fixed-spool reel (Reels)*, which allows the spool to be totally disengaged, lets a fish take line instantly without any danger of it dropping the bait. For general use, a reel line of 10-11lb test is quite sufficient. When exploring large trout reservoirs that open for pike enthusiasts during the winter months, and where monsters in the 30-40lb bracket are on the cards, step up to 15lb test. Either way, use a swivelled, 20in wire trace of 15-20lb test on the business end, holding a brace of size 8 or 6 (depending on bait size) semi-barbless trebles.

For a bouncing ledger rig, an extra 20in monofilament link is added between the wire trace and the bomb-link swivel (fig. 90). This helps to prevent tangles while allowing bounced livebaits maximum movement. Use bombs in the 1-2oz range with a considerably weaker mono link if snags are evident. Deadbaits (mounted head first so that they simulate live fish) can also be presented effectively using the bounced bomb rig, so named because the bomb bounces slowly over the bottom, followed by the bait presented just 2ft above bottom.

The sliding float rig can also present a deadbait but is most effective with a livebait, kept down by a bullet or barrel weight stopped with a bead against the trace swivel. Any large through-the-middle sliding float will support the bait, which should be fished 2-5ft above bottom. As the boat is propelled forwards by the oars, the bait will rise attractively behind and then settle again at the predetermined depth, at which the *sliding stop knot* is tied (*Knots*).

Once a bait has been taken, row slowly backwards with the oars (or put the electric motor into reverse) to minimize resistance, and if need be clear the other rods prior to striking.

TRIGGERFISH

(*Balistes capriscus*)

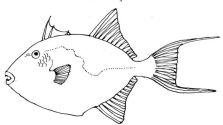

British record: 5lb 5¼oz (2kg 416g)

This rather unusual warm-water oddity is occasionally caught from south and south-western seas around the British Isles, and is common in tropical parts of the Atlantic. It has a deep, thickish, but laterally compressed, greyish body with a steeply angled forehead. The mouth is small, thick-lipped and fitted with sharp, incisor-like teeth that the triggerfish uses to crunch up crustaceans and animals encrusted on coral reefs and rocks. It has a distinct, swallow-type tail and a strange, heavily spined first dorsal that locks into position and can only be made to fold by pressing the third spine. The large second dorsal and anal fins are of equal proportions. There are no pelvic fins - a short single spine replaces them.

TROLLING

Trolling, which entails pulling an artificial lure or a mounted fish bait behind a motorboat at speeds of 1-10 knots, in either fresh or salt water, is in world-wide terms the most commonly practised of all techniques.

Within the British Isles, however, trolling under power in certain areas and types of inland waterways - the tidal waterways of the Norfolk Broads, for instance - is illegal, whereas in the Irish loughs and Scottish lochs it is the accepted - and by far the most productive - method of hooking big brown trout, pike and salmon. In some of the large trout reservoirs that permit pike fishing during the winter months, trolling is allowed but only when using a silent, battery operated electric outboard motor such as the Minn Kota which has variable speeds including reverse. Check with the *National Rivers Authority* about trolling by engine in the area where you plan to fish.

Trolling is so effective because of the amount of water it covers, and the subsequent number of predators that get sight

Due to crystal clear inshore waters, trolling is one of the top methods in Danish seas for catching garfish, sea trout, salmon and cod - yes, cod. Working the coastline two miles off Ebeltoft, Dave Lewis is presenting lures on both flat line and downrigger outfits.

of the lure or mounted bait. Once you have located fish by trolling, you can work the productive area systematically by casting while on the drift, or by anchoring up and offering baits all around the boat. Or you can troll through the area time and again, trying a variety of different lures at varying depths to evaluate which works best and at what depth on the day.

Trolling might sound a rather boring and slow technique, but because you are constantly changing lures and exploring different depth-bands around varying features, and relating these to read-outs on the sonar screen, there is little time to become bored. So much valuable information about each new water can be gathered for future trips, in addition to catching fish. The biggest aid to trolling is the electronic *fish-finder* - not necessarily for locating fish, although those that permit the boat to pass over them in deepish water will show up, but more for the ever-changing bottom contours and the features that attract preda-

tors. Study areas around rock formations, for instance, with pinnacles, deep gullies, peaks and sudden drop offs, either well off-shore or running parallel to the shoreline of islands. These are exactly the kinds of sub-surface features found, for instance, in the Irish and Scottish lochs around which shoal fish gather and predators subsequently patrol. Aimlessly pulling lures through huge areas of featureless water is, by comparison, never likely to produce such immediate action as these veritable hot-spots.

Think of large, deep stillwaters (even wide rivers, estuaries and the sea itself) in cross-section, just like a huge layer cake, and then choose a suitable *artificial lure*. The technique is to allow the lure to be taken back behind the boat under gentle thumb pressure on the spool until it is 50-100ft away. Then put the reel into gear, and either hold the rod at a 45-degree angle, or put it into a rest. In depths from the surface down to around 10ft spinners,

spoons and shallow running plugs are the lures to use.

Non-diving lures, such as big spoons, can be attractively presented by dropping them back every so often to flutter enticingly downwards with the reel in free spool. Then put the reel back into gear again instantly to make the spoon come alive as it suddenly zooms upwards to follow the boat. Big brown trout and pike, especially, can be encouraged to grab hold using this simple ruse.

In depths of 10-20ft, deep-diving plugs such as rapalas and russelures work best. The trolling paravane is an effective addition that allows virtually any lure, including many surface patterns, to work down at these depths. Tie the reel line to the paravane's angled head, and to the other end add a 6-8ft monofilament trace with a link-swivel to facilitate quick changes of lure. As with standard trolling, if pike are expected a 12in, 15lb-test wire trace is imperative. When trolled at a standard 1½-2½ knots, the paravane quickly dives down, pulling the line behind it (fig. 98).

When trolling in wide estuary mouths for bass, the Toby-type lures, which were originally designed on the shape and action of the sand eel, are the best to try. These and other bar-type spoons work effectively, whether used in conjunction with a paravane or flat-line trolled. Bass love rapala magnums, too, especially in blue mackerel.

The last depth band that can be effectively worked by standard or flat-line trolling (as opposed to downrigger trolling), 20-30ft deep, is really only fishable with huge-lipped, deep-diving plugs. Considerably more line must be let out behind the boat to enable these really deep divers to angle steeply down and do the business. Start with a slow trolling speed while the plug is diving down, and increase the throttle very slowly and steadily to around 1½-2 knots. An erratic trolling speed only encourages the plug to turn turtle and pop up to the surface.

It is best to secure the rod or rods (two anglers sharing a boat can work no more than two rods each) in adjustable, custom-made trolling rests (fig. 91). If there are no rests or rod-holders, each angler should only use one rod, holding it at all times while the boat is under power in case a fish grabs hold and takes it over the side. Rods in the 9-11ft category with a fast-tip, medium-to-heavy spinning action (*Rods -*

freshwater) are perfect for trolling. Soft, all-through-actioned models cannot transmit sufficient power to the lure to make the hooks bite home on the strike.

The multiplier reel is the tool for trolling, and the drag should be set firmly for the hooks to bite home on the strike, yet not so tight that line cannot be taken by a big fish. Leave the reel's ratchet on to provide an audible alarm, but quickly flip it off once a fish is hooked.

Trolling puts enormous demands on tackle because hits come so suddenly when fish lunge at the moving lure, so an increase in line strength of 25-30 per cent on what you would normally use to cast the same lure provides a safeguard against break-offs. Most spinners, plugs and spoons used to catch pike, big brown trout and even salmon can be trolled comfortably on a 15lb-test reel line, the only exception being when huge-lipped diving plugs or heavy spoons are in use, as they put enormous pressure on the line, and when downrigger trolling. In both cases line strength should then be increased to 18-20lb test, especially if a sizeable salmon is on the cards.

To troll lures below a depth of 30ft, and

to troll freshly killed whole fish baits slowly in depths of 10-20ft, downrigger trolling provides the answer. Its main advantage is that once a fish is hooked, the fight can be enjoyed on light tackle with no additional weight on the line.

When fishing from a small boat, each angler uses only one rod, with the line going down almost vertically to the 5lb lead trolling ball, set at a pre-determined depth, where it is gripped firmly in an adjustable line clip some 10-20ft in front of the bait or lure (fig. 92).

The lead trolling ball is lowered down from the boat via an 18in steel boom connected to a stainless-steel cable, which is housed on a large-diameter centre-pin spool incorporating a handle. Once the lure is working at the desired depth, line is taken up on the reel and the rod tip wound down into a tight curve. Then, when a predator grabs the lure and yanks the line from the downrigger clip, the rod tip springs back to help pick up slack line, while a strong follow-through strike is made in order to put the hooks home. To help the process of hooking when downrigger trolling in depths of 40ft and more, accelerating the motor by several knots instantly takes up

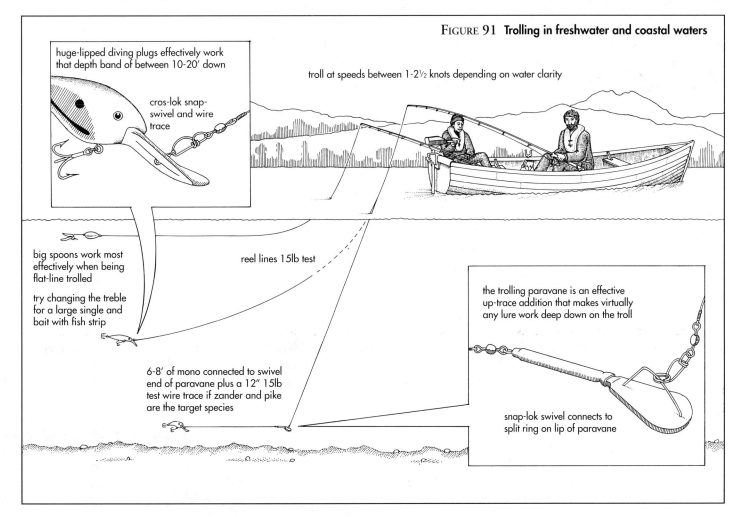

FIGURE 91 **Trolling in freshwater and coastal waters**

huge-lipped diving plugs effectively work that depth band of between 10-20' down

cros-lok snap-swivel and wire trace

troll at speeds between 1-2½ knots depending on water clarity

big spoons work most effectively when being flat-line trolled

try changing the treble for a large single and bait with fish strip

reel lines 15lb test

6-8' of mono connected to swivel end of paravane plus a 12" 15lb test wire trace if zander and pike are the target species

the trolling paravane is an effective up-trace addition that makes virtually any lure work deep down on the troll

snap-lok swivel connects to split ring on lip of paravane

FIGURE 92 **Downrigger trolling in deep rivers and stillwaters**

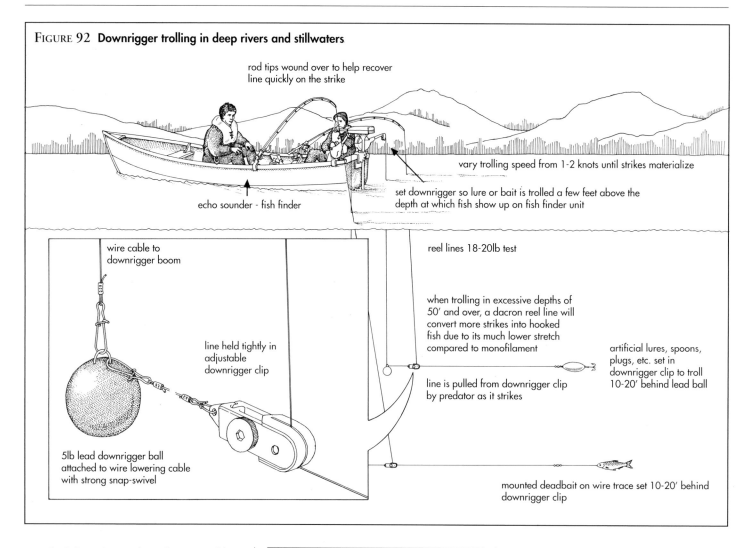

rod tips wound over to help recover
line quickly on the strike

vary trolling speed from 1-2 knots until strikes materialize

echo sounder - fish finder

set downrigger so lure or bait is trolled a few feet above the
depth at which fish show up on fish finder unit

wire cable to
downrigger boom

reel lines 18-20lb test

line held tightly in
adjustable
downrigger clip

when trolling in excessive depths of
50' and over, a dacron reel line will
convert more strikes into hooked
fish due to its much lower stretch
compared to monofilament

artificial lures, spoons,
plugs, etc. set in
downrigger clip to troll
10-20' behind lead ball

line is pulled from downrigger clip
by predator as it strikes

5lb lead downrigger ball
attached to wire lowering cable
with strong snap-swivel

mounted deadbait on wire trace set 10-20' behind
downrigger clip

any slack line. A switch to dacron reel line (*Lines*), which has minimal stretch compared to monofilament, also helps enormously.

Remember that sudden acceleration or deceleration is always a worthwhile ploy to make predators grab a lure or bait when working over known features without success, whether you are downrigger or flat-line trolling.

Downrigger trolling can only be done successfully in conjunction with a sonar/fish-finder unit. A constant eye must be kept on the display screen so that the downrigger ball can be raised instantly and the slack line taken up on the reel whenever the bottom shelves up dramatically, or it could become snagged. Downrigger units with a built-in depth counter are recommended because they register the exact length of cable out beneath the boat and thus indicate at what depth the lure or bait is being trolled.

Quality units that also have built-in rod holders come fitted with 150ft of 150lb-test stainless-steel cable, retrievable on a single-handed control, clutch-and-break system for a steady descent of the lead ball.

TROPICAL FRESHWATER SPORTSFISH

Reaching weights in excess of 500lb apiece, species such as the sturgeon, wels catfish and the aripaima are in all probability the three largest species to be caught from freshwater anywhere in the world. The following species, however, all top 50lb and are easily among the most powerful and exciting of freshwater sportsfish to hook on rod and line.

CHANNEL CATFISH
(*Ictalurus punctatus*)

Average size: 10-25lb
World record: 58lb (26kg 30g)

The channel catfish has a long, smooth body with a short dorsal and long anal fin, plus a rayless adipose fin. It has a depressed head, a small eye and four pairs of barbels. The tail is deeply forked. Colouration is dark grey along the back, fusing into lighter sides and belly. There are pads of bristle-like teeth in both the upper and lower jaws.

It is common in the USA, southern Canada and northern Mexico. It prefers large lakes and rivers with clean bottoms of sand or gravel, but tolerates muddy rivers, and feeds on vegetation, insects, crayfish and fish off the bottom.

Use a medium to heavy spinning rod, 8-9ft long, with reel lines of 10-15lb test and a size 1/0-2/0 hook on a light ledger rig. The best bait is a fresh cutlet from a silver-bodied shoal fish. Bites can be rather gentle so allow line to be taken before striking. Once hooked, however, the channel catfish is an exceptionally hard fighter.

The physical endurance and anguish experienced during the fight are almost over for Nanda Susheel, one of India's most famous shooting and fishing ladies, who has caught numerous mahseer up to nearly 100lb. For over 30 minutes this 40lb mahseer has battled away amongst a torrent of white water between fingers of exposed black bed rock. Now it's time for guide Suban to think about putting his arms beneath one of the world's finest freshwater sportsfish and removing the 6/0 hook before returning it to the Kaveri River.

Trying to lift a really big Nile Perch is often harder than fighting it. This magnificent 125-pounder fell to the rod of travel agent Buckley Hunt (centre) whilst out afloat on Kenya's massive Lake Victoria with the author and Robert Duff (left). It grabbed a Russelure trolled at around two knots and made several spectacular leaps during the 20-minute battle.

DOURADO
(Salminus maxillosus)

Average size: 8-20lb
World record: 51lb 5oz (23kg 30g)

The dourado, which can grow to over 60lb, is bathed all over in golden yellow with a distinct black line through the tail fork. It has a small adipose fin. The jaws are strong and well-armed with teeth. The deep, thick-set body has noticeable horizontal etching on the scales, very similar to the flanks of the African tigerfish.

The dourado is found only in parts of South America - Argentina, Brazil and Paraguay - in deep, wide, fast-flowing rivers that carve their way through dense rainforest. It feeds on crustaceans and fish among rocks close to the bottom and at midwater, and on shoal fish on the surface.

Use a medium salmon spinning rod outfit with 20lb reel line, a 12in wire trace and a size 6/0 hook baited with morinita or any 5-10in local river fish. The best tech-nique is to drift with the boat side-on to the current, casting back upstream and bumping the bait just over rocky edges. Lures worked beside and over features also produce good results - big spoons and Rapala magnum plugs are ideal. The dourado leaps repeatedly when hooked, and has the capacity to crunch the strong-est trebles and artificial lures flat.

MAHSEER
(Barbus tor)

Average size: 20-50lb
World record: 121lb (54kg 885g)

The mahseer is, possibly, the world's hard-est-fighting freshwater fish, and can grow to in excess of 140lb. It has a long, power-ful, fully-scaled body, which looks part carp and part barbel, a large, semi-protrusible mouth and thick, rubbery lips. It sports a pair of long barbels from each corner of the mouth. There are no visible teeth, just huge pharyngeal throat teeth. The scales are huge and thick, and the powerful tail is forked. The large, powerful fins are trans-lucent grey, often with a tinge of orange. Colouration changes from grey brown along the back into sides of brass or pew-ter. The belly is cream coloured.

The mahseer is found throughout In-dia and Burma in fast-flowing rivers. It prefers to inhabit the fastest runs over bed-rock or coarse gravel bottoms, in both deep and shallow areas. It feeds on freshwater crustaceans, particularly crabs, and small bottom-dwelling fishes, including its own kind.

The best techniques are ledgering into fast runs from the bank or spinning, using a heavy spinning rod with 20-40lb line, and 4/0-8/0 hooks. The most productive bait is ragi paste, made from local millet flour, made into chicken's-egg-sized balls and boiled, or small, dead fish.

NILE PERCH
(Lates niloticus)

Average size: 15-50lb
World record: 191lb (86kg 650g)

Commonly caught over 100lb, but grows to over 400lb, this aggressive predator has a thick-set, typical perch-like body with a huge expanding mouth. The top of the head is strongly depressed. It has two dorsal fins, the first with spines, the second with soft rays, a rounded tail, and is brown to greenish-brown above and silver underneath.

It is found only in Africa, in large river systems, namely the Nile and in huge lakes, such as Lake Victoria, Lake Turkana and other large areas of tropical freshwater. It loves features such as sunken, rocky reefs and steep drop-offs close to islands in still-waters, while in rivers it is prolific in the deep, swirling waters of pools. It feeds on crustaceans and shoal fish, including its own kind. It ambushes its prey among rocks, but also chases shoal fish in open water.

The best methods for catching nile perch are trolling large artificial lures and float-fishing livebaits just above rocks. Use a heavy spinning or 20-30lb-class trolling rod with a reel line of 30-40lb test. A 5ft trace made from 100lb-test monofilament, joined to the reel line with a strong swivel, helps to prevent break-offs caused by the line chafing against the fish's jaws.

TIGERFISH
(Hydrochymus forskablii)

Average size: 2-5lb
World record: 37lb (16kg 800g)

This prehistoric-looking predator has a long, compressed body, long, sharp, pointed teeth, a vicious-looking mouth, and relatively long and sharply pointed fins. The large, powerful tail is deeply forked. The silvery body has black spots along the scale rows. The lower body fins are transparent grey with bright orange tips, and the tail is transparent grey to brown, with a broad red margin and a narrow black edge. The adipose fin is black and transparent at base, while the dorsal fin has a pale brown edge with red.

The tigerfish is found only in African tropical freshwaters, in dammed lakes and river systems, notably the Zambezi and Lake Kariba. It feeds on any small fish, including its own kind. The best techniques are to spin or cast small deadbaits with or without a float, trolling artificial lures or mounted fish baits, and even fly fishing. A 30lb-test, 12in wire leader is essential, and a medium spinning-rod outfit with a reel line of 10-15lb test is ideal.

A bunch of local sardines (kapenta), bunches of worms or strips of flesh on a hook or spinner such as Mepps Longue in sizes 3 and 4 provides added attraction when presenting artificials.

The tigerfish is a strong fighter and jumps repeatedly when hooked. Another species (*Hydrocymus goliath*), which actually grows to over 100lb lives in the Congo river system.

VUNDU CATFISH
(Heterobranchus longifilis)

Average size: 30-50lb
World record: 109lb (49kg 45g)

The vundu is a particularly hard-fighting catfish that can grow to well in excess of 150lb. This ugly bottom-feeder has a large, flat, bulbous head and a long, slim, rapidly tapering body. The wide jaws sport eight whiskers. It has a long dorsal fin, a large, rayless adipose fin and a rounded tail. It is brown on top, lighter beneath.

Found in tropical African freshwater, the vundu loves deep water in river gorges and in mainstream or deep areas around dams, where it preys on crustaceans, molluscs and fish.

Use a heavy-action spinning rod and multiplying reel coupled to 20-25lb-test monofilament, presenting the bait on the bottom from the shore or from an anchored boat, or slowly drifting over deep water with the bait trundling along bottom.

Bait a 2/0-5/0 hook with a bunch of sardines (kapenta), small fresh fish, or an egg-sized ball of blue soap (yes - blue soap).

TROPICAL SALTWATER GAMEFISH

Although giant blue and black marlin, which grow to over 1,000lb, are considered the most powerful and exciting blue-water gamefish in the world, pound for pound there are numerous lesser species that have equal appeal. Some of these, even at over 100lb, are considered light-tackle species and are available to anyone who wishes to spice up a holiday in the tropics by chartering a gamefishing boat.

AMBERJACK
(Seriola dumevili)

Average size: 20-50lb
World record: 155lb 10oz (70kg 59g)

This is the largest member of the jack family, sometimes growing to over 150lb. It has a long, laterally flattened body, very small scales, two dorsal fins, and a deeply forked tail fin. The small teeth are set in bands. The back is silvery grey with lighter sides and a silver under-surface. The flanks have a golden iridescence. A diffuse, dark stripe runs from shoulder to eye. The young are yellow with dark vertical stripes and a distinct yellow eye.

The amberjack is found in the Mediterranean, Western and Southern Atlantic, Central Pacific and Indo-Pacific, usually in small, fast-swimming groups. It likes moderate to deep water, usually around rocks or deep sunken reefs, where it feeds on shoal fish, squid and so on.

It can be caught by trolling near the surface, or livebait fishing, and by drifting over a feature in deep water, jigging or with live-bait. Use a 30-50lb-class boat or trolling rod with 6/0 to 8/0 hooks. It fights hard and repeatedly dives for the bottom.

DORADO
(Coryphaena hippurus)

Average size: 8-25lb
World record: 87lb (39kg 46g)

This swift-swimming pelagic species has a deep, compressed body brilliantly coloured in greens, blue and yellow, liberally flecked with small dark spots. Males have blunt foreheads. There is a long, continuous dorsal fin and a deeply forked tail.

The dorado loves open blue water, well offshore, and is found worldwide in tropical and warm temperate oceans, always close to the surface around weed rafts, floating features, flotsam and so on. It feeds on flying fish and other small surface fish.

The best technique is to troll using a 20lb-class outfit, with feathered lures, bubble heads, squid or plugs. It can also be taken on cut bait from a drifting boat once one of a shoal has been taken by trolling. The dorado leaps repeatedly when hooked and it quickly changes colour while on the hook and immediately following death. Once hooked, a fish must be kept in the water while catching others, or the shoal will vanish. It often takes lures intended for sailfish and wahoo.

SAILFISH
(Istiophorus platypterus)

Average size: 60-85lb
World record: 221lb (100kg 24g)

This, at over 60 mph the fastest fish in the sea, grows to over 100lb in the Atlantic Ocean and over 200lb in the Pacific, has a long, slender body, oval in cross-section,

with a large head and long bill. It is silvery white below, deep blue above. The sides often have pale, bluish-grey vertical bars or rows of spots. The slate or cobalt-blue, sail-like dorsal fin is spotted with violet rings, black inside. There is a double anal fin and a huge, swallow-like, tail fin with bevelled shutes at the narrow tail root.

Sailfish are lovers of tropical and sub-tropical oceans near land masses, and are prolific in the Pacific Ocean, Atlantic Ocean, Indian seas including the Seychelles, and along the East African coast. They usually travel alone or in small groups, and feed on squid, octopus and small pelagic fish.

The best technique is trolling, using a 20-30lb outfit with strip baits, whole mullet, plastic lures, feathers, mounted tuna belly, small kona heads and so on. It is an exciting, acrobatic fighter, but tires quickly.

TARPON
(Megalops atlanticus)

Average size: as large as 60-100lb in Florida Keys area
World record: 283lb (128kg 36g)

This huge, herring-like member of the bony fish family can grow to 300lb. It has a long, compressed body with a large mouth, fine teeth and a bevelled jaw hinge, a large, forked tail, and a long trailing filament at the rear of the dorsal fin. Colouration is burnished silver, merging into blue-black on the back. The scales are huge and silver coloured.

Tarpon are found both offshore and inshore, including brackish and fresh waters, lagoons, mangrove swamps and shallow flats. However, it loves the warm, temperate, tropical and sub-tropical waters of the Atlantic Ocean, where it can often be seen in large groups with its dorsal or tail protruding above the surface. It feeds on molluscs, crustaceans and fish, and has a distinct preference for mullet.

After a punishing 40-minute struggle during which this giant tarpon (estimated at 130lb) repeatedly leapt, taking the boat over a mile from where it was first hooked, John's fishing buddy Pete Hazelwood, from Milton in Cambridgeshire, now has time to reflect on the truly wonderful sport found in the Florida Keys. When the guide has the trace in his hand and touches the fish it is claimed by the angler and then it is unhooked and gently released.

Amidst the tropical blue background of the Seychelles, Jo and John Wilson display what trolling in these fertile waters has to offer. A brace of power-packed yellow fin tuna and the cigar-shaped wahoo taken on mounted tuna belly.

To catch tarpon, use a medium to heavy spinning outfit with 20-30lb line. A 6-7ft trace of 100lb abrasion-resistant monofilament or wire trace must be joined to the reel line, or the reel line will be quickly severed by the rough edges of the tarpon's bevelled jaw hinges when it leaps. The best baits are mullet or any other small, silvery fish, crabs, squid and so on. Tarpon can also be caught on a fly rod using streamer flies and jigs. They are hard to hook because of their bony jaws, and they can leap up to 10ft out of the water.

WAHOO
(Acanthocybium solanderi)

Average size: 15-40lb
World record: 155lb 8oz (70kg 53g)

This extremely fast, pelagic species has a long, cigar-shaped body and a swallow-shaped tail. It has a movable upper jaw, and large, strong, laterally compressed teeth. The back is brilliant, deep blue, with bright blue vertical bands down the sides. The belly is silvery.

The wahoo is a lover of blue water well offshore, and feeds in the upper water layers near and on the surface on squid and small pelagic shoal fish. It has world-wide distribution in tropical seas, and tends to be a loner or to travel in small groups of two to six fish.

Use a 20-30lb line class, trolling rod outfit. A wire trace is imperative for wahoo. Good lures are kona heads in small to medium sizes with squid skirts over mounted pin fish or tuna belly, flying fish and so on. It often grabs a kona-head lure or mounted fish intended for sailfish or marlin. One of the fastest fish in the sea, it occasionally jumps on the strike and shakes it head violently when hooked.

YELLOWFIN TUNA
(Thunnus albacares)

Average size: 15-50lb
World record: 388lb 12oz(176kg 35g)

The yellowfin is a hard, powerful and dogged-fighting tuna. The most highly coloured of all the tunas, it has an over-extended, yellowy second dorsal fin. The anal fins extend to the start of the second dorsal fin. The back is blue-black, fading to silver on the lower flanks and belly. A golden yellow or iridescent blue stripe runs from eye to tail. The fins and finlets are golden yellow and the finlets have black margins. There are many vertical rows of whitish spots on the belly.

The yellowfin tuna is found in all warm, temperate oceanic waters. It feeds close to and from the surface on squid, crustaceans and small fish - flying fish in particular.

The most effective technique is trolling, using a 20-30lb outfit and presenting squid, strip baits or artificial lures. Small livebaits are also effective. Where big yellowfin are expected, a 50lb line class outfit is advisable.

Southern trout-rearing supremo Nigel Jackson (left) inspects a holding net full of the beautifully conditioned, jumbo-sized brown trout for which his two-lake day ticket fishery at Dever Springs near Stockbridge in Hampshire has become internationally renowned.

TROUT, AMERICAN BROOK

(Salvelinus fontinalis)

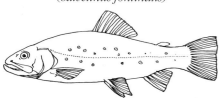

Average size: 1-2lb
Mega specimen: over 3½lb
British record: 5lb 13½oz (2kg 650g)

The brook trout originates from North America, where it is also called a brook charr. It lives in cold, pure streams and rivers and reaches a weight of over 10lb. The overall shape is similar to the brown trout, though a little stockier, with mosaic, charr-like markings along the back and flanks

comprising cream spots on a pewter-grey background. The belly is silvery white, and there are distinct white edges to the pectoral, pelvic and anal fins, with an inner black line - a feature that clearly separates the brookie from other trout, although the tiger trout (a brookie/brown trout hybrid) and cheetah trout (a brookie/rainbow hybrid) also share the same characteristics.

It feeds on all stages of aquatic life, molluscs, crustaceans and small fish.

HABITAT AND DISTRIBUTION

Brook trout are bred and reared by fish farmers in the British Isles on a very limited basis, and are stocked into comparatively few rivers and man-made stillwater fisheries.

TECHNIQUES

Artificial lure fishing - freshwater; Fly casting; Fly fishing; Trolling.

TROUT, BROWN/ FEROX

(Salmo trutta)

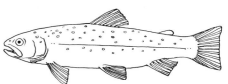

Average size: 1-2lb
Mega specimen: river - over 5lb;
                              stillwaters - over 10lb
British record: cultivated - 21lb 3½oz
                              (9kg 623g); natural - 19lb
                              10½oz (8kg 912g)

The brown trout is more rounded than the salmon, with a classic salmonid body, including an adipose fin and a noticeably thick tail root. The tail itself is squared or slightly concave. Adult male brown trout

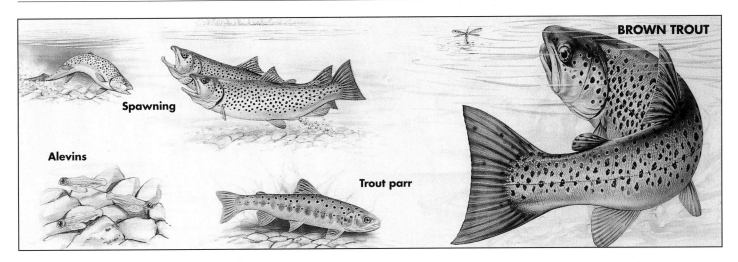

Spawning

Alevins

Trout parr

BROWN TROUT

as they mature, develop a curved lower jaw which, like that of the salmon, becomes kyped during the spawning season. The upper jaw bone extends beyond the eye. There is no standard colour or pattern. The brown trout varies considerably in colouration depending on its condition and the habitat in which it lives. Brown trout living in chalk streams, for instance, might have a golden-bronze back fusing into paler sides, and a buttery yellow belly, and be most exquisitely marked with large spots - red, black or brown, or all three, each ringed in white. Brown trout in the peak of condition from a large river or a clear, deep-water, man-made reservoir might have silver-enamelled flanks overlaid with a sprinkling of asterisk-type spots. Just to add to the confusion, there is nearly always a difference between individual brownies caught from the same fishery on the same day.

Brown trout are aggressive feeders and will happily gobble up small shoal fish, including their own parr, in addition to crustaceans and molluscs, and all stages of aquatic insect life from the nymph to the adult fly on the surface.

Reproduction occurs during the winter months in well-oxygenated, shallow water over a gravel bottom. Large eggs are deposited by the female and instantly fertilized with milt from the cock fish. The resulting fry develop through alevin, fry and parr stages, like all salmonids.

HABITAT AND DISTRIBUTION

Brown trout are indigenous to Europe, and are more widely distributed throughout the British Isles than any other freshwater fish. Provided that high levels of dissolved oxygen are present, brown trout will live happily in the tiniest streams or the largest man-made reservoirs. They occupy individual, choice lies in running water behind or in front of boulders, bridge supports, shallow bars where the water ripples and so on, and in stillwaters always stay much deeper than rainbow trout. The largest concentrations of wild brown trout live in mountainous streams and in the huge loughs and lochs of Ireland and Scotland. The monsters of deep-water Scottish lochs, which become totally predatory and cannibalistic, are given the name 'ferox'.

TECHNIQUES

Artificial lure fishing - freshwater; Fly casting; Fly fishing; Trolling.

TROUT, RAINBOW

(Oncorhynchus mykiss)

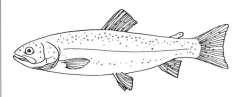

Average size: 1-4lb
Mega specimen: over 15lb
British record: cultivated - 30lb 1oz
                                (13kg 643g); natural -
                                29lb 12oz (13kg 506g)

Rainbow trout have the classic trout shape, but are noticeably more rounded across the snout than brown trout, with an entirely different, unmistakable colour pattern. The back is usually olive pewter, blending into silvery flanks across which runs a magenta flash from gill plate to tail. The belly is silvery white. Rainbow trout from deep, clear waters such as reservoirs, particularly the hen fish, may have flanks like a bar of silver without any trace of magenta. The rainbow, however, is by far the most densely spotted of all trout and the entire body, including dorsal fin and tail (which is

RAINBOW TROUT

slightly concave), is invariably overlaid with a profusion of small, dark spots down to a line level with the pectoral fin. Rainbows leap repeatedly when hooked and are very fast.

The rainbow feeds on all stages of aquatic insect life, molluscs and crustaceans, and preys aggressively on small shoal fish. Reproduction in the wild within the British Isles occurs only in isolated river systems where conditions are perfect. The vast majority of rainbow trout are farm-reared and fed to a stockable size on pelleted food. Both sexes, however, prepare for reproduction (between January and April), the hen fish growing sizeable ovaries containing large, orange eggs, while the cock fish darkens (referred to as black fish) and develops a hook on its lower jaw and a vivid orange magenta flash over the gill plates and along the flanks.

British rainbow trout originate from north-west America, so it is no surprise that they share their classification, *Oncorhynchus mykiss*, with the legendary steelhead trout that lives in the Pacific Ocean but returns to fresh water to spawn, as does the sea trout.

HABITAT AND DISTRIBUTION

Although rainbow trout are cold-water fish, like all salmonids, they have a much greater tolerance of modern, man-made fisheries than brown trout and will thrive in most stillwaters, even gravel pits without feeder streams. For this reason, and for their superb fighting qualities, rainbow trout are now the accepted stock fish for modern trout fisheries from the chalk streams of Hampshire to the largest man-made reservoirs.

TECHNIQUES

Fly casting; Fly fishing.
See also *Artificial flies.*

TROUT, SEA

(*Salmo trutta*)

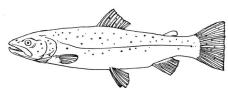

Average size: 1-3lb
Mega specimen: over 10lb
British record: 22lb 8oz (10kg 205g)

As sea trout eggs can be fertilized with milt from a brown trout, and as the sea trout shares the classification *Salmo trutta* with the brown trout, it is no surprise to discover that the sea trout is actually a migratory brown trout that spends the greater part of its life in the sea. However, is has an entirely different behavioural pattern from the brown trout, and is acutely aware of changes in both water and weather conditions. It is identical to the brown trout in body shape, but looks more athletic. When it enters freshwater at the start of its upstream migration to spawn covered in sea lice, it has a silvery sheen of metallic pewter, liberally spotted with small dark asterisks along the flanks, often to a line level with the pelvic root. Spots on the salmon usually only occur above the lateral line. The tail root is thick (unlike the narrow wrist of the salmon), and the tail is either squared or slightly convex. Young sea trout, however, have slightly concave tails. In addition, the sea trout's anal fin, which is more pointed than that of the salmon, has an outer leading edge that is longer than the inner, even when the fin is pressed against the body. When adult sea trout have been in the river for long periods, they darken considerably and look more like the brown trout, except that they lack red spots. As with brown trout, it is common to catch two very different sea trout from the same river, which makes identification all the more confusing.

In the ocean, sea trout feed on crustaceans such as shrimps and prawns and on small shoal fish, sand eels in particular, but they fast on entering freshwater. Reproduction occurs between October and December in the shallow, fast, gravelly bottom reaches of pure, well-oxygenated rivers. The young sea trout develop through the alevin, fry and parr stages, just like other salmonids. Once several inches long (which might take two years) the young sea trout silver up (now called smolts) and run to sea. Some return after only a few months in saltwater, but the majority return to spawn the following year, just like salmon.

HABITAT AND DISTRIBUTION

Sea trout are found all around the British Isles, though rivers along the west coast of Ireland and Scotland and those along the Welsh coastline enjoy the strongest runs of sea trout. They enter freshwater between April and September, travelling far inland into the high upper reaches, often via lochs.

TECHNIQUES

Artificial lure fishing - freshwater; Fly casting; Fly fishing; Spin casting.
See also *Artificial lures.*

Juveniles

Spawning

SEA TROUT

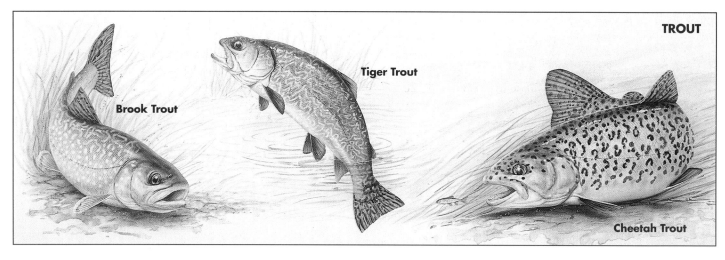

Brook Trout

Tiger Trout

TROUT

Cheetah Trout

TROUT, HYBRID BROWN BOW

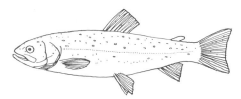

As its name suggests, this sterile hybrid results from crossing a brown trout (*Salmo trutta*) with a rainbow trout (*Oncorhynchus mykiss*) and produces what appears to be a brown trout covered with a profusion of various-sized spots. These hybrids were at one time regularly bred and stocked into man-made stillwater fisheries, but the practice has virtually come to a standstill as they were found to be neither as strong nor as durable as either of the parent trout. Brown bow trout respond to all methods used to catch brown trout and rainbow trout.

TROUT, HYBRID CHEETAH

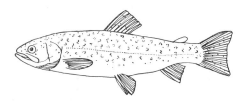

British record: none

A stocky, unusually coloured sterile hybrid resulting from the crossing of an American brook trout (*Salvelinus fontinalis*) with a rainbow trout (*Oncorhynchus mykiss*). It has a bluish-pewter back and flanks overlaid with a faint (rainbow type) magenta or pinkish flash and numerous irregular-shaped spots reaching down to a line level with the pectoral fins. Pectoral, pelvic and anal fins have the distinct white edging of its brook-trout parentage. Like the brook trout and tiger trout, cheetah trout were bred and reared specifically for stocking into man-made stillwater fisheries in southern England during the 1970s and 1980s. Their popularity, however, was short-lived and they are now rarely reared. The cheetah responds to all fly-fishing techniques used for catching brown and rainbow trout.

TROUT, HYBRID TIGER

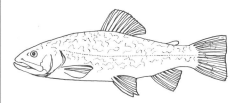

British record: none

A cross between the American brook trout (*Salvelinus fontinalis*) and the brown trout (*Salmo trutta*), and sometimes referred to as zebra trout, this sterile hybrid is only rarely bred, specifically for stocking into man-made stillwater fisheries, due to problems with disease during rearing. It is, however, a strikingly handsome fish that fights well and is very aggressive. The back and flanks are a deep pewter bronze overlaid with golden squiggly markings, fusing into a golden-yellow belly. The pectoral, pelvic and anal fins are edged in white like those of its male parent, the brook trout. It responds to all fly-fishing techniques for brown and rainbow trout.

TROUT, TRIPLOID

Triploids result from subjecting the eggs (usually of rainbow trout) to immersion in hot water. This sudden shock produces a sexless trout that has a wonderful silver sheen along the flanks and grows incredibly deep in the body because it uses all its energy to pack on bodyweight extremely fast, unlike both a hen fish, which produces eggs, and a cock fish, which becomes black and most aggressive towards other cocks during the spawning cycle.

As rainbows rarely breed successfully in the wild, but have to be artificially reared for stocking, fast-growing triploids make economic sense to the owners of trout fisheries. However, massive egg losses can occur during the production of these sexless trout, so triploids are slightly less profitable to rear. They are also harder to transport and more susceptible to oxygen deficiency.

Scottish fish farmers who specialize in rearing cage-fed salmon triploids for the table have enjoyed more success by pressure-treating fertilized eggs than by giving them the hot-water shock treatment, and now a large proportion of fish farmers who rear-on trout for stocking into fisheries use pressure treatment for producing both rainbow and (to a much lesser extent) brown-trout triploids.

TUBE FLIES

Tube flies were designed for sea trout and salmon fishing, but in recent years they have also begun to be used by some people for big, reservoir brown trout. Though large, they are streamlined and therefore less prone to tangle during casting and fishing.

Tubes vary in length from ½in to 3in, and are available in a variety of materials, such as plastic, nylon, aluminium and brass.

Metal tubes - particularly brass ones - fish deep and are used in spring and autumn for salmon. They are used in conjunction with treble hooks, which give greater hooking potential and are harder for salmon to lever out than longshank single or double hooks. The tube runs free on the leader with a treble attached to the bottom end and a swivel to the top. During casting and fishing, water pressure holds the tube tight against the hook, but when a fish takes, the tube runs freely up the line out of the way and in doing so also prevents damage from occurring to the dressing. Some anglers prevent any risk of the treble moving away from the tube (and causing a tangle) until a fish has taken by pushing a piece of rubber tubing over the lower end of the tube and then pushing the eye of the treble into the protruding end of the rubber tubing.

Metal tubes need a polythene lining to reduce wear on the leader cast. Some tubes are produced with flared ends to prevent the dressing from slipping off.

Tube flies are tied with long hair wings, which swirl and pulsate attractively in flowing water. The body is usually whipped with silk and often ribbed with tinsel. Tube flies, like standard salmon flies, come in a wide variety of colours from the virtually all-black Stoat's Tail to the gaudy yellow, red and black Willie Gunn.

TUBES - KEEP

For the retention of particularly long fish, such as barbel, pike, zander or catfish, specialized tubes are more popular and preferable to rectangular keepsacks.

Tubes are made from well-perforated, super-soft, dark green nylon material, and are kept open with 12in-diameter plastic inner rings, just like a keep net. The ET range of tubes have drawstrings at each end, so that the fish can be put in head first at one end and removed or released head first through the other. Provided that the tube is staked out lengthways (using two bank sticks) in the marginal shallows, any large fish will lie quietly, without stress, until released. In running water the tube should be placed so that the fish's head faces the current.

A special, zipped model, with a continuous zip along the top, is also available, and is particularly useful when pike fishing from a boat.

Steadfast models are fitted with plastic-hexamesh covered, round or rectangular 'Protecta' rings at each end for quick release. The main body (18in-diameter tubular or 20x16in rectangular) is constructed from ultra-fine, super-soft, black nylon. The weighted body rings always settle in the vertical position. Both types of 'Protecta' tube are available in 48in and 60in formats, and are fitted with nylon D rings at each end for staking out.

TUNA, BIG EYED
(*Thunnus obesus*)

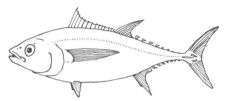

British record: 66lb 12oz (30kg 276g)

This extremely powerful, hard-fighting pelagic species is found in the clear, blue waters of the Indian Ocean, the Pacific and the Atlantic. It characteristically runs deep (often 200-300ft down) during daylight unless shoals of bait fish are sighted above. It has been captured on trolled lures to over 400lb in the Pacific and over 350lb in the Atlantic, but is a rarity on rod and line around the British Isles.

The back is dark grey-blue fusing into paler sides and a light belly. It has two dorsal fins, which are close set, the first being larger. Slightly behind the second dorsal is a similar-shaped anal fin, and between these fins and the powerful tail are several bright yellow finlets. The big-eyed tuna has incredibly long pectoral fins that reach back to the second dorsal. There is a powerful keel on the tail root, situated between secondary keels located slightly further back. The eye is noticeably large, as are the jaws.

Unless global warming drastically changes the movements of these large pelagic species, big-eyed tuna will remain an extremely rare catch from British seas. John visited the island of Madiera to catch these firm bodied battlers which weighed 65lb and 85 lb respectively - part of a five-fish haul taken in a hectic 45-minute spell whilst trotting large squid lures from local charter boat *Anguilla*, skippered by Roddy Hays.

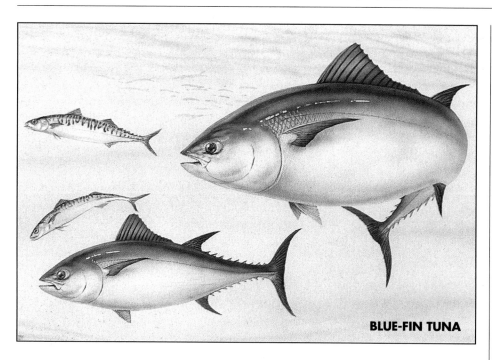

BLUE-FIN TUNA

TUNA, BLUE-FIN
(Thunnus thynnus)

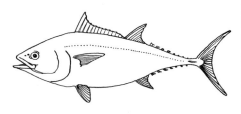

British record: 851lb (385kg 989g)

By far and away the largest fish ever caught on rod and line in British waters, back in the 1930s, tunny (as blue-fin tuna were called then) were regularly caught in the North Sea following the herring fleets. Fishing from small rowing boats close to the nets of commercial fishermen, pioneering sports fishermen like L. Mitchell Henry used herring baits to hook into massive blue-fin tuna, the ensuing fight often lasting several hours. His British record still stands and was once the world record for the species, but the world record has since been smashed by a monster of nearly 1,500lb from Nova Scotia. When the massive concentrations of herring disappeared from the North Sea during the 1950s due to over-fishing, so did any real chance of continuing to catch the giant blue-fin tuna, although isolated groups still migrate into the North Sea.

Blue-fin are built like a blown-up mackerel, with a firm, round body, blue-black along the back fusing into pale blue sides and a light belly. The first dorsal fin is long and noticeably high. The second is high and scythe-like, as is the anal fin directly below it. Between these two fins and the powerful tail is a series of yellowy-grey finlets. The tail is stiff and deeply concave, with a keel on the sides. All fins are grey-blue except the anal and second dorsal, which are brown. The mouth is large and lined with small, strong teeth in both jaws. This extremely powerful swimming machine feeds on herring and other shoal species such as pilchards and mackerel, and squid and crustaceans. Reproduction occurs during the summer months. Small blue-fin respond readily to trolled, artificial, feathered lures and plastic squid.

TUNA, BONITO
(Sarda sarda)

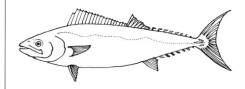

British record: 8lb 13¼oz (4kg 4g)

This member of the tuna, or tunny, family is like a scaled-down blue-fin, though size for size it is not so portly around the middle. It has a large mouth (lined with fine teeth), the jaws extending back to the rear of the small eye. It is coloured steel-blue along the back and upper sides fusing into silvery lower sides and belly. Along the upper sides it is overlaid with dark horizontal stripes, and this feature is the quickest way of distinguishing bonito from skipjack tuna, which have stripes along the lower sides and belly. It has a long first dorsal fin, which almost joins up with the second, and an anal fin that starts in a vertical line with the end of the second dorsal. Between these two fins and the tail are several mackerel-sized finlets. The tail is large, concave, and has a keel at the root with secondary keels both above and below. This pelagic species is most common in tropical parts of the Atlantic, where it feeds on small surface shoaling species and squid, and reaches weights exceeding 16lb.

Occasionally caught from south-western seas around the British Isles, particularly off the west coast of Ireland, the bonito responds readily to trolled feathers and artificial lures such as plastic squid.

TUNA, LONG-FINNED
(Thunnus alalunga)

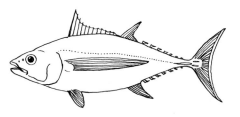

British record: 4lb 12oz (2kg 155g)

Better known in oceans throughout the world as 'albacore', and reaching weights in excess of 80lb, this pelagic member of the tuna family is a rather rare visitor to seas around the British Isles, occasionally taken off the south-western and western coastlines. The adult's most striking feature is the length of the pectoral fins, which reach back to a point beyond the anal fin, distinguishing it immediately from all other tuna.

It has the classic tuna shape, the thickest part of its deep blue body being in a vertical line with the second dorsal fin. There is a bluish flash along the sides and the belly is white. The first dorsal is long and low set. Between the second dorsal and the powerful tail are several yellowy finlets, with similar dark finlets on the underside. There is a powerful keel along the tail root, and the tail has a distinct, light trailing edge.

The long-finned tuna feeds on shoal fish and squid and readily grabs trolled artificial lures and feathers.

Uu

TURBOT
(*Scopthalmus maximus*)

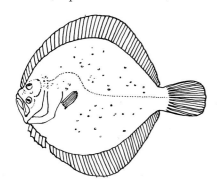

Average size: 4-8lb
Mega specimen: over 20lb
British record: 33lb 12oz (15kg 308g)

This large, hard-fighting and much sought-after flatfish has a broad, thick-set body, a big head, and huge upturned mouth with protruding lower jaw. Turbot are left-eyed flatfish: both eyes are on the left side. Colouration varies to provide camouflage on the sea bed, and is generally sandy brown overlaid with dark spots. Bony bumps are scattered irregularly all over the top side, and are occasionally found on the cream-coloured underside. The tail is large and slightly convex, and both dorsal and anal fin frills are wide, and extend all round the turbot from head to tail.

Turbot feed on other, smaller flatfish, in addition to hunting actively for shoal species such as sand eels, herrings and sprats. They reproduce during the spring and summer, the eggs floating on the surface until they hatch. Young turbot remain on the surface for a few months before dropping to the sea bed and commencing life as flatfish.

HABITAT AND DISTRIBUTION
Turbot love to occupy the downtide side of shingle and sand banks, lying in wait for shoal species to pass by. They can often be caught in comparatively shallow water over offshore banks. Turbot are also occasionally taken from wrecks. Distribution around the British Isles is limited to suitable habitat, and the warm southern, south-western and western coastlines offer the best prospects for catching turbot.

TECHNIQUES
Downtide boat fishing; Drift fishing at sea.

TURBOT

TWITCHER HITTING
See *Ledgering techniques.*

UMBRELLAS

Fishing umbrellas come in rib lengths of 45in, 50in and a giant 60in. Some are made from green, black, blue, camouflage or tan water-proofed nylon in various qualities. Others are made from wavelock, a laminated, vinyl-reinforced material giving 100 per cent waterproof protection. Wavelock is extremely strong, virtually tearproof and has welded seams. It is crack-proof to -30°C, and is available in either light green or camouflage.

Umbrellas are available in a standard, non-tilt format, in a basic locking tilt, and in the versatile Steade-fast Nubrolli tilt. The Nubrolli's lightweight-aluminium centre stem can be unscrewed and removed when it is used in conjunction with an overwrap *bivvi*, or it can be screwed into the brolly top at an oblique angle between the ribs and bellcap, providing more usable space beneath the cover.

A specialized, plated-steel, pile-driver spike with detachable tommy bar is available to replace the standard aluminium spike for really hard ground. This useful accessory also doubles as a bank stick. In strong winds it is advisable to anchor the umbrella with guy ropes. These are available in kit form comprising two pegs, a dog clip and braided cords.

Unconventional, rather specialized brollies with nylon covers, designed for the carp-fishing world by Fox International, include the Ultra 50in model and the Specialist umbrella, both of which have integral storm sides providing double the usable space of conventional brollies. Rigidity is provided by two built-in side poles and a main pole that follow the contour of the cover and support the ribs. The Liteweight model is of a similar design without storm sides, but is still supported with a single pole contoured to the side panel and fitted with solid fibreglass ribs.

UNHOOKING
See *Disgorgers.*

UNHOOKING MAT

Originally developed for large freshwater fish such as carp and pike, these designer mats, available in various sizes and formats, provide maximum protection to any fish that cannot be held during unhooking. When fish flap about over rough ground or gravel banking, their protective body mucus can easily be removed and their scales dislodged, so unhooking mats are an essential tackle item for anyone fishing gravel pits or brick- and concrete-lined reservoirs. They are in fact now regulation on many stillwater pike, tench and carp syndicate fisheries.

The basic mat is a rectangle of 1in-thick foam, around 20x36in, covered in soft PVC-coated material that should be wetted before fish are laid on it. At each end there are elasticated loops so that the mat can be rolled up neatly. Some models also have loops sewn into each end enabling the mat to be pegged down on the ground. Many models designed exclusively for pike and carp are up to 30x50in in size, with either a pocket at one end to accommodate the fish's head (once their eyes are covered fish lie still), or a generous flap with velcro edging to keep the catch still while the hook is removed. Some models have been designed with a velcro flap to enclose the fish fully, transforming the mat into a combined weighing bag, and these are fitted with strong handles for lifting on to the scales.

Top-of-the-range mats can be inflated around the edges (like a rubber dinghy), so there is no chance of the fish rolling or jumping off. Self-inflating unhooking mats featuring an open-cell foam liner, which expands to give extra bankside protection, are also available.

UPTIDE BOAT FISHING

Uptiding is exactly what the term implies. Instead of lowering the rig over the stern of an anchored boat and allowing the current to take it downtide until it reaches bottom (Downtide Boat Fishing), a cast is deliberately made uptide (fig. 93). If several rods are being fished, an enormous area of the ocean floor can be explored all around the boat, not just the limited patch immediately downtide (93A). Uptiding also permits much lighter and more sporting tackle to be used for most species of bottom-feeding fish, including the use of lighter leads.

As a shoal of fish working uptide might divide to avoid an anchored craft, especially in exceptionally clear or shallow water, uptiding puts a bait in front of fish that downtide fishing could never attract. Moreover the longer, 9-11ft, specialized, softer tipped uptide *boat rods (Rods - Sea)* so necessary for casting from an anchored boat permit the fight of even comparatively small species to be thoroughly enjoyed. Small multiplying reels work best - models in the 6000-7000 format holding 200yd of 15-20lb test. In addition to providing smooth casting, they are quite capable of dealing with species such as thornbacks, cod, bass and smooth hounds, as well as larger species like tope.

Several points must be taken into account if tangles and accidents are to be avoided when a party of anglers is boat fishing. Casts should be made from outside

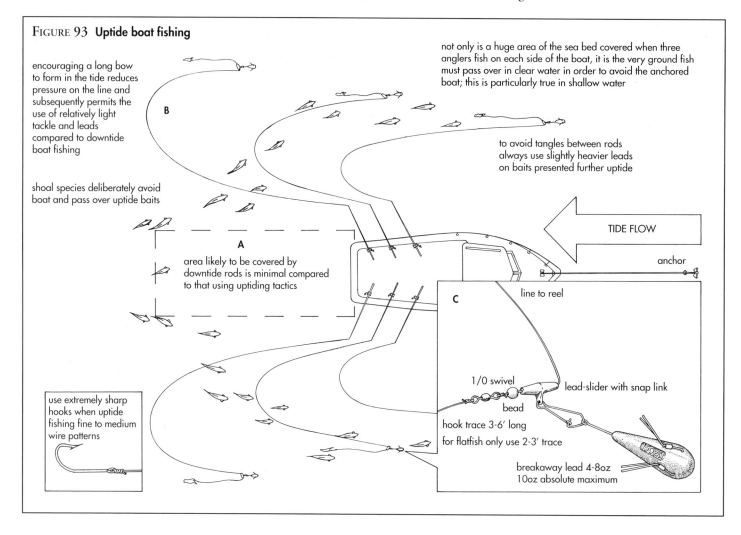

FIGURE 93 Uptide boat fishing

encouraging a long bow to form in the tide reduces pressure on the line and subsequently permits the use of relatively light tackle and leads compared to downtide boat fishing

shoal species deliberately avoid boat and pass over uptide baits

B

A

area likely to be covered by downtide rods is minimal compared to that using uptiding tactics

not only is a huge area of the sea bed covered when three anglers fish on each side of the boat, it is the very ground fish must pass over in clear water in order to avoid the anchored boat; this is particularly true in shallow water

to avoid tangles between rods always use slightly heavier leads on baits presented further uptide

TIDE FLOW

anchor

line to reel

C

use extremely sharp hooks when uptide fishing fine to medium wire patterns

1/0 swivel

bead

hook trace 3-6' long

for flatfish only use 2-3' trace

lead-slider with snap link

breakaway lead 4-8oz
10oz absolute maximum

Local charter boat skipper John Rawle, who works two boats out from Bradwell Marina into the productive waters of the Thames Estuary, nets a nice thornback ray for film director Paul Martingell. It accepted peeler crab on a size 2/0 hook and fought well in a strong tide on a sporting uptide outfit (note the long rod) with a reel line of 18lb.

the boat, aiming uptide and slightly across away from the anchor rope. They should not be made over the boat or from inside it as the lead is liable to hit someone or pick up other lines. Casts of up to 75yd are quite possible using little more than a gentle punch out, although areas closest to the boat should be explored first and subsequent casts made progressively further out. It also makes sense to use slightly heavier leads on the baits being presented furthest uptide, stepping down progressively so that the lightest leads of all are on the extreme downtide outfits.

To ensure that the bait stays in position, use break-away type leads. Once the wires have found purchase in the bottom pay out line to form an exaggerated bow in the tide. As current pressure against the bow is only severe in the middle (93B), this allows light leads to be used. If the line is kept too tight (insufficient bow), the lead will pull free

and bounce the bait downtide regardless of its weight, so remember to pay out more line (creating a larger bow) if the lead drags or step up, say, from a 5oz to a 7oz lead.

The most functional end rig comprises a running lead slider (to take the breakaway) stopped on the reel line by a large bead against a size 1/0 swivel (93C). To the other end tie a 3-6ft hook trace to suit the species expected. For species like bass, where bait movement is advantageous, use as long a trace as you can comfortably cast, but for out and out bottom-feeders such as cod, whiting, rays, flatfish, dogfish and smooth hounds, a 3ft trace is sufficient. One exception is if tope are the target species. To avoid being bitten off by their sharp teeth use a 12in, 60lb wire trace holding a 6/0, uptide-extra hook on the business end and a 1/0 swivel on the other. To the swivel tie 4ft of 50lb monofilament to resist the tope's rough, sandpapery skin and join to

the reel line with another swivel. The lead link and bead go on the reel line immediately above the second swivel.

When uptiding over exceedingly rough ground across which the front section of reel line is bound to lie, add 40ft of 40lb test to the 15-20lb reel line (*Knots - beachcaster*) to prevent the line chaffing. This not only acts as a buffer, but also becomes a shock leader when you are punching out leads of up to 10oz. Weights beyond this are not practical.

Distinct knocks and bangs on the rod tip from fish hanging on to the bait but not pulling the lead should be wound down quickly in order to straighten the huge bow of line hanging out in the tide. The hook will not be set simply by picking up the rod and striking hard. When really positive bites occur, the rod top suddenly nods back and the line slackens, which means that a fish has made off with the bait, causing the lead's wires to fold and bump downtide along the bottom. Again it is essential not to strike. Wind down quickly until you feel the weight of the fish, and then bend the rod firmly back into it. To help the hook to penetrate it is advisable to use strong, fine to medium-wire hooks.

Vv, Ww

VENDACE

(Coregonus albula)

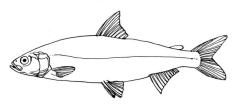

British record: none

A member of the very rare family of white fish, the vendace is now protected under the provisions of the Wildlife and Countryside Act 1981, whereby it is an offence to catch them intentionally.

The vendace is a shoal fish inhabiting deep, cold, clear-water lakes in Scotland and the Lake District, feeding on planktonic crustaceans. Its shape is similar to a herring, with a large eye and an upturned mouth with a protruding lower jaw. The back is greeny-pewter fusing into silvery flanks and a white belly. All fins, including a tiny adipose fin, are grey. It averages 8-12in in length when fully grown.

The vendace is common in Scandinavia and in north-eastern Europe. It reproduces during the spring in deep water.

WADDINGTON

The Waddington is a tempered-steel shank on which a hair-wing salmon fly pattern is tied. It is articulated (fig. 94) where the eye of the treble hook joins the shank of the fly so that the hook can be changed. Slide the silicone band along, removing the old hook, and replace with a new or different-sized one.

Waddingtons are tied in exactly the same way as tube flies, but provide a much lighter large fly for presentation in shallow and slow water.

WADING STICK

This essential game fisherman's aid provides support for wading in fast rivers, and can be used for assessing the bottom structure and for testing the depth. Models vary in length from 48in to 60in and have a cord at the top end that goes over the head and around one shoulder, enabling both hands to be used for casting. Single-stem wading sticks are made of steel, hollow fibreglass, and even traditional built cane with a solid rubber stopper on the bottom for prodding the river bed and a comfortable hand grip at the top. There is also a telescopic, pack-away model made from six 10in hollow-steel sections that are held together by an elasticated cord through the centre.

WALLEYE

(Stizostedion vitreum)

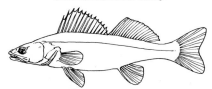

British record: 11lb 12oz (5kg 329g)

This species, an almost identical predatory fish to the *zander*, is prolific in North America and reaches weights of 22lb. A small stock of walleye were introduced into isolated British fisheries as far back as the 1920s, and have now either become extinct

FIGURE 94 **The Waddington**
tempered steel shank with eye at each end upon which fly pattern is tied

treble hook is held in place with silicone band

hair wing pattern is then tied exactly the same as a tube fly

silicone band permits a quick change of hook

or interbred with the European zander stocked into the Great Ouse system in the 1960s. The record walleye was caught in 1934 from the River Delph at Welney, Norfolk, part of the huge interconnecting Fenland waterways, much of which is fed by the Great Ouse.

WATERSIDE FLORA - RIVERS

Some people might think that it is impossible to tell which species lives where simply by identifying trees and plants along the river banks, but they would be wrong. It is also possible to use the waterside flora to work out where top fish-holding features such as undercut banks are likely to be situated, and where gravel runs exist, even when the river is running coloured and the bottom cannot be seen. Such knowledge improves your chances of catching, whether you are crawling on all fours along a clear-flowing overgrown stream after chub or ledgering a fast, deep weir-pool for barbel.

For instance, of the 200 or more willow variants growing in Britain, the tall white willow, the crack willow, the weeping willow and the goat willow - easily identified by those large, fluffy catkins and known affectionately as the pussy willow - are found along river banks. During the summer, willows provide heavy camouflage to the stalking angler, but their overhanging branches also provide shade and a multitude of concealing leaves for fish to bask beneath. Wherever willow branches overhang and lap the surface, a group of chub is likely to be in residence. In rivers that hold them, barbel also love such spots. Exceptionally weedy rivers will have clear sand or gravel bottoms in areas shaded by willow - obvious spots for the bait to be placed.

Where mature willows overhang the outside of an acute bend expect a cavernous, undercut bank harbouring a galaxy of species. During floods, water sweeps around the bend, keeping a deep run clear on the outside of the bend and eroding the clay banking beneath the willows' sub-surface roots, often for a distance of several feet inland (fig. 95). Such undercuts are

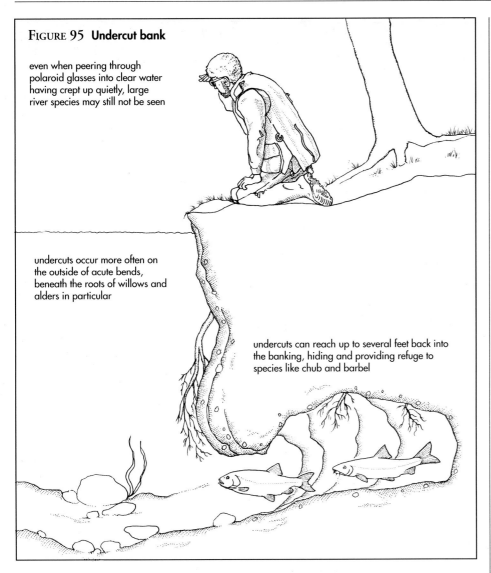

FIGURE 95 Undercut bank

even when peering through polaroid glasses into clear water having crept up quietly, large river species may still not be seen

undercuts occur more often on the outside of acute bends, beneath the roots of willows and alders in particular

undercuts can reach up to several feet back into the banking, hiding and providing refuge to species like chub and barbel

not visible from above, even when you are peering straight down, wearing polaroid glasses, through the crystal-clear water of summer. If you can see absolutely nothing in a spot where you know fish are present, they will be tucked away under the very bank on which you are standing.

Undercuts are also sometimes found beneath large chestnuts, beech, ash and alders. Chub and roach love the shade and clean bottom beneath the thick, low-hanging foliage of alder, in particular. Find mature willows or alders anywhere along a river, and nine out of ten will provide good chub swims. Find a large, wind-blown tree actually in the water, a tree whose lower branches are sunk beneath the surface, and all sorts of debris will have collected around it, forming a large raft. Chub love these rafts, and will reside beneath the smallest of bushes whose branches trail over the surface to provide a dark tunnel - brambles, hawthorn, blackthorn and especially the elder, whose ripe fruits fall in the autumn and are gobbled up immediately (*Baits, freshwater - Particles*). Trout also love tun-

nel swims and, like the chub, use them all year through. Don't look upon overhanging trees and bush hideouts as warm-weather hot-spots only. A tree may look rather naked without its leaves, but to a fish down below hugging the bottom it's better than no cover at all.

Different marginal plants flourish in different conditions, so by identifying the plants in a stretch of river you can work out the speed of flow, the bottom structure and even the water depth. For instance, in slow-moving rivers wherever there is a build-up of marginal silt, expect to find tench browsing between the thick stems of the greater reed mace in depths of 1-3ft. The tall common reed and reedgrass prefer a fairly dense bottom strata, and both send stems up through depths of 2-4ft. So just about every species - roach, perch, pike and in particular barbel - might lie close in to the bank, using the stems both as a current break and a vantage position.

For sheer fish-holding potential nothing matches tall, soft-stemmed plants such as reed sweet-grass and floating sweet-grass.

Both have drooping foliages and are usually referred to as rushes. They grow out from the bank across the water surface, along silty or peaty margins for up to several feet. Sprouting new growth from their creeping, floating rootstock, these plants provide a cavernous floating canopy much loved by species like roach and chub. Beware when walking close beside these marginal plants because what looks like the bank is actually floating rootstock. If your foot suddenly goes through, you could find yourself in water 3ft deep.

In the summer, a large bait such as a big lobworm or piece of breadflake freelined over the edge of the leading foliage will score instantly with chub. In the winter, float-fish over depth allowing the float to rest alongside the outside edge of the foliage so that the bait swings beneath the now brown matting straight to the fish below (*Stretpegging*). Another plant indicative of soft margins is the branched bur reed, easily identified by its odd, spiky-looking fruits or seed pods. One of the most distinct marginal river plants is the true bulrush, easily identified by its tall, dark green, round, onion-like stems, which taper to a point. Bulrushes love gravel between their roots and are often found in huge clumps right in the middle of the river and wherever the bottom is hard. Gravel runs between or alongside these clumps could be anything up to 4ft deep, and in rivers that hold them are much loved by barbel and perch, the latter's stripes blending in well with the vertical stems (fig. 96).

Tempt perch by trotting a brandling or bunch of maggots close alongside the rushes (*Freshwater floatfishing techniques - Long trotting*), and for barbel ledger a cube of meat or three grains of corn over a carpet of hempseed attractor (*Ledgering techniques - Quivertipping*). Where the banks are lined with thick beds, species such as roach, chub and grayling can also be expected. Lying hard on the bottom among the cut-ins or at the very end of each clump where the current pace is much reduced, expect pike to be lying in wait. When the river is well above its normal level and thickly coloured, during the winter, remember exactly where the clumps of bulrushes were situated, because immediately downstream of their brown rotting stems, there will be a very much slower pocket of water. And that's exactly where a ledgered bait will tempt barbel or chub using the bulrush stubs as a refuge.

There are few more exciting locations to explore than an intimate, overgrown stream in its summer clothes, where a basic knowledge of natural history and riverside flora can only help you catch more fish. Under the lapping willow branches for instance, there will be shade where chub love to lie. Beneath the willow's trunk, especially on a bend, the banking below might be carved out into an undercut, harbouring still more chub, a big perch or barbel. Barbel are also attracted to clean gravel runs beside and between beds of bullrushes which have onion-like stems that continually quiver against current pace. The fishing detective has many pleasant hours ahead.

Leaves may well have left the trees at the confluence of these two southern chalk streams, but waterside flora in the shape of tall reeds and sedges hold the key to fish location. Species like dace and roach are often found in pockets of quiet water where reed stems help to break full current force.

When in bloom the water crowfoot, one of the large ranunculus family of water plants, hides species like chub and, in particular, barbel beneath its long, wavering canopy. Many of the ranunculus family form massive beds during the summer, often 20-30ft long, sometimes choking the river from bank to bank with narrow runs between them. Search out these small pockets of clear water, no matter how seemingly difficult to fish they appear, because that is where the fish are. And unless a freelined or ledgered bait is allowed to roll with the current right beneath the floating plant clumps, bites will be few and far between.

In much slower water, such as the meandering fenland rivers and drains, the common yellow water lily will be seen, its large pads and tight yellow flowers smothering the shallow margins, indicating exactly where the drop-off into deep water

starts. This lily can exist in depths up to 8ft, but then only its sub-surface cabbage-type leaves can be seen. Wherever these cabbages are found, expect to find roach, bream and tench. Don't be afraid to put the bait right in among the foliage, because that's exactly where the fish are. Stewed wheat is a great summer bait for tempting cabbage-patch roach. Fish it layed-on or slowly on the drop together with a little loose-fed grains (*Baits, freshwater - Particles*).

WATERSIDE FLORA - STILLWATERS

Whatever type of stillwater you fish in - whether it is a tiny pond, a gravel pit, a lake, a mere or even a reservoir - you can improve your fishing by getting to

know the marginal and floating plants, together with the trees, shrubs and wild flowers found there, because the flora of a stillwater reveals much about its character and about the inhabitants beneath the surface.

Let's start with trees, particularly those found very close to the water, some of which might have branches extending out across the surface. Willows and alder trees are common beside stillwaters and both shade the surface with dense foliage. Many whose lower branches hang beneath the surface sprout enormous, fibrous rootstocks that harbour a mass of aquatic insect larvae, the caddis grub being just one. These dark, fibrous carverns are much loved by carp and chub. Rudd also rest in the shade during the heat of a summer's day. And crouched low among the bankside greenery, the angler is well hidden. Most species lay their eggs on these mats of fibrous roots, so a visit to favourite lakes or ponds during the spawning season, towards the end of May or early June, could prove

FIGURE 96 Bullrushes

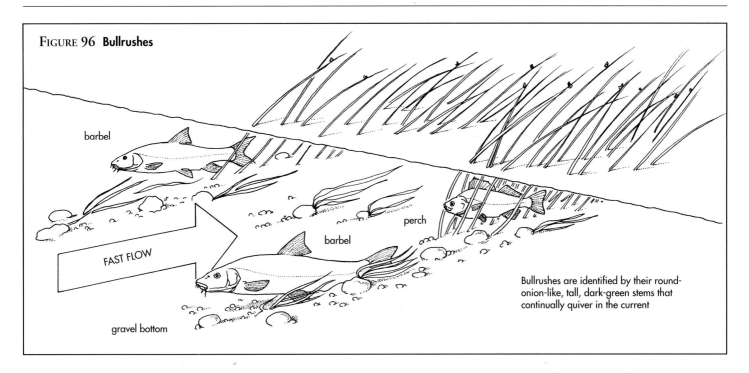

barbel

FAST FLOW

barbel

perch

gravel bottom

Bullrushes are identified by their round-onion-like, tall, dark-green stems that continually quiver in the current

very informative in identifying the exact positions of these root mats.

Above the surface both flies and moths, plus their caterpillars, fall from the leaves into the water. So whenever there is a good hatch of flies or a glut of caterpillars, you can be almost certain that a shoal of rudd will locate them.

Perch love the camouflage provided by sub-surface roots and branches, the vertical stems from the main branches blending in beautifully with their stripes. Be very careful when freelining or float-fishing a bait close to alder foliage because those small, knotty, dark brown cones are strong enough to withstand a pull from the

This is not wilful destruction, simply Wilson removing surplus yellow water lilies from one lake to be planted in another. But just look at the number of stems and subsurface roots sprouting from an average size rhizome. Small wonder care must be taken whilst trying to extract carp from such a hideout.

In this beautiful summer lakeland scene (which is in fact a man-made ex-gravel workings and part of the author's own two-lake fishery in Norfolk) locating carp is all about observing the surface in and around beds of colourful lilies. Look for pads which twitch, stalks that sway when there is no wind, gentle tail patterns and vortexes on the surface proving fish are rooting 2ft below. Beneath sunken willow and alder branches carp will also be present, sucking in nymphs which cling to the white fibrous rootstock sprouting just beneath the surface. The observant, opportunist fisherman should never leave home without polaroid glasses and binoculars.

strongest nylon line. Alder wood, however, snaps incredibly easily - a point worth remembering when climbing up thin branches to a fish-spotting position.

Willow branches can lose sap quickly, and in the case of the giant 'crack' willow they crack loudly as they break. Though sunken branches are generally associated with summer species because of the cover they provide, species like carp and perch still occupy these same snaggy areas throughout the winter months, making them prime close-range hot-spots when there is little surface activity.

Much smaller than willow and alder, and generally found beside small ponds and pits, blackthorn and hawthorn also dip their lower branches beneath the surface. This creates a dense, dark canopy that attracts carp, who can sometimes be heard below the prickly foliage sucking in floating baits that drift beneath it.

Wherever large trees such as oak, beech and chestnut preside over a stillwater, expect a thick layer of leaf mould on the bottom directly beneath them. Even the bottom of a gravel pit soon silts up with a rich, decomposed layer created by heavy leaf fall. Among the top layer of this detritus is an active network of animal life, from microscopic bacteria to freshwater louse and shrimps, that feed on the leaves, helping to reduce them to organic silt. Gasses become trapped between the layers of the detritus as decomposition takes place and are released by bottom-feeding fish such as tench, eels, bream and carp as they root about. This is why observation of the surface beneath tree-clad margins is so important in the early morning and again at dusk. Both are natural feeding times for most bottom-feeding species during the warmer months, and the fish betray their presence by the bubbles they send up.

Because each marginal plant prefers a certain water depth and bottom structure, knowledge of the habitat preferred by each plant can give a fair indication of the water depth close in. For instance, the tall common reed, often called the Norfolk reed because in that county it is still used for roof thatching (*Reed floats*), can sprout up from the bottom through 4ft of water, but the beautiful yellow iris will not. All irises prefer to have their tuberous roots set in a rich, loamy soil covered by little more than a few inches of water. They are, in fact, just as happy out of water in marshy, peaty ground.

The greater and lesser reed mace, often wrongly called bulrushes, are easily identified by their cigar-like seed heads. Tench, especially, love to browse beside their leek-like lower stems, sucking off the snails and nymphs that adhere there. As with the common reed, they can often be seen knocking or twitching when there is not the slightest hint of any wind, as tench and carp manoeuvre and feed below the surface - a wonderful give-away for the observant fisherman, who should always have his binoculars at the ready.

Many sedges, of which the fox sedge with its sharp, triangular leaves is the most common, float and even span outwards from their fibrous rootstock, so beware when walking along soft, spongy margins. One of the most beautiful of all waterside plants, although it does not hold fish, is the Himalayan balsam, often called 'Jumping Jack' because its seed pods 'jump' as they burst, scattering the seeds from the distinct pink and white flowers everywhere. And no angler can resist stopping to admire the rich beauty of the foxglove, with its white or dark red, trumpet-like flowers on erect stems, which is most common beside wooded lakes. There is nothing to stop the angler transporting its seeds, which ripen in the late autumn, to other stillwaters, and the same goes for a host of other lovely flowers.

Just as marginal plants can provide a rough guide to water depth, so can those that have floating leaves. The large, green-leafed, common yellow water lily, for example, can send up leaves to the surface from 6-8ft down provided the water is clear, although it is happier and grows thickest in depths of 2-3ft. This strong plant will survive almost anywhere, quickly criss-crossing the bottom with its huge tubers. From these turnip-like tubers, or rhizomes, sprout soft, sub-surface, lettuce-like leaves, usually referred to by anglers as cabbages, in addititon to the stems supporting floating pads and the small, tight, yellow flowers. All fish from pike to carp and from rudd to tench love this lily and use its maze of underwater tubers and stems for food, refuge or both.

The white water lily and all the coloured hybrids do not have the same, dense, sub-surface superstructure as the yellow lily. They are, nevertheless, sure-fire fish attractors when their pads cover the surface, especially for species such as carp and tench. Most species are easier to extract

from cultivated lilies, which grow most prolifically in depths of 4ft and below, though some of the more vigorous white hybrids will come up from 5-6ft down. Floating plants with oval leaves, such as potomogeton and amphibious bistort, are quick to colonize newly dug stillwaters such as gravel pits. They beautify the otherwise exposed shallow bars up to 4ft deep with a dense covering of green leaves and erect, knotty pink flowers. They attract tench, perch and carp, and because for every twenty or so leaves on top there are only one or two stems below, there is always a good chance of extracting even large specimens.

Another floating plant with very few sub-surface stems supporting a seemingly impenetrable covering of surface pads is the dwarf pond lily, which though not a true lily has tiny, perfectly round, green pads no more than 3in across and bright, buttercup-yellow flowers. This is one of the most dense marginal plants to colonize stillwater and is much loved by tench and crucian carp. Don't be afraid to fish close by or right in the gaps between the leaves. Firm hit-and-hold tactics will soon work a fish up to the surface. Again, this little plant prefers depths of 2-4ft but will, if the water is clear, pop up through 6-8ft of water.

WATER TEMPERATURES

Water temperature directly affects every fish's willingness to feed. In warm weather most species tend to become more active and some, such as rudd, trout, carp and chub, take to searching the upper layers, even taking food from the surface. During severe heat waves, however, fish will seek shelter under overhanging trees, bushes, weed beds or deep water during the day, only venturing forth to feed during the cooler hours of night. In winter, a sudden influx of snow-water into a river or a run of savage night frosts will kill off sport. And even when the weather warms up, it can be a few days before the water temperature rises to a level that the fish consider comfortable.

The water in big, deep lakes can be divided into three horizontal bands: the epilimnion, the thermocline and the hypolimnion. In summer and autumn the upper layer of the lake - the epilimnion - will be the warmest part; in winter, the deepest layer - the hypolimnion - will be warmest. The temperature of the water in these two bands tends to be similar, but shows most variation in the thermocline layer between them. When strong winds blow, these horizontal bands tilt, causing the epilimnion to build up on the lee shore. Species that prefer cold water, such as charr and lake trout, will move progressively deeper as the summer temperatures build.

WEATHER FORECASTS

No angler should ever put to sea without first getting the very latest weather forecast. At best the weather patterns in the UK are fickle. A day that dawns fine and sunny can all too often end with a full-blown gale - certainly not the time to be stuck offshore in a small dinghy.

There are many sources of accurate weather forecasts. The BBC weather bulletins at the end of each news programme have been popular with anglers, in particular the weekend outlook given after the Wednesday lunchtime news, and the look ahead for the following week for farmers and growers on BBC1 at 12.55pm on Sundays. These should be double-checked by watching local weather reports broadcast after local news programmes. Shipping forecasts are broadcast on various BBC radio programmes throughout the day (full details are available in the Radio Times).

Coastguard stations broadcast the local inshore weather forecast at various intervals throughout the day on VHF, with a run-down on the present sea conditions. Coastguards are more than willing to provide the latest weather information if you phone them up prior to sailing, or call them on a VHF radio.

Several angling magazines now run a telephone weather/fishing information service, notably *Sea Angler*'s Coastcall (tel: 0891 600 262), which provides up-to-date information on coastal weather and sea conditions around the country.

Daily forecasts are available from 0600 hours every Friday, Saturday and Sunday, and all English bank holidays. Every Monday a comprehensive weekly forecast for the entire UK is available.

However, this service should be regarded as a supplement to, not a replacement for, the local coastguard report or other sources of local weather information.

WEAVER, LESSER

(*Echiichthys vipera*)

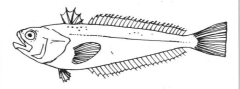

British record: 3¼oz (92g)

Despite its tiny size, the lesser weaver is a species to be wary of. It has a long, laterally compressed, deepish body with a distinctly upturned mouth and a squared tail edged in black. Its eye is set high in the head, and it has a short-spined and poisonous first dorsal fin, which is black. There is also a single poisonous spine on the gill cover. These venom-loaded spines can inflict an extremely painful wound on anglers who unthinkingly grab hold of the weaver to remove the hook. Both the second dorsal and anal fin are long and almost identical. The back and sides are a yellowy-brown overlaid with darker markings fusing into a lighter belly.

The lesser weaver is the most dangerous of the four European weaver species. It is a regular visitor around the British coastline in shallow waters, and is regularly caught by anglers fishing from the beach or piers and jetties. It feeds on crustaceans, worms and small fish, and prefers a sandy bottom. It reproduces during the winter, from January to March.

WEED RAKES

Weed rakes are used to clear channels of water just beyond the marginal growth through areas of soft-roofed plants such as Canadian pondweed, hornwort, mill foil, lilies and so on that have become too dense during the summer, in order to make it possible to float-fish for species such as tench and crucian carp lying close to the bottom.

The most effective way to clear quite shallow, reasonably hard-bottomed ponds and lakes, is to wade in, wearing chest-high waders, and clear out the weed with a long-handled garden rake. Then give the bottom a good going over to colour the water and suspend numerous items of natural food above the silt, which will attract tench,

especially, despite the disturbance.

For deeper swims, two standard, steel garden-rake heads tied back to back and attached to a length of rope will certainly clear out enough weed to make float fishing worthwhile.

Wide (though expensive), double-pronged rake-heads with a hole to take a rope make a much quicker job of weed clearance. Visit the local garden centre for additional ideas.

Specially designed lightweight, stainless-steel weed-cutters with fixed blades, shaped rather like a boomerang complete with throwing cord are available from most tackle shops. In the middle of the cutting head is a ⅜ BSF thread that screws into a collar holding the throwing cord, or into the standard thread of a telescopic landing-net handle.

The Kleerweed cutter is a most useful tool and is small enough to fit into any tackle bag.

WEIGHING SLING/BAG

These semi-circular protective bags with strong handles for lifting fish on to scales are made from soft, super-smooth PVC or strong nylon material, and have drainage holes in the bottom. The standard 30in-long model accommodates all small species, including specimen tench or bream, while the large 40in and extra-large 60in models are designed for carp, pike and catfish.

The interior of the bag should be wetted prior to receiving a fish. To release a fish, submerge the bag and allow the fish to swim off in its own time in order to minimize stress.

WEIR-POOLS

Weir-pools probably contain more fish, and a greater variety of species, than any other type of habitat or feature in running water. And they offer the most exciting and mysterious sport, not just during the summer months but throughout the entire year for both coarse and game fish (fig. 97).

Weir-pools (and to a much lesser extent mill-pools) are meeting places for many species. Some visit for the food brought

This is one of the largest weir pools ever fished by the author. It is called Lockport Bridge Dam, near Winnipeg in Manitoba, Canada, and it holds back the mighty Red River, famous for its enormous stocks of common carp, and channel catfish which are regularly caught between 20 to 35lb.

depending upon the amount of water coming from the upper reaches.

In rivers that have both weir-pools and mill-pools, a steady stream of water bypasses the weir and is channelled beneath the mill building, down into a concrete pit, where it works the mill turbine. The wooden-slatted water-wheels of yesteryear, used to turn the grinding stone for milling flour, still exist although most have been restored purely for public interest.

Small, intimate weir-pools are easy to read because most of the water is usually channelled through a single gate, creating a deep hole immediately beneath the sill. The constant push of water scours the bottom clean, often down the entire run to the point where the bottom shelves up at the tail end of the pool. On either side of this main flush, water slowly circles in back

down from above the weir. Species such as dace, grayling, barbel and trout are attracted by the increased levels of dissolved oxygen and a clean gravel bottom associated with fast, turbulent water. Salmon and sea trout, on the other hand, use weir-pools to hold up and rest for a while during their upstream migration to the spawning beds in a river's upper reaches. Pike and perch love weir-pools because vast gudgeon shoals and dense concentrations of small roach and dace provide a resident larder of food. And eels love weir-pools because a veritable junkyard of discarded human rubbish, such as milk-crates, supermarket trolleys, old fencing and traffic cones on the bottom provide carvernous hideouts for the eel to occupy.

Most rivers have weir-pools created by barriers constructed to hold back and control the water flow, especially during times of severe flooding but also to maintain a mean water level throughout the year. Large rivers such as the Thames, Great Ouse or the Severn have equally large weirs with wide, concrete sills over which water pours into the pool below. Smaller rivers have weirs made up of several gates, each of which can be opened or shut down,

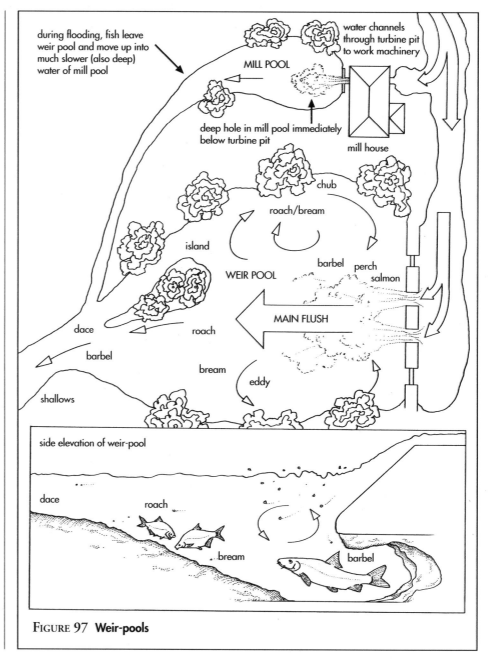

FIGURE 97 Weir-pools

eddies and these are prime holding spots for many species.

Large weir-pools are not so easy to read, and much depends on whether the water is evenly distributed over a wide sill or is funnelled through a limited number of hatch gates. Immediately below wide sills, the bottom usually shelves down deeply, and then gradually shelves up towards the tail end of the pool. Water pouring through hatch gates, however, generally carves out a depression in the bottom for at least a few yards down the pool; the bottom then starts to shelve up slowly towards gravelly shallows at the tail end of the pool. Study surface currents carefully, for at least several minutes, to gain an accurate assessment of where food particles will be deposited. Shoals of quality roach or bream usually prefer to occupy the deep, steady, even-paced water throughout the middle section before the bottom shelves upwards and the current increases in pace. Barbel, trout and chub love the back flow immediately below the sill, where the surface is often white with foam, and those shallow, gravelly runs between long, flowing beds of streamer weeds at the very tail end of the pool, where it invariably starts to narrow and the current pace quickens. Chub also love to lie beneath overhanging trees and in swims where foliage laps the surface, collecting a raft of cut weed and other flotsam. Barbel are also likely to be present.

During high levels of flooding, when the weir-pool becomes tea coloured, full of debris and totally unfishable for days on end, many of the inhabitants will be aware of the quieter life to be had only a short swim away in the mill-pool (if there is one) until the flood waters recede. As only a certain amount of water can be channelled through a mill's turbine pit, the depth of a mill pool increases but has only a moderate current. A disproportionate number of fish will therefore be packed into the pool like sardines until the weir-pool becomes habitable again, and the angler should take advantage of such occasions.

WHITING
(Merangius merlangus)

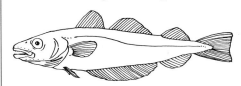

Average size: 12oz-1¼lb
Mega specimen: over 3½lb
British record: 6lb 12oz (3kg 61g)

This commonly caught shoal fish belongs to the cod family. The whiting has a streamlined, soft body with a narrow, pointed snout (no chin barbel in adult whiting, though young fish have a tiny one), three dorsal fins that join up at their bases, two anal fins, a squared tail and a small, dark spot at the base of the pectoral fins. Colouration along the back is sandy-grey fusing into flanks of metallic silver and a white belly. It has a noticeable lateral line.

The whiting feeds on small fish, squid and crustaceans. Reproduction occurs in shallow water between February and June, the resulting fry drifting inshore with the currents.

HABITAT AND DISTRIBUTION
The whiting lives in vast shoals close to the sea bed and are most commonly found over sand, mud or gravel. It is prolific all around the British Isles, but the species is well known for its seasonal appearance and sudden disappearance.

TECHNIQUES
Artificial lure fishing - sea; Beachcasting; Downtide boat fishing; Drift fishing at sea; Feathering; Uptide boat fishing.

WHITING, BLUE
(Micromesistius poutassou)

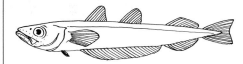

British record: 1lb 12oz (793g)

This small member of the cod family has three well-separated dorsal fins (those of the common whiting are all closely joined at their bases) and two anal fins. It has a forked tail (the common whiting's is squared) and lacks the small black spot at the base of the pectoral fins of the common whiting. It has a pointed snout, and no chin barbel. Colouration is bluish-grey along the back fusing into lighter sides and a belly of silvery white.

The blue whiting feeds on small fish and crustaceans, and is not often caught by anglers. It prefers extremely deep waters, and is found well offshore all around the British Isles.

WIRE TRACES - FRESHWATER

Only when fishing for big eels, zander and pike are wire traces necessary, and they are simple to make.

Most tackle shops stock a choice of cabled alasticum wire and extra-fine braided wire such as Marlin Steel and Seven Strand. The

WHITING

FIGURE 98 Wire traces - freshwater

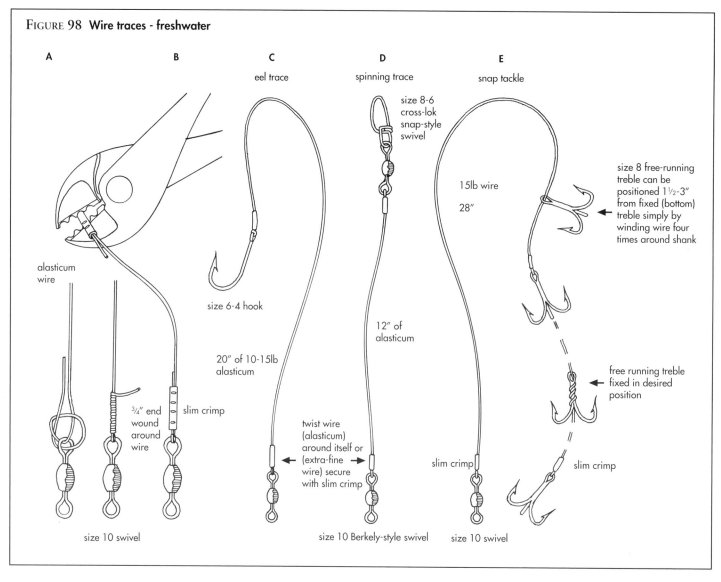

A

B

C

eel trace

D

spinning trace

E

snap tackle

size 8-6
cross-lok
snap-style
swivel

size 8 free-running
treble can be
positioned 1½-3"
from fixed (bottom)
treble simply by
winding wire four
times around shank

15lb wire

28"

alasticum
wire

size 6-4 hook

12" of
alasticum

free running treble
fixed in desired
position

20" of 10-15lb
alasticum

¾" end
wound
around
wire

slim crimp

twist wire
(alasticum)
around itself or
(extra-fine
wire) secure
with slim crimp

slim crimp

slim crimp

size 10 swivel

size 10 Berkely-style swivel

size 10 swivel

difference between these two types is that alasticum can be twisted around a hook and swivel without any risk of it coming undone (fig. 98A), while the thinner wires are more springy and must be joined to a hook and size 10 swivel with slim crimps, using a crimping tool (fig. 98B). Either way, start by threading the wire once through the swivel eye. If using alasticum, thread the wire through the eye again, forming a simple slip knot, then twist the end around the wire; or sleeve a slim crimp on to fine diameter braided wire.

To make an eel trace, use a single, size 6 or 4, eyed hook (depending upon bait size) to 20in of 10lb or 15lb test alasticum, twisting the wire around both hook-eye and swivel (fig. 98C). A spinning trace is made in exactly the same way from 12in of alasticum, twisted round a link swivel one end and a plain swivel at the other; or from 12in of fine wire secured at each end with slim crimps (fig. 98D).

To make snap tackles using two semi-barbless treble hooks, secure the swivel,

thread one of the trebles up the wire, then add the second. The free-running treble can easily be fixed 1in, 2in or 3in above the bottom hook by winding the wire four times around its shank (fig. 98E). Make 28in-long snap-tackle traces with a duo of size 10 trebles for zander and size 8 or 6 for pike, so that if the wire is damaged by the forceps during unhooking the trace is still long enough for the last 3-4in to be cut off and the trebles fixed on again.

WIRE TRACES - SEA

Today the wire trace has a limited application for sea anglers, with only the larger members of the shark family and tope really requiring the use of wire. Wire was once used for the likes of conger, skate and rays as well, but now heavy-duty monofilament, which is available at breaking strains of 150lb or more, is far more popular with top anglers fishing for these species.

Several different types of wire are used, in varying thicknesses and breaking strains, according to the intended species. For tope a 15in trace made from nylon-covered multistrand in breaking stains of 40-60lb is ideal. Above this length of trace use 4ft of 50lb monofilament to act as a buffer against the tope's sandpapery skin. Multistrand wire has far less tendency to kink than single, with many of the best wire-trace lines being marketed for pike anglers. For sharks, a much heavier gauge of wire is a must, up to 300lb BS, holding a pair of 10/0 hooks.

The hooks and a swivel are attached at opposite ends of the trace. When making lighter traces, for example for tope, standard wire crimps are adequate and are easily compressed with a pair of crimping pliers. However, the tremendous force likely to be exerted on the trace during the fight from a shark demands that specialist crimps and ferrules are used, and these need to be attached using heavy-duty crimping gear. Ready-made traces are widely available, but most chandlers have the necessary crimping gear for assembling boat rigging and will custom-make shark traces for a nominal fee.

WITCH

(Glyptocephalus cynoglossus)

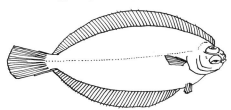

British record: 1lb 2¾oz (533g)

Found mostly around the south-western and western seaboard of the British Isles, and an uncommon angler's fish, this right-eyed flatfish has large eyes, a small head and mouth, and a narrow body. It is perhaps the most slender of all flatfish. The lateral line is slightly curved above the pectoral fin, and the scales are a little rough to the touch. The underside is white and the topside grey-brown. The dorsal and anal fin fringes are long and the tail is rounded.

The witch feeds on worms and crustaceans, and reproduces during the summer. It prefers deep water and a sandy or muddy bottom.

WOBBLING DEADBAITS

The art of retrieving a dead fish through the water in such a way that predatory freshwater species like pike, and to a much lesser extent zander, think it is alive and worth grabbing is also referred to as 'sink and draw'.

The bait is cast out and allowed almost to touch bottom before a crank or two of the reel handle draws it upwards in a lively, juddering, fluttering action (fig. 99A). It is then allowed to sink again before a short retrieve sends it fluttering upwards once more. This erratic, wobbling action is best achieved by mounting the deadbait slightly offset (fig. 99B), with two prongs of the upper treble worked into the eye socket and one prong of the bottom treble hooked into the flank. With small baits (3-4in) such as sprats, dace and gudgeon, set the hooks just 1in apart, but for all larger baits (5-8in) a distance of 2-3in is preferable so than an immediate strike can be made with a fair chance of at least one of the hooks finding purchase.

When working the bait in really shallow water or across the surface through a shallow layer of clear water over dense weed beds, weights on the trace are not required.

But to ensure that the bait dives on cue in deeper areas, pinch one to four swan shot on to the wire trace immediately below the swivel.

Think of pike (and zander) occupying that lower 3ft of water immediately above bottom and endeavour to wobble the bait just within or just above that band. In crystal-clear water, pike might sometimes zoom up from the lake or river bed to grab a bait 10ft above them, but not often. And in coloured water with no more than about 1ft of visibility, the bait almost has to bump a pike on the nose or tail to initiate action.

WOBBLING IN RIVERS

To keep the bait down in the taking zone some 2-3ft above bottom in running water, a bomb link of 36in is tied to the top swivel alongside the reel line (fig. 99C). A snap-swivel on the bomb end allows various weights to be used and quickly changed to suit each new location.

Use only enough weight to just hold bottom and the bomb will bump and slide easily over the river bed on the retrieve. The short, 12in monofilament link between wire trace and the top swivel (to which the reel line and bomb link are tied) helps to prevent tangles.

Work all feature swims likely to hold pike by casting downstream and across the

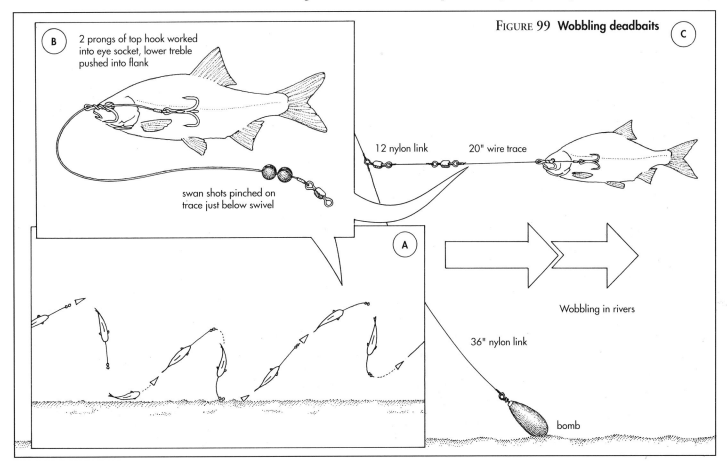

FIGURE 99 **Wobbling deadbaits**

B 2 prongs of top hook worked into eye socket, lower treble pushed into flank

swan shots pinched on trace just below swivel

12 nylon link   20" wire trace

A

Wobbling in rivers

36" nylon link

bomb

For catching large pike in the coloured waters of the Norfolk Broads, John wobbles a fresh deadbait during the winter months, ever so slowly a foot or so above the bottom sediment upon which these predators lie. This superbly conditioned 25-pounder gobbled up a small mackerel mounted on a 20in, 15lb test-wire trace holding a brace of semi-barbless size 8 trebles. In shallow water up to just 4ft deep, add just a single swan shot or two immediately below the trace swivel to ensure the bait is retrieved at the correct level. Add further shots to accomodate greater depths.

flow (just like traditional wet-fly fishing); then tighten up and hold the rod tip high while working the rig towards the bank in gentle twitches and jerks. Start at the upstream end of the area and walk a pace or two downstream between each cast to ensure that every pike has a chance of seeing the bait. If you feel the sudden lunge of a pike grabbing the bait, don't wait for a run to develop. Lower the rod tip until the line tightens and strike hard immediately, keeping the rod fully bent.

WOLF FISH
(Anarchichas lupus)

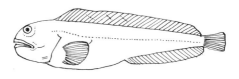

British record: 26lb 4oz (11kg 906g)

Also called 'catfish' and 'stone-biter' because of its ferocious rows of grinding teeth, this long, awesome-looking predator resembles a giant blenny in outline. It is, in fact, related to the blennies, and is not a true catfish. It has a long, smooth body that tapers from a huge head down to a tiny tail. The dorsal frill stretches from above the gill plate all the way to the tail, with an anal fin exactly half the fish's length. The pectoral fins are large and rounded; the pelvic fins are absent. Colouration is dark bluish-brown on top, gradually fusing into a lighter belly. The back and flanks are overlaid with up to a dozen darkish bars.

The wolf fish uses its dog-like teeth for crunching up crustaceans and molluscs. It is generally found over broken or rough ground in deep water in seas around the northern half of the British Isles, but rarely in the south. It is commonly caught in Scandinavian waters, but is only very rarely caught by British boat anglers. It reproduces in the winter.

WRASSE, BALLAN
(Labrus bergylta)

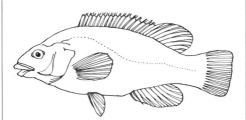

Average size: 1-2lb
Mega specimen: over 5lb
British record: 9lb 6oz (4kg 252g)

This deep-bodied, fully scaled, thick-set wrasse is by far the largest found around the British Isles. It has a small head and pointed snout, with thick-rimmed, cherub-like lips hiding a veritable armoury of sharp teeth. Its exquisite colouration varies according to the habitat and water clarity. It is generally rich bronze across the back and sides fusing into a golden belly, overlaid with blue-white spots that also cover all fins including the traditional, long dorsal, two-thirds of which is spined. There are also spines at the leading edge of the anal fin. The tail is large and rounded.

It feeds on crustaceans, worms and molluscs, and reproduces in the summer, laying eggs in a nest built with plant material.

HABITAT AND DISTRIBUTION
Common around much of the British Isles wherever the coastline is rugged, the ballan wrasse loves rocky ground and reefs in relatively shallow water. The rocky shores along the south-west coast of Ireland and in the Channel Islands are ballan wrasse havens.

TECHNIQUES
Drift fishing at sea; Floatfishing in harbours and off the rocks.

WRASSE, BALLIONS
(Crenilabrus ballion)

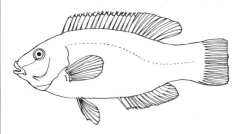

British record: 1½oz (40g)

This tiny, deep-bodied, fully scaled wrasse rarely exceeding 8in long, has distribution limited to the Channel Islands. Colouration is greeny-brown with distinguishing dark spots in the centre of the tail root and at the base of the dorsal fins. There is also a dark blotch on the snout. It feeds on worms, molluscs and crustaceans, and lives among rocks.

Spawning

WRASSE

WRASSE, CORKWING
(*Crenilabrus melops*)

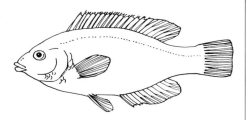

British record: 11¼oz (318g)

The corkwing wrasse has the typical wrasse layout of fins, with a long dorsal fin, the first two-thirds spined, and spines at the leading edge of the anal fin. The body is a deep, warm, green-brown and fully scaled. There is a crescent-shaped, dark mark behind the eye and a distinct, dark mark in the centre of the tail root.

It is found along rugged coastlines all around the British Isles, feeding among rocks on crustaceans, molluscs and worms. It reproduces during the summer, the eggs being laid in a nest made by the male from sea weed.

WRASSE, CUCKOO
(*Labrus mixtus*)

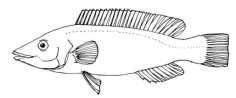

British record: 2lb 13¾oz (1kg 13g)

Though noticeably slimmer in the body compared to the chunky ballan, cuckoo wrasse are the most colourful of all wrasses. The snout is pointed and the mouth large, with sharp teeth and thick lips. The dorsal fin is long, and two-thirds of it is spined. There are more spines to the leading edge of the long anal fin. Females are less highly coloured than males and are distinguished by three dark blotches on the back, at the end of the dorsal fin and tail root. Males have bright yellow bodies with brilliant blue on the head, shoulders and front of the dorsal fin. The middle flanks are also overlaid with blue, and there is blue edging on the pelvic and anal fins and tail.

The cuckoo wrasse feeds on worms, molluscs and crustaceans, and reproduces in summer following a nest-building courtship. It prefers a similar habitat to ballan wrasse of rugged coastlines and rocky inshore waters, and migrates to deep water in winter. It is occasionally caught by anglers fishing for ballan wrasse.

WRASSE, GOLDSINNY
(*Ctenolabrus rupestris*)

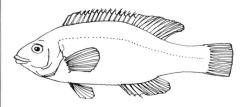

British record: 3¼oz (90g)

This small, fully scaled wrasse is distinguishable by a dark blotch covering the leading rays of the long dorsal fin and a dark mark at the top of the tail root. It has the classic wrasse fin arrangement. The dorsal is spined for two-thirds of its length,

Resplendent in yellow and blue livery, the male cuckoo wrasse is one of the most brilliantly coloured fish that British saltwater anglers are ever likely to catch; the female, however, is drab by comparison. Both readily accept worms or baited feathers fished close to the bottom around rocky coastlines.

and the leading edge of the anal fin also spined. Colouration varies according to habitat between a warm orange-brown and greeny-brown. The head is pointed and the small mouth has large, curved teeth at the front.

The goldsinny feeds on worms, small crustaceans and small molluscs. It reproduces during the summer. It has localized distribution around the British Isles in areas where the coastline is rugged, with rocks close inshore.

WRASSE, ROCK-COOK

(Centrolabrus exoletus)

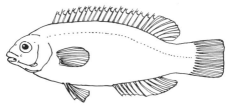

British record: 2¾oz (77g)

This tiny, deep-bodied, fully-scaled wrasse has a typical fin arrangement of a long dorsal (three-quarters of which is spined) and an anal fin with spined leading rays. Small head and mouth with small teeth. Colouration is greeny-warm brown along the back fusing into lighter sides, overlaid with blue stripes and a yellowy belly. There are dark vertical bars on the tail.

The rock-cook wrasse feeds on worms, tiny molluscs and crustaceans. It reproduces during the summer. It has an extremely localized distribution around the British Isles, in inshore waters over rocks.

WRASSE, SCALE-RAYED

(Acantholabrus palloni)

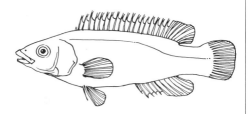

British record: 14¾oz (418g)

This long-bodied, fully-scaled wrasse has a pointed snout, thick lips and a large mouth with protruding teeth. The long dorsal fin, two-thirds of which is spined, has a dark blotch at the junction between spines and soft rays. There is another dark blotch at the top of the tail root. The first half of the anal fin is spined. Colouration

is greeny-brown on the back and sides, with a lighter belly.

It feeds on worms, molluscs and crustaceans, and lives among rocks in deep water. It has a localized distribution around the British Isles.

WRECKFISH

(Polyprion americanus)

British record: 10lb 10oz (4kg 819g)

The wreckfish is extremely thick set and looks very similar to the American large-mouth bass. It has the typical perch-like features of a double dorsal fin (the first half heavily spiked) and a large expanding mouth with protruding lower jaw. The back is brownish-grey with silvery grey sides and belly. The tail is broad and powerful, and there are spines along the leading edge of the anal fin.

Although it is a common Atlantic species, it is only occasionally caught along the southern and south-western coastline of the British Isles. Young wreckfish are attracted to floating rubbish or weed rafts and wreckage, but adult fish, which grow to over 100lb, are deep-water predators. It feeds on squid, fish and crustaceans.

WRECK FISHING

A wreck lying on an otherwise barren sea bed can be considered an oasis of life in a featureless desert. Within a very short time a wreck becomes a foundation block on which the entire marine food chain can build. Various types of marine growths form very quickly, attracting small crustaceans and fish species, which take refuge in the wreck's complex structure. These in turn draw the larger predatory species, such as conger, pollack, coalfish, ling and cod.

There are many different ways of fishing wrecks, depending on the size of the wreck, the depth of water, the strength of the tide and, of course, the target species. Over the

years these methods have been honed to perfection and now, with the advent of exceptionally accurate electronic navigation systems, even more boats are visiting offshore wrecks.

PIRKING

Pirking was one of the first methods that anglers used to catch fish from wrecks. Pirks are widely used in Scandinavia, where they are known as pilks, and the considerable range available to the angler covers all colours and sizes, from 2oz up to more than 24oz. Pirks are fished on traditional downtide boat rods matched to the weight of the pirk in use. For example, at the heaviest end of the scale the angler will need a 50-lb class rod, while a 12-20lb-class rod will suffice with the lightest *pirks (Artificial Lures)*.

Pirks are fished on the drift. The skipper positions the boat uptide of the wreck (or up wind if that is stronger), and instructs the anglers when to lower their pirks. The pirks should be lowered quickly to the bottom, and retrieved a few yards to prevent them snagging on the sea bed. The skipper keeps an eye on the depth-sounder and warns the anglers when the boat starts to drift over the wreck so that they can retrieve slightly and avoid getting snagged. Many fish strike the pirks on the drop. However, a steady but not erratic jigging technique will give the pirk, which simulates an injured fish, sufficient action to attract the fish.

Pirks must be fished as close as possible to the bottom because that is where most fish are found. They must also be fished vertically, not streaming out behind the drifting boat, which will nearly always result in snagging. Some anglers fish two or three redgills or muppets above their pirks (known as 'killer gear'), but this practice is branded unsporting by many, and is certainly not advisable if there are sizeable fish on the wreck.

ARTIFICIAL SAND EELS

Pollack, coalfish, bass and cod rank among the most sporting British species, and one of the most pleasurable methods of catching them is by using an artificial sand eel fished on a long trace. Like pirking, this method invariably involves drifting across the wreck, but the advantage over pirking is that it is possible to use much lighter tackle. A 12-20lb-class outfit is ideal *(Artificial lure fishing - Sea)*

The basic rig consists of the artificial eel

Zz

attached to a long hooklength - usually 6-12ft of about 20lb bs monofilament. Tie on a small, good-quality swivel half way along the hooklength, and attach the hooklength to the main line with a second swivel. Use either a French boom or a long, tube-type, sliding boom to attach the lead. This will also help to prevent the eel tangling around the main line as the lead descends to the bottom (fig. 9). Allow the lure and hooklength to straighten out in the tide before lowering them; then lower the eel steadily to prevent tangles.

When you feel the bottom, re-engage the reel and retrieve the eel at a slow to moderate rate. Retrieve for about 20-30yd off the bottom, then re-lower the eel and start again. Fish will swim up and strike at the eel, usually hooking themselves as they turn and dive back into cover. Do not strike, just continue a steady rate of retrieve until you are sure that the fish is hooked. A correctly set clutch is essential. If you let the fish gain too much line, it will usually snag in the wreck.

FISHING AT ANCHOR

The last method commonly used over wrecks is fishing at anchor. The boat is anchored just uptide of the wreck, in a position that allows the anglers to trot their baits downtide towards it. Owing to the excessive depths at which many wrecks lie off the British coast, it is only possible to fish over the high- and low-water slack periods, and then only on the smallest neap tides.

Hauling big conger up from deep-water wrecks is gut-busting action, as skipper of Sussex charter boat *Helen Louise*, Brian Joslin, knows only too well.

Most of the biggest conger eels recorded have been taken by anglers fishing at anchor over wrecks. However, many wrecks, and the hollows scoured out of the adjacent sea bed by the tide, are inhabited by many other desirable species, including bream, plaice and turbot, and it is always worth experimenting with smaller baits and rigs in addition to heavy-duty conger gear.

ZANDER
(*Stizostedion lucioperca*)

Average size: 2-5lb
Mega specimen: over 12lb
British record: 18lb 10oz (8kg 448g)

Often referred to as a pike-perch, the zander is, of course, not a hybrid but an entirely separate, predatory species. Its introduction into the Great Ouse relief channel in the early 1960s caused great controversy. Zander were labelled indiscriminate killers and were blamed by some angling officials as the cause of worsening sport among shoal fish such as roach and bream throughout the Fenland drainage system. However, zander have always had a place in the balanced ecosystems of European freshwater fisheries, where all species flourish, and now that they have settled down in various types of British inland waterways, a state of equilibrium exists.

The zander has a long, athletic body covered in extremely rough scales. The head is small with large, glassy eyes (for hunting in bad light) and strong jaws fitted with four large canine teeth at the front. Colouration is bluish-grey along the back fusing into metallic brassy-pewter below the distinct lateral line. The belly is silvery white. Several dark vertical bars reach down to the lateral line. These, however, only seem to be evident on zander living in clear water. The fins are large, especially the double dorsal, the first of which has strong spines and the second soft rays. Both are flecked with dark spots. The pectoral, pelvic and anal fins are pale, translucent grey, often with a warm tinge. The tail is large and forked.

Zander usually feed close to the bottom, most actively in low light conditions and especially at night. They hunt in packs, searching for small shoal fish (including their own young) and have an excellent sense of smell in addition to superb vision.

Reproduction occurs in the early spring, when eggs are deposited around reed or rush stems in gravelly shallows. The fry hatch after 2 weeks.

HABITAT AND DISTRIBUTION

Zander prefer to inhabit the deepest areas in both rivers and lakes, and by far the largest concentrations exist within the interconnecting network of drainage channels fed by the Great Ouse in Cambridgeshire, Lincolnshire and Norfolk. They are absent from Wales, Scotland and Ireland.

TECHNIQUES

Artificial lure fishing - freshwater; Drift fishing in stillwater; Freshwater floatfishing techniques - Sliding-float fishing for predators, Drift-float fishing for predators; Ledgering techniques - Livebaits and deadbaits; Wobbling deadbaits.

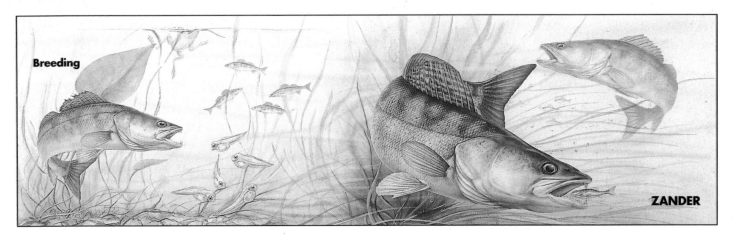

Breeding

ZANDER

As artist and fishing companion Dave Batten helped John in the initial preparation of this encyclopaedia, it is only fitting that he appears at its end with these two fine zander, taken on float-fished livebaits from a shallow, reed-lined mere. Note the vaned drift float rig used in their capture, strikes invariably coming between 60 and 80yd away from the boat.